MW00355287

THE
LINGERING
CONFLICT

REVISED EDITION

THE LINGERING CONFLICT

ISRAEL, THE ARABS, AND THE MIDDLE EAST 1948–2012

ITAMAR RABINOVICH

A SABAN CENTER AT THE
BROOKINGS INSTITUTION BOOK

BROOKINGS INSTITUTION PRESS
Washington, D.C.

First edition copyright © 2011
Revised edition copyright © 2013
THE BROOKINGS INSTITUTION
1775 Massachusetts Avenue, N.W., Washington, DC 20036
www.brookings.edu

All rights reserved. No part of this publication may be reproduced or transmitted in any form or by any means without permission in writing from the Brookings Institution Press.

The Library of Congress has cataloged the hardcover edition as follows
Rabinovich, Itamar, 1942–
    The lingering conflict : Israel, the Arabs, and the Middle East, 1948–2011 / Itamar Rabinovich.
        p.   cm.
    Includes bibliographical references and index.
    Summary: "A detailed history and analysis of Arab-Israeli relations and the conflict between two peoples claiming the same land, exploring through firsthand experience how these relations have been shaped over the years and assessing the prospects for a peaceful future"—Provided by publisher.
    ISBN 978-0-8157-2228-1 (cloth : alk. paper)
    1. Arab-Israeli conflict—1993– I. Title.
    DS119.76.R329 2011
    946.08—dc23   2011041176

ISBN: 978-0-8157-2437-7 (pbk : alk. paper)

9 8 7 6 5 4 3 2 1

Printed on acid-free paper

Typeset in Sabon

Composition by Cynthia Stock
Silver Spring, Maryland

In memory of my mother
TOVA BUCHSBAUM RABINOVICH

Contents

Preface

This book is based on my book *Waging Peace,* first published by Farrar, Straus in 2000 and then in 2004 by Princeton University Press in a revised and updated paperback version. Several colleagues who have assigned the book in their classes and other interested individuals have urged me in the past few years to update it once again given the massive changes that have occurred in Arab-Israeli relations since 2003. When I finally decided to undertake the task, it soon transpired that more than just an update was required.

This volume includes two and a half new chapters that cover Ariel Sharon's last two years in power, Ehud Olmert's tenure, and Barack Obama's and Benjamin Netanyahu's record in Middle Eastern diplomacy thus far. In addition, I have updated and revised other chapters where necessary. *The Lingering Conflict* differs from the editions of *Waging Peace* in two main respects. *Waging Peace* was a study of Arab-Israeli relations since 1948, but its core was the peace process of the 1990s. This is not the case with *The Lingering Conflict.* Also, as the change of title and subtitle implies, the new book reflects a harsher reality—a decline of the peace process, a festering of the conflict, and a broadening of the arena with two Muslim, non-Arab regional actors, Iran and Turkey, assuming more prominent roles in Middle Eastern politics and Arab-Israeli affairs.

Of the book's nine chapters, seven are written as a narrative and the final two are analytical. I chose this structure so that I could let the narrative flow without too many digressions and yet be able to elaborate on substantive issues in the analytical chapters. This choice entails a bit of repetition, but it seems to me on balance that the book and the readers end up benefiting.

It is a pleasant duty to thank several individuals and institutions for their help and support. I am grateful to Haim Saban and Charles Bronfman for sponsoring my fellowship at the Saban Center and for their friendship over many years. Strobe Talbott, Martin Indyk, Ken Pollack, Dan Byman, and many others at Brookings and the Saban Center have offered friendship and professional support. It was a genuine pleasure to collaborate with Bob Faherty, the director of the Brookings Institution Press, and with the editorial team: Janet Walker, Martha Gottron, and John Felton. I am grateful to the management of Princeton University Press and to my former editor, Hanne Winarsky, for facilitating the transition from *Waging Peace* to *The Lingering Conflict*. At Tel Aviv University, several colleagues at the Dayan Center and the Institute of National Security Studies have been generous with their time and expertise. I am grateful to Dov Weissglas, Yoram Turbowicz, and Shalom Tourheman for valuable insights. Special thanks go to my associate Dr. Tamar Yegnes and to my assistants Moran Azoulay and Nitsan Dori.

Tel Aviv
October 2011

1

THE BACKGROUND

The Arab-Israeli conflict is now in its seventh decade. An earlier conflict between the small Jewish and the much larger Arab community in Palestine had first erupted in the late Ottoman period. It became fiercer and more significant after the First World War, the publication in 1917 of the Balfour Declaration (in which the British government supported the "establishment in Palestine of a national home for the Jewish people"), and the establishment in 1920 of a British Mandate over Palestine on both sides of the Jordan River. During the next three decades, Arabs and Jews fought over rights and control, their conflict culminating in a war that broke out after the United Nations' decision in 1947 to partition Palestine between a Jewish state and a Palestinian-Arab one.[1]

Throughout the decades of low-level conflict, the indigenous Palestinian Arabs were supported and helped by a large part of the Arab world, but the conflict widened following the establishment of the state of Israel in 1948 and the immediate invasion by five Arab armies. Israel's victory, the consolidation of its existence and expansion of its original territory, the Arabs' military defeat, the failure to establish the Palestinian Arab state envisaged by the UN resolution, and the consequent problem of Palestinian refugees were the fundamental facts in the process that transformed the Arab-Jewish conflict in Mandate Palestine into the Arab-Israeli conflict we still know today.

The conflict's history is divided by the October War of 1973. For twenty-five years after the creation of Israel, the old wounds festered as efforts to heal them or at least address some of their causes failed for reasons that I analyze. But after the Israeli victory in October 1973, diplomatic procedures were inaugurated that developed into an Israeli-Egyptian peace process, which in March 1979 produced Israel's first peace treaty with an Arab state. This process subsequently came to a grinding halt, and the ensuing stasis lasted through the 1980s. Then a new phase of peace negotiations was inaugurated in October 1991 at the Madrid Conference. These negotiations gave birth to a second Israeli peace treaty in 1994, with Jordan, to a Palestinian-Israeli breakthrough, and to a significant degree of Arab-Israeli normalization. Even in the heyday of the "Madrid process" in 1993–95, this phase failed to bring about a comprehensive settlement of the Arab-Israeli conflict or to end the political disputes and the bloodshed between Israel and parts of the Arab world. New developments in 1996 slowed negotiations and in 1998 brought them near collapse.

The Madrid process represents the first sustained international effort to resolve the Arab-Israeli conflict.[2] It is significant that no comparable effort—as distinct from short-lived attempts, various mediation efforts, and partial settlements—had been undertaken before, and that nearly forty years of an uneven peace process have still failed to produce a comprehensive settlement. The Arab-Israeli conflict has indeed been one of the most complex and difficult international problems of the second half of the twentieth century and into the current century. The first step to understanding its complexity is to recognize that there is no single Arab-Israeli dispute but a cluster of distinct, interrelated conflicts:

—The core conflict between Israel and the Palestinians. This is a classic conflict between two national movements claiming historical title to and vying for possession of the same land. This original strand in the Arab-Israeli dispute was overshadowed for some fifteen years (1949–64) by the pulverization of the Palestinian community that had been dispersed during Israel's war of independence, and by the preeminence then of pan-Arab ideologies and Arab state interests. The resurgence of Palestinian nationalism in the mid-1960s and, ironically, the establishment in 1967 of Israeli control over the whole of Palestine west of the Jordan River restored a major role to the Palestinians in the Arab world. Their new importance was reinforced by the Palestine Liberation

Organization (PLO) offensive against Israel, conducted with the defeat of the established Arab armies in the background.

—A broader dispute between Israel and Arab nationalism. This is a national, political, cultural, and increasingly religious conflict. Both sides came into this conflict carrying their historical and cultural legacies. The Jewish people's national revival in their historic homeland in the immediate aftermath of the Second World War and the Holocaust, and after millennia of exile and persecution, unfolded during a head-on collision with an Arab national movement seeking revival, renewal, and power after a century of soul-searching and humiliation at the hands of Western powers. Unfortunately, most Arabs have perceived Zionism and Israel as either part of the West or, worse, a Western bridgehead established in their midst.

—A series of bilateral disputes between Israel and neighboring Arab states created by geopolitical rivalries combined with other factors. Thus Egypt was drawn into war with Israel in 1948 by the Palestinian problem, but its decision to join the Arab war coalition and its subsequent conflict with Israel were also affected by the ambitions of Arab and regional leaders, by Egypt's sense of competition with Israel as the other powerful and ambitious state in the region, and by a desire to obtain a land bridge to the eastern Arab world through the southern Negev Desert. Similarly, Syria's bitter relationship with Israel has expressed both its genuine attachment to Arab nationalism and to the Palestinian cause and its acute sense of rivalry with Israel for hegemony in the Levant.

—The larger international conflict. The Palestine question has long been an important and a salient international issue. The interest and passion aroused by the Holy Land (*Falastin* to Arabs and Muslims), the saliency of what used to be called the Jewish question, the rivalries of colonial powers and later the superpowers in the Middle East, and the overall geopolitical importance of the Arab world are some of the considerations and forces that have accounted for the significance in international affairs of the evolving Arab-Israeli conflict. The conflict was not originally nor subsequently allowed to be a merely local squabble. Arabs and Israelis from the outset sought international support for their respective causes, while foreign governments and other actors—out of genuine commitment to one of the parties, in search of gain, or for the sake of peace and stability—have always intervened.

The Cold War magnified and exacerbated these international factors. The Middle East, because of its intrinsic importance, its geographical closeness to the Soviet Union, and its openness to change, became an important arena of Soviet-American competition. In the early 1950s, the Soviet Union shifted from initial support for Israel to sweeping support for the Arab states, and it exploited the Arab-Israeli conflict in order to weaken the Western position in the Middle East and enhance its own. After about a decade of fluctuation, the United States decided on a policy of open cooperation with Israel and other Middle Eastern allies against the region's radical and pro-Soviet regimes. So, in the Arab-Israeli wars in 1967 and 1973 and in other Middle Eastern crises, the two superpowers contended by proxy. Israel's power was increased dramatically by American aid and support, but the Soviet Union's military assistance to its allies and clients, the prospect of Soviet military intervention, and Soviet help in rebuilding the defeated Egyptian and Syrian armies were important in denying Israel the political fruits of its military power and achievements.[3]

Whereas in the 1950s and early 1960s it was the Soviet Union that tended to take advantage of the Arab-Israeli conflict, the equation was altered by Israel's victory in the 1967 war. Within a few years, the Arab world grasped that Washington held the key to regaining the territories Israel had captured in that war. American endorsement of the principle of exchanging land for peace, and an occasional willingness and ability to act on it, were the basis on which the United States was able to orchestrate the Arab-Israeli peace negotiations and register several impressive achievements. For example, the Egyptian-Israeli peace process initiated after the 1973 war—the first major breakthrough in the Arab-Israeli conflict—was intimately linked to one of Washington's greatest Cold War accomplishments: Egypt's transition from a Soviet ally to a nation in the American orbit.[4] After the Soviet Union's collapse and the end of the Cold War, the international and regional landscape in the Middle East was transformed. Washington's interests in the Middle East were no longer shaped to a large extent by its rivalry with the Soviet Union; regional actors like Iraq, Iran, and Turkey began to play larger roles and in recent years a reassertive Russia began to make fresh inroads in the Middle East.

1948–67

This was the formative period of the Arab-Israeli conflict. The 1948 war that gave birth both to the state of Israel and to the Arab-Israeli conflict ended with a series of armistice agreements, not with a peace settlement. This fact has in recent years been the focus of a fierce debate in Israel among three schools of opinion: an orthodox, establishment-oriented, almost official historiography that blames this failure on the Arab world and its refusal to accept Israel's existence; a revisionist school that considers these critical years through a contemporary ideological prism, relying on several newly opened archives, primarily Israel's state archives, and that lays much of the blame on Israel and its first leader, David Ben-Gurion, for refusing any sensible compromise or concession; and another school of postrevisionists, also using newly available archival and other sources, that shuns both the apologetic tendency of the first historiography and the blunt revisionism of the second.[5]

This third group is interested less in allocating blame and discovering "missed opportunities" than in trying to understand the stalemate produced by the Arab-Israeli clash of interests and outlooks and in their asymmetries. Israel sustained heavy casualties in the 1948 war, believed that in the aftermath of the Holocaust the Jewish people were entitled to a secure homeland, and maintained that a belligerent force defeated in a war that it had itself initiated could not reasonably demand a reversal of its outcome.

Israel was also guided by a genuine, albeit sometimes exaggerated, existential insecurity and a fear that a second round of conflict might be initiated by its Arab adversaries, who had refused to accept the war's outcome and Israel's entrenchment in their midst. Under Ben-Gurion's leadership, Israel sought to stabilize the status quo on the assumption that, once it had consolidated its existence and absorbed the postwar wave of Jewish refugees and immigrants, peace could later be made on better terms. In a series of exploratory and then real peace negotiations conducted after the 1948 war, Israel offered some concessions, though not the ones demanded by its Arab interlocutors.[6]

From the Arab nationalist perspective, Israel was an illegitimate state that threatened the Arab world culturally and geopolitically. The few

Arab leaders who agreed to negotiate with Israel insisted on far-reaching concessions—giving up the southern part of the Negev Desert, allowing a corridor to link Gaza to the West Bank, permitting the return of Palestinian refugees, and jurisdiction over part of Lake Tiberias (or the Sea of Galilee). These leaders made such demands both to legitimize any prospective agreement in Arab eyes and because they believed that only significant and painful Israeli concessions could redress some of the injustices done them by Israel's very establishment and the expansion of its original territory, the defeat of the Arab armies, and the disintegration of the Palestinian community.[7]

A close look at the various attempts to arrive at peace settlements between Israel and its Arab neighbors after the 1948 war will point to many reasons and forces responsible for their failure, but at the root of the difficulty is the truth that the Arab and Israeli perspectives were irreconcilable. In the circumstances obtaining at the war's end, any concession that could possibly satisfy at least some of the Arabs was perceived by Israel's leaders as an existential threat. This state of affairs continued until June 1967, when Israel's victory in the Six-Day War gave it territorial assets that it could use as bargaining chips in peace negotiations. Until then, the conflict had lingered and festered. The limitations and shortcomings of the armistice agreements, friction over unresolved issues, the impact of radical ideologies espoused by certain Arab army officers on Arab politics, Israel's response to these developments, and the Soviet Union's influence in the region combined to shape a full-blown Arab-Israeli conflict by the mid-1950s. This meant a virtual absence of normal contacts between Israel and the Arab world; a complete Arab boycott; border clashes; individual and organized group Arab violence against Israel and an Israeli policy to retaliate against both; a second Israeli-Arab war in 1956 shaped by Israel's cooperation with Great Britain and France, two declining colonial powers, versus revolutionary pan-Arab nationalists; an arms race; and perennial fear of still more war.[8]

Soon events and developments occurred that led to the crisis of May 1967 and the Six-Day War in June. One was the completion of Israel's overland water carrier, bringing water from Lake Tiberias in the north to the more spacious but arid lands in the south, and the Arab decision to thwart a project designed to enhance Israel's capacity to absorb more people and thus consolidate its existence. A second was the return of the Palestinians and the Palestinian national movement to a directly active role in Middle Eastern politics with the emergence of various groups and organizations that subsequently assembled under the umbrella of the PLO. Third was the radicalization of Syrian politics under the Ba'ath Party's regime and the exacerbation of rivalries among various Arab states, particularly with regard to issues relating to Israel. Fourth was the intensification of Soviet-American rivalry in the region. And lastly there was a leadership crisis in Israel after David Ben-Gurion's second and final retirement in 1963.[9]

1967–73

Although the June 1967 war created a potential for a political settlement by gaining Israel new territorial assets, it also escalated the Arab-Israeli conflict to hitherto unfamiliar levels. Right after the war, Israel indeed considered the Sinai Peninsula and the Golan Heights as, essentially, temporary holdings to be used to obtain a genuine peace. As time went by and peace failed to come, however, the situation progressively acquired the trappings of permanency, and the temporary holdings were tied to Israel by a variety of bonds and vested interests.

The West Bank and the Gaza Strip, which Jews considered parts of the historical Land of Israel and which had been parts of Mandate Palestine, were treated from the outset on an entirely different basis. Sovereignty over the West Bank and Gaza was, unlike that over the Sinai and the Golan, according to the Israeli interpretation at least, an open issue. Control over and title to these territories raised fundamental issues of security and identity—these were the lands of the Bible (much more so, in fact, than the coastal plains where most of Israel's population actually lived). In them lay the key to a historic compromise with Palestinian nationalism or, alternatively, to yet another effort to make an agreement with Hashemite Jordan; but neither the shape of such a settlement nor an available partner was readily apparent. Moreover, Israel's politics were altered by the powerful wave of messianic-mystical nationalism generated by Israel's acquisition of Judea and Samaria. (In the coded language of Israeli politics, the term "West Bank" is neutral but the biblical term "Judea and Samaria" expresses a claim to the heartlands of

Jewish history.) This wave was reinforced by the Israelis' unprecedented sense of power after their great and swift military victory, and their determination never to return to the vulnerable borders of the prewar period or to a trauma like the one they had endured in May 1967, when on the eve of the war many in Israel feared a disaster.[10]

The military might that Israel displayed in June 1967 convinced the Arabs, at least temporarily, that they could not reasonably hope to end the conflict through a military victory, although limited wars and wars of attrition could still be launched. The effect of the 1967 defeat was qualitatively different from that of the defeats in 1948 and 1956—Israel's swift and stunning victory could not be explained away by the Western powers' direct participation or by the decay of the old order in the Arab world, for though Jordan's King Hussein was a traditional Arab monarch, the Nasserite regime in Egypt and the Ba'ath regime in Syria were paragons of revolutionary Arab nationalism. In the Arabs' ensuing soul-searching, several alternatives were fiercely debated—return to the Islamic fold, further radicalization, or stay with the familiar status quo. But a recommendation to draw yet another conclusion from the repeated failure to defeat Israel—to seek a political settlement based on a historic compromise—was not made.[11]

These Israeli and Arab frames of mind were chiefly responsible for the diplomatic stalemate over the next six years. Meanwhile, the Soviet Union hastened to rebuild and resupply the Egyptian and Syrian armies, while the United States supported Israel's insistence that its victory should lead to nothing less than a genuine settlement of the Arab-Israeli conflict. The United Nations' lengthy deliberations in the summer and fall of 1967 ended with the adoption of Security Council Resolution 242, an epitome of constructive ambiguity: it has served ever since as the basis for the several efforts to resolve the Arab-Israeli dispute precisely because its careful formulation (along with the differences between the English, French, and Russian versions of it) has enabled all parties to claim the validity of their own interpretations.

The initial efforts at international mediation having failed, Egypt, with its armed forces rehabilitated with Soviet aid, resumed hostilities in late 1968. Limited fighting with Israel spread along the Jordanian and Syrian fronts; this war of attrition lasted until the summer of 1970. The Arab states' eagerness to regain the territories they had lost in June 1967 was supplemented and enhanced by Palestinian nationalism's quest for self-determination. Thus the Six-Day War gave new scale and impetus to a process that had already begun: the Arab states' formation of the original PLO, the challenge presented to the PLO by authentic Palestinian groups, the formulation of the Palestinian National Charter—in short, the return of the Palestinian issue to the forefront of the Arab-Israeli conflict.

After the June war, the relationship and balance between the Palestinian national movement and the Arab states changed, the latter losing power and prestige while the former seemed to offer new hope—of defeating Israel through a popular war of liberation, and inflicting unfamiliar blows on it through a series of spectacular terrorist acts. In addition, the Palestinians built virtually independent territorial bases in Jordan and Lebanon, at the expense of these states' sovereignty. An authentic Palestinian organization led by Yasser Arafat, Fatah, took control of the PLO, ending the rivalry of the previous four years. Arafat became an important Arab leader, wielding influence in summit conferences and at other Arab meetings.[12]

In theory, some of these developments might have been the basis for an Israeli-Palestinian accommodation. Israel was in control of all of Mandate Palestine, but it was not eager to add the Palestinian population of the Gaza Strip and the West Bank to its body politic. Palestinian leaders had the authority and credibility to make a compromise agreement that their predecessors had refused to consider. But accommodation and compromise remained only theoretical options. Israeli attachment to the West Bank intensified, while the PLO was carried away by its initial successes to an inflated view of its power and prospects.[13]

By the summer of 1970, it had become clear that the PLO's efforts to organize a popular uprising in the West Bank and the Gaza Strip were unsuccessful. Still more significant, the Arab states' war of attrition against Israel had run its course, and Egypt's president, Gamal Abdel Nasser, responded positively to Secretary of State William Rogers's "initiative" for a cease-fire. The PLO's radical wing fought a rearguard action against what it viewed as capitulation. Western airliners were hijacked to Cairo and Jordan. In Jordan this defiance triggered a final showdown between the Palestinians and the Hashemite regime. For three years, King Hussein had tolerated the gradual erosion of his authority and sovereignty in Jordan by a movement that enjoyed the support of both the Palestinian majority among his own subjects and the larger Arab world. In September 1970, the Palestinians overplayed their hand, humiliating him and his loyalists, but the Jordanian army crushed the Palestinian opposition and expelled the PLO's fighting units from Jordanian territory without incurring significant criticism from Nasser, who had just made his own truce with Israel. A halfhearted Syrian intervention on behalf of the Palestinians ended ignominiously: Hafiz al-Asad, commander of the Syrian air force, refused to commit his planes to what he regarded as a senseless adventure, and without air cover the Syrian armored column invading Jordan fell easy prey to Jordan's small air force and was forced to turn around.

There was more to this episode than a minor military clash between Jordan and Syria. It was also a Soviet-American conflict by proxy. In the Cold War context, a Soviet client had invaded the territory of an American client and had apparently been defeated by the latter's armed forces, though it was also deterred by the mobilization of Israeli land and air forces in case they were needed to support Jordan in its battle against the Syrians. Israel's moves were closely coordinated with the United States, which viewed this coordination as a successful implementation of the Nixon doctrine—resolving a regional crisis with local allies and without American troops. This was the first in a series of exploits by Henry Kissinger that defined his spectacular Middle Eastern diplomacy during the next years.

In Israel a retrospective policy debate followed this episode. Henry Kissinger's chief partner on the Israeli side had been Yitzhak Rabin, who was serving as ambassador to Washington—a preparatory phase in his transition from a military career to a political one. He and the government of Prime Minister Golda Meir took pride in what they considered a clear demonstration of Israel's strategic value to the United States, its contribution to pragmatism and stability in the region, and the reinforcement of Israel's community of interests with the Hashemite regime in Jordan. Curiously, the government's right-wing critics took exception to this latter point. In their view, Israel should have remained neutral in the Jordanian dispute and allowed the Palestinians to defeat the Hashemite regime and take over the Jordanian government, for they believed that, once the Palestinians had their own state in Jordan, Israel could press its claim to the West Bank. Thus the maxim: Jordan is Palestine.[14]

But this Israeli debate seemed almost academic. The successful conclusion of the Jordanian crisis, the end of the war of attrition, Nasser's subsequent death, and the partnership and intimacy with the United States combined to generate a feeling that the status quo could be indefinitely perpetuated. This, however, came from a false sense of security.[15]

The war launched in October 1973 by Egypt and Syria against Israel differed from those of 1948 and 1967. They did not go to war in support of the Palestinians or drift into it in an uncontrolled process of escalation. Rather the Sinai Peninsula for Egypt and the Golan Heights for Syria were parts of their national territories, and Israel's control of them seemed unbearable. The real driving force behind planning and executing the war was Nasser's underestimated successor, Anwar al-Sadat.

Sadat's new policy toward Israel was predicated on his underlying decision to liberalize Egypt's politics and economy and to reorient that nation from a Soviet to an American focus. To implement these changes, he had to disengage from the conflict with Israel. His concepts for a diplomatic settlement with Israel were very modest (and very distant from the peace treaty he ended up signing years later), but they were unacceptable to Golda Meir in 1971, and Sadat decided to launch a limited war to break the deadlock.

Sadat relied on two partners. One was Syria's new ruler, Hafiz al-Asad, who had seized full power in his country in November 1970 after an internecine debate over Syria's debacle in Jordan two months earlier. Asad, a senior member of the Ba'ath regime since its inception in March 1963, headed its more pragmatic wing. He did not believe in the ill-defined notion of a "popular war of liberation" championed by his radical rivals, but instead advocated cooperation with other Arab states against Israel. When Sadat approached him in 1972, he agreed to join Egypt in a war coalition, although he did not share Sadat's concept of the war as a prelude to negotiations or relish Syria's junior-partner position. Sadat's other partner was the group of conservatively governed, oil-producing Arab states. By the early 1970s, the first signs of the energy crisis were visible, and the balance was shifting among the oil-producing nations, the international oil companies, and the Western powers. Sadat knew that in launching a war he could rely on the increasing political and economic power of the Gulf Arabs.[16]

The PLO was not part of or privy to these preparations. Having been evicted from Jordan, it was busy building a new territorial base in Lebanon. The weakness of the Lebanese state, the sympathy and support of several factions within Lebanon, and the backing of other Arab governments enabled the PLO to build a state within a state there—with virtual control over Palestinian refugee camps in Beirut and in the south, autonomous political and operational headquarters in Beirut, and an extensive infrastructure in southern Lebanon, which it could use as a base of operations against Israel.

1973-77

The October War of 1973 did indeed break the deadlock and opened the way to a lengthy, intermittent effort to convert the potential created by the 1967 Six-Day War into peace negotiations that would settle the Arab-Israeli conflict. The transition from violence to diplomacy was facilitated by the absence of a clear outcome to the 1973 war, which ended with Israeli troops on the Egyptian side of the Suez Canal, a hundred kilometers from Cairo, and also in Syrian territory, within artillery range of Damascus to the north. Only forceful diplomatic intervention by the United States saved Egypt from a total military defeat. But Egypt did effect a successful crossing of the Suez Canal and managed to keep some troops inside the Sinai Peninsula. And Syria, before its troops were pushed back toward Damascus, had overrun the Golan Heights. Owing to an intelligence setback caused by political shortsightedness and a bureaucratic mind-set, Israel had been caught by surprise, and at first its armed forces performed poorly. Its recovery and subsequent performance were most impressive, but the impact of the war's early phases could not be forgotten: the large number of Israeli casualties, the need for American resupplies, and therefore the collapse of an important element in strategic U.S.-Israeli cooperation—the belief that Israel could hold its own against any Arab coalition so long as the United States deterred the Soviet Union.

Given the war's ambiguous outcome and the danger of resumed hostilities, the chief protagonists sought an accommodation, and their early agreements became the starting points for a new Arab-Israeli diplomacy led and driven by President Richard Nixon and Secretary of State Kissinger, whose sense of urgency derived from several sources: the energy crisis, the quadrupling of oil prices by Iran and the principal Arab oil-producing states (which clearly took advantage of the war to effect a change they had been planning for some time), and the danger of a confrontation with the Soviet Union if war broke out again.

Beyond these immediate considerations, additional forces were at work. The debacle and shock of the early days in the October War disabused many Israelis of the sense of power they had enjoyed ever since their victory in 1967 and paved the way for significant changes in domestic politics and national-security policies. The full extent of this domestic change was manifested only in 1977, when the Labor movement, after fifty years of hegemony in prestate and independent Israel, lost power to the right-wing Likud alignment. In the meantime, a yearning for peace and a weariness with bloodshed provided public support for the concessions made in foreign policy by Prime Minister Meir and her successor, Yitzhak Rabin, in 1974 and 1975.

The Arab states were buffeted by contradictory forces. The Egyptian and Syrian armies' initial success, and the swelling of Arab economic power and political influence, tilted many Arabs against the notion of a compromise with Israel. These were the years (1973–82) of the Arab Decade, when the rest of the world sought Arab oil and money and Arabs could reasonably hope that as a result Israel's base of international support might be undermined. Other Arabs were more cautious. If Israel could not be defeated even when caught by surprise, as it had been in 1973, with its military machine out of gear, what was the point of waiting for some prospective opportunity to fight it in the future? From that perspective, there was no value in a long-drawn-out effort to erode Israel's position when significant concessions might be obtained through diplomacy.[17]

After the October War, Sadat completed the move he had begun in 1972, when he expelled the Soviet Union's military advisers from Egypt and placed his country squarely within the American orbit. Indeed, for Henry Kissinger, his partner in this transition, the Israeli-Arab peace process was not only a mechanism for preventing another war, for directing Arab-Israeli relations on the path of resolution, and for calming the Arab oil-producers, but also part of a strategy designed to facilitate precisely this shift of allegiance. And the success of that strategy was one of the United States' greatest achievements during the Cold War. But Kissinger's effort to apply the same rule to Syria met with only limited success. Asad concluded one military disengagement agreement with Israel and began negotiating with Washington, but he refused to abandon his pro-Soviet orientation.

Alongside the American mediation, a direct channel of communication between Egypt and Israel was opened after the October War: talks between Generals Abd-ul-Ghani al-Gamasi and Aharon Yariv at Kilometer 101, a site named for its sign marking the distance from Cairo. The talks revealed the potential for reconciliation inherent in the relationship between the two countries, but at the end of the day both preferred to have Washington's mediation. With American help, Egypt and Israel signed a number of agreements that culminated in a disengagement-of-forces agreement in January 1974. This stabilized the situation and indicated the direction further peace negotiations could take: the agreement stipulated Israel's withdrawal from the Egyptian mainland and from the banks of the Suez Canal. Egypt thus emerged from the war with its first concrete achievement, while Israel could relish the opportunity to regroup and contemplate its next moves, taking comfort in the notion that a withdrawal from the Suez Canal was a sine qua non for starting a peace process with Egypt. (Israel could also ask itself whether it had been necessary to go through the October War to come to that conclusion.)

Kissinger's mediation efforts and the three accords they yielded—disengagement agreements between Israel and Egypt and then Syria in January and May 1974, and the Israeli-Egyptian interim agreement of September 1975—were referred to at the time as step-by-step diplomacy. As this implied, U.S. policy was to aim not for a comprehensive settlement of the Arab-Israeli conflict but for a series of partial, interim agreements. The pessimistic presumption was that a comprehensive, final settlement that met Arab demands and expectations and also addressed Israel's needs and concerns was not feasible under prevailing circumstances. Though almost everyone paid lip service to the idea of a comprehensive settlement by coming to a brief Arab-Israeli peace conference held in Geneva under UN auspices in December 1973, this was an essentially ritualistic affair designed to placate the Soviet Union and Arab nationalist opinion, both of which resented Washington's control of the negotiations and its preference for partial bilateral agreements.[18]

Syria boycotted the Geneva conference but was eager nonetheless to collaborate with the United States in negotiating a disengagement agreement with Israel. The negotiation was protracted and arduous. Syria had fewer bargaining chips than Egypt, but Asad was determined to obtain an equivalent agreement, and he bargained hard, reinforcing his diplomacy with a minor war of attrition. The agreement finally reached in May 1974 provided for Israel's withdrawal from the territory it had captured beyond the Golan Heights in October 1973 and from Quneitra, the provincial capital there. Like Sadat, Asad thus managed to win back a slice of the territory his country had lost in 1967. But whereas in the Egyptian case the postwar disengagement agreement was only a first step in a phased process, the Israeli-Syrian agreement of May 1974 had no sequel.

In the early summer of 1974, it was clear that Israel and Egypt were ready for the next stage of their negotiations, but the substantive issues were compounded by a procedural problem. Sadat was willing to defy the Arab nationalist demand for a comprehensive agreement with Israel, but he was not willing to go it alone. Syria had been Egypt's partner until now, but the idea of pairing the two again did not appeal to anyone; Asad had acquired the reputation of being a tough, meticulous negotiator, and the Golan Heights' limited terrain offered limited choices. A short-lived effort was made to bring in Jordan: Kissinger's idea was to offer Jordan a bridgehead in the area of Jericho as a prelude to its getting back the West Bank. To Rabin, Israel's new prime minister, and to the Labor Party as a whole, Jordan was preferable to the PLO as a partner in resolving the Palestinian problem. However, Rabin was not ready to make a bold move that would address this underlying issue in Israeli politics and public life, for though partnering with Jordan might possibly provide a satisfactory solution it would certainly generate bitter controversies at home. This was not Rabin the mature statesman of the 1990s, but a political novice still, entrusted with ultimate responsibility at a very difficult time. So Rabin rejected Kissinger's initiative. Shortly thereafter, the Arab states, in a consensus formulated in a summit conference at Rabat, formally denied Jordan's claim to the West Bank and recognized the PLO as "the sole legitimate representative of the Palestinian People" and as the rightful claimant to those parts of historical Palestine that Israel might give up in future negotiations.[19]

Given this sequence of events, Egypt decided to go it alone in negotiations with Israel. After nearly a year of arduous work, an interim agreement over the Sinai Peninsula was signed in September 1975: Egypt regained its oil fields there and the strategic Mitla and Gidi passes; a collateral U.S.-Israeli memorandum of understanding was also signed that advanced the two nations' strategic and diplomatic cooperation still further.

The interim agreement represented the high point of Kissinger's step-by-step diplomacy, but it also marked its end. At least one additional phase might have been planned in the Sinai, but it was not at all clear that Sadat was able or willing to face an angry Arab chorus led by Syria. Kissinger showed his own ambivalence when he allowed a senior State Department official, Harold Saunders, to state in a congressional hearing in November 1975 that the Palestinian issue was "the core of the problem." If this was indeed the case, negotiations that did not deal with that problem had only limited value. In any event, the outbreak of civil war in Lebanon in 1975–76 and the Ford administration's preoccupation with the presidential election in November 1976 resulted in a virtual suspension of Middle Eastern diplomacy.[20]

1977–82

Jimmy Carter's election and the inauguration of his administration in January 1977 began a new phase in Israeli-Arab relations. President Carter and his team—Secretary of State Cyrus Vance, National Security Adviser Zbigniew Brzezinski, and Harold Saunders and William Quandt as the bureaucratic experts on the Middle East—were motivated by a host of new considerations: an open desire to distance themselves from their predecessors' policies, a genuine belief that a final and comprehensive settlement of the Arab-Israeli conflict could be made, diminished interest in East-West Cold War rivalries and a concurrent preoccupation with tensions between North and South, concern about the supply and price of oil, and a religiously inspired sense of mission. Carter's new Middle East policy not only reversed Kissinger's but turned a comprehensive settlement of the Arab-Israeli conflict into a major goal. His administration's concept of comprehensiveness meant an international conference, cooperation with the Soviet Union, and the allocation of significant roles to Syria and the PLO. Carter made no secret of the fact that, in line with a Brookings Institution report that inspired his policies, he believed that Israel should withdraw practically all the way back to its pre-1967 borders and should allow for the establishment of a Palestinian state, in return for diplomatic recognition and peace that Israel would obtain from the Arab states.

These views and policies pitted Carter against Prime Minister Rabin and, after May 1977, his successor, Menachem Begin. But they also confounded President Sadat, who could not understand why the United States would want to bring the Soviet Union back to center stage in the Middle East and relegate Egypt, Washington's newfound ally, to a role secondary to that of uncooperative Syria. Egypt's and Israel's concern with these developments led to their forming a direct channel of communication. By means of it, the groundwork was laid for Sadat's historic journey to Jerusalem and for the negotiations that led to the Camp David Accords of September 1978 and to the Egyptian-Israeli peace treaty of March 1979.[21]

Shared exasperation with the policies of the Carter administration certainly helped to start this direct Egyptian-Israeli dialogue, but both parties were also moved by more significant considerations. Sadat wanted, of course, to regain the whole of the Sinai Peninsula. In 1977, he understood that this was a realistic possibility but full peace had to be offered in return. Early in his presidency, Sadat had decided that disengagement from the conflict with Israel was integral to a realignment of Egypt's policies and politics. However, he had not thought through a plan and had only a sense of direction, some rudimentary notions, and an understanding of the Egyptian public's weariness. By 1977, he had several years' experience, self-confidence gained in the October War and its sequel, and a clearer idea of what had to be done.

In Menachem Begin, Sadat found a surprising, not to say unlikely, yet effective partner. On May 17, 1977, after successive defeats in previous elections, Begin finally won and became Israel's prime minister, a victory that ended Labor Zionism's hegemony and represented the first genuine transfer of power in Israeli politics. The accession to power of a nationalist right-wing politician was widely expected to exacerbate

Arab-Israeli tensions. But this expectation failed to take account of two significant changes in Israeli politics: as a newcomer, Begin was less constrained by convention than his predecessors had been; and as a nationalist ideologue, he was totally committed to the idea of the Land of Israel (*Eretz Yisrael*) but not to the Sinai Peninsula—from which, it turned out, he was willing to offer full withdrawal to achieve peace.

A separate peace with Israel was not what Sadat had in mind. The discrepancy between his and Begin's ideas of what peace meant produced an early crisis in their direct negotiations that was resolved by the United States. Washington initially responded coldly to the direct Egyptian-Israeli dialogue, but the president and his team soon understood that, whatever their own hopes, once Egypt and Israel were in direct negotiation, both opportunities and dangers presented themselves that U.S. policy had to address. The unusual gathering at Camp David in September 1978 was the culmination of a process that made the United States a third, often dominant, partner in the negotiations and introduced a kind of mediation-cum-arbitration into what originally had been direct give-and-take.

The Camp David Accords turned Arab-Israeli diplomacy into a fullblown effort to achieve peace. By extending diplomatic recognition to Israel, signing a peace treaty with it, and establishing normal relations with it, Sadat and Egypt violated a taboo that an Arab consensus had strictly enforced for more than three decades. There were two parts to the Camp David Accords—an Israeli-Egyptian agreement terminating the bilateral dispute between them, and a framework laying down the principles for resolving Israel's conflict over the Palestinians and its disputes with other Arab neighbors. But the two parts were not of equal importance. Begin and Sadat were primarily interested in their bilateral agreement, and both leaders saw to its strict implementation. Indeed, this was how the Arab world perceived the agreements: as Sadat's having broken ranks and made a separate peace with Israel. He was denounced and vilified, Egypt was ousted from the Arab League, and most Arab states severed diplomatic relations with Cairo.[22]

Sadat reacted angrily to this criticism. He viewed himself not as a traitor to the Arab cause but as a pathfinder showing the Arab world the only course open to it for regaining territories lost in 1967. When Asad and other critics accused him of being a careless and ineffective negotiator, he retorted that they were small-minded men who focused on minor details and failed to see the overall picture. He kept saying that his loudest critics would end up following in his footsteps—a judgment that was vindicated posthumously.

As for Begin, he exploited part of the potential created in June 1967 to resolve the "conflict of 1948" on the Egyptian front. His far-reaching achievement—Israel's peace agreement with Egypt—was the most significant breakthrough in Arab-Israeli relations to date, but the price was commensurate. Sadat was willing to offer Israel full peace and generous security arrangements in the Sinai, but he insisted on regaining the whole territory, every last square inch. By agreeing to this, Begin not only conceded the whole of the Sinai but established a precedent (in fact explicitly): full withdrawal for full peace.

Furthermore, if Begin expected Sadat to treat the Palestinian dimension of the agreement as a mere formality and allow Israel a free hand in the West Bank, he misunderstood. In the Israeli-Egyptian negotiation of 1977–78 Sadat had pressed for recognition of the Palestinians' "national rights." Begin, worried by the potential ramifications of this abstract principle, had put forth a plan for Palestinian autonomy, to which Sadat had reacted coldly. But once it was agreed on, Egypt pressed hard for a liberal interpretation of full autonomy for the Palestinians. A deadlock was reached on this issue, and relations between Israel and Egypt soured.

The failure to implement the Palestinian component of the Egyptian-Israeli peace treaty allowed Sadat and his successors a convenient justification for keeping bilateral relations between the two countries at a low level, or, as it came to be known, the cold peace. Egypt has kept its principal commitments to Israel (full diplomatic relations, a security regime in the Sinai, free access to Egypt for all Israeli tourists) but has imposed severe restrictions on the development of normal relations in the economic and cultural spheres and has continued its political and diplomatic rivalry. Thus the collapse of the "autonomy negotiations" in 1980, which seemed at the time only a temporary setback, was perpetuated over the next decade, aided by several events and developments: Jimmy Carter's loss in his reelection campaign, Sadat's assassination, the Lebanon war, the Iran-Iraq war, the changes in the PLO's standing and position, and new trends in Israeli politics.

1982–91

Israel had two aims for the war it launched in Lebanon in June 1982. One was to resolve permanently the host of problems presented by the collapse of the Lebanese state in the civil war of 1975–76. On another level, the war's plan reflected a much more ambitious effort to bring about a sweeping change in the whole region. As Ariel Sharon, architect of the war, saw it, Israel could transform its regional position by inflicting serious blows on Syria and the PLO and by installing a friendly regime in Lebanon. This flawed plan failed on both levels. Israel's regional position was not transformed, and the general challenge of the Lebanese problem has continued and even worsened. The confrontation with the PLO has been replaced by a confrontation with the Shiite community in Lebanon and two Shiite militias—Amal and, subsequently, Hizballah. The latter is a political movement and also a militia and terrorist organization controlled by Tehran. During and after the conflict with Israel and the United States in 1982–84, Syria consolidated and further institutionalized its hegemony in Lebanon; as part of its strategic alliance with Iran, Syria afforded Tehran access to the Shiite community in Lebanon and acquiesced in its control of Hizballah, although it imposes some limits on Iran's activities.[23]

The Islamic revolution in Iran in 1979 that brought Ayatollah Khomeini and his fundamentalist regime to power was a cardinal event in the modern history of the Middle East. For Israel, it put an end to a vital relationship Israel had established with the shah of Iran and placed Iran's considerable potential at the service of the Muslim world's radical wing. Ever since, the Islamic Republic of Iran has agitated against Israel and against the notion of Arab-Israeli reconciliation, has used its extensive networks in the Middle East and other parts of the world for anti-Israeli terrorist activities, and has introduced new elements, such as suicide bombings, into the Shiite-Lebanese and Palestinian conflicts with Israel. But at first these negative effects were mitigated by other developments. The fall of the shah and the rise of the ayatollahs also upset a delicate balance of power in the Persian Gulf region. It had always been difficult to maintain stability in a region made up of several rich but weak states and two wealthy powerful states: Iran, a conservative monarchy, and Iraq, a radical republic. When the conservative monarchy in Iran was taken over by revolutionary clerics, the balance became impossible, and indeed Iraq in 1980 launched a war against Iran that lasted nearly eight years. The war gave the weaker Arab states in the Gulf region a breathing spell, but the end of the Iran-Iraq war in 1988 inevitably shifted the tension elsewhere; this happened in 1990, when Iraq invaded Kuwait.

During this period, a substantial change occurred in the agenda and priorities of the conservative oil-producing states of the Arabian Peninsula. In the 1960s and 1970s, they had been genuinely concerned about the Arab-Israeli conflict and its radicalizing effect on their own polities. By the 1980s, different dangers were emanating from Iran and Iraq, which meant a change of attitude toward the conflict with Israel, as well as the peace process. Concerns about Israel were dwarfed by existential threats posed by Iran and Iraq. The peace between Egypt and Israel— the object of sharp criticism in 1978–79 when it was first struck—now seemed more positive, having stabilized the western part of the region and freed Egypt's armed forces to defend the Arabian Peninsula against the two radical republics. This change of perspective facilitated a reconciliation between Egypt and the other nations of the Arab world and enabled Sadat's successor to rejoin the Arab League in 1989 without having to give up the new relationship with Israel.[24]

At the same time, American leadership during Ronald Reagan's eight years in the White House lacked the drive, conviction, and determination that his two predecessors (and eventually his successor) displayed in matters concerning the Middle East. Reagan seemed warmly disposed toward Israel, but he lacked any emotional commitment to the Camp David Accords, his rival's great achievement. He also lacked the messianic zeal that drove the Carter administration's quest to bring peace to the Middle East. Reagan's administration was damaged badly by a series of negative experiences in the Middle East—a crisis in Lebanon, the virtual rejection of his September 1982 Reagan Plan, and the Iran-Contra affair—and turned its foreign-policy efforts elsewhere, mostly to the great struggle against the Soviet Union. Secretary of State George Shultz did invest time and ingenuity in his efforts to revive the Arab-Israeli peace process, notably in 1987 and 1988, but drive and muscle were lacking. The effort to broker an Israeli-Jordanian agreement (the London Agreement of 1987) and to turn the PLO into an acceptable negotiating partner (in 1988) failed.

In Israel, the debacle following the 1982 invasion of Lebanon was the beginning of the end of the Begin era in Israeli politics, but the Likud alignment's decline was not matched by a return to Labor ascendancy. The elections of 1984 and 1988 produced six years of power sharing under two versions of national-unity governments: the first gave a domestic political base for an (almost complete) Israeli withdrawal from Lebanon, but efforts by the Labor leader Shimon Peres to revive the peace process, whether as prime minister (1984–86) or as foreign minister (1986–88), were to no avail. Then Labor brought down the second national-unity government in 1990, when it believed that Likud was not responding to efforts by Secretary of State James A. Baker III to restart the peace process.

At the core of the Likud-Labor disagreement were two conflicting approaches to an Israeli-Arab, or Israeli-Palestinian, settlement. Tactically, these differences were translated into a debate over the acceptability of various Palestinian negotiators and their affiliations with the PLO. Likud's opposition to the PLO was absolute. The Labor Party's leaders also refused to accept the organization as a legitimate negotiating partner but were willing to accept certain Palestinian negotiators whose relationships with the PLO were not direct or explicit. Still, in the end, it was Likud and its right-wing allies who were able to form a new government, and the Labor Party went back to the opposition.

Not every twist and turn in Israeli politics during the 1980s derived from the Likud-Labor rivalry and their respective ideologies, but a significant pattern could be identified: between 1977 and 1992, Israel was governed for thirteen years by a Likud prime minister and for only two years by a Labor prime minister. This shows the preeminence, however slight, of conservative nationalist forces in the Israeli body politic. Thus it was a right-wing Israeli government that confronted the massive changes of the early 1990s.[25]

On the other side, three forces had contended since 1967 to be the effective and legitimate representation of the Palestinian cause: the PLO, Jordan, and ill-defined local forces in the West Bank and the Gaza Strip. The PLO was dealt a severe blow in the Lebanon war of 1982; the subsequent removal of its headquarters and fighting forces to Tunis and to Yemen was a severe handicap. But there was no one else to take advantage of its predicament. The London Agreement of 1987 was the last time

an effort was made to have Jordan be Israel's principal partner in resolving the Palestinian issue, but it failed before its feasibility could be tested.

When the Palestinian uprising, the intifada, broke out spontaneously
in 1987, it was sustained by individuals and groups that were not part
of the PLO's hierarchy. The PLO ultimately captured the political capital generated by the intifada, but only after traveling a road that was
far from straight: first, acceptance in 1988 of a formula for a two-state
solution, then the establishment of a dialogue with the United States, the
breakdown of that dialogue after the PLO's fresh drift into sponsorship
of terrorism, and finally its misguided support of Saddam Hussein's Iraq
after his invasion of Kuwait.

THE TURNING POINT OF THE MADRID CONFERENCE

The Madrid Conference of October 1991 finally placed the Arab-Israeli
peace process on a qualitatively different footing. This first sustained
effort by the international community to resolve the old conflict[26] was
the product of three principal developments.

First, the decline and dissolution of the Soviet Union ended the Cold
War's deleterious effects on Arab-Israeli issues. The United States was
left as the sole power capable of exercising influence for settlement,
while the Soviet Union's Arab clients lost their chief source of aid for
their subsidized weapon systems. Rulers like Syria's Asad found themselves looking for substitutes, seeking out the United States, and dealing
with the repercussions of the fall of Eastern European dictators. Israel,
on the other hand, was a clear beneficiary. Soviet and Eastern bloc hostility was replaced by normal (in several cases friendly) relations.

Also, the arrival in Israel of nearly a million immigrants from the
former Soviet Union had a very significant substantive and psychological effect on the Arab-Israeli balance. In absolute terms, the addition
of a million Jews to the Arab-Israeli demographic equation may not
seem very impressive. Still, the disappearance of Soviet support and the
resulting influx of one million Jews (who constitute 20 percent of the
population) to Israel sufficed to persuade many Arabs that time was not
necessarily on their side.

Second, the United States, having already benefited from the Soviet
Union's decline, saw its position and standing in the Middle East rise

to a new level after the world witnessed its willingness and ability to field half a million soldiers and build an international coalition for the liberation of Kuwait and the defense of Saudi Arabia. The Persian Gulf War weakened Arab radicals and the PLO. (The PLO leaders, aware of their diminished position, consented to being demoted, as it were, to only indirect representation at the Madrid Conference.) The United States also emerged from the war determined to take advantage of its enhanced influence and prestige to seek a comprehensive solution to the Arab-Israeli conflict. The administration of President George H. W. Bush saw resolution of the conflict as a prerequisite for stability and for a reorganized Middle East. It also believed, given Iraq's launching of Scud missiles against Israel in the Gulf War, that the danger had increased that weapons of mass destruction would be used in future wars, making a political settlement all the more vital.

Third, the Palestinians' first intifada in the West Bank and in Gaza beginning in late 1987 had a long and profound effect on the Israeli public. Ever since the 1967 war twenty years earlier, Palestinians had failed to devise an effective strategy for their struggle against Israel, and whenever Israeli society weighed the costs of keeping the status quo or working out a new compromise, the balance had tilted toward maintaining the status quo. But in 1988 a significant body of opinion in Israel was no longer willing to pay the costs of a perpetuated status quo. It is impossible to understand Prime Minister Yitzhak Shamir's acceptance of the Madrid framework or the Labor Party's victory in the 1992 elections without understanding the effect of this change in attitude.

It took several months of hard work by Secretary of State Baker, including nine trips to the Middle East, to build upon these developments and put together the formula for convening an international conference. A compromise had to be worked out between Arab and Israeli points of departure. As I have already noted, a weakened PLO had to give up hopes for direct participation in the conference and in ensuing negotiations. Syria, which for years had hoped for significant roles for the Soviet Union and the United Nations, one single Arab delegation, and continuous negotiation thereafter, finally agreed to a process cosponsored by the Soviet Union but dominated by the United States, and on comparatively loose coordination among four Arab-Israeli negotiating tracks. Israel accepted the notion of an international conference and was willing to turn a blind eye to the Palestinian delegation's real source of authority (the PLO).

The final texts of the letter of invitation to the Madrid Conference and of the different letters of assurance given by the United States to the participants clearly expressed the bitter arguments over these principles and terms, and the nature of the compromise solutions finally worked out by Secretary Baker and his team. Thus the phrase "territories for peace" was not included in the text of the letter of initiation to the Madrid Conference or in the specific letter of assurances sent to Israel, but it was mentioned in the letters of assurance addressed to the Arab invitees. For Shamir's government, the fact that the Palestinians formally had no separate representation but were present only as part of a Jordanian-Palestinian delegation was an achievement.

Another Baker achievement (and Syrian concession) was the formation of a second, multilateral negotiation to supplement the bilateral one. Working groups were established to focus on five regional issues: water, refugees, arms control and regional security, environment, and economic cooperation. The original idea was to generate discussion of how to achieve regional cooperation on these matters and paint visions of a better future, which would facilitate the concessions that all the parties on the bilateral track would have to make. This plan proved to be particularly fruitful, even though Syria and Lebanon refused to join these multilateral talks. It enabled a group of states from outside the region to take an active part in the peace process, bringing in Arab states from the Gulf, the Arabian Peninsula, and North Africa, and accelerating Arab-Israeli normalization.

At the Madrid Conference—where for the first time the international community, led by the United States, committed itself to a sustained effort to resolve the Arab-Israeli conflict—a framework and a set of rules were accepted by all parties. As we have seen, a measure of ambiguity was maintained, but the Madrid formula was more explicit than, say, Security Council Resolution 242 had been. Diplomatic ambiguity and various protestations notwithstanding, it was clear that Israel wanted full peace with the Arabs, and the Arabs wanted massive territorial concessions. Territories for peace of course did not mean all of Israel's occupied territories for peace, but the phrase was nonetheless unacceptable to Shamir's government, although its leaders had come to understand that their advocacy instead of "peace for peace" was unrealistic.

The Madrid formula also showed that a new balance had been struck between the Palestinian and larger Arab components of the conflict. Earlier, choices had to be made in practice between Palestinians and the Arab states. Both the Geneva Conference and Kissinger's step-by-step diplomacy had been predicated on a conscious policy to bypass the Palestinians and the Palestinian issue. President Carter's attempt to put the PLO and the Palestinian issue at the center of a comprehensive settlement was an important reason for the failure of that aspect of the Camp David Accords. True, the Camp David Accords and the Egyptian-Israeli peace treaty incorporated the notion of an interim or transitional Palestinian self-government, but this remained a dead letter. The Bush administration had, before the Gulf crisis, focused exclusively on the issue of Palestinian autonomy. But in 1991 the idea of dealing simultaneously with the Palestinians and with the Arab states was one of the keys to Baker's success.

Yet the forces that produced the Madrid successes could not take them beyond a certain point. The opening conference was impressive, but during the next nine months and five rounds of negotiations in Washington, no progress was made. It was clear from the outset that a breakthrough could happen only on the Syrian or the Palestinian track, and that progress with Jordan and Lebanon would have to come later. However, the Syrian and Palestinian protagonists were unwilling to make the concessions needed for progress, let alone for a breakthrough. The Bush administration, having invested a great deal of effort and political capital in Madrid, was not ready for the cost and pain entailed in goading the parties on; it was openly critical of Shamir and his government and was willing to wait for the Israeli elections of June 1992, hoping that a Labor victory would lead to change.

2

MADRID AND OSLO:
YEARS OF HOPE

As the twentieth century drew to a close, the four-year period from June 1992 to May 1996, shrouded as it was by both nostalgia and controversy, loomed ever more distinctly as a notably significant chapter in the evolution of Arab-Israeli relations. A hospitable regional and international environment, the newly formed Madrid framework, American leadership and support, and, above all, the determination of two Israeli prime ministers to move toward peace and the positive response of several Arab partners produced the most ambitious and sustained effort yet to settle the Arab-Israeli conflict.[1] These ambitions endowed the period with significance, and a number of important breakthroughs changed the contours of Arab-Israeli relations; these produced negative reactions, though, and underlined the limits to achieving a notion of peace that would be acceptable to both Arabs and Israelis.

The term "peace process" is often used rather loosely, but in those years it had a very concrete meaning: four formal tracks of bilateral negotiations supplemented by discreet informal ones, five working multilateral groups, a concerted international effort to give financial and economic support to Arab peacemakers, and two economic conferences (in Casablanca and Amman). These led to the Oslo Accords between Israel and the PLO, a peace treaty between Israel and Jordan, semi-diplomatic relations established between Israel and four other Arab states, a significant degree of less formal Israeli-Arab normalization, and a widespread sense that the Arab-Israeli conflict was finally on the way to reconciliation and resolution.

Yet the negative reaction to the same set of developments was hardly less significant.[2] Palestinian opponents of the peace process, some of them encouraged and supported by Iran, conducted a terrorist campaign designed to undermine it. Radical Israeli opponents of their government's peace policies perpetrated and condoned a massacre of Palestinian worshippers at the Tomb of the Patriarchs in Hebron in February 1994 and, separately, the assassination of Prime Minister Rabin in November 1995. Violent conflict between Israel and Hizballah continued along the Israeli-Lebanese border, exacting a high toll of casualties on both sides and culminating in Katyusha rocket attacks on northern Israel and two large-scale Israeli military operations in Lebanon. This conflict in Lebanon had local causes, but it should be seen in the context of Iran's effort to undermine the peace process and of the failure to reach an agreement between Israel and Syria. The peace process was not well received by large segments of public opinion in the Arab world and was bitterly criticized and rejected by the Arab intelligentsia. In Israel it was pursued by a government that relied on a very slim majority, and opposition rose to the agreement made with the PLO and to the agreement contemplated with Syria. This culminated in the assassination of Rabin and the subsequent election of Benjamin (Binyamin, in Hebrew) Netanyahu, who promised to respect the agreements made by his predecessors but also to shift the peace process to an entirely different premise.

The progress made during 1992–96 had one additional and unanticipated effect. Israelis and Arabs had been familiar for some fifteen years with the benefits and limitations of the separate peace between Egypt and Israel, but a comprehensive Arab-Israeli peace remained remote and abstract. The peace process of 1992–96 brought a comprehensive peace close and made it more palpable; the process also showed both sides the limits to a concept of peace that would be acceptable to their societies and political systems.

It may seem odd that the period should be defined by two Israeli elections. But in fact, that configuration determined the ebb and flow of the peace process. Yitzhak Rabin's electoral victory in June 1992 marked the beginning of a new chapter, and Benjamin Netanyahu's triumph in 1996 brought it to an end. The 1992–96 peace process unfolded through four distinct phases: from the Israeli elections of June 1992 to the signing of the Oslo Accords in September 1993; then to the signing of the Israeli-Jordanian peace treaty in October 1994; then to Rabin's assassination in November 1995; and then to the Israeli elections of May 1996.

THE ROAD TO OSLO

Yitzhak Rabin's electoral victory in June 1992 was universally interpreted as the first step in a revived peace process, and Rabin himself stated clearly that he could produce an agreement on Palestinian self-rule within nine months. But at the time neither Rabin nor his eventual partner, Yasser Arafat, envisaged himself signing an agreement like the Oslo Accords in a festive ceremony in Washington fourteen months later. And yet both leaders, in their different styles and within their different environments, adjusted and made new choices.

Rabin arrived in the prime minister's office in Jerusalem in July 1992 as a mature, experienced, and authoritative political leader. His first tenure as prime minister, from 1974 to 1977, had been rocky and had ended with his resignation after a personal scandal. Fifteen years later, he had eradicated the memories of that period and now projected the image of a confident senior leader who was Israel's ultimate authority on matters of national security because of his military background. He was widely seen as a direct and trustworthy man, a political leader who was a reluctant politician.[3]

Rabin won two political victories in 1992. In February, having failed in earlier challenges, he defeated Shimon Peres in the Labor Party's primaries and became the party's leader and its candidate for the premiership. He had finally succeeded in persuading not only the rank and file but much of the party apparatus that he alone could defeat Prime Minister Yitzhak Shamir and the Likud, and thus return Labor to power. The conventional wisdom in Israeli politics was that Israeli voters had shifted to the right, that they thought Peres was too dovish. Only Rabin, it was felt—identified as he was with national security and more centrist policies—could attract swing votes in the center of the Israeli political spectrum. So Labor's campaign in the subsequent general elections presumed that, although a significant number of voters might be ready to switch their votes away from the Likud, they remained reluctant to cast them for Labor. Accordingly, the campaign focused on the candidate and not on the party.

In the general election, Rabin hammered away on two principal issues: Shamir's inability to move the Madrid peace process forward, and his mismanagement of Israel's relationship with the United States, as evidenced by the manifest tension between his government and the Bush administration. Rabin promised that if elected he would galvanize the peace process and argued that an agreement to give the Palestinians some kind of autonomy could be reached within nine months. (A settlement with Syria did not seem realistic to Rabin at the time and did not arise as an issue in the campaign.)

Rabin won, but only barely so. An analysis of the voting figures in June 1992 shows that the Israeli body politic remained evenly divided between right and left; in fact the right received several thousand more votes than the rival bloc but ended up with a slightly smaller representation in the Knesset. Rabin formed a coalition with the left-wing Meretz and with Shas, the latter being an unusual combination of an ultra-Orthodox party and a grassroots movement of Israelis of North African extraction.

The key term in the new government's agenda was "a change of national priorities." Rabin, who did not believe that a comprehensive Arab-Israeli peace was likely in the near future, was ready to offer concessions in order to reach an accommodation with the Arabs, but not to return to the 1967 borders. Nor did he believe in simultaneous negotiation with Israel's four Arab protagonists, in which the Arab position would be dictated by the most radical Arab party while Israel would have to make simultaneous concessions on several fronts. Rabin preferred a gradual approach, and in the meantime Israel's domestic, regional, and international positions could be improved.

As minister of defense only a few years earlier, Rabin had conducted Israel's campaign against the intifada sternly and severely, but its lessons were not lost on him. He knew that the cost of holding on indefinitely to the West Bank and Gaza had become prohibitive. An ultimately futile effort was diverting too many resources to the West Bank from Israel proper and exacerbating Israel's relationship with the rest of the world, most significantly with the United States. For Israel's new prime minister, it was essential that peace negotiations begin again, that good relations be restored with the United States, that Israel obtain the $10 billion in loan guarantees that the Americans were willing to underwrite and invest that money in expanding the economy and strengthening infrastructure. Israel needed not only to absorb its new immigrants from the former Soviet Union but to prepare for the future.

Yet Rabin was not enamored of the format established in Madrid. Simultaneous formal negotiations with four Arab delegations were not likely to lead to the kind of breakthrough with the Palestinians or Syrians that he wanted. (Lebanon and Jordan could not be counted on to act first, since Lebanon was subordinate to Syria, and the diplomatically weak Jordan would need the covering legitimacy of a prior Syrian or Palestinian agreement.) But for the time being, he saw no reason to insist on a format different from Madrid. His initial preference was to move first on the Palestinian track. In 1989–90, he had cooperated with Secretary Baker in trying to start an Israeli-Palestinian negotiation; given what he knew from that experience, his own readiness, and Arafat's diminished stature, he thought an agreement on self-rule could be reached within nine months. One factor in his reasoning, carried over from Madrid, was that the Palestinian negotiators would be acceptable to the PLO but not representing it directly. Self-rule would not, of course, "solve" the Palestinian problem, but it would take the edge off the confrontations, move people onto a course of accommodation, open up the larger peace process, and improve Israel's international standing.

Yet there were significant advantages to predicating the peace process on an early agreement with Syria—a powerful state ruled by an authoritarian government—in contrast to the fragmented Palestinians. Hafiz al-Asad was difficult to negotiate with, but Israel's experience showed that once he made an agreement, he kept it. An agreement with Syria would also resolve Israel's problems in Lebanon, encourage Jordan to seek agreement, and thus strengthen Israel's hand with the Palestinians. Still, Syria was likely to insist on discussing only a final settlement, to settle on nothing short of Israel's full withdrawal from Syrian territory (the Golan Heights), and to offer less in return than Israel had in mind.

Rabin's original preferences were modified during what turned out to be Secretary Baker's final trip to the Middle East in July 1992. Baker went first to Damascus and then, in Jerusalem, impressed Rabin both with his account of Asad's willingness to come to a genuine peace agreement and with the Bush administration's willingness to help in reaching it. From that point on, Prime Minister Rabin realized that the only practical course open was to forget about the comparative advantages of this or that possible breakthrough and explore instead the possibilities afforded by the new circumstances.[4]

To begin with, the new government decided to cease building new settlements for Jews on the West Bank. To Syria it offered an implicit acceptance of the principle of withdrawal as a component in a prospective settlement. The effect of these small but significant gestures was felt during the sixth session of Madrid-inspired talks held in Washington from August 24 to September 2. The format did not change, but those sessions were marked by a new atmosphere, and substantive progress was made.

Syria responded to Israel's opening gambit by presenting, on September 1, 1992, a draft of a proposed Declaration of Principles for a Syrian-Israeli peace agreement. The concepts underlying this draft and the positions presented in it were all totally unacceptable to Israel, but, in contrast to Israeli-Syrian relations during the previous four rounds of Washington talks—an acrimonious dialogue of the deaf—its very presentation and its mention of a Syrian-Israeli peace agreement were emblematic of significant changes.

By the end of 1992, this good momentum had been all but dissipated. The Palestinian delegation to the Madrid process talks in Washington, operating under instructions from the PLO leaders in Tunis, and the Israeli delegation were at cross-purposes. (The Palestinian delegation, composed of residents of the West Bank and the Gaza Strip, was headed by a distinguished Palestinian nationalist, Dr. Haidar Abdul Shafi from Gaza, but it was common knowledge that for all intents and purposes the group was controlled and monitored by the PLO leaders in Tunis.) And the Israelis and Syrians were bogged down by Syria's insistence on Israel's commitment to a full withdrawal from the Golan Heights as a precondition to any further give-and-take. In December Israel cracked down on the radical Islamic opposition in territory under its direct control by deporting some four hundred members of Hamas, the Islamic Resistance movement, to Lebanon. The Arab parties at the Washington talks knew very well that Hamas was challenging them, too, but they responded to Israel's move by suspending their participation in the negotiations.

What were the principal forces that were slowing down or stalling the hoped-for peace?

One was the continued discrepancy between Israeli and Arab outlooks. Syria tried hard to rally the four Arab negotiating parties, and indeed the larger Arab world, behind its own concept of a prospective settlement with Israel and of the procedural aspects in the negotiations. Asad was determined to maximize Arab coordination and to seek a comprehensive settlement or at least an approximation of one. When, in late July 1992, the Arab foreign ministers were invited to Damascus to formulate their strategy in the aftermath of the Israeli elections and in anticipation of the sixth round of the Washington talks, their joint statement of July 25 alluded to some flexibility (the term "peace agreement" was used for the first time), but it also foreshadowed Syria's and the PLO's opposition to the main thrust of Israel's peace policies. The statement noted approvingly the new Israeli government's "relative change in tone and approach" but criticized its failure to declare "its commitment to the basic principles of comprehensive, just and lasting peace in the region through full implementation of Security Council Resolutions 242 and 338 and the principle of the return of all occupied Arab land, including Jerusalem, in return for peace." The foreign ministers "emphasized anew the . . . principles and elements on which the peace process is based." This meant, overall, a "commitment to the objective of comprehensive peace in the region." But the foreign ministers also pledged to "respect and ensure the Palestinian people's right to self-determination and [to] set up their independent state on their national soil"; they stressed "the linkage between the transitional and final stages in the Palestinian track," and pledged to work to eliminate not only "the obstacles that block completing the Palestinian representation to include the inhabitants of Jerusalem and the diaspora," but also the obstacles to "PLO participation in an official manner in the peace process." They also insisted on "the illegitimacy of all forms of Israeli settlement" in the West Bank and Gaza and called for a "comprehensive solution in all fronts and in all tracks . . . rejecting any attempt to fragment and deal with each party individually."[5]

During the next few months, Syria and the PLO succeeded in upholding these principles. The PLO was, indeed, concerned to obtain formal legitimacy for itself in the peace process and to block any interim
agreement that was not linked to a final arrangement that met Palestinian nationalism's basic expectations. It made sure that no progress
was made in Washington so long as these two principal goals were
not met. Genuine progress between Syria and Israel was obstructed by
Asad's insistence on an Israeli commitment to a full withdrawal from
the Golan Heights. Outside the conference room, Asad objected to any
informal, discreet contacts with Israeli diplomats, refused to engage in
public diplomacy, and declined to exercise a restraining influence on
Hizballah's activities in and from Lebanon.

A second difficulty concerned political developments within the
United States. The revival of the Madrid process in the summer of 1992
coincided with the diminishing diplomatic effectiveness of the Bush
administration. Shortly after Secretary Baker's trip to the Middle East
in July, President Bush asked him to leave the State Department and
move to the White House as his chief of staff. It was a desperate effort to
salvage Bush's ailing campaign for reelection. Dennis Ross, Baker's chief
aide in Israeli-Arab matters, went with him to the White House. Deputy
Secretary Lawrence Eagleburger was appointed acting secretary of state.
Eagleburger, an authoritative diplomat and policymaker, had at his disposal an experienced "peace team," but the reality and perception of a
waning presidency undermined his effectiveness. Asad, for one, went on
participating in the talks as much to build a new relationship with the
Americans as to arrive at a settlement with Israel and regain the Golan
Heights. But Asad saw no sense in offering concessions to a president
whose future prospects appeared increasingly uncertain or, later, after
Bill Clinton had defeated Bush, in making concessions in anticipation
of working with a new president about whom Asad knew practically
nothing. This transitional phase ended only in February 1993, when
Clinton's new administration signaled its assignment of high priority to
the Arab-Israeli peace process.

A third difficulty was the direct challenge presented by the radical
Islamic opponents of peace with Israel. Hamas and the smaller Islamic
Jihad were inspired by several sources: opposition to the very notion of a
peaceful settlement with Israel, a more specific opposition to the Madrid

process, opposition to and criticism of Yasser Arafat and his team, and Iranian encouragement. The actions of Hamas, the more active and effective of the two, were shaped by a terribly effective logic—violence and terrorism against Israeli targets would undermine the Israeli people's support for peace and would force Israeli counteractions that would disrupt it.[6] And, indeed, by stepping up its deadly activity—Hamas killed three Israeli soldiers in the Gaza Strip on December 7, 1992, and an Israeli border-police officer was abducted and murdered on December 13—Hamas provoked Rabin into his radical effort to emasculate, if not destroy, the Hamas infrastructure in the West Bank and the Gaza Strip: the deportation of some four hundred Hamas activists to Lebanon.

Warren Christopher, the new secretary of state, went to the Middle East in February 1993, marking the revival of the peace process, which by April was fully back on track. Rabin had his first working visit to the Clinton administration in March, and the Washington talks were resumed in April. Rabin's March visit to Washington was especially important, for it laid the foundation for a warm personal relationship between Clinton and Rabin and for a close working relationship between their governments. But progress was clearly neither smooth nor linear. Rabin completed his work in Washington but had to cut short his visit to the United States because of a wave of terrorist knifing attacks in Tel Aviv.

Coherence and clarity marked the architecture of the new American administration's Middle East policies: a dual containment of Iraq and Iran in the east and pursuit of Arab-Israeli peace in the west, two mutually reinforcing policy prongs. By cultivating an Arab-Israeli peace, Washington hoped to make it easier for its conservative Arab allies to support dual containment, and fostering Israeli-Syrian and Israeli-Palestinian reconciliation should diminish the ability of Iran and other fundamentalist Muslim states to agitate and subvert.[7]

The administration also believed that this Middle East policy had an unusual asset: an authoritative Israeli prime minister who was determined by his own choice to move toward peace and who was ready to offer indispensable concessions. During the previous twenty years, the United States and Israel had cooperated for much of the time, but as a rule American presidents and secretaries of state had to extract concessions from reluctant Israeli prime ministers (including Rabin himself during his first tenure). Here was a unique opportunity.

In their discussions with Rabin in March, Clinton and his team were quite explicit about their preference for effecting a breakthrough first on the Israeli-Syrian track, which seemed eminently feasible given Rabin's willingness to offer a significant (though still not specific) territorial concession and assuming Asad's willingness to make peace. They believed that Asad could deliver on an agreement he would sign and that an Israeli-Syrian peace could be a prelude to an American-Syrian rapprochement; this would detach Syria from Iran's sphere of influence, as it were, and be the key to a desirable realignment in the Middle East. Rabin was responsive to this view, but he reminded the Americans that from Israel's point of view a breakthrough would be welcome on either track.

In April the State Department official in charge of the peace process, Edward Djerejian, was dispatched on a secret mission to President Asad. He bore a letter from President Clinton that was intended to persuade Asad to open additional discreet channels to Israel and to adopt a bolder, more forthcoming approach in the negotiations. Djerejian's mission, then a second letter from Clinton, a meeting in Vienna between Secretary Christopher and Syrian Foreign Minister Faruq al-Shara, and further work between the Israeli and Syrian delegations in Washington all failed to produce results.

Nor did U.S. diplomacy succeed in helping the Israeli and Palestinian delegations reach accommodation. Israeli diplomacy, resorting to unorthodox methods, produced a final breakthrough on this track only by means of secret bilateral negotiations that went on in Oslo for several months. The Oslo talks began, like several similar informal and unauthorized Israeli and Palestinian dialogues, in January 1993. On the Israeli side it had the sponsorship of Deputy Foreign Minister Yossi Beilin, who operated through two of his academic protégés. Beilin took his time before briefing his superior, Foreign Minister Shimon Peres, about these talks, and Peres took his time in reporting to the prime minister.[8]

Rabin's response was complex. He himself was not enamored of the Madrid format and had lost faith in the formal negotiations in Washington. He had authorized some of his own confidants to deal indirectly with the PLO and in March 1993, during his visit to Washington, had agreed to have Faysal Husseini, the most prominent Palestinian leader in East Jerusalem, join the Palestinian delegation to the Washington talks. Husseini was known to have close ties with the PLO, and his participation in the talks could conceivably be construed as a crack in Israel's adamant claim that Jerusalem's status as an Israeli city was not negotiable. This latter point was finessed by the admittedly weak argument, familiar since 1989, that since Husseini had a West Bank address he could be regarded as a West Banker and not necessarily as a Jerusalemite. As for the PLO connection, Rabin felt that the pretense of dealing with presumably independent local leaders was wearing thin. Husseini was an authentic local leader, whatever his affiliation with the PLO, and his participation in the Washington talks was a last-ditch effort to see whether there was any value to dealing with local leaders by bypassing the PLO. In retrospect, it is clear that Rabin was not really surprised to discover that Husseini, too, received his marching orders from Tunis. For him, the whole episode was a transition to the ensuing negotiation with the PLO.

So in May 1993 Rabin agreed to formalize and elevate the status of the still-secret Oslo talks and dispatched the director general of the Foreign Ministry, Uri Savir, to head the Israeli team there. Rabin's concession was dual: he agreed in fact to negotiate with the PLO, an organization he had until recently demonized, and he assigned the principal work in this negotiation to Shimon Peres and his team. The original division of labor in Rabin's government had reflected the lingering rivalry between the prime minister and the man he had defeated in the party primaries just five months earlier: Rabin had taken charge of the four tracks of bilateral negotiations with the Arabs, while Peres was left with the five working groups in the multilateral talks. Now Rabin was altering the internal balance in his government, but he regarded this as a secondary issue compared with the prospect of a breakthrough with the Palestinian nationalists.[9]

The Oslo negotiations continued into early August. The Palestinian delegation, composed of Abu Alaa (or Ahmed Qurai), a senior member of the PLO hierarchy, and two associates, at Israel's insistence provided ample proof that they were valid and effective PLO representatives. On the Israeli side, Savir was reinforced by Joel Singer, a retired international lawyer with the Israeli Defense Forces. Rabin kept his own close aides and the defense establishment in the dark, and Singer's participation (in addition to Rabin's own overseeing of the negotiations) was intended to ensure that security issues would be covered. By early August, the broad lines of an agreement had indeed been put together.

The core of the agreement was predicated on the model established by the Camp David Accords in 1978. Palestinian self-rule was to be established in the West Bank and the Gaza Strip for a transitional period of five years. At the end of the second year, negotiations would begin over final-status issues. Israeli military forces would be redeployed in several stages—first from Gaza, then from Palestinian cities in the West Bank, and then in a series of "further redeployments" during the final-status negotiations. Israeli settlements on the West Bank would not be affected, and their future, as well as the issues of Jerusalem, of water rights, and of refugees, would be addressed in the final-status negotiations.

But the agreement taking shape in Oslo was different from the autonomy plan of 1978–79 in several significant respects. For one thing, the PLO had earlier refused to endorse the autonomy agreement, and Israel was then led by a government determined to prevent Palestinian statehood. But the Oslo Accords were signed by the PLO and by Israeli leaders determined to effect a historic compromise with Palestinian nationalism and aware that an agreement on self-rule would likely lead to Palestinian statehood.

It was precisely his realization of the magnitude of the issues involved in the Oslo Accords that led Rabin to resort to an unusual measure: before an agreement was concluded in Oslo, he wanted to establish whether Israel had any option vis-à-vis Syria. On August 3, during a meeting in his office in Jerusalem with Warren Christopher, he asked the secretary of state to use the "hypothetical-question" technique when he went next to Damascus. As we have seen, the effort during the previous few months to develop an effective Israeli-Syrian communication had been made to no avail. Rabin now asked Secretary Christopher to inquire of Asad whether, "on the assumption that his own demand would be met," he would be willing to make peace with Israel on the basis of terms acceptable to Israel.

Rabin modeled the terms of his question on the Israeli-Egyptian peace treaty of 1979: contractual peace, full diplomatic relations, normalization, security arrangements, implementation in phases over a five-year period, and what he called interface—a heavy dose of normalization at the outset in return for a very small withdrawal on Israel's part, to enable Israel to test the new relationship before withdrawing from the rest of the territory it had seized in the war. Rabin emphasized to

Christopher that his question must remain secret, that it was a hypothetical question, and that, since Rabin had not presented it as part of his platform in the 1992 elections, he would have to submit such an agreement to a referendum before it had legitimacy.

Secretary Christopher and Dennis Ross presented Rabin's hypothetical gambit to Asad on August 4 and returned to Rabin's office on August 5 with a response that they regarded as positive but he viewed as disappointing. Asad envisaged an implementation period of six months rather than five years; he took exception to the term "normalization"; security arrangements were welcome as long as they were for both parties and "on equal footing;" and the notion of interface was unacceptable. Asad clearly thought he was beginning a protracted bargaining process, but his response was totally unacceptable to Rabin. Not only did Rabin not want a lengthy and arduous tug-of-war over every issue, big or small, but he felt it was an inherently flawed process. Since Syria regarded full Israeli withdrawal from the Golan Heights as a given, the bargaining process would be restricted solely to Israel's terms, which were bound to be whittled down. Christopher and Ross went back home and left on their summer vacations—only to find out later in August that Israel had gone ahead and concluded the Oslo Accords.[10]

The Clinton administration had been briefed in general terms about the secret negotiations between Israel and the PLO. In fact, Rabin and Christopher had discussed them on August 3, but the briefings were vague enough that the Oslo breakthrough was a surprise. The Clinton administration wasted no time in being surprised, disappointed, or angry: most of its decisionmakers and policymakers had thought a Syrian-Israeli agreement was the best starting point, but they recognized the historic significance and policy implications of Israel's agreement with the PLO. After the Israeli and Norwegian ministers of foreign affairs briefed Christopher and Ross in California, the administration decided not only to endorse the Oslo Accords but to endow them with the added value of an impressive signing ceremony on the White House lawn on September 13.

From that point on, the Israeli-Arab peace process was predicated on the Israeli-Palestinian agreement, while prospects for an Israeli-Syrian agreement diminished. Hafiz al-Asad's positions and attitudes, as revealed by the hypothetical exercise in August, had had a chilling effect on Rabin, who also felt that he could not "overload the circuits" in Israel itself, that the Palestinian settlement had to be digested before a second painful concession could be accepted in Israel.

But Asad and the Clinton administration had a different idea. Asad chose to ignore the distinction between a hypothetical deposition with an honest broker and an actual commitment made in the course of a negotiation. His position was reinforced by Christopher's view that a promising start had been unnecessarily nipped in the bud, and by his determination to go ahead with Israeli-Syrian talks once the Oslo Accords were signed. The Americans invested considerable effort in placating Asad, persuading him not to agitate against Oslo and in fact to send his ambassador in Washington to the signing ceremony. They also promised Asad to resume the work begun in August, and indeed they obtained Rabin's commitment to cooperate in new talks in four months. This is how the term "commitment"—as a description of Rabin's hypothetical question—was introduced into the vocabulary of the Israeli-Syrian negotiation.

Fourteen months after taking office, Rabin thus effected the first breakthrough toward peace with the Palestinians. The Oslo Accords and the Washington signing ceremony were momentous: the ground had been laid for a historic compromise between Israeli and Palestinian nationalism. By addressing this core issue and by going through the rites of mutual recognition with the PLO, Israel also laid the groundwork for normalizing its relations with other Arab states and its own international position, while Palestinians for the first time since 1947 had a real chance for statehood.

The prospects were exhilarating, but the euphoria of the moment could not conceal the gravity of the remaining problems or the difficulties inherent in the very wording of the Oslo Accords. Compromises and concessions generated criticism on both sides; criticism and opposition were bound to increase after the initial shock wore off and problems of implementation came to the fore. There was an ironic symmetry to the criticism leveled at Rabin by his Israeli critics and at Arafat by his Arab ones. Rabin was accused of making an agreement with the leader and organization he himself had demonized, endowing them with legitimacy, giving away parts of the Jews' historic homeland, and undermining the security of Israel and Israelis. Arafat was charged with having sold out, offering Israel legitimacy and recognition in return for mere self-rule under Israeli tutelage, abandoning the Palestinian diaspora, and relegating Palestine's crucial final status to an ill-defined future moment.

Now the principles in the Oslo Accords would have to be converted into detailed, agreed-on implementations. This required a sense of partnership and genuine cooperation. In the absence of clarity about the future, both leaders would have to win each other's confidence while keeping the support of their own constituencies. Yet, throughout the West Bank and the Gaza Strip, Israeli settlers and Palestinian Arabs would pursue different, often contradictory agendas. The PLO's former foot soldiers were to become a gendarmerie entrusted with keeping law and order but also with foiling attacks against Israel and Israelis. Important questions would have to be answered by both parties. Would Arafat actually move to Gaza and turn the new Palestinian Authority (PA) there into the center of Palestinian life, or would he keep the PLO headquarters in Tunis and its "embassies" and offices around the world as the real locus of Palestinian nationalism? Would the Israeli public reelect the government that had signed the Oslo Accords, or would the critics come to power to stop the process before the final-status negotiations?

THE CRUCIAL YEAR OF 1994

Some of these questions were answered during the following year, which Israel and the PLO spent negotiating the implementation agreement for a Gaza and Jericho plan (it was signed on May 4, 1994, in Cairo), and the Paris Agreement, which regulated economic relations between Israel and the Palestinian Authority. This was arduous work, and yet the first phase was concluded successfully. By the summer of 1994, there was a functioning Palestinian administration in Gaza and a less significant extension of Palestinian control in Jericho. Arafat had moved to Gaza and was spending most of his time there.

But some of the anticipated difficulties arose as well. Chief among them were violent efforts made to derail the peace process. On February 25, a Jewish settler killed twenty-nine Muslim worshipers at the Tomb of the Patriarchs in Hebron; a few weeks later, on April 6 and 13, Hamas killed twelve Israelis in suicide bombings in two Israeli towns.

Israel's next major initiative was to seek a full-fledged peace settlement with Jordan. This was a popular, noncontroversial move that would require only moderate concessions in return for which Israel would have peace along its longest border, the prospect of warm relations and actual cooperation with King Hussein's friendly regime, and increased leverage with both Syria and the Palestinians.[11] But several significant obstacles had to be overcome. These included the Clinton administration's reservations. It felt beholden to the Syria track and wanted to hold Rabin to his commitment to resume serious give-and-take with Asad once the agreement with the PLO was in place. The administration also doubted that Jordan would make a full peace; after all, the Hashemite kings had not yet done so despite decades of secret diplomacy. Also, disputes over land and water had to be resolved, and to resolve them Jordan would have to defy Syria (which had similar issues with Israel) and move on its own.

But Rabin persisted. He saw the advantage in several developments. King Hussein was not pleased with the Oslo Accords and the resulting prospect of a Palestinian state on Jordan's border claiming the allegiance of the majority of his subjects, who were Palestinian. But once the king and his entourage overcame their initial anger, they understood the advantages of having a close working relationship with Rabin during this crucial period. The Americans, despite their reservations and different priorities, also were finally persuaded to support the process by offering Jordan debt relief, the possibility of strengthening and modernizing its armed forces, and, not least, an opportunity to erase the negative legacy of its support for Iraq during the Gulf War period.

Israel had experienced a long tradition of secret personal diplomacy with Jordan. So the talks in Washington were sidestepped during 1994 by personal diplomacy at the highest level, which achieved the breakthrough; the official delegations resumed work in earnest only at the final phases, and not in Washington. The warm personal relationship between King Hussein and Prime Minister Rabin was indispensable in the completion of a peace treaty in one year; it was signed in October 1994.

The character and pace of Israel's negotiations with Syria were very different. In late April, when the Cairo Agreement with the Palestinians was about to be signed, Rabin was stunned to hear from Secretary

Christopher that Asad had a new precondition for resumed negotiations: Israel's full withdrawal from the Golan Heights—conditionally and hypothetically suggested by Israel via the United States in August 1993—must mean withdrawal to the lines of June 4, 1967, that is, before the 1967 war. This demand raised a difficult truth about borders in the Middle East. A line separating Mandate Syria from Mandate Palestine had been drawn in 1923, and was generally accepted by the international community but did not represent an official border between the modern states of Syria and Israel. The 1948 war had ended with an armistice agreement, signed in 1949, that in certain respects was ambiguous: it referred specifically to an "armistice line," leaving the border issue for future settlements. Then, between 1949 and 1967, Syria took advantage of controlling the high ground to establish itself in the al-Hamma enclave in the southern foothills of the Golan Heights and on the eastern shore of Lake Tiberias, Israel's most important water reservoir. The term "lines of June 4, 1967," which presumed this territory was Syrian, had appeared before in the Israel-Syria negotiations, but the cutting edge of Syria's demand had all along been "full withdrawal." Syria's insistence now on the June 4 lines could be explained as tactical (a desire to do better than Egypt, which had made its peace according to the international border) or principled (in line with Asad's traditional railing against the region's partition by the colonial powers). But in any event Rabin viewed it as unjustified and illegitimate; to him it cast doubts on Asad's intention actually to conclude an agreement, let alone swiftly, and it reinforced Rabin's sense that an Israel-Syria agreement was not likely during his first term.

Still, Rabin was not interested in pushing Asad into a corner or in straining his relationship with the Clinton administration, which, from its remote and lofty vantage point, saw little difference between the acknowledged international border and the June 4 lines. By July 19 a formula had been found for grafting the lines of June 4 onto the original hypothetical, conditional suggestion made in August 1993. Asad now authorized his ambassador in Washington, Walid Muallem, to open an ambassadors' channel with his Israeli counterpart, the present author. We met regularly and frequently for several months, always in the presence of one or two American diplomats. This ambassadors' channel proved to be most effective: the two nations could with relative ease explore each other's real positions and establish the possibilities and limitations of any future relationship.

Casablanca and After

On October 31, 1994, shortly after Jordan and Israel signed a peace agreement, the first Middle East Economic Conference opened in Casablanca. Several themes converged here: one was the notion of Arab-Israeli normalization, which Israel's agreement with the PLO had made much easier to implement; another was the idea of having multilateral talks in which Israel, various Arab countries, and other nations discussed regional issues and means of cooperation that among other things would facilitate any concessions made in bilateral negotiations. A third idea, identified closely with Foreign Minister Peres, was that a durable Arab-Israeli peace should rest on a common effort to resolve regional socioeconomic problems and to elevate the general population's standard of living. A calmer and better integrated Middle East was a positive idea for everyone.

In many respects, the Jordan-Israel peace treaty and the Casablanca Conference were the high-water marks of the 1992–96 period. Soon, several negative trends became apparent, two of which were devastating. But first there was the signing on September 28, 1995, of Oslo II— the agreement that extended Palestinian self-rule to the West Bank. The negotiations had been more difficult and more protracted than expected. The implementation of the Cairo Agreement (concerning Gaza and Jericho) had been considered fairly successful, and a sense of partnership did develop at least among some of the Israeli and Palestinian decisionmakers and negotiators, but several obstacles obstructed the next phase. To begin with, the implementation of Palestinian self-rule was a more complex and difficult matter in the West Bank than in Gaza, a more compact area with fewer Israeli settlements and settlers. The West Bank is close to Israel's main cities, contiguous to Jerusalem, and dotted with Israeli settlements large and small. The Palestinian negotiators were eager to control as much territory as possible before the final-status talks began and before the Israeli elections, both scheduled for 1996.

Rabin and Peres were equally determined to keep as many bargaining assets as they could for as long as possible.

The core of the agreement finally reached stipulated a division of the West Bank into several categories: Area A would consist of the main cities, in which a full transfer of civil and security authority to the Palestinian Authority would take place gradually as Israel withdrew; Area B would include more than 450 villages under the PA's civil authority, but with Israel maintaining overall responsibility for security until mid-1997; Area C would include Israeli state lands, thinly populated areas, and the Jewish settlements, which would remain under full Israeli security jurisdiction, with a limited PA jurisdiction over the area's sparse Palestinian population. All told, less than 30 percent of the West Bank would be transferred to direct Palestinian control at that phase.

Later on, Israel was to continue its withdrawal in three further redeployments. Israeli negotiators agreed to this scheme, which the Palestinians argued was predicated on the autonomy plan in the 1978 Camp David Accords ("a withdrawal of Israeli armed forces will take place and there will be a redeployment of the remaining Israeli forces into specified security locations"), but only at a later date and in circumstances that have since become controversial in Israel. The logic underlying Israel's acceptance of the arrangement was intimately linked to its anticipation of the final-status negotiations: every Israeli withdrawal should facilitate a concession that Arafat would have to make if those negotiations were to succeed. Another important stipulation of the Oslo II agreement concerned the election, under international supervision, of an eighty-two-member Palestinian legislative council, to be held twenty-two days after Israeli soldiers had withdrawn from the main cities of the West Bank (except Hebron).

This Oslo II agreement was a particularly important milestone. The original Oslo Accords had had far-reaching potential consequences, but actually getting through the first phase of implementation to the second was not inevitable. The second agreement provided for that transition and brought the Palestinians to the verge of statehood. Israeli negotiators defined it as "a historical agreement that put an end to the Israeli domination of the Palestinians and to the concept of the 'Land of Israel' and which set in motion the beginning of cooperation between the two peoples who decided to divide the land between them for the sake of the mutual object of peace, security and economic development."[12]

The next phase of negotiations coincided with the temporary collapse of talks between Israel and Syria. Between November 1994 and June 1995, significant efforts were made to develop a dialogue between the security establishments of the two countries; the relatively open discussion between the ambassadors in Washington had clearly demonstrated that this dialogue was indispensable to any real progress. So, in December 1994, a first meeting was held between the army chiefs of staff of Israel and Syria. This important and "normal" act revealed the depth of the gap separating the two protagonists' views of the security issue. Syria insisted on full Israeli withdrawal from the Golan Heights, of course, but maintained that Israel would not need extensive security arrangements, which would be invasive and humiliating for Syria given that Israel enjoyed overall military superiority. For Israelis who viewed the Golan Heights primarily as a security necessity, withdrawal from most, let alone all, of it would obviously have to be offset by an impressive array of other security arrangements.

President Asad, unhappy with what he regarded as excessive Israeli expectations and demands, suspended further negotiations between the military officers and insisted that a set of underlying principles be agreed upon before they met again. Most of the principles important to Asad were quite acceptable to Israel, as it happened, but for more than four months Asad's insistence that Israel agree to so-called equality as an underlying principle proved to be an insurmountable obstacle: Rabin held that, though most security arrangements could be implemented on an equal basis, their territorial dimensions could not be equal, because of the two countries' differences in size and topography. In May 1995 a compromise formula was finally worked out, which led to the drafting of a "nonpaper" on "the aims and principles of the security arrangements."

After this, the Syrian and Israeli chiefs of staff met again, in Washington in June (in the meantime General Amnon Lipkin-Shahak had replaced Ehud Barak as the chief of staff of the Israel Defense Forces). A genuine give-and-take developed in the course of that meeting, but afterward misunderstanding and disagreement recurred. Asad now wanted Israel to give up its demand for a manned early-warning station on the

Golan Heights before any further discussions ensued. Rabin refused to comply with this negotiating style and insisted that the sequence agreed on in May be kept. On this sticking point the negotiation was stalled, and it was renewed only after Rabin's assassination.

By the time the talks stalled, however, several other negative developments had occurred. Foremost among them was a string of terrorist attacks launched by Hamas. In October 1994 twenty-two Israelis were killed by a suicide attack on a bus at the very center of Tel Aviv; in January 1995 twenty-one Israeli soldiers were killed when two explosive charges were detonated in a bus station; and in July five Israelis were killed in another suicide bombing in a bus in the city of Ramat Gan, near Tel Aviv.

These terrorist attacks had a devastating effect on the Israeli public's attitude toward the unfolding possibility of peace with the Arabs. Not all of the attacks originated in areas under the Palestinian Authority's control, but the prevailing perception was that they did and that Arafat and his colleagues were not totally committed to preventing anti-Israeli terrorism by Muslim fundamentalist opponents of the peace process. The attacks led Israelis to believe that Arafat did not consider Hamas a dangerous challenge whose infrastructure and ideology had to be uprooted lest his own strategy be destroyed, but instead as a legitimate, significant political force he would rather co-opt than fight head on and as a potential partner if his agreement with Israel collapsed.

Arafat's familiar proclivity to equivocate in difficult and complex situations was, indeed, compounded by issues that grew out of the Oslo Accords, though not exactly as the Israeli public perceived it. Oslo, being a phased conditional formula for resolving the Israeli-Palestinian conflict, required Arafat to deal simultaneously with two conflicting constituencies. He had to persuade Israel that he had buried the hatchet and was a partner solicitous of Israeli security, but he also felt that he had to keep the Palestinians mobilized and motivated for the tug-of-war with Israel that lay ahead. Whatever his sense of partnership with the Rabin-Peres government, Arafat knew well that profound disagreements could be expected over the final-status issues. Meanwhile, his promises and exhortations to his Palestinian constituency—the struggle continues, it's a *jihad* (holy war), we know from Islamic history that agreements made with infidels may not be binding, Jerusalem will be liberated—were noted and amplified by Israeli opponents of the very idea of making peace with the Palestinians.

This posturing by Arafat was embarrassing to the Israeli government, but not as devastating as was the reformulation of the security issue, which occurred as an unanticipated consequence of the Oslo Accords. Rabin, a leader preoccupied with national security, oversaw the government's effort to guarantee that reconciliation with Palestinians would have no adverse effects on Israel's national security. He also believed that peace with the Palestinians and Israel's other immediate neighbors would set the stage for dealing with the more serious, even existential threats presented by Iraq and Iran. But he failed to foresee that a terrorist campaign in Israel proper might be launched by Arab and Muslim enemies of the peace process, and Israel had no answer to the suicide bombings. During the six years of the intifada, 172 Israelis were killed; by contrast, during the peak years of the peace process, 1993–96, close to 300 Israelis were killed by terrorists. As a result, many Israelis began to equate the Oslo peace process with an actual loss of personal security. Whatever the immediate or more remote benefits accruing to Israel and to its citizens from the Oslo Accords, they were less palpable and seemed less significant than the perceived security threat, not to mention the apparent new dependence on the Palestinian Authority's cooperation for security, not only in the West Bank but in general.

By the summer of 1995, public disenchantment with the implementation of the Oslo Accords and growing opposition to the idea of withdrawal from the Golan Heights began to erode the government's support base and legitimacy. The Oslo II agreement was approved only barely in the Knesset, and the government was only barely able to fend off an attempt by the Golan Lobby to entrench the 1981 Golan Law, which extended Israeli law to the Golan Heights. This would have been a mortal blow to the beleaguered Israeli-Syrian negotiation.

More ominously, domestic opposition to the government's peace policies was becoming still uglier and more vehement. There were violent demonstrations, calls for civil disobedience (a concept imported from the United States), disruption of public order, and much incendiary rhetoric. As it turned out, in this context of violence, delegitimization, and demonization, a small fanatical group was operating with the belief that the only way to stop the peace process was to assassinate Yitzhak

Rabin. One of its members acted on November 4, 1995, and his action proved, indeed, to be terribly effective.

The declining fortunes of the peace process in Israel were matched by growing opposition and eroding support on the Arab side. Euphoria had not been part of the Arab response to the Oslo Accords from the outset, of course, and most of the Arab world wanted simply to get the conflict with Israel over with and turn its attention to other issues. Many Arabs were grudgingly willing to endorse Oslo and to offer Israel a measure of acceptance and normalization, but even this grudging acceptance was never universal. Soon it was further clouded by criticism of the Oslo Accords themselves, by Syria's unhappiness with the failure to achieve progress, by Islamic and other radical agitation, and by both popular and official fear that normalization might lead to Israel's domination of the Middle East. Israel's decision to send a very large delegation to the Casablanca Conference and some less-than-tactful rhetoric in Israel fanned these anxieties. The term "New Middle East," used by Shimon Peres as the title of a book outlining his vision of peace in the region, became the focus of this criticism of Israel's intentions.[13] Peres had wanted to propose a future in which Israelis and Arabs worked together to resolve the region's underlying problems, first and foremost poverty and scarcity of natural resources. However, his book and the ideas it expounded were received by a suspicious Arab world as paternalistic at best or, more commonly and at worst, as demonstrating Israel's quest for hegemony. As Asad put it in an interview in the Egyptian newspaper *al-Ahram*:

> I believe that they want a dark future for us. . . . I believe that the long-term goal of the others is to cancel what is called the Arabs, what is called Arabism. . . . I mean canceling our feelings as a nation, canceling Arab feelings, canceling pan-Arab identity. . . . We, as Arabs, certainly reject this because . . . Arabism is not a commodity to trade in even though this is what the others seek.[14]

Egypt played a significant part in the development of this attitude. During the previous fifteen years, Egypt had been embarrassed by its separate peace with Israel and criticized Israel for failing to implement the Palestinian part of it. Now, with a larger peace process unfolding, and when an Israeli-Palestinian agreement had been signed, with Egypt's help and support, Egypt was visibly unhappy with the restructuring of regional politics, and Cairo, too, saw Israel as striving for regional hegemony at its expense. It did nothing to improve its own bilateral relationship with Israel and waged a vociferous campaign against Israel's potential as a nuclear power, noting its policy of studied ambiguity about nuclear weapons and its refusal to sign the Treaty on Non-Proliferation of Nuclear Weapons. Egypt tried to obstruct Washington's policy of extending the terms of that treaty indefinitely upon the expiration in 1995 of its original time frame and, when this failed, suspended its participation in the multilateral working group on arms control and regional security. In the event, this Egyptian policy resulted in the suspension of all the multilateral tracks on which Israeli-Arab negotiations had been proceeding.[15]

Rabin's assassination thus happened when the peace process he had launched was already receding, and his death dealt it a near-fatal blow. Peres's attempt to revitalize and accelerate peace negotiations can be viewed in retrospect as its Indian summer.

AFTER RABIN

Throughout this period, and for everyone involved, Israel's domestic politics and foreign policy were closely intertwined. This was especially true between Rabin's assassination and the Israeli elections of 1996. Shimon Peres, as Rabin's successor, had to make an early dual decision: when the next Israeli election should be held, and on what platform he would run. If he called an early election, he would run as Rabin's avenger and the principal issues would be the government's support of the Oslo Accords and its efforts to assign responsibility for the assassination. Or he could keep the original date—late October 1996—by which time he would have to run on his own terms and on the strength of new policy decisions he would make during the intervening months.

Peres chose the latter option, which presented him with the next decision to be made: should he seek to finalize an agreement with Syria, or should he try to speed up final-status talks with the Palestinians (scheduled to begin in May) and seek to telescope them into a few months?

One of Peres's closest associates, Yossi Beilin, had just concluded another secret, unauthorized negotiation with the Palestinians: he and Arafat's deputy Mahmud Abbas (Abu Mazen) had drafted a final-status agreement, which offered the Palestinians statehood and sovereignty over most of the West Bank, although it kept most of the Jewish settlements and settlers under Israeli rule. It also proposed an ingenious solution to the issue of Jerusalem: Abu Dis, a village (or suburb) bordering Jerusalem on the east would be named al-Quds (the Arabic name for Jerusalem) and become a capital for the Palestinian state, contiguous to Jerusalem proper. Beilin argued that by using this draft, final-status negotiations could be completed by May, and that such an agreement would win the support of a majority of Israelis and would give the government a program both for winning the elections in October and for consolidating the peace process.

Peres was not convinced. He preferred a different plan favored by some of his other aides and by the Clinton administration: to get a swift deal with Syria and to use it to achieve a comprehensive settlement of the Arab-Israeli conflict. Peres's idea of an Israeli-Syrian settlement was quite different from what Rabin's had been. He was interested not in a lengthy phased implementation but in rapid execution, he did not see security as the key issue, and he did not believe in assigning military officers an important role in the negotiations. In keeping with his larger view, the new prime minister believed that the way to build a durable peace was to create a web of common economic interests and to increase Syria's own prosperity. There was also a significant difference in his view of normalization. Rabin had not believed that Syria would willingly offer more normalization than Egypt had, and he thought Israel could settle, for the time being, on a formal peace. Peres held that Israel should insist on early engagement and economic cooperation, that this was the only way to deal with the underlying issues and place an ensuing settlement on a solid foundation.

Peres's preferences and his sense of urgency ran against the grain of Asad's character and style: cautious, suspicious, and deliberate. Asad was attracted by Peres's apparent willingness to deemphasize the security dimension, but he was taken aback by Peres's insistence that normalization and direct economic cooperation with Israel were crucial.

Just as Rabin's gambit via Secretary Christopher in August 1993 had been a breakthrough, Peres's interest in making a swift deal with Asad provided the opportunity for a second breakthrough. But prospects for an agreement soon faded. Peres explained to Secretary Christopher and his team that his willingness to come to terms with Syria was conditional on Asad's agreement to an early meeting: he knew that Asad would make peace only on the basis of Israel's full withdrawal from the Golan Heights, and he was willing to bite this bullet, but only if his own terms were met, which could be established only through high-level negotiations. Peres wanted an early indication of seriousness, and he knew he could hardly go into the election campaign as a prime minister who had given up the Golan and gotten nothing in return.

A public meeting between himself and Asad was the litmus test. But Asad rebuffed the idea. He, too, favored swift negotiations and was agreeable to some relaxation in their format, but he would not upgrade the negotiations significantly, would not engage in serious public diplomacy, and certainly would not meet Peres before an agreement was reached.

Relations deteriorated further during negotiating rounds that took place at a conference center at the Wye River Plantation (later to become much better known), near Washington, where Israel and Syria were represented by mixed civilian and military delegations. Together with a group of American diplomats, the two teams stayed for several days at a time under the same roof, shared meals, and talked more freely than they ever had before. Progress was made, but too slowly for the Israeli government's domestic political agenda and timetable. Peres, grappling with the question of whether to move up the elections to late May, needed to know in January whether an agreement might be reached by the spring, so as to fit into a political schedule leading to October elections, and the reports he received from Wye were not clear. Some progress was made, but not much on security issues, and Syria resisted Israel's new insistence on genuine economic cooperation.

Peres therefore decided to move up the election to May 29. This displeased Asad (eventually, his spokesmen would argue that an agreement had been well on its way and that Peres's decision destroyed that prospect). But he agreed to continue the negotiations at Wye in anticipation of the vote. Israel suspended them in early March, however, after suicide bombings staged by Hamas and Islamic Jihad in three Israeli cities in late February and early March and the Syrian delegation's refusal to condemn them.

This terrorist wave in February and March exacted a large number of victims, and it inflicted a deadly blow on the peace process. Benjamin

Netanyahu's victory over Shimon Peres in the May elections was the result of several forces at work, but there can be little doubt that the suicide bombings were the single most important one. Before them, Peres enjoyed a comfortable lead (some twenty percentage points) in the polls, but by early March that had gone, and he never fully recovered. Netanyahu's campaign, on the other hand, used the terrorist attacks to assail the credibility of Peres and his policies and to offer the Israeli voter a magic formula of "peace with security." Netanyahu pledged to respect the Oslo Accords but to replace Peres's policy with a more aggressive insistence on Israeli security and Palestinian compliance and a more deliberate pace in the peace negotiations. If the suicide bombings were designed by Iran and its Palestinian clients to stop the 1992–96 peace process, they proved to be morbidly effective.

Iran's offensive against an Arab-Israeli peace was mostly focused on Lebanon, where Hizballah had long been Tehran's principal instrument both for expanding its influence in and through the Shiite community, and for launching attacks against Israel's security zone in the south and against Israel itself. Together with the cycles of terrorist attacks within Israel, the continuing violence along the Israeli-Lebanese border cast an ominous shadow on all the diplomatic maneuvers aimed at peace. And Israelis were hard put to accept Syria's complex conduct in this matter. As the dominant power in Lebanon, Syria could have put an end to Hizballah's attacks, but Asad had no intention of doing so, believing as he did in negotiating from a position of strength and in applying pressure tactics. If Israel was vulnerable to a steady stream of losses in southern Lebanon, that was all the more reason to keep the pressure on until a satisfactory agreement was reached. All the arguments made by U.S. and Israeli diplomats that this policy was undermining Asad's credibility in Israeli eyes and Israeli public support for a settlement with Syria were to no avail. Nor was Asad interested in prematurely jeopardizing his strategic alliance with Iran. If an agreement with Israel came and if a diplomatic dialogue with Washington began, Damascus might change its stance toward Tehran, but the prospect seemed remote.

At various points over the years, this complex Syrian policy in Lebanon became untenable. When, in late July 1993, Israel had launched a large-scale operation in southern Lebanon—Operation Accountability—Asad responded positively to Secretary Christopher's urging that he get Hizballah to accept understandings on the basis of which a cease-fire could be worked out. And from December 1995 to January 1996, at the height of its negotiation with Peres, Syria did put serious pressure and limitations on Hizballah's activities—to the point of having Iran look for alternative supply routes to its Lebanese clients rather than always sending supplies by air through Damascus.

But in early 1996, yet more events—those that brought an end to the Wye River Plantation negotiations—led to further deterioration in Israeli-Syrian relations. After the terrorist attacks in February and March, and to stabilize the situation and to shore up the Peres government, the Clinton administration launched a global campaign against terrorism, inaugurated in an impressive international summit meeting at Sharm al-Sheikh, at the tip of the Sinai Peninsula, and continued in Washington. This effort pushed Syria into a dangerous corner: the campaign had a clear anti-Iran purpose, but Asad regarded it as a hostile American-Israeli action also aimed at isolating Syria. An emerging strategic understanding between Israel and Turkey further exacerbated his paranoia. He responded by giving Hizballah the green light to accelerate activity in southern Lebanon and to launch Katyusha rockets against northern Israel, in disregard of the understandings of July 1993. In so doing, he did much to draw Prime Minister Peres to decide on yet another large-scale operation in Lebanon—Operation Grapes of Wrath.

That military operation in April 1996 is remembered primarily for one of its tragic unintended consequences—the death of more than a hundred Lebanese civilians by misguided Israeli artillery shells. But it had several other significant consequences: the alienation of Israel's Arab voters, many of whom decided not to vote in May, and Asad's humiliation of Secretary Christopher, who was laboring to arrange a cease-fire and a new set of understandings. Ironically, an improved set of understandings and a monitoring mechanism were eventually worked out.

The monitoring agreement was drafted by diplomats representing five countries: the United States, France, Israel, Syria, and Lebanon. It was the second text agreed upon by Israel and Syria in a four-year negotiation that failed to produce the broader agreement both countries were after. The draft was actually completed during the final days of the Peres government but was signed by Benjamin Netanyahu's government in early July. By then the Arab-Israeli peace process had shifted to a new phase.

3

YEARS OF STAGNATION

On October 24, 1998, a memorandum was signed in the East Wing of the White House after nine days of tripartite American-Israeli-Palestinian negotiations at the Wye River Plantation conference center. At the core of it was an Israeli agreement to transfer control within three months of 13 percent of the West Bank to the Palestinian Authority. In return, the latter agreed to wage a genuine campaign against the fundamentalist Islamic and terrorist opponents of the peace process, once again to make a ceremonious revocation of the offensive paragraphs of the Palestinian National Charter that called for the elimination of the Israeli state, and, apparently, also to abstain from proclaiming statehood on May 4, 1999, which was the end of the five-year transitional period stipulated at Oslo. This agreement ended nearly two years of stalemate during which the very future of the Oslo Accords and of peace in the Middle East was in question. It brought Israeli-Palestinian relations back to the track charted by the Oslo Accords and, in so doing, set the stage for final-status negotiations; it postponed, although it did not eliminate, the dangers of a crisis erupting once the transitional period came to an end.[1]

It was significant that a right-wing Israeli prime minister had in early 1997 grudgingly handed over the city of Hebron to the Palestinian Authority and committed his country to further implementation of the Oslo Accords, and then in October 1998 signed a broader agreement in which he once again committed himself to the Oslo process, now modified to meet his demands and requirements. Yet Benjamin Netanyahu's words and actions after signing the Wye Agreement did not reflect a conversion to a belief in a genuine political settlement with the Palestinians or a sense that Yasser Arafat was and should be his partner in this process. It was difficult to know whether Netanyahu's rhetoric after signing the memorandum was reflecting a lingering resistance in an ideological leader who had journeyed from the right wing to the pragmatic center, or was a political tactic designed to keep together his reluctant cabinet and uneasy coalition.

By the same token, it was difficult to know how authentic was Yasser Arafat's commitment to dealing with the Palestinian foes of the peace process and to ending the ambiguity and ambivalence that he himself had exuded about reconciliation with Israel. It was important for Arafat to rally his own constituents and not to appear as an Israeli accomplice and collaborator. But did he decide to establish a single line of authority to confront the fundamentalist opposition and to reach out to the Israeli public? Or, was he merely offering temporary concessions to a right-wing Israeli leader in order to get an additional 13 percent of the West Bank on the road to statehood and independence?

It is easier to understand and explain Arafat's acceptance of the terms of the Wye Agreement than to trace the path that led his Israeli counterpart to it, after total opposition to the Oslo Accords and to any territorial concessions in the West Bank. More than two years after coming to power, Benjamin Netanyahu remained an enigmatic figure, the object of bitter controversies, a prime minister who led his country through a complex and crucial period without a clear and credible articulation of his goal.

A great deal happened in the Middle East and in Arab-Israeli relations in the aftermath of May 1996—with the electoral defeat of Shimon Peres and the peace policies he represented, the Arab world's complex reaction to Netanyahu's victory, and a different U.S. policy about the peace process taken by the Clinton administration during its second term. But the dominant developments were two interrelated ones: the deliberate slowdown of the peace process, which brought it to the verge of collapse; and the effective, albeit reluctant, endorsement of the Oslo process by part of the Israeli right wing. Netanyahu was central to both developments.[2]

Netanyahu came to power at the age of forty-six, Israel's youngest prime minister. His victory in the elections of May 29, 1996, was the culmination of a stunning thirteen-year drive for political power that began in 1983, when Netanyahu was drafted as an aide by Moshe Arens, then Israel's ambassador to the United States and a future defense and foreign minister in Likud governments. Arens was making a systematic effort to bring back to the fold the offspring of former Revisionist Movement or Herut Party leaders who had distanced themselves from the Likud over the years. Netanyahu was the son of Professor Ben Zion Netanyahu, an eminent historian of medieval Spanish Jewry and a prominent disciple of Ze'ev Jabotinsky, the founder of Revisionist Zionism. The elder Netanyahu, when he pronounced on Israeli politics, revealed a classic formulation of right-wing Zionism, hardly affected by the passage of time and articulated with great authority and conviction.[3] Arens brought Benjamin Netanyahu, who had lived much of his life in the United States, to the Israeli Embassy in Washington as deputy chief of mission. He subsequently served as Israel's ambassador to the United Nations, entered full-fledged politics through the Likud primaries, served as deputy foreign minister, and, in 1992 (right after Likud's electoral defeat and Rabin's election) made a successful bid for the party leadership.

In 1992–93, Netanyahu, then still leader of the opposition, wrote a book published as *A Place among the Nations: Israel and the World,* in which he elaborated his view of Jewish history, Zionism, and the Arab-Israeli conflict and peace process. For the most part, the text consists of familiar Israeli right-wing views and arguments rehearsing the case against Israel's making territorial concessions, against the notion of a Palestinian state, and in favor of the "peace-for-peace" formula. Netanyahu was clearly assisted by researchers and professional writers, but the book reflects his personal style and formative experiences—as a politically oriented diplomat in Ronald Reagan's Washington and as an exponent of Likud views at the United Nations and at the Madrid Conference.

Genuine peace, Netanyahu argued, could be made and maintained only between democratic governments. In the absence of democracy in the Arab world, Israel could not hope for a Western European or North American type of peace. Peace in the more modest sense of the term—absence of war—could be made and kept in the Middle East only from a position of strength and had to be predicated on a bedrock of security and deterrence. The problem in the Middle East, in

Netanyahu's view, was not an Arab-Israeli territorial dispute but the Arabs' refusal to accept the reality of Israel's existence and its right to exist. But if Israel stood firm and received full support from the West, the Arabs would come around to accepting both Israel's reality and its right to exist. The West Bank and the Golan Heights were a defensive wall crucial for Israel's survival and could not be surrendered. A Palestinian state in the West Bank would present a mortal danger to Israel, and in any event there was already a Palestinian state—Jordan. The demographic argument made against this viewpoint—that if Israel held onto the West Bank and the Gaza Strip, it would cease to be either Jewish or democratic because of the faster-growing Arab population—was a "demographic demon; a false argument."[4]

In 1993 Netanyahu's book, published during the time of the Madrid process, laid out a particular strategy for Israel. The emphasis was on the Palestinian issue. The Gaza Strip was seen as the easier part: "Since administration of Gaza by its Arab residents does not pose an extraordinary security risk for Israel, it makes sense for most of the territory (with minor modifications for Jewish settlements) to be granted the fullest possible autonomy." Netanyahu wrote that he envisaged "an arrangement whereby Israel would be in charge of security and foreign policy while all other areas of authority would be transferred to the self-administering authority under the rubric of Israeli sovereignty." He further envisaged an international effort to invest in Gaza's economy, thus sparing both Gazans and Israelis the need to have Gazan workers making their daily trips to and from jobs in Israel's cities. After an interim trial period of at least ten years, "Israel could consider offering the Arabs of Gaza an even greater degree of self-rule."[5]

With regard to the far more complex problem of Palestinians in the West Bank, whom Netanyahu called "the Arab residents of Judea and Samaria," he offered a particular interpretation of the Camp David Accords. Limited autonomy for those Palestinians would give them "the ability to conduct their lives with a minimum of interference from the central government." But Israel's needs and expectations in the West Bank were far greater than in the Gaza Strip; there were security needs and the imperatives of Jewish settlement. The powers of Palestinian self-rule had to be curtailed, and freedom of movement for Israel's security forces had to be guaranteed. There could not be a contiguous area of

Palestinian self-rule but "a system of four self-managing Arab counties: Jenin, Nablus, Ramallah, Hebron . . . together these counties encompass the great majority of the West Bank's Arab population and they take up no more than one-fifth of the land . . . control over vital matters would have to remain in the central Israeli government's hands."[6]

This would be an interim arrangement, he argued. Later, following twenty years of cooling off, the discussion of a final settlement could consider whether West Bank residents should be offered Israeli citizenship. Israel would justifiably insist on an oath of allegiance and on military service and full payment of taxes, Netanyahu speculated, and most residents of the West Bank would probably opt to retain their Jordanian citizenship.

Shortly after the publication of his book, Netanyahu had to formulate his response to the Oslo Accords. For several months he was hard put to cope with a dual challenge: not only had the Rabin government signed an agreement that ran against the grain of everything Netanyahu stood and argued for, but it appeared to be riding on the crest of a major historical wave. Later, when a backlash developed in Israel and terrorist acts undermined the Israeli public's support for the Oslo Accords, Netanyahu led the opposition to the government's policies. Public opinion polls in 1994 and 1995 showed him running neck and neck with Rabin.

Rabin's assassination in late 1995 had an immediate and devastating effect on Netanyahu's standing. The Israeli public's revulsion with his political and personal affiliation with the political campaign against Rabin and with the radical right wing gave Rabin's successor, Shimon Peres, an advantage. However, after Peres's decision in January 1996 to advance the elections to May, a wave of terrorist attacks in three Israeli cities in late February and early March completely erased Peres's lead and placed him and Netanyahu in more or less the same position some ten weeks before the elections.

With that campaign a new electoral system was also introduced in Israel—a direct election of the prime minister. Netanyahu's victory by a very slim edge can partly be explained by the effect of the new system, by the superiority of his campaign, and by other personal, political, and social forces at work. But the May 29 elections were also a referendum on the peace process, and in that referendum the line expounded by

Netanyahu won—by only sixteen thousand votes in the total electorate (including Arab voters), but by a significant margin of some 10 percent among Jewish voters.

Netanyahu's campaign relied on mutually reinforcing positive and negative messages formulated on the basis of a shrewd reading of the average Israeli voter's frame of mind. Netanyahu continued with criticism of the Oslo Accords, yet he undertook to accept them and continue the peace process with modifications that would make it more deliberate and "secure." The Oslo Accords were binding international agreements that had been undersigned by the United States, and Netanyahu well understood that, as a serious contender for power, and certainly if elected prime minister, he could not renounce his predecessors' contractual obligations. He also understood that, if he refused to commit himself to respect the Oslo Accords and proceed with the peace process, he could not expect to attract the floating votes at the center of the Israeli political spectrum. The slogan "secure peace" proved to be extremely effective for this crucial bloc of Israeli voters.[7]

The negative part of Netanyahu's and Likud's platform included harsh criticism not only of the Oslo Accords and the subsequent diplomatic work, but of numerous developments during the Oslo period. These included Arafat's failure to comply with his commitments and Peres's willingness to ignore this, the accords' shift of some of the responsibility for security to the Palestinian Authority, the Israelis' ensuing loss of any sense of personal security, and Netanyahu's opponents' alleged intention to "divide Jerusalem" and acquiesce in the formation of a Palestinian state. This vilification of Netanyahu's rivals and their policies proved to be very effective, as was his promise to deliver a secure peace. But many Israelis and Israel's diplomatic partners wanted to know more about the candidate's specific ideas regarding the unfolding Arab-Israeli relations in the future. As election day drew closer, Netanyahu—in a series of interviews, in a television debate with Shimon Peres, and through the Likud Party's written platform—outlined the following strategy.

To resuscitate the stalled peace process, Netanyahu said he would try, if elected prime minister, to reconvene the Madrid Conference, at which he would

YEARS OF STAGNATION 61

... suggest emphasizing several new channels through which to reduce the level of tension in the region, minimize the arms race and find ways to supervise the introduction of certain weapons. ... This, in any event, is the right approach to dealing with Syria. An agreement based on withdrawal from the Golan in return for a peace treaty and normalization has no value. Furthermore, Syria is in fact not interested in such an arrangement. For Asad regaining the Golan is a fourth priority.[8]

A normal peaceful relationship with Israel would open up Syria and endanger Asad's rule, and a peace agreement signed by Syria would be no more than a piece of paper, Netanyahu implied. Under these circumstances, a "nonterritorial" negotiation on issues such as security and water would suit both sides, he argued.

In a different vein, Netanyahu sought to employ, as both a stick and a carrot, Washington's aversion to identifying Syria as a sponsor of terrorist groups.: "Just as there are no American technology transfers, oil sales or trade with Iran and Iraq, Syria should be warned that it would be subject to the same sanction," he said. But if Syria expelled Palestinian terrorist groups from its territory and dismantled Hizballah in southern Lebanon, "there should be no reason why, after a period of time, Syria should not be removed from the State Department's terror list."

As for the Palestinians, "the Oslo Accords established facts on the ground. I am forced to accept them as starting points. A government I will lead will hold negotiations with the Palestinian Authority on a fair concept of peace. As for Arafat, it is not my heart's desire to meet him. I will meet him only if he meets all his commitments to us and if Israel's interests require that I do so."[9]

The Likud Party's platform expanded further on this issue: "The Government of Israel will carry out negotiations with the PA to achieve a permanent peace arrangement on condition that the Palestinians fully honor all their obligations. Most important among these are the clauses in the Palestinian Charter which call for the destruction of Israel and that they prevent terror and incitement against Israel." Israel's commitment to the Oslo Accords under a Netanyahu government was thus made contingent on the PA's compliance with its own commitments.

The notion of an Israeli-Palestinian settlement was given a very narrow interpretation:

> The Government of Israel will enable the Palestinians to manage their lives freely within the framework of self-government. However, foreign affairs and defense and matters which require coordination will remain the responsibility of the State of Israel. The government will oppose the establishment of an independent Palestinian state. . . . Israel will keep its vital water resources in Judea and Samaria. . . . The IDF and other Israeli security forces will enjoy complete freedom of action . . . in all places in their struggle against terror. . . . Security areas vital for the defense of Israel and Jewish settlements will remain under full Israeli sovereignty. . . . The Jordan River will be the eastern border between the State of Israel and the Hashemite Kingdom of Jordan. The Kingdom of Jordan may become a partner in the final arrangement between Israel and the Palestinians in areas agreed upon in the negotiations. . . . United and undivided Jerusalem is the capital of the State of Israel. Activities which undermine the status of Jerusalem will be banned and therefore PLO and PA institutions in the city, including the Orient House, will be closed.[10]

With regard to the policy of allowing Jews to establish settlements in the West Bank, Netanyahu was careful and evasive:

> I certainly don't rule out new settlements, that's obvious. But my view about settlement activity has always been . . . that it has to be built on economic infrastructure which means larger urban centers." This settlement activity need not be a burden on the Israeli taxpayer: "One of the things I intend to do is to allow [settlement activity] through market forces. . . . I will not subordinate the government budget to it . . . but allow it simply through the release of public lands and transportation lines and allow natural growth.[11]

The positions Netanyahu presented stood in stark contrast to the policies Rabin and Peres had pursued and were clearly unacceptable to Israel's negotiating partners in the three unfinished tracks of the peace process—the Palestinians, Syria, and Lebanon. In the case of Syria, the substantial negotiations conducted by the Rabin and Peres governments had not produced a written agreement, and the issue was strictly one of policy: since, contrary to what Netanyahu had said, Asad was interested only in a territorial negotiation, what would both nations choose to do if Netanyahu won? Would a formula be found for resuming negotiations, would the conflict by proxy in Lebanon deteriorate into a full-blown conflict, or would the familiar mixed pattern of muted conflict and quest for negotiation continue?

The issue with the Palestinians was far more complex. Netanyahu's public positions were inconsistent with the Oslo Accords and with his promise to respect them. His commitment was couched in terms sufficiently broad to attract many Israeli voters worried that the pace of the peace process was too rapid and worried by the loss of personal security. These voters were willing to settle for a vague promise to negotiate for peace in a deliberate, secure way that would be acceptable to the Palestinian leadership. Alongside his public position, Netanyahu gave private assurances to the Habad movement (associated with the U.S.-based Lubavitch branch of Hassidic Jewry) that he would not cede any territory in the West Bank to the Palestinians. The Habad movement was particularly active in the final phase of his campaign. Insistence on the PA's full compliance with its contractual commitment could not be faulted—after all, agreements are signed in order to be respected—but it also provided an escape mechanism, should a new prime minister decide to suspend implementation of the Oslo Accords.

Victory only slightly moderated Netanyahu's stated positions. He realized that at least some of his convictions would have to be modified. Necessities of statecraft required him to polish some of the rough edges in the original draft of the new government's platform. But it still stated that the government would "insist on preserving [the Golan Heights] under Israeli sovereignty," though it stipulated elsewhere that "the Israeli Government will hold negotiations with Syria without any preconditions." The assertion that "the Jordan River will be Israel's eastern border" (implying continued Israeli control of the West Bank) was omitted, but opposition to Palestinian statehood was retained, as was a fairly narrow concept of Palestinian self-government.[12]

But when his government's platform was published, Israel's new prime minister had in fact headed in a direction bound to lead him away from the principles and policies he had advocated before his election. It is not known what Netanyahu had in mind when he announced, on the eve of the elections, that despite his own opposition to the Oslo Accords he would respect them if elected. It was first and foremost a (successful) bid for centrist voters, but did Netanyahu also feel that he would in fact be fortunate to inherit a compromise with Palestinian nationalism rather than to have to make it himself, that while continuing to criticize the Oslo Accords and seeking to modify them he might actually proceed on the road to peace? Or did he perhaps toy with the idea that one could profess to accept the Oslo Accords but in effect emasculate, perhaps even destroy, the process they had set in motion?

Netanyahu's assumption of ultimate responsibility for Israel's policies in June 1996 was not a simple linear process. If he had not known it before, Israel's prime minister soon discovered that it was extremely difficult to get off the Oslo track. The reality of Israeli-Palestinian relations had been altered permanently—once by the intifada and then by the initial implementation of the Oslo Accords. To suspend further implementation was likely to lead to conflict. Israel was infinitely stronger than the Palestinian Authority, but could it afford the price of a military victory over the Palestinians? The direct cost—the effect on Israel's relations with Jordan, Egypt, and the other Arab powers and on Israel's international relations, particularly those with Washington—was prohibitively high. But there were numerous countervailing forces: Netanyahu's personal and party legacy, the opposition of right-wing members of his cabinet and coalition, and mistakes made by the Arab participants in the peace process.

Netanyahu took a step forward and soon thereafter seemed to backtrack. He signed (in January 1997) an agreement to withdraw Israeli soldiers from Hebron, and then immediately authorized construction of a new Jewish neighborhood in the Har Homa section of Jerusalem that was intended to drive a wedge between the city and Arab Bethlehem. He sent messages to Syria expressing interest in renewing negotiations and then endorsed legislation sponsored by the Golan Lobby intended to entrench Israel's presence on the Golan Heights. To some extent this was political maneuvering by a prime minister trying to preserve a precarious coalition, but there seemed also to be personal vacillation. As late as August 1997, Netanyahu delivered a speech to the graduating class of Israel's National Security College in which he fell back on his

1993 book and argued that peace agreements and normalization made no sense in the Arab-Israeli context: "As long as the regimes around us are not democratic and inherently peace-seeking we will not be able to afford any arrangements in which the security dimension is not dominant. No arrangement will survive if we fail to keep security and defense zones." And yet, fourteen months later, the very same leader signed the Wye River Memorandum and initially carried his cabinet and coalition with him. The path that took them from the formation of Netanyahu's government to that historic point unfolded in three phases.

Early Transition and Adjustment

Benjamin Netanyahu's adjustment to the reality and responsibility of power was matched by the Arab world's complex, evolving reaction to Israel's new government: initial shock and concern, followed by gradual adjustment. Public opinion polls had indicated since early March that Peres and Netanyahu were running neck and neck, and yet the Peres defeat came as a surprise. Arabs thought of Netanyahu as a foe of the peace process and assumed that a radical change in Israeli policies would ensue. An Arab summit conference on June 21–23, 1996, issued an explicit warning to the new Israeli government:

> The Arab leaders affirm that any violation (*ikhlal*) by Israel of these principles and bases on which the peace process is founded, any retraction on the commitments, pledges, and agreements reached within the framework of this process, or any vacillation in implementing them will set back the peace process and will entail dangers and consequences that will plunge the region back into a spiral of tension and will compel all the Arab countries to reconsider the steps they have taken toward Israel within the framework of the peace process. The Israeli Government alone will be fully responsible for these consequences.[13]

But there were nuances in the various Arab reactions. Yasser Arafat was the most anxious. He depended on Israel for implementation of the next phases of the Oslo process, and he had come to trust Shimon Peres and his team, with whom he presumed a final-status agreement could be negotiated. What was he to make of Netanyahu's criticism of the Oslo process, his opposition to Palestinian statehood, his narrow concept of Palestinian autonomy, and the assignments in his government given to people and parties widely perceived as implacable opponents of the PLO: Ariel Sharon, Rafael Eytan, and the National Religious Party?

Egypt was more ambivalent. On the one hand, as patron of the Palestinians and needing to defend its own peace with Israel, it feared the prospect of a deep crisis, but there was also an element of relief. Egypt had been visibly uncomfortable with the sweeping scope and rapid pace of the peace process over the previous eighteen months, and was especially wary, as we have seen, of Peres's vision of a new Middle East. President Hosni Mubarak and his government had genuinely hoped for a Peres victory, but they could see a silver lining in his defeat: a more modest scope and a more deliberate pace to the unfolding developments, with Israel clearly responsible for both.

Syria was particularly strident in its criticism of the new Israeli government. Syria had been unhappy with the two Labor prime ministers, although both had seriously negotiated with its representatives. Having refused to listen to friendly advice about the wisdom of concluding a deal with either of them before the elections, it now confronted an Israeli prime minister who was openly hostile and who seemed to rule out the possibility of an Israeli-Syrian settlement. Angry commentaries expressed Syria's frustration, but in private its diplomats were willing to meet with representatives of the new government to divine its real intentions.

Jordan stood in a category by itself. King Hussein and his government were the only Arab party to have supported Netanyahu during his election campaign, being concerned that a victorious Peres would proceed swiftly to a sweeping agreement with Syria and to the establishment of a Palestinian state. Netanyahu managed to persuade Hussein that he would keep the peace process going at a level and pace suitable to Jordan's political needs.

According to the Oslo process's agenda and schedule, final-status talks, launched formally in May 1996, were actually scheduled to begin in September. The interim arrangements were supposed to end five years after the Cairo signing of the implementation agreement (Oslo II), which meant that May 4, 1999, became the target date. A major item on the agenda was Israel's withdrawal (or redeployment, to use the vocabulary of the peace process) from most of Hebron. Unlike the other cities of the West Bank, Hebron, a city with about 120,000 Palestinian inhabitants, had a Jewish settlement in its midst. The presence of this group of radical Orthodox settlers, the city's general historical and religious significance, and the memory of the massacre perpetrated against the city's Jewish population in 1929 only worsened the complex issue of the Israeli Defense Forces' redeployment. Peres had not been keen on going through with the redeployment after the election, and he passed this issue on to Netanyahu.

Upon completing the redeployments from the six main cities of the West Bank, Oslo II committed Israel to proceeding with three "further redeployments" before final-status negotiations. The origin of that idea was in the Camp David Accords, which stipulated that during final-status negotiations Israel would withdraw its troops to "security locations." In the summer of 1995, at a late phase of the negotiations leading to the second Oslo accord, Israel had agreed to three "further redeployments," a concession that made sense only in the context of a genuine final-status negotiation: if Israel were to hand over most of the West Bank to Palestinian Authority control, it might as well do it in phases, and use the phasing as a way of facilitating the concessions Arafat would have to make, too. But for Netanyahu's government—formally opposed to Palestinian statehood and committed to a narrow view of Palestinian self-government—this notion made little or no sense.

Netanyahu was, indeed, determined to change both the agenda and the pace of Israeli-Palestinian diplomacy. He refused to meet with Arafat and wanted the latter to settle for meetings with lesser officials—first Netanyahu's own policy adviser (June 28), then the foreign and defense ministers (July 23 and September 18, respectively). He indicated several times that he was in no hurry about redeployment in Hebron, a complex issue. Most significantly, he insisted on "reciprocity" and "compliance," themes that had figured prominently in his election campaign, when he had accused Peres of being too lenient and of being willing to overlook Arafat's and the Palestinian Authority's failure to discipline or control terrorist organizations that struck at Israel, failure to complete the revision of the Palestinian National Charter, and failure to cease issuing hostile propaganda against Israel. Netanyahu now demanded that the Palestinians comply "fully" with these commitments before Israel took another step.

A demand for full compliance with an agreement is, of course, perfectly valid. But, given the context in which the demand was made, Palestinians, Arabs in general, and the world at large saw it as an attempt to change the rules of the Israeli-Palestinian game. Rabin and Peres had argued that Israel, as the senior and more powerful party to the agreement, did not have to insist on a literal interpretation and implementation. The shift from that approach to a strict insistence on "full compliance" was widely perceived as a manifestation of the new government's negative attitude and of its proclivity to use Israel's preponderance vis-à-vis the Palestinians to impose rather than negotiate a settlement.

The awkwardness of Israel's relationship with the Palestinians was matched by dim prospects for peace with Syria. The new prime minister was now fully briefed on the course of the 1993–96 negotiation. He knew that Hafiz al-Asad was willing to make peace with Israel but only on the basis of the latter's complete withdrawal from the Golan Heights. Asad now demanded also that the new government endorse the whole legacy of the negotiation conducted by its predecessor and commit itself to that full withdrawal. Netanyahu knew very well that the positions he himself had advocated with regard to Syria and the Golan Heights were not realistic, but he was not willing to accept this demand. Asad, grasping the full significance of the change in Israel, chose to dig in more firmly rather than modify his position.[14]

In late July Netanyahu tried a different approach. An agreement would be worked out that would have Israel withdraw its soldiers from the security zone in southern Lebanon, which Israel had occupied for fourteen years at an enormous cost. This agreement would be conceived and perceived as a first, confidence-building phase in a broader Israeli-Syrian settlement (hence the name "Lebanon First" given to this initiative). The idea was stillborn. In fact, it was not a new idea, and Syria had systematically obstructed earlier attempts to break the logjam in this fashion. As Syria saw it, Israel's predicament in Lebanon was Syria's most effective instrument for pressuring Israel to withdraw from the Golan Heights, and Asad was not about to give this up. Furthermore, Syria suspected that a separate Israeli-Lebanese negotiation would be used to lure Lebanon away from Syria. It lost no time in foiling the new Israeli initiative.

Nor was Netanyahu successful in building his relations with Jordan's King Hussein and Egypt's President Mubarak. With the passage of time, and as Netanyahu's Palestinian policy became more evident, Cairo and Amman expressed disappointment and criticism; both could live with a virtual suspension of Israeli-Syrian negotiations, but neither could accept Israel's new policy toward the Palestinians. Egypt's anger was contained. Cairo had a stake in Arafat's success but was content to take advantage of the new turn of events in order to slow down normalization of Israel's position in the region. For Jordan the political challenge was much more acute. Given that the majority of Jordan's citizenry was Palestinian and given the criticism the king had endured for making a peace with Israel, he believed that a suspension or collapse of Israeli-Palestinian efforts could undermine his own position. He expected subtlety from Netanyahu; he had wanted more deliberation and modesty in Israeli diplomacy, but he had not expected such a dramatic reversal of policy.[15]

This transitional phase was terminated in September 1996 by two unrelated developments, the first between Israel and Syria, which brought the two countries to the verge of military confrontation.

This was a classic case of an unintended escalation nourished by misperceptions and mutual suspicions—all exacerbated by the new Israeli leaders' inexperience and the Syrian leaders' unfamiliarity with their counterparts. A redeployment of Syrian troops from Beirut to the Beqaa Valley in eastern Lebanon, close to the Syrian border, had been planned for some time as a demonstration of the incremental normalization of life in Lebanon. But south of the border, it was seen as a potential buildup for a surprise attack against Israel. In turn, Syrians, knowing they had no offensive intentions, saw Israel's deployment for such an eventuality as preparation for a potential attack. This spiral of mutual suspicion threatened to escalate into real hostilities. The tension eventually eased, but the episode demonstrated the dangerous potential in the Israeli-Syrian relationship, particularly when there was no ongoing direct dialogue between the two.

The other development was much graver. On September 24 the Israeli authorities opened for public viewing and to promote tourism the Hasmonean Tunnel, which runs from the Western Wall along the base of Temple Mount in Jerusalem. The tunnel, of immense archaeological interest, had been readied for opening during Rabin's tenure, but government policy then had been to open the tunnel only in coordination with the Palestinian Authority. Given Arab, Muslim, and international sensibilities regarding anything that had to do with the holy places in Jerusalem, it was decided to wait for the right moment; the tunnel and its opening would not in any case interfere with the status quo in Jerusalem. The Netanyahu government's decision to disregard these considerations and to open the tunnel on September 24 as an assertion of Israel's sovereignty in Jerusalem was yet another symptom of its inexperience, and it played directly into Arafat's hands. Arafat saw a golden opportunity to reverse the rules of the game that Netanyahu had played since June. He called for protest marches denouncing the tunnel opening as a "big crime against our religion and our holy places." In the following five days of violence, fifteen Israeli soldiers and sixty Palestinians were killed. Some of the violence was spontaneous, but there is little doubt that the Palestinian security officers who took an active part in the fighting were in most cases authorized if not encouraged to do so by Arafat.

By reacting in this fashion, Arafat may well have damaged his cause in the long run. For many Israelis it was proof that the Palestinian Authority could not be trusted to be a genuine partner in protecting Israeli security, that Arafat gave his cooperation only so long as his expectations were met, and that violence could be expected if final-status negotiations were deadlocked. But in the short run his action was most effective. Netanyahu was now anxious to talk to him. President Clinton invited both men, as well as King Hussein and President Mubarak, to Washington for a meeting on October 1 and 2. The Jordanian monarch accepted the invitation; Egypt's president declined.

THE ROAD TO THE HEBRON AGREEMENT

The Washington summit conference quickly accomplished two important goals: it defused the crisis that had erupted after the tunnel opening, and it resuscitated Israeli-Palestinian negotiations. But these talks were arduous, and it took three more months to reach further agreements about Israel's redeployment in Hebron and future relationship with the Palestinian Authority. Also, the Washington conference demonstrated important changes in Washington's outlook on and role in the Israeli-Arab peace process.

Ever since the formation of the first Clinton administration in January 1993, the Israeli-Arab peace process had been high on Washington's foreign policy agenda. The president, the secretary of state, and their assistants invested a significant portion of their time in it, and its achievements were among their most notable foreign policy successes. Indeed, the Clinton administration's cooperation with the Rabin and Peres governments was a unique phase in American-Israeli history. In earlier stages, American pressure on reluctant Israeli prime ministers to make territorial and other concessions was invariably required to effect progress (even Begin's negotiation with Sadat, which had originated as an Israeli-Egyptian initiative, could not be concluded without American participation). Under Rabin and Peres, however, the main force was an Israeli leadership determined to move toward peace and reconciled to the notion that both sides had to make concessions to reach and implement an agreement. During the Rabin years, this was buttressed by an unusually warm and intimate relationship between the president and the prime minister, and the Clinton administration openly supported Peres in the 1996 election campaign.

After Netanyahu's victory, the administration felt that it had lost this secure Israeli footing. Its nervousness was exacerbated by Secretary of State Warren Christopher's disenchantment with Syria, and by changes in the Middle East (the formation in 1996 of an Islamist government in Turkey and unrest the same year in Saudi Arabia) that made the region less hospitable to a major investment of U.S. efforts. As the presidential elections of November 1996 drew closer, the prospect of open disagreement with an Israeli prime minister openly allied with conservative Republicans grew more alarming. It remained important for the Clinton administration to preserve the American achievements in the Arab-Israeli peace process and to avoid its breaking down, but American willingness and ability to invest significant resources were limited.

This calculus was altered by the outburst of violence in September related to the opening of the Hasmonean Tunnel. Just a few weeks before the election, President Clinton took the political risk of convening a summit that could end in failure. In the event the meeting was successful, but Netanyahu's mobilization of the organized right-wing Jewish community in the United States and the Republican leadership in Congress to keep the administration at bay was a harbinger of future developments.

The Washington summit was followed by a round of intensive negotiations held at the Erez checkpoint between Israel and Gaza. Secretary of State Christopher presided at the outset, but as the negotiations lingered on, leadership passed to the principal American negotiator, Dennis Ross. In the absence of mutual trust and effective communication between the Israeli and Palestinian leaders, the United States had to go from being a facilitator to being a combined mediator, partner, and guarantor.

One level of the negotiation dealt with the redeployment in Hebron. On another level, Arafat and the Palestinian Authority—while eager to obtain control over Hebron—wanted also to ascertain that this would not be a final act of a moribund process but would be fitted into a broader agreement on the implementation of Oslo II. More specifically, they demanded that a date be set for resumption of final-status negotiations, that a timetable be set for the implementation of Israel's three further redeployments, and that agreement be reached on other issues pending since 1995: the opening of air- and seaports in Gaza, the establishment of a safe passage between the West Bank and the Gaza Strip, and the release of Palestinian prisoners from Israeli jails.

Benjamin Netanyahu, in turn, faced numerous dilemmas and problems. Many Israelis would see Israeli withdrawal from Hebron as an act of withdrawal from part of the historical, biblical Land of Israel. By going through with the withdrawal agreement, he would be the first Likud leader to offer and implement such a concession. And even if he were to argue that he had no choice but to fulfill the contractual obligation undertaken by his predecessors, what was he to do about the sweeping commitment to three more redeployments?

The problem was not limited to Netanyahu's personal soul-searching. He was the first Israeli prime minister to have been elected by a direct popular vote, but as he and the Israeli political system soon discovered, the new election law did not mean that the prime minister was immune to pressure from his own cabinet and coalition. Although the law made it more difficult to unseat a prime minister than before, he still had to form and maintain a parliamentary coalition if he was to accomplish anything. Netanyahu's not very large coalition (it originally consisted of sixty-six members out of one hundred and twenty in the Knesset) had a rightist complexion; within it, several of his Likud colleagues and members of the National Religious Party formed a hard core of opposition to any territorial concessions in the West Bank. The argument that governments are constrained by domestic political opposition has been used all too often in Arab-Israeli negotiations, but Netanyahu did face a genuine, significant opposition within his own party and coalition.

Netanyahu understood that he had no choice—he had to redeploy in Hebron, and he had to reiterate the basic Israeli commitments at Oslo II—but he fought to recast these commitments in terms that would be, or at least appear to be, new and more congruent with his own outlook. By mid-January 1997 an agreement had been reached that was embodied in three documents: a protocol to implement the redeployment in Hebron; a "note for the record" prepared by Dennis Ross as a summary of a meeting between Netanyahu and Arafat; and a letter from Secretary Christopher to Netanyahu. These three documents were supplemented by a letter from Dennis Ross to the secretary of the Israeli cabinet that formalized the original compromise worked out by King Hussein, suggesting that the term "mid-1998" (the agreed-upon date for Israel's final withdrawal from Hebron) be left vague.

The security arrangements detailed in the Hebron protocol were different enough from past ones to enable Netanyahu to argue that he had obtained a better, indeed satisfactory, security regime in Hebron. In the note for the record, Israel reaffirmed its promise to proceed with implementation of Oslo II, which meant first and foremost the three further redeployments. It undertook to carry out the first redeployment during the first week of March 1997, to negotiate the other pending issues, and to resume the permanent-status negotiations within two months of the implementation of the Hebron protocol. Arafat, for his part, reaffirmed the following principal promises: to complete the revision of the Palestinian National Charter, to fight terror and prevent violence, to strengthen security cooperation, to prevent incitement and hostile propaganda, and to combat terrorist organizations and infrastructure systematically and effectively. The note also stipulated that "the exercise of Palestinian governmental activity and location of Palestinian governmental offices will be as specified in the Interim Agreement" (in the coded language of Israeli-Palestinian relations, this meant the Palestinian Authority's undertaking not to engage in "governmental" activity in Jerusalem) and that Oslo II should be implemented on the basis of "reciprocity."

That last point was repeated and reinforced in Secretary Christopher's letter to Netanyahu. The letter was essentially intended to assuage Israelis, but it addressed a major Palestinian concern by stating the American administration's "belief that the first phase of further redeployments should take place as soon as possible and that all three phases of further redeployment should be completed within twelve months of the implementation of the first phase of further redeployments but no later than mid-1998." Israel, it was implied, would determine the scope of the redeployments.

The Palestinian Authority and the United States could note with satisfaction that a Likud prime minister was about to withdraw Israeli soldiers from most of Hebron and that he formally reaffirmed the principal commitments of Oslo II. Netanyahu, in turn, could claim that he had committed Arafat to respond to his criticisms of the Oslo Accords and that he had formalized the principle of reciprocity and established a formal link between Arafat's compliance with these commitments and Israel's own further undertakings. In fact, although Israel's redeployment in Hebron was carried out in accordance with the protocol, the larger agenda addressed in the note for the record and the secretary's letter was not implemented. Further progress in Israeli-Palestinian relations was delayed for nearly two years.

In other words, the Hebron Agreement ended up being only and precisely that—an agreement on Israel's redeployment in Hebron. To address and implement the larger agenda—reaffirming and implementing the unfinished components of Oslo II—the three partners to the Hebron Agreement had yet to make some fundamental decisions.

Israel's prime minister felt ill at ease with the agenda itself, which required those three further redeployments by mid-1998, leaving less than a year before the end of the five-year transitional period specified by the original Oslo Accords. Israel could not realistically expect to complete the process without ceding a significant portion of the West Bank. For the first redeployment, scheduled for March 1997, Netanyahu offered to withdraw from 2 percent of the West Bank, an offer that Arafat scornfully rebuffed. Netanyahu and Arafat thus were miles apart, bridging the gap was likely to take a long time, and from the

Israeli vantage point, giving up land in three predetermined moves made little if any sense.

Thus, in March 1997 Netanyahu proposed that Israel and the Palestinian Authority telescope the whole process and, instead of proceeding with the implementation of Oslo II, meet for a Camp David–style conference, allocating three to six months for completing the final-status negotiations. The underlying argument was quite persuasive. The Oslo process, it was said, had been intended to move in phases to build confidence between the parties. Whatever its initial achievements, Oslo by this point clearly was not building confidence and should be replaced by something else. This valid argument was briefly endorsed by the new U.S. secretary of state, Madeleine Albright, but it was rendered useless by one problem: mistrust. Arafat and many other Arabs had no trust in Netanyahu and his government, and they saw his offer as a transparent maneuver to extricate himself from the Oslo commitments.

This policy problem was exacerbated by a political one. Even if Netanyahu wanted to go through with genuine implementation of the Hebron Agreement, he might lose a working majority in his cabinet and coalition. One right-wing member of his party and cabinet, Benny (Binyamin) Begin, resigned after the agreement was signed. Menachem Begin's son refused to remain a member of a government that had voted to hand over part of what he considered the Land of Israel to foreign control. Nor did Begin conceal the contempt he had for Netanyahu. Other right-wing Likud coalition members and members of the National Religious Party threatened to topple the government if it decided on further withdrawals in the West Bank. Their threat was aggravated by the dissension of other cabinet and coalition members—Finance Minister Dan Meridor resigned in June 1997 and Foreign Minister David Levy in January 1998—and others distanced themselves, owing to personal differences with Netanyahu or unhappiness with his style and performance.

As time passed, pressure built among more moderate or pragmatic members of the government, who began to suspect that Netanyahu had no intention of implementing the Hebron Agreement. Netanyahu himself was increasingly preoccupied with his government's survival, and his perpetual maneuvering created a zigzag effect. After Netanyahu signed the Hebron Agreement in January, he tried to balance it in February by placating his right-wing critics with the Har Homa construction in Jerusalem. The Palestinians considered this a provocative act, and Arafat responded by suspending the negotiations.

As might have been anticipated, the principle of reciprocity also obstructed rather than facilitated progress. Arafat had been reluctant to take on the Islamic fundamentalist opposition to his negotiations with Israel, to complete the revision of the Palestinian Charter, to stifle anti-Israeli rhetoric, or to engage overtly in security cooperation with Israel. Even when the peace process had been at its best, he was determined to keep the option of joining forces with the fundamentalists if things turned sour, to keep his people mobilized, and to refrain from appearing as an Israeli accomplice. By 1997 he must have realized this conduct had alienated part of the Israeli public and had helped to undermine Peres and bring Netanyahu to power. If he considered a policy change, however, he was discouraged by his—and many others'—suspicion that Netanyahu was actually seeking to emasculate the Oslo process, in which case Arafat was not about to alter his own conduct. And thus, throughout this period, Arafat persisted both in presuming that the Oslo process offered the best way to achieve the historic goal of Palestinian statehood, and in refusing to take any further steps to act on the Hebron Agreement commitments. In turn, Netanyahu argued that, given this Palestinian failure to offer reciprocity and compliance, he was not about to have Israel make additional withdrawals.

At the core of the original Oslo process had been the idea that time was needed to make a transition from conflict and hostility to a settlement predicated on compromise and partnership. These last elements had not always been present during the brief golden period of Israeli-Palestinian relations, but they were glaringly absent after June 1996. Any concessions made and cooperation secured were offered grudgingly. Both parties presumed they were locked in conflict, and each acted to maximize its position in the West Bank and in East Jerusalem.

Under these circumstances, it was difficult to get them to cooperate in the crucial and sensitive area of security. Given the devastating effectiveness of the Islamic terrorist campaigns of 1994–96 and the significance attached to this theme by Netanyahu, terrorist attacks were now particularly agonizing. During the first thirty months of Netanyahu's government, two suicide bombings occurred in Tel Aviv and Jerusalem, though they did not have the impact of the earlier ones—partly because of effective countermeasures taken by Israel and at least some-times by the Palestinian Authority, and also through sheer luck and, perhaps most important and ironic, the slowdown in the peace process. Iran, Hamas, and Islamic Jihad did not have to invest an effort com-parable to that of the previous years to obstruct a peace process that was now faltering.

The security cooperation between Israel and the Palestinian Author-ity was erratic. Conducted both bilaterally and trilaterally (with the Central Intelligence Agency as the third party), it affected and expressed the fluctuations of the general Israeli-Palestinian relationship. Security, after all, was at the core of the reciprocity and compliance issues. Arafat, in offering some cooperation some of the time, withholding it at other times, and occasionally tolerating or encouraging anti-Israeli violence, was walking a very fine line. Throughout this period he continued to act on the assumption that the Oslo process still offered the best prospects, but favoring it was not a policy he pursued with enthusiasm or con-sistency. As time went on, his motivation changed. His primary effort became to cultivate a new relationship with the United States and, spe-cifically, with the Clinton administration. The primacy of obtaining con-trol over additional land in the West Bank was clear, but as long as that was not feasible, Arafat was willing to settle, as an interim goal, for the dividends earned in a new relationship with the world's leading power.

President Clinton had made a personal political investment in Israeli-Palestinian relations and had taken some political risks to defuse the crisis in September 1996. But if it took three months to negotiate the Hebron Agreement, only to encounter fresh difficulties and disappoint-ments when it came to implementation, what were the prospects for the United States in the much-more-difficult final-status negotiations?

Warren Christopher's successor, Madeleine Albright, had a different order of priorities, as was seen in her decision to delay her first trip to the Middle East (in sharp contrast to Christopher's trip to the region less than a month after the inauguration in 1993). During her first weeks in office in 1997, it became evident that only part of the Hebron Agreement would be implemented and that a fresh effort would have to be made to get the three additional redeployments. This prospect was not attractive, and it was made even less so by the Israeli govern-ment's demonstrable willingness and ability to mobilize conservative

Republicans in Congress and a significant part of the organized American Jewish community against it.

In theory, a president who had just been reelected should have been immune to such considerations. But political circumstances in early 1997—and a Republican majority in both houses that enhanced the influence and importance of every single member of Congress—dissuaded the administration from open confrontation with the Israeli government. President Clinton and several of his aides made no effort to hide their criticism of Israel's prime minister and his government, but they avoided an outright showdown. The United States lowered its profile in the peace process but, despite criticism and advice to the contrary, refused to walk away from it. Clinton believed that the United States must make real and visible efforts to prevent the collapse of a diplomacy closely identified with the American position, and that at the end of the day Netanyahu would go through with the second redeployment.

The end of the day came nearly two years later, when four factors converged in the fall of 1998 to bring about that result:

First, Washington made it abundantly clear that, even if Arafat and the Palestinian Authority did not fully comply with their own commitments, it expected Israel to provide the key to further progress and to implement the redeployments. The American peace team established a middle ground of 13 percent as the effective range of Israel's next withdrawal in the West Bank. It brought Arafat down from his initial demand for a withdrawal from some 40 percent, it subsequently obtained Netanyahu's personal agreement to the lower figure, and then it set to work on constructing an agreement into which this withdrawal could be fitted and on helping Netanyahu to bring along the rest of his government and coalition.[16]

In the course of this protracted process, President Clinton was going through the first stages of his worst personal-political crisis. The Lewinsky affair (which eventually led to Clinton's impeachment, but not expulsion from office) exploded during Netanyahu's visit to Washington in January 1998, when the question of U.S. pressure on Israel was at the fore, and began to simmer down in the early fall of 1998, when Clinton summoned Middle East leaders to a conference at the Wye River Plantation. There, the president was first and foremost trying to solve a difficult and dangerous problem in the Middle East, but he was also trying to conduct normal presidential business and demonstrate his own personal effectiveness. By making the conference possible, by sustaining Clinton's personal participation, and by making their own political contributions, the president and his administration exerted an unusually effective influence on Israeli-Palestinian relations.

A second important consideration was the imminence of May 4, 1999, the end of the transitional period envisioned by the Oslo Accords. This date had seemed quite remote when the Hebron Agreement was completed in January 1997, but now all parties were dangerously close to the end of what was supposed to be a transition to a permanent settlement between Israel and the Palestinians. Arafat began to threaten publicly that he would announce Palestinian independence and statehood unilaterally; Israel threatened to respond with its own unilateral actions. Israel, indeed, was not short of potential responses, but a major crisis over a unilateral Palestinian declaration of independence would be undesirable for any Israeli prime minister. Arafat's and his colleagues' consternation with Israel and their own rhetoric notwithstanding, they still preferred to reach their goals by an agreement with Israel and were worried about the repercussions of a unilateral declaration. The explosive potential in this situation was fully exploited by U.S. diplomacy in bringing the parties together at the Wye River Plantation.

Third, a deal was gradually crystallizing. After all, the territorial aspect of the agreement had been put together by mid-1998; it then had to be matched by a political structure that would meet Netanyahu's requirements. On the face of it, Arafat had done this when he signed the Hebron Agreement. What was the value in yet another undertaking to revise the Palestinian Charter or the practical and political value of further reaffirmations of all the old points? Yet, in substantive and political terms, it was important for Netanyahu to be able to show that Israel's territorial concession would be matched by something; on a deeper level, he and his associates had to ask themselves about the rationale of giving up an additional 13 percent of the West Bank at that particular juncture. Keeping a commitment, mending relations with the United States and other nations, keeping the peace process going—these were all weighty reasons, but they had been for years. A new prospect was now needed for Netanyahu's government to agree to a new situation in which the Palestinian Authority would control a total of 40 percent of the West Bank and have an international airport in Gaza.

Last, Netanyahu needed to assemble the domestic political base in Israel for implementing the 13 percent withdrawal. The link between Netanyahu's personal and domestic political calculus and the implementation was an especially intricate business. Netanyahu had concluded earlier that what had already been implemented as part of the Oslo process was irreversible, and that at least part of the remaining Israeli commitments had to be implemented as well. These conclusions were linked to a presumption that in a reelection bid Netanyahu would need centrist as well as right-wing votes, that he would run as a leader who had lived up to his promises. But when would the next election be held? Could Netanyahu keep his coalition together until 2000? Could he, more specifically, withdraw from 13 percent of the West Bank *and* keep the National Religious Party (the settlers' movement's closest ally) in his coalition? Or did he perhaps want an early election, right after an agreement, in which he might lose the votes from the radical right wing but steal the Labor Party's thunder?

For many months, Netanyahu seemed to think of and try every political option and maneuver: creating a "national-unity government" with the Labor Party; attempting to split the Labor Party by attracting part of its parliamentary caucus into his coalition under the banner of "saving the peace"; buttressing his current coalition by promising its right wing he would avoid, delay, or fail to implement an agreement, and promising its more pragmatic members he would make the deal and carry it out. Finally, in September 1998 he decided to make Ariel Sharon (then serving as minister of national infrastructure) his main ally and to rely on this leader of the radical right in the final stage of negotiating the agreement.

On October 14 Netanyahu appointed Sharon as foreign minister. Sharon immediately announced that he would not vote for any agreement stipulating a withdrawal from the West Bank of more than 9 percent, but he made it clear that he would be the prime minister's partner in negotiating such an agreement at the Wye River Plantation.

Sharon's own journey from right-wing radicalism to this position paralleled and supplemented Netanyahu's shift from his preelection positions to his postelection policies. Sharon had grown up in the tradition of Labor Zionism's activist school. In 1973, having retired from the armed forces as a general, he joined Likud; he left his mark on Israel's relationship with the Arab world as the architect of the subsequent war in Lebanon and as the secular patron of the settler movement.[17]

By 1998, at the age of seventy, Sharon was acting under the influence of multiple considerations. He clearly remained critical and dubious of the ongoing peace process and specifically of the two Oslo Accords. But he was also eager to rehabilitate his reputation and image that had been tarnished during Israel's debacle in Lebanon in 1982–83. He also clearly relished his standing as the one substantial person in Netanyahu's government, though his relationship with Netanyahu was awkward. As a rule, Sharon criticized the prime minister from the right, but when he was in charge of resolving disputes between Israel and Jordan over water rights, he proved to be most accommodating.

Sharon's work in resolving the water issue and the Jordanians' exasperation with Netanyahu made Sharon a pivotal figure in Israeli-Jordanian relations. For years, this Likud leader most closely identified with the slogan "Jordan is Palestine" had been anathema to the Jordanians. But in the circumstances of 1998, they were willing to hold on to him as a pillar of effectiveness and pragmatism in the confusing landscape of Israel's new politics. As for Sharon himself, he regarded his new relationship with the Hashemites as a model for the kind of accomplishments he envisaged for himself in Israeli politics. Why couldn't he, drawing on his nationalist credentials and his gift for plain, tough talk, cast himself as the senior, mature figure of Israel's right wing who could offer the key to a reasonable compromise, a compromise for which he alone could mobilize sufficient support?

A glimpse into Sharon's thinking at that time is afforded by the synopsis of a presentation distributed by his office in May 1998 (before he became foreign minister) under the title "Security and Coexistence: An Alternative Approach to Breaking the Deadlock between Israel and the Palestinians." The final two paragraphs—"a summary"—read as follows:

> The way I view the situation today, it is possible to reach an agreement with the Palestinians in the interim phase, which would be somewhat similar to the concept of non-belligerency. This will give Palestinians the possibility of keeping and holding to the Oslo

Accords, and Israel the necessary time to examine and see that conditions for a true and lasting peace have materialized.

Finally, I wish to emphasize that this alternative approach of crisis avoidance, and the concept of "less than peace" agreement, which I have presented here, should be considered as a fallback position: if at a certain point it becomes clear to all parties that the current efforts to reach an agreement fail, then I believe it would be in the interest of both Israel and the Palestinians to adopt this approach as a means of breaking the deadlock and reviving the peace process.[18]

It is apparently with this view in mind that Israel's new foreign minister went to the Wye River Plantation. He is reported to have argued that any agreement reached there should be seen as an interim one, lasting for some twenty years. This is clearly not what the Palestinians, the rest of the Arab world, and the United States had in mind. Nor was it clear how Sharon and Netanyahu really viewed the agreement they ultimately concluded. Did they believe that they could freeze the status quo for so long, or did they realize that this was not the last stop in their journey toward the middle ground of pragmatism and compromise? Whatever they believed, the agreement they accepted at Wye was a limited one that commited Israel to withdrawing from 13 percent of the West Bank, but it was not intended to postpone a final agreement for anything like the twenty years Sharon reportedly had in mind.

In stark contrast to the partial progress made during this period in Israeli-Palestinian affairs, there was no movement whatsoever in Israel's relationship with Syria. The negotiations suspended in March 1996 were not renewed, despite several attempts by the American peace team, the European Union's special envoy, and a whole host of private intermediaries. Technically, the chief obstacle was Syria's insistence that "the negotiations be resumed at the point at which they had been interrupted" and Israel's rejection of this demand and of the interpretation on which it was based. This terminology was coded language for a very sweeping demand: Syria's version of the 1993–96 negotiations insisted that Prime Minister Rabin had committed Israel to withdraw from the Golan Heights, that Peres had reaffirmed this commitment, that these commitments were legally binding, and that fresh negotiations must proceed from this point of departure. The Israeli version was that there was no commitment, agreement, or promise to withdraw; and that a hypothetical, conditional position had been deposited with the United States to be matched by Syrian acceptance of a settlement package, which never happened. Netanyahu had a letter from Secretary of State Christopher in September 1996 expressing the view that the only agreement reached during the negotiations—the nonpaper on the security arrangements—was not legally binding. Oral exchanges were surely even less binding than this nonpaper.

The gap between these two positions could in fact have been bridged, but the real obstacle was substantive rather than procedural. As the negotiations of 1993–96 had clearly established, President Asad was willing to sign a peace treaty with Israel but insisted on a full Israeli withdrawal from the Golan Heights, and the peace package he had offered did not meet Israel's criteria. The hypothetical formula facilitated negotiation, but suspension of the talks left Syria with nothing achieved. Starting in June 1996 Asad faced an Israeli prime minister elected on a platform that explicitly precluded full withdrawal from the Golan Heights. Therefore Asad came to insist on an explicit (not hypothetical) American or Israeli commitment as a precondition for renewing the negotiations, but he was not anxious and certainly not desperate for this. He also was not interested in negotiations for their own sake. In his view, the very fact of holding a Syrian-Israeli negotiation would have played into Netanyahu's hands, enabling him to argue that the peace process had been revived and, on that basis, to advance the cause of Arab-Israeli normalization. Asad therefore demanded that a new phase of negotiations be predicated on Israel's explicit commitment to withdraw from the Golan Heights.

This was not acceptable to Netanyahu, for two main reasons. Like his predecessors, on procedural and practical grounds he resented Asad's attempt to dictate conditions and to open a negotiation with a guaranteed bottom line, thus leaving the Israeli side with very little leverage. Then there was the substantive, and ultimately most important, obstacle: Was Netanyahu interested in and could he deliver an agreement with Syria that was predicated on Israel's withdrawal from the Golan Heights? For more than two years the prevailing assumption was that Netanyahu would not and could not do this. Asad had only to watch the

Palestinians make limited progress in their arena and continue his pressure on Israel by extending support and encouragement to Hizballah in its ongoing campaign against Israel in South Lebanon.

Only after Netanyahu's electoral defeat in 1999 was his secret negotiation with Asad in the summer and fall of 1998 exposed.

In the annals of Arab-Israeli diplomacy, this negotiation, which came to be known as the Lauder Mission, stands out as a particularly peculiar episode. For several months the Jewish-American cosmetics magnate Ronald Lauder shuttled between Jerusalem and Damascus, conveying messages between Netanyahu and Asad. Lauder was accompanied by his personal aide and by a Lebanese-American, George Nader, a man of many connections who for several years had been acting in the gray zone of Arab-Israeli relations. Netanyahu did not advise the Clinton administration of his negotiations with Asad, nor did Lauder, who as a Republican political appointee had served as Ronald Reagan's ambassador to Vienna. The negotiation itself was quite interesting. Netanyahu conveyed through Lauder his willingness in principle to withdraw from the Golan to the lines of June 4, 1967. Asad, who negotiated directly with Lauder, agreed to keep the Israeli monitoring station on Mount Hermon (adjacent to the Golan Heights) as long as it was manned and operated by the United States (he may also have agreed to include some Israeli personnel dressed in American uniform). Netanyahu's choice of Lauder for this complex and delicate mission was curious and apparently based their friendship and Lauder's financial support of Netanyahu. Asad agreed to deal with him as such, but he was also intrigued by the prospect of dealing directly with a representative of an American big business, which held a peculiar attraction for this former Arab revolutionary.

The episode ended when Asad decided after several rounds that he wanted a concrete proof of Netanyahu's seriousness and told Lauder that he must not return unless he brought along a map with Netanyahu's lines of withdrawal marked on it. At this point Netanyahu brought his defense and foreign ministers, Yitzhak Mordechai and Ariel Sharon, into the picture. Both objected and Lauder never returned to Damascus.[19]

In December 1998 the situation changed again with the collapse of Netanyahu's coalition. It is moot whether the prime minister could (and should) have stayed the course or whether his government was doomed by the tension between policy (the need to come to an agreement after nearly two years of procrastination) and politics (the refusal of several right-wing coalition members to support the government through implementation of the Wye Agreement). Netanyahu got the cabinet and the Knesset to approve the agreement, but his coalition ran out of steam soon thereafter. On December 21 the coalition and opposition joined forces in a vote that dissolved the Knesset and stipulated an early election, called for May 17, 1999, with June 1 as the date for a possible second round in the prime ministerial election.

During the next few weeks the stage was set for a lengthy, contentious election campaign. The formation of a new Center party meant that for the first time in Israel's political history there would be a three-way race. Netanyahu and his election advisers chose to focus their campaign on the peace process and the prime minister's character while avoiding domestic socioeconomic issues that had been festering. The strategy was to repeat the success of 1996 and to depict Netanyahu as a resilient, uncompromising leader who, despite the recent Wye Agreement and in contrast to his meek competitors, would not yield to Arab and, specifically, Palestinian pressures.

Aside from a minor Israeli redeployment and several meetings of joint committees established by the Wye Agreement, implementation was suspended in anticipation of the elections. Some protests notwithstanding, Arafat agreed to this and to delay his threatened declaration of Palestine's independence and statehood. For one thing, he (and for that matter the Clinton administration) was reluctant to affect the Israeli election adversely. Whatever their sympathies, each had discovered in 1996 that an overt Palestinian effort to help Netanyahu's rivals could backfire; passive communication of one's preferences seemed the safer option. Inasmuch as Arafat was concerned, this meant that he was not going to overtly support the Labor candidate, Ehud Barak, or the centrist Yitzhak Mordechai or be critical of Netanyahu. Likewise, he was determined not to embarrass Israeli supporters of the peace process by staging a major crisis before the elections.

In Arafat's strategy, investment in Washington's goodwill remained cardinal and continued to yield handsome dividends, notably when in mid-December 1998 President Clinton visited Israel and the Gaza Strip—as agreed on and announced at the Wye River conference. The visit was meant to reinforce the implementation of an agreement that was likely to encounter difficulties. Yasser Arafat and the Palestinians could easily note the political and diplomatic advantages of having the president of the United States visit Gaza, while Netanyahu was promised that Clinton's presence would be used to guarantee a definitive public abrogation of the offensive anti-Israel paragraphs of the Palestinian National Charter. Chairman Arafat registered yet another milestone on his way to hoped-for Palestinian statehood, and the Israeli prime minister could claim he had obtained the final revision of the document for which he had chided Peres in 1996.

4

EHUD BARAK AND THE
COLLAPSE OF THE PEACE PROCESS

Ehud Barak was elected Israel's prime minister on May 17, 1999; on July 6 he presented his coalition government to the Knesset. He had conducted his election campaign as Yitzhak Rabin's heir—a high-ranking military man and a former chief of staff of the Israel Defense Forces (IDF)—who went into politics to provide Israel with peace embedded in a solid new security regime.[1] But as prime minister, Barak adopted a style radically different from Rabin's. Rabin moderated his bold decisions through his preference for gradualism; Barak sought to cut the Arab-Israeli Gordian knot with one bold stroke. He concluded that the phased approach to Israeli-Arab peacemaking had run its course and acted out of a deeply held conviction that the failure to reach a swift comprehensive Arab-Israeli settlement would inevitably lead to a large-scale collision.

Barak set a formidable challenge for himself by formulating, in his public statements, ambitious goals and a rapid timetable. During his first visit to the United States as prime minister, Barak's spokesmen told Israeli reporters, he had presented President Clinton with a program for a final peace agreement that would resolve all outstanding issues among Israel, the Palestinians, Syria, and Lebanon. These issues included the most intractable problems, such as Jerusalem and the resettlement of the Palestinian refugees. The Israeli reporters were told that "Barak wants to remove the phased approach once and for all off the agenda and proposes that Arab leaders come to discuss the whole gamut of issues. . . . The Barak plan sets a timetable of fifteen months, until October 2000, to reach a breakthrough on all tracks: a final-status Israeli-Palestinian agreement, peace agreements with Syria and Lebanon, and regional arrangements for the refugee and water problems."[2]

On other occasions, Barak emphasized that he was setting a fifteen-month deadline to find out whether Israel had a "real partner" on the Arab side. Barak and his spokesmen did not elaborate in public on the essential components of his plan, but they let it be understood that he estimated an agreement could be reached on terms that were quite acceptable to both Palestinians and Israelis. This agreement would include an independent Palestinian state, contiguous in the West Bank and connected to the Gaza Strip through an elevated bridge; a unified Jerusalem under Israeli sovereignty; the Jordan River serving as a security border; and refugees rehabilitated in their countries of residence without "right of return" to Israel. Barak was said to be willing to predicate the peace settlement with Syria on Israel's withdrawal from the Golan Heights, while insisting that the border be pushed back from the shoreline of Lake Tiberias.[3]

Barak's domestic political moves reflected his decision to devote his first two years in office to completing—or at least significantly advancing—the peace process. The elections of May 1999 were conducted by the two-ballot method, which meant that each voter cast one ballot for the direct election of the prime minister and another for a party list of candidates for the Knesset. Barak won an impressive personal majority (56.08 percent) but emerged with weak support in parliament. His own Labor Party list won only twenty-six of one hundred and twenty seats, and the larger bloc of center-left parties, the natural supporter of his peace policy, failed to obtain the requisite number of seats for building a coalition on its own.

Against this backdrop the prime minister-elect had two choices. One option was to form a coalition government with the Likud, whose parliamentary caucus had been decimated to nineteen; to settle on modest progress in the peace process; and to seek to turn the Likud into a partner for an ambitious program of domestic sociopolitical reform. The second option was to add the Orthodox Sephardi Shas (the third-largest party, now holding seventeen seats) to his governing coalition alongside the left-wing Meretz Party, in the hope that in return for accommodating the Shas agenda on handling a separate school system and "church and state" issues, that party's leadership would overcome the nationalistic proclivities of its voters and support Barak's bold vision for ending the Arab-Israeli conflict.

Barak chose the second option, working on the assumption that under the leadership of Rabbi Ovadya Yosef, Shas would become an effective partner to his peace policies. On July 6, 1999, he introduced a government resting on a coalition composed of seventy-three members of the Knesset. He also assumed that a government conducting an energetic peace policy could rely on the votes of the Arab members of the Knesset without adding them to the coalition.

This strategic choice was supplemented by a second major decision: to focus the initial and main effort of the government's peace policy on the Syrian, rather than Palestinian, track. Barak did not advertise this choice, however. According to his own public statements, he remained committed to the idea of reaching final-status agreements with both Syria and the Palestinians within a reasonable time frame, but he clearly preferred a "Syria first" policy, seeking to obtain an early agreement with Syria and then proceed to negotiate with the Palestinians from a better bargaining position.

This premise—as well as the whole tenor of Barak's policy—was questioned by a significant portion of Israel's foreign policy and national security establishment. Questions were raised about whether a government resting on a fragile coalition would be able to complete agreements entailing significant concessions on both the Syrian and Palestinian tracks. More specific questions concerned Barak's ability to achieve an agreement with Syria, based on withdrawal from the Golan and approval by a referendum, with the Palestinian issue hovering in the background.

Barak's preference for the Syrian track was shaped by the same considerations that had guided his three predecessors—Rabin, Peres, and Netanyahu—to choose a "Syria first" policy. The Syrian-Israeli conflict was perceived as less complex than the Israeli-Palestinian dispute, as an essentially territorial conflict between two sovereign states rather than a nationalist and communal conflict over land and rights. Hafiz al-Asad was also seen as a better partner than Arafat for a swift negotiation. Barak, in a typically determined fashion, pushed from this vantage point to an early resumption and conclusion of the Israeli-Syrian negotiations.

Given the comparatively cordial welcome both the Syrian government and media offered to Israel's new leader, the prospects of an Israeli-Syrian agreement began to seem better in the latter half of 1999 than they had been in the previous decade. And yet the efforts to resume the negotiations met with a series of unanticipated difficulties. It took a full six months—until December 1999—to restart the negotiation.[4]

Two of the difficulties were of an apparently technical nature. For one, Asad continued to insist (as he had done with Netanyahu) that the negotiations be resumed only "at the point at which they had been interrupted," with that "point" including an Israeli agreement to withdraw to the lines of June 4, 1967. Barak was familiar with the history of the Israel-Syrian negotiations and well knew that Asad would not sign a peace treaty with Jerusalem without a full Israeli withdrawal from the Golan. Even if Barak accepted this as part of the negotiation's end result, he was not willing to accept it as the point of departure. By effectively surrendering his trump card before the start of the negotiations, he would be left without any leverage or bargaining chips once the negotiations began to unfold. Barak also wanted to establish the degree of flexibility in the Syrian insistence on Israel's withdrawal to "the lines of June 4, 1967." Such lines had never been drawn on a map. Barak wanted to ascertain Asad's willingness to settle on a formal Israeli acceptance of his demand, in return for Syrian flexibility regarding the actual location of the lines. When this issue was first put on the agenda in the mid-1990s, the Israeli negotiators and their colleagues on the U.S. peace team assumed that what mattered to Asad was the principle of obtaining an Israeli withdrawal from land on Syria's side of the 1923 international boundary, that he was primarily interested in Israel leaving the al-Himmeh salient (south of Lake Tiberias), and that he would be willing to accommodate Israel's needs regarding the shoreline of Lake Tiberias and the northern Jordan River. It was made amply clear to Asad that this was a "red line" for a country preoccupied with its water supply.[5]

A second difficulty arose from the loose ends left from the aftermath of the Lauder mission. Barak's team was given a cursory briefing on this issue by Netanyahu's team, and Lauder, to protect Netanyahu, initially told the Clinton administration that Asad had negotiated with him on the strength of Netanyahu's willingness to withdraw to the 1923 international boundary, as distinct from the lines of June 4. This led Barak to believe that he could restart negotiations on terms that were relatively comfortable from an Israeli point of view. It took several weeks to discover that Lauder's report—and the set of assumptions it produced—were erroneous. (The Syrians continue to deny this version of events and have sought to belittle the significance of the whole Lauder episode.)

Beyond these particular issues lies the more fundamental question of Asad's intention ever to consummate negotiations with Israel. A school of thought had argued throughout the 1990s that Asad never intended to reach an agreement with Israel, and that his participation in the peace process was motivated purely by the political dividends he expected to reap in Washington simply by negotiating. But even those who did not share this view had to contend with the question of the extent to which—and the conditions under which—Asad was interested in resuming and completing negotiations with Israel in 1999–2000.

The principal change during this period was the decline of Asad's health and the subsequent urgency that was now vested in the issue of succession. Asad died in June 2000. During the preceding months his physical and mental decline was all too evident and was matched by a loss of authority and political power. The process of promoting his son, Bashar, and building him up as heir apparent, was accelerated. Some of Hafiz al-Asad's closest friends and associates were removed and replaced by younger men who were closer to Bashar and viewed as better partners for the new ruler. Asad's gradual decline gave Syria's foreign minister, Faruq al-Shara, a degree of authority and freedom of action that he had not known in the past.

Hafiz al-Asad's power remained unchallenged while he was still alive, but the removal of several former partners and associates, the widespread unhappiness with the adoption of the dynastic principle, and the discontent with Bashar's persona created significant pockets of domestic criticism of and opposition to the government for the first time in many years. Part of the criticism was directed at the very idea of settlement with Israel and the compromises and concessions it entailed; these were easier targets than Asad's nepotism. Asad, aware of his decline, chose to focus on his chief priority: ensuring the succession of his son.

But domestic politics was not the only set of forces brought to bear on Syria's negotiations with Ehud Barak. Asad's desire to regain the Golan before stepping offstage, the need to secure Washington's goodwill and cooperation at this sensitive juncture, and the potential for conflict in Lebanon (given Barak's pledge to the Israeli public to get the IDF out of Lebanon within his first year in power) all modified and affected the Syrian-Israeli negotiations.

Barak first made that Lebanon pledge during the election campaign, and it was, indeed, dismissed by many as a mere campaign promise. But he did repeat it after his election and thereby changed the dynamic that had shaped the Israeli-Lebanese-Syrian triangle throughout the 1990s. Israel's policy had been predicated on the assumption that its problems in south Lebanon could be resolved only through an agreement with Syria. The hegemonic power in Lebanon, Syria in fact encouraged Hizballah's attacks in order to extract greater concessions from Israel. Barak's promise (or threat) to take Israel out of south Lebanon by July 2000 altered this equation. How would Hizballah conduct itself if Israel were to withdraw unilaterally from south Lebanon? How should Syria act on its own and with regard to Hizballah and its Iranian sponsors? Could Damascus risk escalation along the Israeli-Lebanese border, given the complex state of affairs in Syria's domestic politics?

Against this backdrop, the quiet diplomacy of the summer and fall of 1999 yielded a positive outcome. In December 1999 the resumption of the Israeli-Syrian negotiations was announced. Moreover, Asad agreed to upgrade the negotiation from the bureaucratic to the political level and nominated Foreign Minister Shara as the Syrian negotiator. Barak, in turn, decided to overlook the difference in rank and status and put himself at the head of the Israeli delegation. Negotiations began in Washington on December 15. Barak was accompanied by his foreign minister, David Levy; the minister of tourism (and former chief of staff of the IDF), Amnon Shahak; and a team of negotiators headed by Reserve General Uri Sagi (who, like Barak and Shahak, had participated in earlier phases of the Israeli-Syrian peace process).

In December 1999 and January 2000 two rounds of negotiations were held under President Clinton's aegis in Washington and in Shepherdstown, West Virginia. The Washington talks were overshadowed by Shara's sulking conduct, notably his refusal to shake Barak's hand and his strident speech.[6] Such details may seem trifling within the larger context of two enemies making an effort to move from a state of hostility and belligerency to a state of peace, but symbols and rituals are significant both in conflict and during a transition to peace. This was particularly true for the Israeli-Syrian relationship. It was widely assumed that in the event of an agreement with Syria, Barak would have to hold a referendum. It was also assumed that to win this referendum, he would have to persuade Asad to engage in public diplomacy—a series of gestures designed to persuade the Israeli public that Syria had had a change of heart and was now ready for genuine peace with yesterday's enemy. But during the Washington talks and throughout this period, Syria held on to its familiar position: refusal to engage in any public diplomacy, and continued pressure exerted on Israel in the Lebanese and Palestinian arenas as long as an agreement had not been reached.

In the closed sessions held in Washington, however, Shara was more forthcoming than his public conduct suggested. Furthermore, the strident tone notwithstanding, he incorporated two intriguing phrases in his public statement: that the conflict with Israel was no longer existential but territorial, and that peacemaking with Israel constituted a transition from struggle to competition.[7] This motif was essential to Syria's concept of a prospective settlement with Israel—Israel would no longer be an enemy but would remain an adversary and a competitor. By signing a peace treaty with Israel, Syria could end active conflict with the Jewish state but not reconcile itself to its legitimacy. The struggle would therefore continue in other (that is, nonmilitary) ways. This concept of peacemaking with Israel is, in fact, not so different from the policies pursued by Egypt, although the latter's leaders stopped short of an explicit adoption of the notion of "an ongoing struggle," preferring to use cautious terms such as cold peace and opposition to normalization.

The Shepherdstown talks lasted longer than the brief meeting in Washington but ended in failure. The chief obstacle was familiar: Syria's insistence on an explicit Israeli commitment to withdraw to the lines of June 4, 1967, as a precondition to any progress. Barak alluded to his willingness to withdraw, and to start preparing Israeli public opinion for withdrawal to the lines of June 4, 1967, as an abstract concept, but he refused to make an explicit commitment before assessing Asad's flexibility regarding the actual demarcation of the June 4 lines and in particular the shoreline of Lake Tiberias. According to American diplomats who participated in the talks, Foreign Minister Shara indicated that Syria could be flexible in this matter. But he refused to elaborate, and, as it turned out during a Clinton-Asad meeting in Geneva in March 2000, his statement had no real value.

The failure of the Shepherdstown talks subsequently became a bone of contention between Barak and his critics. Participants such as the U.S. Ambassador to Israel, Martin Indyk, and Barak's own chief negotiator, Uri Sagi, have argued that Barak developed cold feet. They felt that his failure to make an explicit commitment prevented a breakthrough with a Syrian partner otherwise ready to make a deal. Raviv Druker's critical book on Barak's tenure claims that pollsters warned Barak that Israeli public opinion was opposed to the concessions demanded by Syria.[8] Robert Malley, a former official of the National Security Council, argued that Clinton was resentful of Barak's conduct at Shepherdstown—so much so that, angered by a change in Barak's position during the subsequent Camp David Summit in July 2000, he told him: "I can't go to Arafat with a retrenchment! You can sell it. . . . This is not real. This is not serious. I went to Shepherdstown . . . and was told nothing by you for four days. I went to Geneva [to meet with Asad] and felt like an Indian doll doing your bidding. . . ."[9]

Barak still insists that it would have been a grave mistake to offer Asad an explicit commitment to withdraw, and that it was Asad's insistence on this precondition that obstructed the talks. Barak also attributes great importance to the fact that an American draft of a proposed text for an Israeli-Syrian peace treaty was leaked to the Israeli press. The U.S. peace team prepared the draft in an effort to demonstrate how close the parties were to agreement. The Syrians leaked a doctored version of the text, to show that the draft was in fact closer to a "nonbelligerency" agreement than to a peace treaty. Later, a different version of the text, more attractive to Israel, was leaked to an Israeli journalist. Indeed, in the postmortem of the Shepherdstown talks, the Syrians complained that the latter leak embarrassed Asad and made it difficult for Syria to resume the negotiations.[10]

As had been the case in earlier instances, the very fact that a high-level Israeli-Syrian meeting took place agitated the Israeli political system. The prospect of an agreement with Syria predicated on a full Israeli withdrawal from the Golan seemed close and realistic. The Golan Lobby had become powerful during the previous decade, and its campaign against Barak's Syrian gambit was facilitated by two crucial forces:

Hafiz al-Asad's refusal to invest any effort to win over Israeli public opinion, and the inherent difficulty of persuading the public to endorse an agreement that had yet to be made.

In hopeful anticipation, Barak's government began a campaign to build support in the United States for a massive aid package, to be received when an agreement with Syria was signed. It suggested that the Clinton administration should ask Congress for a special aid package of up to $17 billion, allowing Israel to build up and modernize the IDF to compensate for the loss of the Golan.[11] This was a staggering amount that would be difficult to get endorsed by any Congress, let alone a Republican one explicitly hostile to Syria and reluctant to assist the Clinton administration in attaining its foreign policy objectives. Moreover, during the brief period of high expectations of an Israeli-Syrian breakthrough, the Golan Lobby in Israel and its allies in the American-Jewish community launched a campaign against U.S. support of a would-be Israeli-Syrian agreement. The campaign was reminiscent of the one conducted in the mid-1990s. As it turned out, the campaign was superfluous—cut short by the collapse of the negotiations in March 2000.

In contradistinction to the familiar arguments of Israeli and American opponents of a Syrian-Israeli settlement were the novel voices of a domestic Syrian opposition to accommodation with Israel. There had been some indications of such opposition in the early and mid-1990s, but they had seemed marginal and muted. The domestic criticism of Asad's policies that surfaced in late 1999 and early 2000, however, was systematic and sustained. He and his regime were taken to task for their very willingness to accept the state of Israel, as well as for their apparent readiness to withdraw from some of Syria's original positions in negotiations. An article published by Ali Aqleh Arsan, a Ba'ath Party member and chairman of the Arab Writers Union headquartered in Damascus, was a particularly harsh example of such criticism. Arsan stated, "We reject and will continue to reject any recognition of Zionism."[12] Echoing the bitter tone of Syria's great poet, Nizar Qabbani, Arsan asked rhetorically, "Are we to remain with nothing but a sense of despair and possibly the bitter memories of our defeat? Will the ghosts of millions of Palestinians who were expelled from their homes disappear?" He asserted that he and his colleagues saw the struggle against the "Zionist enemy" as an existential conflict—and not as a conflict over borders—in a clear, sardonic reference to Faruq al-Shara's statement in Washington.

On February 13, Shara delivered a speech to the members of the Arab Writers Union explaining and defending Syria's policy toward Israel. It was an uncharacteristic speech for a foreign minister to make. In ordinary circumstances, it would have been Asad's responsibility to offer an authoritative exposition of his regime's policy. But Asad's health had deteriorated to the point that he was incapable of exercising his customary leadership role.

Shara's speech was not a coherent, focused text but rather a patchwork of ideas and arguments that constituted an effort to address different constituencies—and was therefore full of contradictions. In defense of the regime's policies, he explained that the Arabs had been defeated by Israel and that Syria had been abandoned by its Arab partners. Therefore Syria had no choice but to make peace with Israel. In a similar apologetic vein, Shara repeated in a modified version the statement he had made in Washington in December 1999 that the conflict with Israel had been transformed from an existential to a territorial dispute and was accordingly ripe for resolution. The foreign minister also repeated another motif from his Washington speech in stating that peace, in fact, meant a transformation of the military conflict into a political, economic, and cultural competition—one in which the Arabs stood a better chance.

In other segments of the February 13 speech, however, Shara denounced Israel and Zionism, pledging his allegiance to the original vision and long-term goals of the Ba'ath Party. In response to a question from the audience, Shara went so far as to revive the "phased approach" of the 1970s: "The Ba'ath Party believes that regaining the whole of Palestine is a long term strategic goal that could not be implemented in one phase ... the Ba'ath Party's doctrine draws a distinction between the different phases of the struggle for the liberation of Palestine."[13]

The failure of the Shepherdstown talks resulted in a stalemate that lasted for about two months. Both the Clinton administration and the Barak government were worried by this passage of time. The planned date in May for Israel's withdrawal from Lebanon was getting closer, and Asad's health continued to deteriorate, exacerbating the Israeli debate on a prospective agreement with Syria. Proponents argued that it was preferable to conclude the agreement with a leader who commanded the stature and authority necessary to both make and implement the agreement. They also believed that the majority of Syria's political system and public had come to accept the notion of peace with Israel, so an agreement made by Asad would be kept by his successors even if he died shortly after signing it. They further argued that if an agreement was not signed during Asad's lifetime, it would take his successor a long time to establish enough sway to complete the peace process with Israel. On the other side of the debate, opponents of a settlement with Syria reinforced their original criticism by arguing that handing over the Golan to a dying autocratic ruler would be an egregiously reckless act.

In any event, the United States and Israel reached the conclusion that a face-to-face meeting between Presidents Clinton and Asad was the only possible way to break the deadlock and reach a swift agreement. Washington and Jerusalem therefore acted on the assumption that Asad alone possessed the authority to make crucial decisions required for breakthrough and accommodation, and that absent the prospect of a meeting between Barak and Asad, the closest approximation to an Israeli-Syrian summit was an American-Syrian one. Clinton was familiar with Barak's position and could be trusted to present and represent it well. Furthermore, Asad was believed to be more interested in a dialogue with Washington than in making peace with Israel.

This technique constituted a new version of Rabin's interaction with Warren Christopher in August 1993. Like that original deposit of Israel's willingness to withdraw from the Golan, Barak's reliance on Clinton reflected his exasperation with his repeated failure to reach Asad directly. Barak had also learned from the Lauder episode that it was easier to persuade Asad to make concessions when negotiating with him in person. But Christopher's meeting with Asad in August 1993 had been a first step calculated to set a process in motion. The Clinton-Asad meeting in March 2000 was rather a final measure, a last-ditch effort to prevent total collapse of the Israeli-Syrian negotiation.

The March 26 meeting in Geneva ended in swift, resounding failure. We have yet to learn the full extent of the efforts invested to secure the success of the meeting and to save Clinton from another embarrassment. Clearly, the U.S. president acted on the assumption (derived from statements made by Faruq al-Shara in earlier discussions) that

Asad would be willing to show flexibility in drawing the lines of June 4, 1967, and to allow a strip of land along Lake Tiberias and the Upper Jordan to remain under Israeli sovereignty. The strip would be wider than the ten meters stipulated by the 1923 agreement, which established the boundary between the British Mandate in Palestine and the French Mandate in Syria.

In Geneva Asad rejected these ideas out of hand. He made it amply clear that if Shara had spoken to that effect, he had exceeded his authority. And so the ten-month effort launched in May 1999 collapsed—under the weight of Asad's insistence on obtaining part of the Lake Tiberias shore, and under Barak's insistence that even if Israel agreed to withdraw from the Golan Heights and to give up the al-Himmeh enclave, it could not and would not give up full sovereignty over the lake. Barak viewed full control of Lake Tiberias as key to Israel's water regime. He also sensed that this represented a political red line that the Israeli electorate would not cross in a referendum or a fresh election.[14]

The collapse of the fourth effort toward an Israeli-Syrian resolution in the final decade of the twentieth century had several causes. Asad's uncompromising position and tactical errors by Washington and Jerusalem were two of them. But the prime reason seems to have been Asad's physical and mental decline. During the last months of his life, Asad focused his residual powers on securing the succession of his son. He felt weak and vulnerable and was sensitive to criticism that he was willing to sacrifice his principles for a compromise with Israel. This criticism may well have reflected a minority view and was probably also an expression of opposition to the introduction of the dynastic principle into the political system of a formerly revolutionary republic. Nonetheless, on the eve of a problematic transition, Asad and his loyalist core were defensive. Had Israel succumbed to all his demands and provided him with "the peace of the victors," he might have signed an agreement—but for Ehud Barak this was not a viable option.

The failure of the Geneva summit provided fresh ammunition to those who had argued since the early and mid-1990s that Asad never intended to consummate the negotiations with Israel, and that he was merely interested in the political dividends accruing to participants in the peace process. For advocates of this interpretation, the Geneva meeting in March 2000 was a moment of truth that illuminated Asad's conduct throughout the previous decade. An entirely different interpretation argues that the failure of the 1999–2000 negotiation could have been avoided altogether. My own view is that, given the profound change in Asad's outlook once he realized that his death was imminent, the events during the spring of 2000 do not necessarily explain the previous decade.

Several attempts were made to revive negotiations in the aftermath of the failed summit in Geneva, but they were nipped in the bud by two developments: Israel's withdrawal from Lebanon in May and Asad's death in June.

Israel's withdrawal from south Lebanon ended a nine-year link between the Israeli-Syrian negotiations and the security issues along the Israeli-Lebanese border. Israel no longer expected an agreement with Syria to also provide a fundamental solution to its Lebanese dilemma. It also reached, independently, the conclusion that large-scale military operations in Lebanon, attacks on Hizballah, and indirect pressure on Beirut were all ineffective strategies. Syria was the hegemonic power in Lebanon, and Israel's quest for security along its northern border would now rest on a classic deterrence equation. Attacks on Israel across an internationally recognized border would lead—it was suggested—to a full-fledged Israeli-Syrian collision.[15]

From Barak's point of view, the unilateral withdrawal from Lebanon was a risky gamble. There was no guarantee that either Syria or Hizballah would act cautiously. In the event, however, the gamble proved to be at least a short-term success. Hafiz al-Asad died three weeks later, on June 10. Bashar's succession proceeded smoothly, and the new president was clearly interested in consolidating his position at home rather than engaging in risky adventures involving Israel. Nor were Tehran and Hizballah interested in provoking a wave of violence in south Lebanon at that time. For them, Israel's withdrawal was a great victory—a vindication—and they were determined to exploit it politically by bolstering Hizballah's standing in Lebanon.

For nearly five months, Hizballah's leadership did indeed refrain from initiating dramatic attacks against Israel. Instead, it dug in along the border and encouraged Lebanese civilians to come to the fence in an effort to defy and provoke IDF guards. While Israel claimed that its withdrawal from Lebanon was final and definitive, Hizballah argued

that the issue remained open as long as Israel continued to hold Lebanese prisoners and failed to withdraw from the Shaba Farms, a disputed
area near the juncture of the Israeli-Lebanese-Syrian borders. According to Israel (and the United Nations), the Shaba Farms were on Syrian
territory and should be dealt with by Israel and Syria. Hizballah (and
eventually other Lebanese actors), however, saw fit to argue that this
was Lebanese territory and that Israel's refusal to withdraw from it constituted an act of occupation and aggression. The organization was thus
laying the groundwork for new attacks on Israel at some future date.

That future date came in early October 2000. After the outbreak of
Palestinian-Israeli violence in late September, Hizballah was confronted
with both opportunity and pressure to join the fray. From Iran's and
Hizballah's perspective, the Palestinians were inspired by their success in
making Israel's occupation of south Lebanon untenable and applied the
lesson that there was no need to make concessions to Israel. If one stood
one's ground and fought for one's rights, the Israelis would pack up and
leave. How could Hizballah's leadership remain an idle spectator under
these circumstances? Hizballah's radical proclivities were reinforced
by two developments: its poor performance in Lebanese elections and
Bashar al-Asad's weakness as a new, untested leader. Bashar not only
failed to restrain Hizballah but seemed to be under its leadership's spell.
For Hafiz al-Asad, Hizballah had been an actor on the Lebanese scene,
an arm of the Iranian government, and an occasional ally of Syria's
policy. But while he had sought to use and manipulate the organization,
his son seemed to admire it.

Against this backdrop of events, Hizballah launched an offensive
against Israel by abducting three Israeli soldiers who were patrolling the
border on October 7. A week later it abducted an Israeli businessman
in Europe. Israel, reluctant to open yet another front, decided to refrain
from a military response.

Israel's policy changed after Ariel Sharon defeated Barak in the election of February 2001. Hizballah attacked twice, and on both occasions
Israel retaliated by attacking Syrian positions. Sharon thus implemented
the deterrence equation established by Barak and underscored the view
that Syria was the effective address for Israel's deterrence. Given his
own experience in Lebanon in 1982, Sharon had no appetite for becoming heavily involved in that arena. In both cases Syria refrained from

responding despite pressures reportedly exerted on Bashar al-Asad by his more radical associates.

The calming effect of Israel's actions evaporated after a few months. The Palestinian-Israeli war of attrition intensified, as did Iran's determination to destabilize the region. Hizballah's attacks grew in scope and boldness.

The tension and violence along Israel's northern border in 2001 and 2002 provided yet another manifestation of the "shifting horizon" phenomenon in Arab-Israeli relations. Even when Israel withdrew from Lebanon—and did so in cooperation with the United Nations— Hizballah (and subsequently Lebanon's government) argued that the withdrawal was less than complete. Furthermore, the Arab summit conference in Beirut in March 2002, meeting to adopt the Saudi peace initiative, endorsed this position as well.

BARAK AND THE ISRAELI-PALESTINIAN TRACK

Only in the early summer of 2000, after the final collapse of the Syrian negotiations and Israel's unilateral withdrawal from Lebanon, did Barak devote his full attention to negotiations with the Palestinians. In retrospect it is clear that Barak's focus on the Syrian track during his first year in office had been to the detriment of Israel's dealings with the Palestinians.

These dealings consisted of several meetings with Yasser Arafat, of give-and-take with him through a discreet channel, and of a formal negotiation on the implementation of the Wye Agreement signed by Netanyahu's government in October 1998. Barak confronted a double dilemma: how to preserve Arafat's and the Palestinians' goodwill while assigning a clear priority to the Syrian track, and how to proceed with the implementation of the Wye Agreement without spending territorial assets that he would rather use in the final-status negotiations. Barak viewed himself as a leader possessed of capabilities and style different from those of Netanyahu and believed in his ability to accomplish final-status agreements with both Syria and the Palestinians. The agreement with the Palestinians would perhaps be reached and implemented in phases, but Barak was reluctant to offer massive concessions during the interim phases. (As a member of Rabin's cabinet during the summit of

1995, he abstained during the vote on the Oslo II Accord in disagreement with the phased withdrawals that were built into it.)

In any event, on September 4, 1999, five months after he came to power, Barak and Arafat signed the Sharm al-Sheikh agreement for the implementation of the Wye Agreement. Israel's withdrawal from 13 percent of the West Bank, which had originally been envisaged in two phases, was now to be implemented in three, but the Palestinians were compensated by a verbal promise that they would be given contiguous "quality" territory. Agreement was also reached regarding a familiar set of issues including the seaport in Gaza, safe passage between the West Bank and the Gaza Strip, and Israel's release of Palestinian prisoners. The parties agreed on a continuous accelerated negotiation with a view to reaching agreement in two phases: a framework agreement during 2000 and a final-status agreement within a year.

The final-status negotiations were conducted in two channels: an open channel led, on the Israeli side, by Ambassador to Jordan Oded Eran, and a more significant secret one in Stockholm. The Palestinian delegation to the secret channel was headed by Abu Alaa [Ahmed Qurai), chairman of the Palestinian Authority's Legislative Council and Arafat's chief negotiator in Oslo. Barak was represented by Shlomo Ben-Ami, minister of domestic security, and Gilead Sher, an attorney who negotiated the Sharm al-Sheikh agreement on Israel's behalf. In May 2000, details of the secret Israeli-Palestinian negotiation began to leak. Natan Sharansky, minister of the interior in Barak's government and a prominent member of the right wing of the coalition, publicized these details and began to build up opposition to what he saw as excessive concessions on Israel's part.[16]

The formulas supporting the understandings that coalesced in Stockholm were reminiscent of the core of the Beilin-Abbas draft agreement put together in the fall of 1995: Israeli readiness to withdraw from the bulk of the West Bank and the Gaza Strip, and Palestinian acceptance of Israeli annexation of the large settlement blocs in return for an asymmetrical exchange of territories. Barak felt that a swift final-status agreement with Arafat was within reach on the basis of this formula, and he began to urge President Clinton to summon the parties to a summit modeled on the 1978 Camp David conference, in order to reach such an agreement.

Barak was acting under the pressure of two ticking political clocks. In the United States President Clinton's second term was drawing to a close. The presidential election was scheduled for early November, and Clinton's own assessment was that he could be effective only through September in helping the parties reach agreement and mobilizing support in Congress for the financial aid packages indispensable for its implementation. In Israel Barak was acutely aware that his coalition was shrinking with the passage of time and that a hostile majority was coalescing in the Knesset. These calculations were reinforced by the prime minister's sense that tensions were building between Israel and the Palestinians and that, barring an agreement, the two were on a collision course. The eruption of Palestinian violence on Nakba Day (the term used by the Palestinians to designate Israel's independence and their defeat) in May 2000 lit a significant red light. The level and intensity of the violence indicated the potential for greater conflict, as well as the fact that Arafat did not fully control the Palestinian "street" and that the popular rage was directed in part at him and at the Palestinian Authority.

In the summer of 2000, an intricate and intriguing link developed between the dynamics of Israeli domestic politics and Israel's conduct in its negotiation with the Palestinians.

As mentioned, the elections of May 1999 had produced a discrepancy between Barak's impressive personal victory and the further fragmentation of the Knesset and weakening of the two large parties. Three major conclusions could be drawn from this outcome. First, the Israeli public gave Barak an impressive personal victory but denied him the possibility of forming a stable coalition government. Second, Netanyahu was personally defeated, but his coalition suffered only a minor loss and commanded fifty-eight seats in the new Knesset. And last, with regard to the principal issue on the national agenda—Israel's relationship with the Arab world—the Israeli body politic remained more or less evenly divided.

With these conclusions setting the stage, it is quite possible that Barak's choice of Shas as a principal partner to his "peace coalition" was doomed to fail. This inherent difficulty was then compounded by Barak's failure to learn from Rabin's mistake in 1992. At the time, Rabin had formed a coalition government with Shas and Meretz and assigned the education portfolio to the latter's leader, Shulamit Aloni. Friction soon erupted over the budgeting of Shas's independent educational system (one of the party's principal mainstays). This was one of the main reasons for Shas's decision to withdraw from the coalition in 1993. In 1999 it was Meretz's new leader, Yossi Sarid, who became the minister of education. A tug-of-war soon started between Sarid and Shas, damaging the Shas relationship with Barak and keeping that relationship on the edge of a permanent crisis. In June 2000 Meretz withdrew from the coalition, promising to support the government "from the outside." By this point Barak's relationship with Shas was beyond all repair.

Nor did Barak fare well in his relations with the other coalition partners. The ultra-Orthodox Yahadut Hatorah party left the coalition as early as 1999; Natan Sharansky, the former anti-Soviet activist, was openly critical of Barak's style of governance and his willingness to offer far-reaching concessions to reach agreements with Syria and the Palestinians. The effect of these tensions in the coalition's ranks was magnified by endemic criticism and challenges to Barak's leadership in his own party.[17]

The disintegration of Barak's coalition was accelerated by the decision to go to the Camp David conference. Shas, the National Religious Party, and Sharansky and his faction were all opposed to the anticipated concessions and left the coalition. Foreign Minister David Levy was offended by the fact that the minister of domestic security, Shlomo Ben-Ami, was put in charge of the negotiations and was accompanied by his brother Maxim. Barak was left with a coalition in the Knesset of only thirty seats. He managed to keep his government afloat for several more months through parliamentary maneuvers and owing to the reluctance of several Knesset members to end their term and face a new election. But by late November, Barak had reached the end of his rope and called for a new election. On December 9, he formally resigned and became the prime minister of a transitional government.

One important outcome of this chain of events was that Barak conducted both the negotiations at Camp David and the crisis that broke out at the end of September 2000 without a parliamentary majority and through a diminished cabinet. It was an extraordinary set of affairs. A prime minister preoccupied with his own political survival and devoid of parliamentary support could hardly be expected to manage a profound and sustained national security crisis.

When Barak lost his coalition on the eve of his departure for Camp David in July 2000, he established an unhealthy connection between his own political future and the success of the negotiations. The conventional wisdom at the time stated that a majority of Israelis supported an agreement with the Palestinians but opposed the concessions that such an agreement entailed. It was widely assumed that the Knesset would approve neither an agreement based on massive concessions nor a referendum that would endorse such an agreement. To overcome this kind of opposition to an agreement, Barak would have had to dissolve the Knesset and bring about a fresh election. Barak's supporters and opponents alike estimated that in that situation, he would be reelected. However, when the Camp David conference failed, the issue remained moot.

The expectations generated by the very term "Camp David," as well as the changes in Israel's position in the negotiations, turned this second Camp David conference into the high (and eventually low) point of Ehud Barak's effort to reach an accord with the Palestinians. Despite its saliency, the July summit should be seen as a phase in a negotiation that lasted for almost a year—from the spring of 2000 to the eve of the February 2001 elections.

As time goes by and accounts of that negotiation accumulate, it increasingly appears to have been a journey by Barak and his government from the center-right of the Israeli political spectrum to its left wing. This journey did not produce either a comparable shift on the Palestinian side or an agreement. Furthermore, since the end of September, the effort had been overshadowed by Arafat's attempt to exploit the outbreak of violence as another means of pressure on Israel. The Barak government's journey unfolded through five main phases.

The Stockholm Talks

After the final collapse of his negotiations with Syria, Barak decided to accelerate the Palestinian track. Barak chose to negotiate through Shlomo Ben-Ami and Gilead Sher; Abu Alaa was their counterpart. The chief venue for the secret negotiations was near Stockholm, under the auspices of a Swedish government inspired by Norway's successful role in the 1993 Oslo breakthrough. Barak did not adopt the Beilin-Abbas formula from 1995, but its essential components were clearly reflected in the understandings reached in Sweden. According to Ben-Ami's own testimony (in his interview to *Ha'aretz,* quoted at length below), he and Barak quickly abandoned Israel's opening position ("sort of an Alon Plan . . . if I am not wrong it would offer the Palestinians a mere 66% . . ."). Instead, the Israelis presented a map in Stockholm partitioning the West Bank between Israel and the Palestinians at a ratio of 12 percent to 88 percent (the Gaza Strip was to be fully or almost fully evacuated). Israel insisted on keeping the three large settlement blocs and on holding onto the Jordan Valley for twenty years. Barak did not authorize his negotiators to speak about territorial exchanges—he was wary of leaks that could jeopardize his government's survival. Nothing was formally agreed, but the Israeli negotiators felt that their Palestinian counterparts understood the need for Israel to keep the large settlement blocs and for flexible security arrangements.

With regard to the refugee issue, "a whole concept was constructed for finding the solution in host countries, in the Palestinian state and in third countries and family reunification in Israel." Ben Ami and Sher spoke of ten thousand to fifteen thousand refugees who would be absorbed in Israel over the years. Abu Alaa and his associate, Hasan Asfoor, did not agree to figures but were willing to enter into a business-like discussion of this particular issue.[18]

The negotiations continued through the period leading up to the Camp David summit. In a meeting in Jerusalem, Abu Alaa agreed to give up 4 percent of the West Bank. In the preparatory talks with the U.S. team, the Palestinians gave President Clinton a 2 percent deposit. Ben-Ami, in turn, further reduced Israel's territorial demand to 8–10 percent of the West Bank. It was felt that a compromise could be reached somewhere between 4 percent and 8 percent. Regarding the Jordan Valley— or the future Palestinian state's eastern border—the Palestinians rejected any notion of concession.

At the same time, according to Ben-Ami, an "informal discussion" of the Jerusalem issue began. In a meeting held in Nablus, Arafat promised Ben-Ami that "the Wailing Wall and the Jewish Quarter were ours [Israel's]." Other Palestinian spokesmen alluded to potential flexibility on Jewish neighborhoods in East Jerusalem. But the Palestinians seemed to have taken a step back on the refugee question. According to Ben-Ami's detailed account, "Abu Mazen [Abbas] persuaded Abu Alaa not to discuss any numbers and to insist on the principle of the Right of Return."[19]

Camp David

At the Camp David conference, Israel endowed its earlier concessions with a greater formality. It also accepted the principle of exchange of territories (though not at a one-to-one ratio), and, most significantly, it agreed to far-reaching concessions on Jerusalem (as compared with its original positions). These concessions were not made formally but were offered in simulation games, or given as a "deposit" that could be revoked in the absence of an appropriate response. At this point, Israelis and Palestinians alike knew that once a concession was laid on the table, the impact of that idea could not be obliterated even if the concession was formally withdrawn.

Barak's greatest concessions at Camp David concerned Jerusalem and the Jordan Valley. He discarded one of the sacred slogans of Israeli politics ("One Jerusalem, unified, under Israeli sovereignty") and agreed to partition and compromise, not only in East Jerusalem, but also in the Old City and the Temple Mount. By agreeing to give up a permanent Israeli presence in the Jordan Valley, he crossed both an Israeli and a Jordanian red line. Jordan would rather have had Israel continue to postpone the establishment of a Palestinian state; however, if that were to change, Jordan would prefer an Israeli presence in the Jordan Valley as a buffer.

Barak was more willing to cross these lines after Arafat's promise to Clinton on July 16 that he was ready to give up 8–10 percent of the West Bank and to display flexibility on other main issues. But Arafat retracted his promise the next day, and this left Barak vulnerable. The question of whether Arafat made his statement to Clinton merely to extricate himself from a tight corner—or whether it was a more sophisticated maneuver designed to lead Barak to open up the Jerusalem issue for discussion—still remains unresolved.

The conference ended in failure and left the Israeli participants with the sense that Arafat rejected Barak's gambit of agreeing to an "end of conflict" and "end of claims" in return for the compromise formula on Jerusalem. Arafat also refused to withdraw the Palestinian demand for the right of return in exchange for the compromise formula for a resolution of the refugee problem.[20] In the immediate aftermath of the summit's failure, both Clinton and Barak publicly charged Arafat with responsibility for the failure.

Negotiations under Fire: September–December 2000

The limited Palestinian-Israeli war—commonly (but inappropriately) called the second intifada, or the al-Aqsa intifada—broke out on September 28, 2000. It was triggered by the visit of Ariel Sharon (then head of the opposition) to the Temple Mount and the ensuing Palestinian riots.

The question of responsibility for the outbreak of the violence is as controversial as the debate over the collapse of the negotiations. Sharon's decision to visit the Temple Mount had more to do with his intraparty rivalry with Benjamin Netanyahu than with a quest to embarrass Ehud Barak. Sharon advised the government of his plan, and the government, in turn, notified the Palestinian Authority. In the tense atmosphere of those days it was clearly an uncalled-for visit. But by the same token, there was no real reason to respond to it with violence. Did Arafat plan the violence in advance, as some of his Israeli critics argue?

It was apparent that Arafat for some time had prepared for a violent confrontation. The events of Nakba Day in May 2000 revealed the potential violence threatening to erupt in the Israeli-Palestinian relationship. According to his own testimony, Barak had acted in the shadow of such impending violence—whether spontaneous or organized—since his election. The available evidence suggests that Arafat did not order the violence, but once it broke out he chose to mount "the tiger's back" rather than try to calm things down. He undoubtedly saw the tactical advantages offered by the new turn of events: he could extract himself from a tight diplomatic corner as the apparent culprit in the collapse of the peace process, mobilize Arab and Islamic opinion over the Temple Mount, and expect a meek Israeli response and further concessions.

The spreading of violence into Israel proper, the large-scale confrontation between the Israeli-Arab population and police, and the killing of thirteen Arab citizens of Israel added a particularly ominous dimension to the latest Israeli-Palestinian crisis. Calm was restored only after Ehud Barak issued a statement promising to form a judicial commission of inquiry to investigate these events.

It was at that very same time that Hizballah tried to ignite the conflict on the Lebanese-Israeli border. Barak, as we saw, decided to ignore the new rules that he himself had set after the withdrawal from Lebanon so as not to open a third front in the midst of crisis.

During the first few weeks of this mounting violence, several attempts to settle were made through direct Israeli-Palestinian discussions and in two international meetings, in Paris on October 4 and in Sharm al-Sheikh, Egypt, on October 16. Although these attempts failed, the Sharm al-Sheikh meeting did produce the Mitchell Commission. Named for the former U.S. senator who headed it, George J. Mitchell Jr., the commission was established in response to the Palestinian demand that an international commission of inquiry be formed to investigate the outbreak of violence. The mission of the Mitchell Commission was transformed by the United States and Israel into an effort to chart a course out of the crisis. (Ultimately, the commission issued a report in May 2001 that spread wide blame for the violence and called on both Israel and the Palestinians to take confidence-building steps so peace talks could resume).

The most dramatic attempt to reach an Israeli-Palestinian cease-fire was Shimon Peres's nocturnal visit to Gaza. Barak was initially reluctant to engage his rival, Peres, but eventually yielded to public pressure. On October 31, Tourism Minister Amnon Shahak and Israel's unofficial envoy to Arafat, Yossi Ginosar, held a preparatory visit to Gaza. On November 1, Peres was accompanied to Gaza by Gilead Sher, who had in the meantime become Barak's chief of staff. Their meeting with Arafat ended with a set of understandings and a joint communiqué. Despite this, the violence continued and was in fact intensified.

In December Barak announced his resignation. New elections for prime minister (but not the Knesset) were set for February 6, 2001. In the United States the presidential election had taken place on November 7, but it was not until five weeks later that the Supreme Court finally ratified the election of George W. Bush. During this confused global scenario, an Israeli-Palestinian conference met in Taba, Egypt. It was a last-ditch effort to reach an agreement on the eve of the Israeli election, which the right-wing candidate (either Netanyahu or Sharon) was expected to win.

President Clinton's Bridging Proposals

Despite the glaring failure of the Camp David conference in July, the negotiations continued in an effort to consolidate and formalize points of agreement. The talks were not interrupted by the outbreak of violence, despite Israel's formal refusal to negotiate under fire. On December 23, a month before the end of his term, President Clinton took an unusual step and "laid on the table a bridging proposal of sorts." Clinton emphasized that this was not an American proposal but "a presentation of my own understanding as to how an agreement could be reached within two weeks. These ideas go off the table once I leave the White House." According to Gilead Sher's version, Clinton's ideas concerned five areas:

1. Borders and territory. Eighty percent of the settlers would remain in the settlement blocs annexed by Israel. Israel would annex 4 percent to 6 percent of the West Bank unless an agreement was reached on the leasing of additional territories by Israel. Israel would transfer to the Palestinians 1 percent to 3 percent of its own territory, probably close to the Gaza Strip, and would provide safe passage between the Gaza Strip and the West Bank.

2. Jerusalem. The underlying idea on this issue was that Arab areas of the city were to have Palestinian sovereignty and Jewish areas to have Israeli sovereignty. The idea would be applied to the Old City as well as the rest of East Jerusalem. A special sovereignty arrangement would be developed for the Old City and the larger "holy basin." The Haram al-Sharif (the Muslim term for the Temple Mount) would be placed under Palestinian sovereignty, while the Wailing Wall and the area around it would be placed under Israeli sovereignty.

3. Security. To balance Israel's security needs with the Palestinian quest for maximum sovereignty, Clinton proposed that the future Palestinian state would be "nonmilitarized"; the only military forces on its soil would be the Palestinian police, security services, and an international force that could not be withdrawn without Israel's consent. The IDF would continue to hold positions in the Jordan Valley for an additional period of six years, and Israel would be permitted to retain three early-warning stations in

the Palestinian state's territory. The status of these stations would be reexamined after ten years. In the event of a concrete threat to Israel's national security, it would be permissible for Israel to deploy additional forces in the Jordan Valley upon notifying the international force. Arrangements would be made to negotiate the Israeli Air Force's use of Palestinian airspace. Israel would have three years to complete the evacuation of those settlements and army bases designated for evacuation.

4. The Refugees. The refugee settlement was governed by the notion of two states for two peoples: Israel is the homeland of the Jewish people, and Palestine is the homeland of the Palestinian people. This meant that the settlement must not affect Israel's Jewish identity or its sovereign decisionmaking in matters of immigration into the country. According to Clinton's ideas, the principle of "the right of return" would be addressed by the Palestinians' right to return to "historic Palestine" or their "homeland." With regard to the refugees' ultimate place of residence, Clinton proposed five alternatives: the Palestinian state, the territories offered by Israel as part of an exchange, the host states, third parties, and Israel proper. With regard to the first two categories, no quantitative limits would be set.

5. End of Conflict and End of Claims. President Clinton stated explicitly that the signing of the agreement would signify an end to the conflict, and its implementation would terminate all claims.[21]

The Israeli cabinet held a formal discussion of Clinton's ideas and decided to respond with a "yes, but. . . ." In other words, it accepted them in principle but submitted a list of reservations and proposed modifications. Arafat in turn took his time equivocating between his reluctance to respond with a blunt rejection and his unwillingness to give a positive—albeit reserved—answer.

This, then, was the state of affairs in early January, just days before the end of Clinton's presidency. Israel's relationship with the Palestinians was in crisis—negotiations were deadlocked and there was violent confrontation; Barak's coalition and government had disintegrated and were practically bound to be defeated in the February 6 elections. Diplomatically, efforts continued to negotiate an end to the violence and to establish at least a measure of political understanding, a sine qua non for a durable cease-fire. It was against this backdrop that the Taba Conference was opened on January 21, 2001.

The Taba Conference

Within the tortuous course of events in the July 2000–January 2001 period, the Israeli-Palestinian meeting in Taba (an Egyptian border crossing with Israel) stands out as a particularly peculiar and controversial episode. Was there a chance to reach an agreement on the eve of an Israeli election in which Barak was expected to be defeated owing to the collapse of his negotiations with the same Palestinian partners and the ensuing violence? Was Arafat likely to moderate his position in this context? And what could be expected as a new president, who emphasized his intention to keep away from Clinton's legacy in the Middle East, entered the White House? Was the Taba meeting an attempt to confront the Bush administration and the presumed new Israeli government with a fait accompli? And if so, how valid would that attempt be?

Memoirs of Israeli policymakers depict a pathetic picture of a sinking political boat. The acting foreign minister, Shlomo Ben-Ami, later shared a surprising secret with the readers of *Ha'aretz*: Ehud Barak was blackmailed by one of his ministers. "There was a minister who threatened Barak that if he failed to go to Taba, he would publicly denounce him as refraining from making peace," he wrote. Barak's chief of staff complained about the license taken by some of the Israeli participants in Taba: "In the meantime, it transpired that in other rooms Israel's positions as given orally to the heads of the delegations were being eroded," Sher later wrote.[22]

The actual course of events in Taba is equally contested. Barak's current position claims that the meeting had no importance. Gilead Sher argues that little progress was made in Taba, while Yossi Beilin (at the time Barak's minister of justice) claims that much was accomplished and more could have been. Beilin himself was criticized for ceding too much ground regarding the right of return. The European Union's special emissary to the Middle East, Miguel Moratinos, published an optimistic summary of the discussions, but it is not at all clear how he arrived at his conclusions. Political considerations led the Israeli and Palestinian delegations to publish an unusually upbeat final communiqué: "[The Taba

Talks] were unprecedented with regard to the positive atmosphere . . . but given the circumstances and the time constraints, it was not possible to reach an understanding on all issues, despite the substantive progress reached in all matters under discussion. The parties declare that they were never closer to reaching an agreement."[23]

This clearly was an attempt by both parties to provide Ehud Barak with some assets for the imminent election. But in the ensuing internal Israeli debate, the argument was made that in the months following the Camp David Conference and particularly in Taba, gaps in fact were closed, and in Yossi Beilin's view "had the negotiators had a few more days. . . ."[24]

Be that as it may, if Abu Alaa and his colleagues tried to generate a sense of optimism to help Ehud Barak, Arafat certainly chose to do the opposite—and did so dramatically and effectively. He appeared with Shimon Peres at the World Economic Forum in Davos, Switzerland, and blasted Ehud Barak and Israel's policies before international cameras, inflicting a deadly blow to the effort to salvage a ray of hope from the debris of the stormy Israeli-Palestinian negotiations.

CONTROVERSY OVER CAUSES OF THE COLLAPSE

The conflicting interpretations of these events became a matter of acute controversy in the immediate aftermath of the Camp David summit. The numerous published accounts of the collapse of the peace process and the ensuing violence fall into four main categories.

The Orthodox School

This version can be defined as orthodox owing both to its early dominance and to the fact that it was first articulated by President Clinton and Prime Minister Barak. After the collapse of the Camp David Summit, Clinton broke a long-standing American diplomatic tradition and placed the blame squarely in Arafat's court. He contrasted Arafat's refusal to budge with Barak's boldness and willingness to cross red lines to reach an accord. Clinton later moderated his statements, either because of the criticism he received for pushing Arafat into a corner or because he wanted to preserve his position as a patron of the peace process and a leader who could communicate with both sides. But in private forums, Clinton continued to criticize Arafat. Thus at a party held at the home of Richard Holbrooke, his former ambassador to the UN, Clinton is reported to have spoken at length and freely about his failure to broker an Israeli-Palestinian agreement. According to a *Newsweek* account, Clinton, during a telephone conversation three days before his departure from the White House, told Arafat that he had turned Clinton into a "colossal failure" and "told Arafat that by turning down the best peace deal he was ever going to get . . . the Palestinian leader was only guaranteeing the election of the hawkish Ariel Sharon. . . . He described Arafat as an aging leader who relishes his own sense of victimhood and seems incapable of making a final peace deal. . . . Clinton also revealed that the key issue that torpedoed the talks was not the division of East Jerusalem . . . but the Palestinian demand for a 'right of return' of refugees into Israel. . . ."[25]

In contrast to Clinton, Barak intensified his public criticism of Arafat with the passage of time. The prime minister did continue to negotiate with Arafat up until the eve of the February 2001 elections and conducted his election campaign on a platform supporting the peace process. But Barak had argued from the outset that Arafat was responsible for the negotiations' failure. Barak justified his willingness to offer concessions by the need to establish whether Arafat was a genuine partner and thus felt vindicated by the fact that "the mask has been removed from Arafat's face." Later Barak came to argue that Arafat was not a partner for a negotiated settlement, that Israel should draw the conclusion and opt for a unilateral separation from the Palestinians. In Israeli journalist Ran Edelist's book *Ehud Barak and His War against the Demons,* drawn from long conversations with Barak, the author explains that Barak felt that he had to test whether Palestinians under Arafat's leadership were ready for a final-status agreement that would renounce the right of return and would include an explicit commitment to the end of conflict. His conclusion at the end of the Camp David conference was clear: Arafat does not want such an agreement and certainly did not come to Camp David in order to conclude one.[26]

A similar version of events was presented by Shlomo Ben-Ami, Barak's chief negotiator with the Palestinians and eventually his acting foreign minister. Ben-Ami, though, drew different policy conclusions from the same interpretation. In an eloquent and revealing interview granted to the Israeli journalist Ari Shavit, Ben-Ami joined those who argue that Arafat had not signed the Oslo Accords with clean hands: "It transpired that for Arafat, Oslo was a sort of a huge camouflage act behind which he has been exercising political pressure and terror in varying portions in order to undermine the very idea of two states for two peoples."

According to Ben Ami, the Camp David summit and the whole process of negotiations was doomed to failure because of Arafat:

> At the end of the day, Camp David failed because Arafat refused to make his own proposals and because he failed to indicate to us that there was a terminal point to his demands. . . . One of the important things we did at Camp David was to define the very core of our vital interests: To emerge out of the deceitful discourse of Israeli politics and to define to ourselves what was really crucial. . . . We therefore did not expect to meet the Palestinians halfway, not even two-thirds of the way, but we expected to meet them somewhere. . . . Barak is a rational, Cartesian man and in Camp David we found out that Arafat was a mythological man. Today, I am of the opinion that no rational Israeli leader could have reached an accommodation in such a meeting. Arafat is not a leader connected to the ground, he is a religious man. . . . In Camp David it was clear that he was not looking for practical solutions but was focused on the mythological issues: the "right of return," Jerusalem, the Temple Mount. He is hovering in the heights of the Islamic ethos, the ethos of refugeeism and the Palestinian ethos. . . . [27]

Dennis Ross, the coordinator of the peace process in the State Department (in the Clinton administration) spoke and wrote in a similar vein on several occasions. Soon after he left the State Department after the formation of the Bush administration, Ross granted an interview to Clyde Haberman for the *New York Times Magazine*. Ross feels, writes Haberman, that "when all is said and done . . . those negotiations failed because they ran into a brick wall called Yasser Arafat. Barak was willing to give up a lot, including virtually the entire West Bank and sovereignty over the Temple Mount. . . . He was willing to yield so much that it cost him his job in February. . . . [S]ome senior Palestinian officials were not blind to the opportunity of statehood that was within their grasp—I had one Palestinian negotiator say to me, 'If we can't do an agreement under these circumstances we ought to be fired.'"

"Ross is convinced," Haberman continued, "'that in his own heart of hearts, Arafat wants peace. But I have come to the conclusion that he is not capable of negotiating an end to the conflict because what is required of him is something he is not able to do. It is simply not in him to go the extra yard.'"[28]

Several months later, in another press interview, Ross elaborated further and also explained Arafat's rejection of Clinton's bridging proposals:

He [Arafat] had, frankly, an unprecedented opportunity, given the ideas President Clinton put on the table. He had a historic moment and he could not seize it . . . even though he had the possibility of having the essence of Palestinian needs being met on every issue . . . on borders, on Jerusalem, on security arrangements, and even of refugees, he couldn't do it. Now I will say he had to make some hard decisions himself. Arafat had to give up one of the animating beliefs of his movement and that was the right of return to Israel. . . . [N]ow in 1988 he adopted a two state solution . . . the idea of a two state solution and the right of return, not just to your own state, but to Israel: those two ideas are contradictory. . . . You had an Israeli government prepared to stretch further than anybody thought possible and many in Israel thought wise, but they were prepared to live with it. You had an American President prepared to put his ideas on the table. And he [Clinton] also made it clear that those ideas would be withdrawn if they were not accepted. So I don't think you can recreate those circumstances so easily.[29]

In the summer of 2001 after the publication of Robert Malley and Hussein Agha's revisionist account of events (see below), Ross spearheaded a counteroffensive. In a letter to the editor of the *New York Review of Books,* Ross wrote that he had read the piece by Malley and Agha with "some dismay." He found their account "glaring in its omission of Chairman Arafat's mistakes. One is left with the impression that only Barak did not fulfill commitments. But that is both wrong and unfair, particularly given Arafat's poor record in compliance. However, while striving to prove that the reality was far more complicated than Israel offering and Palestinians rejecting, they equate tactical mistakes with strategic errors." Clinton and Barak made mistakes, but they were not responsible for the failure to make a deal, Ross said.

While Clinton and Barak rose to the occasion and took risks, said Ross, Arafat failed to respond in kind. His conduct at Camp David— and in its aftermath—cannot be explained merely by suspicion and fear of entrapment. Arafat refused to prepare for the conference, or to initiate or react during it, and he even went so far as to invent a new myth: that the Jewish Temple's site had not been in Jerusalem but in Nablus.

According to Ross, as the United States was about to submit bridging ideas at the end of September, Arafat refrained from restraining the outbreak of violence. He knew it was imminent and yet did nothing. In brief, Ross said, "I simply do not believe he is capable of doing a permanent status deal."[30]

In March 2003, the orthodox school was joined by an unexpected member—Prince Bandar bin Sultan, Saudi Arabia's ambassador to Washington. Speaking to Elsa Walsh for a *New Yorker* profile, Bandar complained about Arafat's refusal to complete a deal with Barak: "Clinton . . . really tried his best . . . and Barak's position was so avant-garde that it was equal to Prime Minister Rabin . . . it broke my heart that Arafat did not take that offer."[31] During the following years, President Clinton and most members of the U.S. peace team published memoirs and books which deal, among many other issues, with the failure of the Camp David summit and, on the whole, reinforce the orthodox school.[32]

The Revisionist School

This school rejects the orthodox school's main assertions. It lays the burden of responsibility for the negotiation's failure on Israel and its policies, criticizes the conduct of the negotiations by Israel and the United States, and presents the Palestinian side and its actions in a more positive light. This version is held by the Palestinians and by part of the Israeli left, but its principal articulation can be found in an essay published in the *New York Review of Books* by Robert Malley and Hussein

Agha. Malley was a member of Clinton's National Security Council staff in charge of Arab-Israeli affairs; Hussein Agha is a Lebanese intellectual living in England who had helped Mahmud Abbas during his negotiations with Yossi Beilin. Their essay was published in August 2001 under the title "Camp David: The Tragedy of Errors." Its main points were published in a shorter, blunter version in the *New York Times*.[33]

Malley and Agha open their *New York Review of Books* essay with a statement of intent. Their purpose is to undermine the version of events at Camp David in which "Israel is said to have made a historic, generous proposal which the Palestinians once again, seizing the opportunity to miss an opportunity, turned down. In short, the failure to reach a final agreement is attributed, without notable dissent, to Yasser Arafat. For the authors "as orthodoxies go, this is a dangerous one," because it leads to policy conclusions such as "that there is no peace partner" and that Arafat is an obstacle to a "possible end to the conflict."

To discredit this interpretation, Malley and Agha offer an apologetic view of Arafat's conduct and devote the bulk of their essay to criticism of Barak, his policies, and Clinton's uneven attitude to the parties when he should have been an honest broker.

Any defense of Arafat's policies at the time must deal with the argument that even if Barak did not put a clear proposal on the table in Camp David, Clinton did present a compromise formula on December 23 that Arafat rejected. Thus, Malley and Agha argue,

> unlike at Camp David as shown both by the time it took him to react and by the ambiguity of his reactions, Arafat thought hard before providing his response. But in the end, many of the features that troubled him in July came back to haunt him in December. As at Camp David, Arafat felt under pressure, with both Clinton and Barak announcing that the ideas would be off the table—would 'depart with the President'—unless they were accepted by both sides. With only thirty days left in Clinton's presidency and hardly more in Barak's premiership, the likelihood of reaching a deal was remote at best; if no deal could be made, the Palestinians feared they would be left with principles that were detailed enough to supersede international (UN) resolutions yet too fuzzy to constitute an agreement.

The most telling paragraph in Malley and Agha's essay is the one seeking to explain the Palestinians' passive stance at Camp David and their refusal to offer counterproposals:

> For all the talk about peace and reconciliation, most Palestinians were more resigned to the two-state solution than they were willing to embrace it; they were willing to accept Israel's existence, but not its moral legitimacy. The war for the whole of Palestine was over because it had been lost. Oslo, as they saw it, was not about negotiating peace terms, but terms of surrender. Bearing this perspective in mind explains the Palestinians' view that Oslo itself is the historic compromise—an agreement to concede 78 percent of mandatory Palestine to Israel.

The Israeli version of the Revisionist School derives from two sources: the segment of the Israeli public left who hold Israel responsible for the collapse of the negotiations and for the outbreak of violence and, in a different vein, most Israeli authors of the Oslo Accords who criticize Ehud Barak for the substance of his policies as well as for his conduct of the negotiations. The latter group is quite naturally preoccupied with the argument that the events of 2000–01 revealed deep flaws in the Oslo Accords. Their theory is twofold: the failure was the result of Barak's policy, style, and specific decisions, as well as the cumulative effect of Israel's policies since the mid-1990s. This criticism is sometimes tempered by mild criticism of Arafat and Palestinian policy.

The two senior figures identified with the Oslo Accords were not direct contributors to this version of the story. Shimon Peres made no secret of his criticism of Ehud Barak and his policies, or of Peres's own preference for a different approach. He did, however, refrain from coming out with a full-fledged direct critique. Yossi Beilin, a member of Barak's cabinet and a sometime partner to his policies, offered a more complex and nuanced explanation for the failure in his book *Guide for a Wounded Dove?*[34] But in subsequent publications, Beilin became openly critical of Barak. Unlike Peres and Beilin, Uri Savir, the president of the Peres Peace Center, vented his frustration with Barak and his policy in a press interview.

Uri Savir's criticism was wide ranging—starting with his former partner Yossi Beilin, who found a place on Barak's team, through Sharon and Netanyahu, who, Savir said, acted overtly against the Oslo Accords, and culminating with Ehud Barak:

> Then came someone who was supposed to represent Oslo, Ehud Barak, but he was opposed to the agreement, spoke against the agreement, acted against it, wasted a year on the Syrian track and when he finally came to deal with the issue, refused to speak to the Palestinians. Barak conducted the negotiations with the Americans. . . . He acted in an arrogant fashion, no one would tolerate such behavior. . . . With regard to Camp David, there was a huge campaign of disinformation . . . and yet today the story breaks out from all directions . . . the root of the problem is our attempt to keep educating them [the Palestinians]. We left Gaza, we left the West Bank, we did not leave the occupation. . . . [T]he bulk of Palestinian society in return for genuine freedom and independence is willing to give up the bulk of the right of return.[35]

The most comprehensive articulation of the Israeli revisionist school can be found in Ron Pundak's essay in the British journal *Survival* under the title: "From Oslo to Taba: What Went Wrong?"[36] Pundak participated in the early phase of the Oslo negotiations together with Yair Hirschfeld and under Yossi Beilin's supervision. He then worked for ECF, an Israeli nongovernmental organization, and was until recently the director of the Peres Peace Center.

In his essay, Pundak states that "there was in fact an opportunity for peace, but it was squandered through miscalculations and mismanagement of the entire process." As a result of the policies conducted by Netanyahu and Barak, the Palestinian public and "street"—as reflected in the Fatah movement—reached the conclusion that "Israel did not in fact want to end the occupation and grant the Palestinian people their legitimate rights."

According to Pundak, the clock began ticking toward an explosion with the expiration of the interim agreement (Oslo II) in May 1999. The only way to avoid that explosion would have been to swiftly and seriously implement signed agreements, but "Barak failed to understand this. . . . His error was twofold: he decided not to implement the third redeployment [from the West Bank] . . . which represented the most important element in the Interim Agreement; and although he entered

into permanent status negotiations currently and in good faith, he did
so on the basis of a faulty basic assumption and in a dilettante fashion
which caused their collapse."

Pundak agreed that the Palestinian leadership "shares considerable
blame for the crisis," but like Malley and Agha, he argued that "the
story of the Camp David Summit that is often told in Israel and the
U.S.—of a near perfect Israeli offer which Arafat lacked the courage to
grasp—is too simple and misleading."

Pundak, while also critical of the Palestinians, was crystal clear with
his bottom line in his conclusion: "The insincere and incomplete implementation during Netanyahu's administration and the mismanagement
of permanent status negotiations under Barak were the two main obstacles to reaching an agreement."

The Deterministic School

This position is dominated by the critics of the Oslo agreement, who
tend to come from the right wing of Israeli, American, and American-
Jewish politics. Those who argued as early as 1993 that the Oslo
Accords were flawed, that it was a terrible mistake on Israel's part to
sign them, could quite naturally argue in 2001 that the collapse of the
Oslo process was predictable and in fact inevitable. This is one of the
principal themes of an article titled "Oslo—The Peacemongers Return"
by Norman Podhoretz, one of the American Jewish right's most eloquent spokesmen.[37]

Podhoretz asserted, "The inescapable conclusion reached by many
Israelis was that Camp David and its violent aftermath exposed the
fraudulence of Arafat's expressed desire for coexistence between Israel
and a new Palestinian state. He had no intention of making peace with
Israel and never had. . . . Entering into the 'peace process' had been
nothing more than a change of tactics in the overall strategy of destroying Israel."

Podhoretz offered a detailed analysis of the Palestinians' tactics at
Camp David and during the subsequent months. To reinforce his argument, he quoted from an (indeed puzzling) interview granted by the
most prominent Palestinian leader in Jerusalem, Faysal Husseini, shortly
before his death in May 2001. Husseini referred to Oslo as a "Trojan
horse." It, "or any other agreement, is just a temporary procedure or just

a step toward something bigger," namely, the liberation of all historical Palestine from the Jordan River to the sea. "Palestine in its entirety is an Arab land, the land of the Arab nation, a land no one can sell or buy."

In a more nuanced fashion, part of Israel's national security establishment has maintained that in 1993, Arafat had not budged from the red lines of his own definition of what constituted a legitimate and satisfactory resolution of the Palestinian issue. According to this view, Arafat signed the Oslo agreement (and by the same token the Oslo II agreement in 1995 and the Wye Agreement in 1998) because by signing interim agreements, he was not required to cross those red lines. But when it came to negotiating and signing a final-status agreement, there was no escaping the final dilemma. Since Arafat could not and would not give up his principles, the negotiation was doomed to fail. This analysis leads to conclusions similar to those of Ben Ami and Ross, but it was presented much earlier. Gilead Sher's book tells us that in the corridors of the Israeli government, this view was dubbed "The Military Intelligence's concept (or mindset)."

The chief and most consistent articulator of this view was General Amos Gilead, who, since the signing of the Oslo Accords, continued to argue that Arafat had not relinquished his four basic principles: a Palestinian state within the June 4, 1967, lines; a capital in Jerusalem; sovereignty over and control of the Temple Mount; and implementation of the right of return. This being the case, Gilead continued, stalemate and crisis should be expected once the moment of truth (namely, final-status negotiations) came, unless Israel was willing to concede.[38]

Gilead also warned that Arafat was actually preparing for such an inevitable clash. Positions similar to those of Gilead were expressed, though less systematically, by Israel's former defense minister, Shaul Mofaz, and Israel's former chief of staff, General Moshe Ya'alon. An Israeli journalist, Ronen Bergman, was given access to a large volume of captured Palestinian documents, some of them taken from Arafat's headquarters in the Muqata'ah in Ramallah. Based on these documents Bergman wrote a book denouncing the Palestinian Authority and its chairman's corruption and arguing that the Palestinians had no real intention of settling the conflict with Israel. In 2008 General Ya'alon, who joined the political fray through the Likud Party and became a cabinet member in Netanyahu's government (see below), published a memoir titled *The Longer Short Road*. In it he argued that Arafat never intended to implement the Oslo Accords and that as early as September 1999 he (Ya'alon) warned the Israeli government that Arafat was preparing for a military confrontation to be launched in September 2000.[39]

A deterministic element can also be found on a different level in Henry Kissinger's book *Does America Need a Foreign Policy?* In Kissinger's view, "a conflict defined in this manner is rarely subject to compromises—at least not within the short time limits of an American election year; in fact it is generally concluded by exhaustion, either physical or psychological. It is unlikely to be settled definitively by an agreement (even if there should be one). The most realistic proposal is for a definition of coexistence. To seek to go farther is to tempt violence, as was experienced by the July 2000 Camp David Summit. . . ."[40]

Kissinger goes on to state that

> the prime obstacle to culmination of the peace diplomacy is the differing conceptions of it held by the parties. Israeli and American leaders define peace as a normality that ends claims and determines a permanent legal status—in other words they apply the concepts of twentieth century liberal democracy. But the Arabs and especially the Palestinians consider the very existence of Israel an intrusion into "Holy" Arab territory. They may accept territorial compromises for lack of a better alternative, but they will treat it in the same way that France acquiesced in the German annexation of Alsace-Lorraine in 1870—as a necessity leavened by the determination to regain what has been lost (to be fair, sacred rhetoric has been part of the Israeli discourse as well—for example regarding the indivisibility of Jerusalem).

Having reviewed the history of Israeli-Arab peacemaking, Kissinger noted that

> once Arab-Israeli negotiations reached the subject of Palestine, however, the different perceptions of peace emerged as a nearly insuperable obstacle. . . . [I]n the negotiations with the Palestinians the Israeli perception of peace became like a mirage that evaporates the more one appears to approach it. . . . After Ehud Barak had made concessions inconceivable by any previous Israeli

Prime Minister . . . Arafat found it impossible to accept the Israeli quid pro quo without inflaming his own constituencies. Another obstacle was the Israeli insistence that, after regaining the offered territories, the Palestinians would make no further demands. However reasonable that might sound to Americans and Israelis, Arafat shrank from its finality. He might have been willing to defer some demands for quite some time, but he could not bring himself to abandon them altogether and forever.

Kissinger supplemented these pessimistic fundamental observations with a critical analysis of Clinton's and Barak's policy during the year preceding the Camp David conference, during the conference itself, and in its aftermath. He characterized the relationship between the two leaders as a "symbiotic psychological analysis," in which Clinton was exercising pressure in order to extract concessions and Barak was anxious to demonstrate Israel's cooperation. Kissinger agreed with the decision to relinquish the phased approach but criticized the sense of urgency and eagerness displayed by both Washington and Jerusalem. This conduct, in turn, served only to whet the appetite of Yasser Arafat, who found Israel's insistence on finality and end of claims unacceptable. Camp David thus became "a dialogue of the deaf."

The Eclectic School

This category refers to a number of authors who, for various reasons, refrained from expressing the distinctive and pointed judgments that would have placed them in one of the first three categories. One such author is Yossi Beilin, whose book, *A Guide for a Wounded Dove,* is marked by dissonance. The book is dedicated to Ehud Barak, "who acted boldly for peace," but Beilin is in fact critical of Barak's actual conduct and policies. The book was published soon after the February 2001 elections. As time went by and Barak escalated his criticism of Arafat, Beilin drew further from him and became more critical.

Another critic who can be placed in the same category is Dr. Menachem Klein. His book, *Shattering a Taboo,* deals primarily with the specific effort to resolve the issue of Jerusalem. But in his book and press interviews granted at the time of its publication, two larger themes were also given prominence: criticism of Israel's two senior negotiators,

Barak and Ben-Ami (Klein served as adviser to the latter), and the idea
that the al-Aqsa intifada had a significant intra-Palestinian dimension
that was the product of frustration and antagonism directed at the corrupt, authoritarian leadership that had been accumulating since 1994.
Klein subsequently applied Darby and MacGinty's model for analyzing
peace processes, and demonstrated that most of the criteria they identified as determining success (in South Africa and Northern Ireland) are
absent from the Israeli-Palestinian conflict. Thus, in a "deterministic"
mood, Klein implied that the Israeli-Palestinian negotiation was doomed
to failure.[41]

Ironically, *Within Reach,* the memoir published by Gilead Sher—
Ehud Barak's confidant, negotiator, and, briefly, chief of staff—can also
be placed in the eclectic school. Sher's book offers a detailed "Sher version" very different from a "Barak version" and is critical of several of
the principal Israeli actors, including Barak. Sher's book is an invaluable
source for the history of this period but does not offer a clear-cut thesis.

As I see it, Ehud Barak presented to the Palestinians a far-reaching offer
that could serve as the basis for a mutually acceptable final-status agreement. It cannot be argued that there was no "real" or "binding" offer;
after all, even if the offer was not made in this fashion at Camp David,
it was laid on the table in a clear and concrete manner through President
Clinton's bridging proposal in December.

There were undoubtedly significant flaws in the conduct of the negotiations by Israel and the United States. The Camp David summit convened without adequate preparation and was held too close to the U.S.
presidential election. In the circumstances surrounding the summer of
2000, a final-status agreement was simply not within reach. It would
have been preferable to prepare another interim agreement as a fallback
option—or at least an exit strategy.

Ehud Barak's sense that the negotiating parties were on a collision
course was truly perceptive. He was right to try to establish whether
Arafat was a sincere partner in brokering a final-status agreement. However, once he found out that Arafat was not, Barak's adoption of an "all
or nothing" approach was erroneous. Also, by arguing that he "tore the
mask off his [Arafat's] face," he cast a shadow on the sincerity of his
own (genuine) quest for a definitive agreement.

Yasser Arafat failed the test of statesmanship. A statesman is defined by his ability to read correctly the trends of unfolding history, to make the right decisions in that context and to build the requisite support for implementing those decisions. If Arafat had been guided primarily by the desire to establish a Palestinian state on reasonable terms, he should have exploited the "window of opportunity" that was opened between July and December 2000. There is no way to ascertain the veracity of the claims of Shlomo Ben-Ami and Dennis Ross, who argue that Arafat failed to "cross the Rubicon" for lack of will or capacity. Regardless, Arafat's conduct can be explained without reference to this underlying question.

It is certain that Arafat's and his associates' concept of the time dimension in Arab-Israeli relations changed between August 1993 and July 2000. In 1993, and through the mid-1990s, they acted on the assumption that for the first time in decades time was on Israel's side. This change in perspective derived from several developments: the collapse of the Soviet Union, the U.S. victory in the Cold War, the Persian Gulf War, and the wave of immigration to Israel from the former Soviet Union. But by the decade's end, the perspective had changed again. The impact of the dramatic events of the late 1980s and early 1990s faded. The United States acted softly in its conduct toward Iraq, Syria, and the Palestinians, and the demographic gap between Palestinians and Israelis was reopened.

The Israel of the late 1990s was perceived by many Palestinians as a rich, soft society that had lost the will to fight. Leafing through the Israeli press of the period, one is easily impressed by the meek and passive response to daily break-ins or car thefts. A. B. Yehoshua's *The Liberating Daughter-in-Law,* a novel dealing with Arab-Israeli and Palestinian-Israeli relations, offers a vivid literary expression of the encounter between an eager, hungry society and a soft, tired one.

In this context two events assumed a particular significance. One was the Hasmonean Tunnel crisis in September 1996, when a few days of rioting and shooting transformed Netanyahu's attitude toward Arafat. Another was Israel's unilateral withdrawal from Lebanon in the spring of 2000. Hizballah, Iran, and many Palestinians drew the lesson that it was wrong to make concessions to Israel; that Israel, when confronted with durable opposition, will blink first. This sensibility was reinforced by the Israeli-Palestinian negotiations of 2000, often described as a journey in which Israel made most of the concessions and at a rapid pace without adequate reciprocity. If Israeli moved within such a brief span of time from offering 66 percent to nearly 100 percent of the West Bank, why not keep pressing for additional concessions? And why conclude a complex final-status agreement with an outgoing U.S. president and an Israeli prime minister who had lost his coalition?

The effort to reach an Israeli-Palestinian agreement was also set back by the interplay between the Syrian and Palestinian tracks as it developed in 2000. The United States and Israel spent too much time in a futile effort to come to terms with Hafiz al-Asad and were late to arrive at a crucial phase in the negotiation with the Palestinians. By that point, Clinton was too close to the end of his term and Barak had lost his coalition. The fact that Asad rebuffed Clinton's gambit in Geneva and did so with impunity was not lost on Arafat and emboldened him to do the same four months later. Israel's willingness to accept the principle of withdrawal to the lines of June 4, 1967, on the Syrian front reinforced the Palestinian demand for a full withdrawal in the West Bank. If Israel believed that the Palestinian case was different from those of its neighboring Arab states, it should have been clear and assertive in formulating its position. A single attempt, by the government's legal adviser, to argue that Security Council Resolution 242 did not apply to the territory of Mandate Palestine ended lamely. An Israeli claim for a portion of the West Bank should have been predicated on a sound basis.

Israel also erred in accepting the very term *right of return* as a legitimate part of the vocabulary used to address the refugee problem during the effort to reach a final-status agreement. There can be no final-status agreement without a mutually acceptable formula regarding refugees. The formula included in Clinton's bridging proposals of December 2000 may well be or come close to being the "magic formula." But by accepting this term, Israel acquiesces implicitly in the Palestinian and Arab claim of an "original sin" and leaves the door open for fresh demands in the future. In the conduct of negotiations, it is important to be flexible and inventive at most times, but it is equally important for both sides to clarify what their red lines are.

5

SHARON, BUSH, AND ARAFAT

At the core of this chapter lie three interlocking personal-political narratives. The first belongs to Ariel Sharon, whose passage from marginality and controversy to the center of Israeli politics brought him to a point where he had to make choices that ran against the grain of his biography. The second is that of Yasser Arafat, who for thirty-five years had been successful in building and keeping for himself the positions of symbol and interpreter of Palestinian nationalism. Throughout this period he was able to impose his vision of the goals of that nationalism, discarding several opportunities to settle for less. The years 2000–05 put that personal role into particularly stark relief. And the third is that of George W. Bush, who began his presidency reluctant to deal with Arab-Israeli affairs but soon found himself immersed in the politics of the Middle East and in the effort to resolve the Palestinian-Israeli conflict.

Ariel Sharon became the sixth Israeli prime minister within a decade who sought to grapple with the dual challenge of managing both the Israeli political system and Israel's relationship with the Arab world. Of those predecessors, Yitzhak Rabin was assassinated by an Israeli fanatic and the four other prime ministers—Yitzhak Shamir, Shimon Peres, Benjamin Netanyahu, and Ehud Barak—were all defeated at the ballot box.

The very fact of Sharon's election and subsequent four-and-a-half years in office as prime minister provides several layers of significance and irony. Sharon, who for decades had been knocking on the inner doors of Israel's political establishment, finally reached the ultimate position of power when he defeated Ehud Barak on February 6, 2001, winning 62.38 percent of the vote under the slogan "Sharon alone will bring peace." This was the culmination of a political career for the military officer–politician, who had once failed to become chief of staff of the Israel Defense Forces and was removed from the post of minister of defense. Sharon's election was the product of the failure of Barak's policy and the ensuing crisis of the Israeli left and moderate left, his own political skills, and his cunning exploitation of rival Benjamin Netanyahu's miscalculations during the campaign. After six years of leadership by two prime ministers who represented a new generation and a new style in Israeli politics, power shifted back to a member of the generation that had founded Israel in 1948.

Sharon, whose September 2000 visit to the Temple Mount had sparked the outbreak of the second, or al-Aqsa, intifada, now obtained from the Israeli public a sweeping mandate to end that intifada and restore normal life in Israel. Sharon came into office as the patron of the West Bank settlements, possessed of a distinctive concept of Israeli national and national security agendas.[1] He had the aura of a bold, creative military commander from the 1950s and 1960s—the general who had also quelled Palestinian violence in Gaza in the early 1970s and crossed the Suez Canal in October 1973. Sharon viewed the Arab-Israeli conflict in terms of a war against terrorism, often referring to "a century of Arab terrorism." He believed in diplomacy backed by force and power and was opposed to the Oslo Accords and to the course they charted for Israel.

But a pragmatic strand could also be identified during Sharon's career. This pragmatism was manifested in his role in the evacuation of the Israeli settlements in the northern Sinai (as Menachem Begin's defense minister); in the signing of the Wye Agreement in October 1998 (as Netanyahu's foreign minister); and in fulfilling his preelection promise by forming a national unity government and making Shimon Peres—the Israeli most identified with the Oslo Accords—his chief partner, as foreign minister.

Shortly after Sharon came to power, it became clear that although he had no magic formula himself for defeating the Palestinians, he would still check the efforts of Peres to reach an interim agreement with the Palestinian Authority. Sharon's proclivity for radical choices was moderated by two principal considerations: his determination to preserve the partnership with the Labor Party in the national unity government, and the constraints imposed by Israel's international relations—primarily the relationship with the United States. As a consequence of this dynamic, Sharon was ironically positioned in the middle of the political spectrum, on the one hand restraining the extreme right wing's pressure to conduct an all-out war against the Palestinian Authority, and on the other hand blocking (at least temporarily) a return to negotiations.

Early in his tenure as prime minister, Sharon occasionally spoke of his readiness for "painful concessions" at the right time and of accepting the idea of a Palestinian state—without elaborating on its size and character. At that point this was untested rhetoric, not necessarily grounded in a clear, long-term vision. Still, the man who for many years had been perceived as a fighter, a leader of Israel's radical right, an advocate of radical change and power-oriented thinking—a leader who "does not stop at the red light"[2]—was able to transform himself into the patriarch of Israeli politics. He managed this feat both by ably navigating Israel's political currents and by building a close and effective relationship with the Bush administration. In January 2003, despite continuing violent confrontations with the Palestinians and a lingering economic crisis, Sharon was reelected by a huge majority, owing largely to three perceptions held by the Israeli public: that Arafat was not a credible partner for a political settlement, that Sharon was unusually successful in managing what was seen as Israel's most important relationship—with the United States—and that he was also successful in contending with the enormous challenge of the second intifada.

THE BUSH ADMINISTRATION AND THE MIDDLE EAST

George W. Bush's election to the presidency and the formation of his administration, combined with the collapse of the Israeli-Palestinian peace process, the outbreak of the second intifada, and Ariel Sharon's election in February 2001, changed the landscape of Arab-Israeli relations dramatically.

When Bill Clinton had replaced George Bush senior in the White House in 1993, he chose to adopt the essence of Bush's Middle East policy: dual containment vis-à-vis Iran and Iraq and the Madrid framework to promote an Arab-Israeli settlement. Eight years later, George W. Bush and his team did their utmost to disown Clinton's legacy. The new administration made it abundantly clear that it had no intention of becoming immersed in Israeli-Palestinian peacemaking. The Bush administration believed America's efforts in the Middle East should be invested in the region's eastern flank, where the job—begun in Iraq in 1991—had yet to be completed. Iraq and Iran, administration officials felt, should be denied access to weapons of mass destruction. This was a goal that likely could not be reached without regime change in both countries. This new stance was demonstrated bluntly in a directive issued by Secretary of State Colin Powell to his subordinates: they were no longer to use the term "peace process"—a term that was particularly current (and somewhat overused) in the vocabulary of the Clinton administration. The post of special Middle East coordinator was abolished and the conduct of the State Department's Middle East policy shifted back to the Bureau of Near Eastern Affairs.

If Yasser Arafat and other Arab leaders had expected the new president to distance himself from Israel and draw closer to the Arab world, they were disappointed. Bush's father, the forty-first president, had been tied to Republican groups identified with "Arabist" policies, oil interests, and oil-producing Arab countries, all with a view of the Middle East that perceived Israel as an obstacle to a natural friendship with most of the Arab world. The son, however, was connected to other Republican groups—namely, the party's conservative right wing and fundamentalist Christians—who were very supportive of Israel. And having barely won the election of 2000, he and his advisers were particularly mindful of the "Jewish vote."

Elected shortly after George W. Bush, Ariel Sharon skillfully exploited these trends in the administration and built a good rapport with the new president and his staff. But this auspicious beginning was replaced by a more complex relationship during Bush's first months in office. Some of Washington's traditional Arab friends, headed by Saudi Arabia, began to exert pressure on the administration to distance itself from Israel, publicize its criticism of Israel's policy toward the Palestinians, and become more actively involved in efforts to resolve the Israeli-Palestinian conflict. Their argument was quite familiar: a policy that is perceived as pro-Israeli undermines America's position in the Middle

East and threatens the stability of moderate regimes—regimes already hard put to deal with an agitated Arab "street" galvanized by images of Israeli-Palestinian violence broadcast by the ubiquitous Arab satellite television channels.

Under this pressure in the early summer of 2001, the Bush administration took a series of measures designed to demonstrate some distancing from Israel, a rapprochement with Washington's traditional Arab friends, and support for the idea of a Palestinian state. During Sharon's visit to Washington in June 2001, the White House made a special effort to display a slight measure of tension in its relationship with Israel.

These trends, however, were suddenly both checked and reversed by al-Qaeda's terrorist attacks against the United States on September 11, 2001. The "war on terror" became the defining issue on the administration's agenda. A presidency that initially was seen as passive and unfocused was immediately transformed. George W. Bush began to radiate leadership, turning crisis and adversity to his advantage. Before September 11, his tendency to reduce a complex reality into black-and-white issues had been seen as a flaw; this ability now proved most useful as the public had to be mobilized for the struggle against an unfamiliar and ill-defined enemy.

The interplay between this development after September 11 and Washington's policy toward the lingering Israeli-Palestinian conflict was complex. The emergence of the war on terror as the major issue on America's national agenda immediately generated a debate between two distinct schools. The first argued that Palestinian terrorism and al-Qaeda's terrorism were of the same family, even if a direct organizational or operational link did not exist between them. Therefore, now that the United States had been attacked by a terrorist organization, it should understand the nature of the challenge Israel faced. It should be clear that the attack made on the United States by a group of Arab-Muslim terrorists was unrelated to its support for Israel. Israel and the Palestinian issue were occasionally mentioned by al-Qaeda's leaders, but the organization's hostility to the United States was rooted in its hatred of the Egyptian and Saudi regimes buttressed by the United States, in its opposition to the presence of the American military in the Arabian Peninsula, and, broadly speaking, in radical Islam's grudge against the West and the leader and embodiment of the West—America.

The other school of thought produced by September 11 was a near mirror image of these arguments—that is, there was no comparison or connection between terrorist acts perpetrated by al-Qaeda and those that represented the Palestinian "struggle for national liberation"; that there was no doubting that the United States' support for Israel was a major source of anger and restlessness in the Arab world and of the rage directed at Washington; and that there were no inherent reasons for anti-Americanism in the world of Islam. The supposition, therefore, was that, once the United States ceased its sweeping support of Israel, it should be able to establish sound relations with Muslim states.

The debate soon shifted from the theoretical to the practical level. The Bush administration began to plan a military campaign in Afghanistan, where al-Qaeda's leaders were headquartered, and the planning process raised numerous tactical questions. Did the United States want to build a coalition similar to the one assembled against Iraq in 1990? If so, what Arab states could be expected to join it and what would the United States expect of them? Direct participation, or logistical and political support, or both? And what could be done to avoid popular protest in the Arab world when the United States attacked a Muslim country such as Afghanistan, and possibly, at a second stage, an Arab country like Iraq?[3]

The early phase in the planning of the campaign in Afghanistan placed Israel in an awkward position. The Bush administration clearly was not interested in Israel as a partner in the campaign, nor did it wish to have Israel associated with a U.S.-led military operation in a Muslim country. At the same time, the United States was seeking the cooperation of states like Iran and Syria and of the Palestinian Authority—all seen by Israel (and many others) as intimately linked to terrorist networks and activities. From the Bush administration's point of view, at that stage, everything was subordinate to the success of the anticipated military campaign. The administration tried to gloss over the inherent contradictions and dissonance of that policy by drawing a distinction between "local terrorism" and "terrorism with a global reach." In other words, a suicide bombing in Tel Aviv or Jerusalem was a "local" event, while an attack on New York or Washington was a "global" matter.

The Bush administration also decided to move forward with some of the measures discussed earlier in the summer to obtain the Arab world's cooperation or at least a calm atmosphere in the Arab street. In early October 2001 Secretary of State Powell let it be known that he was contemplating when and how the U.S. plan for an Israeli-Palestinian settlement should be publicly introduced. Originally, this plan was to be brought to the UN's General Assembly in September, but that gathering was postponed owing to the events of September 11. The U.S. plan was reportedly designed to manifest support for the idea of a Palestinian state and to address the major final-status issues: borders, Jerusalem, and the right of return.

Powell's intimation provoked a particularly sharp response from Sharon. On October 6 he called upon the "Western states" to learn a lesson from the failure of the "appeasement policy toward Germany on the eve of World War II," and asserted that "Israel will not be [a second] Czechoslovakia." The White House was irritated by the allusion to Neville Chamberlain but chose to refrain from a public retort.[4]

In any event, this phase ended swiftly. The United States reached the conclusion that its military and technological capabilities were sufficient to topple the Taliban regime in Afghanistan without the help of Middle Eastern allies. Furthermore, alarm bells notwithstanding, there were no signs of agitation among the Arab populace As the military campaign in Afghanistan was unfolding successfully and the administration's self-confidence continued to grow, some voices in the Pentagon began to mention transitioning to the second and third phases of the war on terror. Tension between the United States and the Arab world now centered on two issues: which Arab state or states could become a target in the next phase (Iraq and Syria were mentioned); and the American anger—both official and public—directed at Egypt and Saudi Arabia for the roles their nationals had played on September 11. These developments facilitated a mending of fences between Bush and Sharon and contributed to the decision to delay publication of the American plan Powell had first mentioned publicly in October 2001.

Yasser Arafat's growing identification with "the other side" in the war on terror reinforced this dynamic. In the immediate aftermath of September 11, Arafat made a series of moves designed to placate American opinion, denouncing the attack and publishing repeated public directives for Palestinians to cease fire against Israel. But as time went by, these efforts petered out. Palestinian attacks on Israel—including suicide attacks—continued, and the American distinction between local terrorism and terrorism with a global reach began to lose its significance. The Israeli capture in January 2002 of *Karin A,* a ship carrying weapons from Iran to Gaza, was of particular importance. It clearly was an event of global reach and therefore a great embarrassment to Arafat, who began by denying any connection to the ship and ended by informing the secretary of state that, as president of the Palestinian Authority, he would take responsibility. On other occasions, Israel and the U.S. intelligence community provided President Bush with evidence linking Arafat directly to the financing of specific terrorist acts against Israel. These occurrences were all important links in the chain of events leading President Bush to the conclusion that unless Arafat was removed from power, there would be no prospect for a political settlement.

On June 24, 2002, having consulted with the Sharon government, President Bush presented the U.S. plan for an Israeli-Palestinian settlement. Here was the harbinger of good news in the long term for the Palestinians: the plan outlined the establishment of a Palestinian state alongside Israel; Israeli withdrawal from much of Gaza and the West Bank; and resolution of the major issues of borders, Jerusalem, and refugees through a final-status agreement. Bush also reiterated Washington's commitment to the Mitchell Commission's plan that once progress was achieved regarding Israeli security, the Israel Defense Forces would be required to withdraw from the parts of the West Bank it had reoccupied following the outbreak of violence in September 2000, and that in any event, Israel should stop all settlement activity in "occupied territories."

But in the short term, the main challenge in the Bush plan belonged to the Palestinians: they were to halt and fight terrorism, as well as replace their current leadership. "In order to achieve peace and for a Palestinian state to be established, a different leadership is required. I call upon the Palestinian people to choose new leaders who do not compromise on the issue of terror," said Bush. He went on to anchor his statement in a position associated with the right wings in both the United States and Israel. Bush asserted that the emergence of a viable Palestinian state depended on fundamental rather than cosmetic changes in Palestinian society, meaning a democratic government, a market economy, and opposition to terror. In practical terms, he drew a distinction between the establishment of a Palestinian state—whose borders and other aspects of sovereignty would be provisional—and subsequent permanent arrangements.

This important speech laid the ground for U.S policy and Israeli-Palestinian diplomacy in the next six years: the formation of the "Quartet" (the United States, the United Nations, Europe, and Russia), the publication of the "Road Map," the cultivation of Mahmud Abbas and Salam Fayyad as alternatives to Yasser Arafat, and the 2007 Annapolis conference.

Several components of the Bush administration's policy were at odds with Sharon's own ideas and preferences. The potential tension rarely came into the open, however, and was well disguised by a close, often intimate, working relationship.

The course of events can now be reviewed and analyzed against this backdrop in four major areas: the Israeli-Palestinian war of attrition; the attempts to reach a settlement; the road to war and the war in Iraq; and the effort to renew the Israeli-Palestinian negotiations in its aftermath. This review sets the stage for an evaluation of the dramatic shift in Sharon's policies in the last months of 2003.

THE PALESTINIAN-ISRAELI WAR OF ATTRITION

The term "intifada" implies a spontaneous popular uprising. A spontaneous element can, indeed, be discerned in the violent confrontation that erupted between Israel and the Palestinians in late September 2000, as well as popular anger at and criticism of the Palestinian Authority. But the confrontation was quickly transformed into an organized campaign orchestrated (at least in part) by the Palestinian Authority. With the passage of time, the Palestinian Authority lost both power and authority to the radical opposition and to local groups. The outbreak of violence pitted the Palestinians, who sought to extract additional concessions, against an Israel determined to show that its resolve had not been eroded and to use its overwhelming military advantage for a clear victory.

The conflict unfolded through six phases between 2000 and 2003.

The first phase, during the fall of 2000, lasted for several weeks. It was characterized by the distinctive manifestations of a popular uprising such as demonstrations and marches toward Israeli roadblocks. But the calculated use of firearms was integrated into these activities to provoke an Israeli response as well as to create casualties that would heighten anger against Israel. Israel was, in fact, well prepared for this initiative, having predicted it by intelligence assessments, and the IDF correctly applied the lessons derived from the violent clashes after the Hasmonean Tunnel opening in September 1996. During this early phase, Israel suffered a small number of casualties; the Palestinians' casualty rate was high. This had two principal outcomes: the significant improvement in the international standing of the Palestinians, who were once again perceived as victims and the weaker party to the conflict, rather than as the political party that had recently rejected Israel's offers at Camp David; and an increased Palestinian motivation to press on and escalate the combat.

During the second phase, which began at the end of 2000, manifestations of Palestinian popular resistance were virtually abandoned and the conflict began to be conducted between armed (though uneven) Palestinian and Israeli entities. Among the Palestinians, two main camps emerged. The first included the radical Islamic groups Hamas and Islamic Jihad, later joined by the Popular Front for the Liberation of Palestine. This camp sought to undermine the quest for a settlement by initiating attacks—including suicide bombings—in Israel proper. The second camp, led by the Tanzim (a radical offshoot of Arafat's Fatah movement), focused activities in the West Bank and Gaza, attacking both the IDF and Jewish settlers. Their definition of victory was a settlement on their terms.

In the third phase of the conflict the distinction between these two Palestinian camps became increasingly blurred. This change reflected a new approach on the part of Arafat and his associates. The quest for improved terms in a negotiated settlement was replaced by the assessment that the Palestinians could use force to drive Israel from the West Bank and Gaza, without relinquishing the notion of a two-state solution. Escalation on the Palestinian side bred corresponding escalation of Israel's activities, including incursions into Palestinian areas, longer stays in those areas, and "targeted killings" of leaders of radical Palestinian groups. Still, as prime minister, Sharon displayed an unexpected degree of pragmatism and restraint. This restraint stemmed from the considerations mentioned earlier—his sense of ultimate responsibility, his partnership with the Labor Party, the importance of Israel's relationship with Washington—as well as from Sharon's reluctance to play into the Palestinians' attempts to "internationalize" the conflict by inviting the European Union or the UN to play an active role or seek an imposed solution.

The fourth phase was defined by the terrorist attack on the United States on September 11, 2001, and the wave of attacks inside Israel in the spring of 2002. The events of September 11, America's declaration of a war on terror, and the central position assigned to the issue of terrorism on the international agenda all had a complex impact on the Palestinian-Israeli war. Yasser Arafat and his associates immediately (and correctly) sensed that it was important to establish a clear distinction between their war against Israel and organizations such as al-Qaeda and Hizballah that were seen by the United States as the chief instruments of "international terrorism." This Palestinian recognition, however, was not consistently applied in practice.

Arafat initially did act to reduce the violence in the Palestinian-Israeli conflict, but only to limited effect. Most important, he failed to impose his authority on Hamas and the other Islamic organizations. Israel, in turn, felt that the weakening of Arafat's position (and, more broadly, the Palestinian position) enhanced its freedom of action. It thus chose to eliminate Raid Karmi, the head of the Tanzim in Tul Karam, on January 14, 2002. After a comparatively long lull, this step renewed the radical groups' quest to step up the escalation.

The fifth phase of the conflict unfolded from late March 2002 to December 2002. A wave of suicide bombings led to an Israeli counter-offensive that culminated in two massive operations: "Defensive Shield" and "Determined Way." The Israeli counteroffensive resulted in renewed control over most of the West Bank and emasculated the control and presence of the Palestinian Authority in the region. Israel refrained from reoccupying the main cities and chose instead to dispatch army units for longer stays. The Palestinian Authority's physical emasculation was notably demonstrated in the virtual destruction of the Muqata'ah, Arafat's headquarters in Ramallah. Israel was less active in the Gaza Strip. A security fence separating Gaza from Israel proved very effective in preventing suicide bombings. Even if Israel had contemplated military action in Gaza, it was deterred by the difficulty of operating in one of the world's most densely populated areas.

Israel's consistent pressure reduced the operational capacity of the terrorist groups, but their residual capabilities allowed them to continue occasional suicide bombings and other attacks. The level of violence was kept below that of March 2002 (when a Palestinian suicide bombing killed twenty-nine people during a Passover observance in Netanya), but even the subsequent reduction of violence sufficed to keep the conflict going and exact a heavy price from both societies. The virtual collapse of the Palestinian Authority and the renewal of Israeli military control over most of the West Bank raised the question of whether it might be necessary to rebuild the Israeli military administration there, which had been dismantled with the implementation of the Oslo Accords. But Israel was not forced to make a decision regarding this complex matter. Instead, international aid organizations and the remnants of the Palestinian Authority's apparatus provided the population with a minimum level of service.

The sixth phase of the Israeli-Palestinian violence unfolded over a longer period and is described in detail below. By 2003 Sharon was able to defeat Arafat and quash the second intifada. Occasional, significant suicide bombings and other terrorist acts still occurred in 2003 and 2004 but normal life was gradually reestablished in Israel.

In Israel the continuing conflict created growing pressure for separation from the Palestinians—a fence between the two societies—in both the territorial and the physical sense of the term. As a rule, Israel's right wing opposed the construction of a fence along the green line (on the pre-1967 maps), arguing that it would be tantamount to a renunciation of Israel's claim to the West Bank (or at least a sizable portion of it). The net result of this counterpressure was slowly paced construction of a security fence along segments of the green line.

Meanwhile, criticism of Yasser Arafat and the Palestinian Authority intensified among the Palestinians. The familiar complaints of corruption and arbitrary government were reinforced by the public critique of a strategy that was exacting a high cost from society, leading to the loss of autonomous rule, and seeming to go nowhere. One particularly strident example of such criticism was the speech Mahmud Abbas delivered in a closed session in mid-November 2002. The text, eventually made public and published in the Arab press, included statements such as: "We should have sat down to the negotiations table and pushed him

[Sharon] to a corner where we are more able to act than he is, rather than allowing him to drag us into an arena in which he excels and outshines not only us but the entire Arab world, namely that of military power and the force of arms."[5]

Demands by Palestinian intellectuals and political activists for an end to the authoritarianism and corruption of Yasser Arafat and the Palestinian Authority had preceded Bush's own demand (in June 2002) for Palestinian reform and for Arafat's removal from power. In fact, the pressure exerted by the United States actually played into Arafat's hands. Arafat was adroit enough both to evade that pressure and to exploit it to embarrass his critics (who, he charged, were accomplices of the Bush administration). One critic, Dr. Khalil Shikaki, a political scientist and pollster from Nablus, vented his exasperation in a *New York Times* op-ed piece entitled "How to Reform Palestinian Politics":

> If you were Mr. Arafat, you would certainly have no incentive to step down. After all, he would be doing nothing more than leaving his people with a despicably corrupt and rightly friendless Palestinian Authority, keeping for himself only a political farewell colored by shameful defeat. He might also be leaving his people to the mercies of a politically strengthened fundamentalism. These do not have to be our alternatives. Mr. Arafat does need to give up some power and a great many Palestinians want him to. But neither he nor they will yield to curt demands from Washington or anywhere else.[6]

The Ongoing Quest for a Settlement

Efforts to establish a cease-fire and to renew the Israeli-Palestinian negotiation did continue under the shadow of the violent conflict, albeit in an intermittent and indeterminate fashion. But these efforts were doomed throughout this period. Sharon's concept of a settlement was modest. At that point he was determined to replace the terms established by Barak's failed negotiations of 2000 with a framework that was acceptable to parts of the Israeli right wing, and he preferred to obtain such a settlement after a clear victory. Arafat, in turn, insisted on finding hope within the ebb and flow of the Israeli-Palestinian conflict and was not willing to offer the concessions that would have forced Sharon's hand.

Furthermore, it became quite evident during the latter half of 2002 and the early months of 2003 that the Bush administration was determined to go to war against Iraq. It was therefore widely assumed that a serious effort to seek a political solution to the Palestinian-Israeli conflict would have to wait for the larger changes in the region that could be expected in the aftermath of that war.

The quest for settlement during this period was pushed forward by four principal actors: Shimon Peres, as foreign minister in the national unity government, along with a small part of the Israeli political spectrum who held on to the idea that a settlement was still feasible and still Israel's best option; the UN, a number of European states led by France, and, to some extent, the State Department; Arab states such as Egypt, Jordan, and Saudi Arabia; and that segment of the Palestinian political establishment which felt that the armed struggle had failed and that the public was paying an unacceptable price for the continuation of a futile effort.

The quest for settlement was resisted by an array of vocal and tacit opponents on both the Israeli and Palestinian sides. At the height of its success, the Palestinian radical camp was swept into believing in its ability to expel Israel from the West Bank and Gaza; a larger number of Palestinian militants sought more temperate goals, hoping to wear Israel down or garner enough support for an imposed settlement in the international arena. Israel's right wing argued in a number of different ways that the events of 2000–02 demonstrated the failure of the "Oslo concept," that there was no point in renewing the negotiations and certainly not within the Oslo framework, and that in any event it was essential for Israel to emerge victorious from the confrontation initiated by the Palestinians. The Bush administration, as is described below, did not speak in a single voice or pursue a coherent line.

What mattered most, however, was Yasser Arafat's failure to cope effectively with the cardinal importance George W. Bush assigned to the war on terror after September 11. As we saw, a series of mistakes by Arafat led the president and several of his aides to view him as part of "the terror camp" and to endorse Sharon's view that he was not a legitimate partner for a renewed negotiation.

During 2001 and 2002, four main efforts were made to reach an agreement, or at least a cease-fire. The first was a U.S.-led effort to find a formula for a cease-fire and the resumption of negotiations. This effort began with an international commission formed after the Sharm al-Sheikh conference of October 2000, headed by Senator George Mitchell (whose report was submitted in May 2001). It was continued by the director of the CIA, George Tenet, who in June 2001 had submitted a "recipe" for achieving a cease-fire and renewing Israeli-Palestinian security coordination, and had culminated in the appointment of retired General Anthony Zinni as a U.S. special envoy for the Middle East.

The Mitchell Commission was a well-balanced group whose report analyzed the crisis of late September 2000 and offered a reasonable scenario for ending the violence. George Tenet's mission had been predicated on the experience and credit assembled by the CIA during the 1990s when it helped build the Palestinian security services and mechanisms for coordinating with their Israeli counterparts. General Zinni was expected to translate his predecessors' recommendations into an actual course of action. All three efforts were essentially technical in nature, rather than quests for a fundamental, political resolution. The goals were to end violence, renew security coordination, get the IDF to withdraw from the positions captured after September 28, 2000, and (in a more political vein) halt new settlement activity by Israel. Zinni's mission collapsed in March 2002 under the wave of Palestinian suicide bombings in Netanya and several other Israeli cities. It was not until June 2002 that President Bush presented his comprehensive plan for an Israeli-Palestinian settlement.

The second main effort was the negotiation conducted between Shimon Peres and Abu Alaa throughout 2001 in an attempt to reach an interim agreement that would be linked to an ensuing permanent-status negotiation. In December the "Peres–Abu Alaa Understandings" were assembled. The main points were these: cease-fire within six weeks; Israeli recognition of a Palestinian state in more than 40 percent of the West Bank; and a negotiation on final-status issues to be completed within one year and implemented within two.

It is not known how much support Abu Alaa had for this plan among Palestinian leaders, but Sharon—who had authorized his foreign minister's give-and-take with Abu Alaa—rejected out of hand the product of their negotiations, in public on December 23, 2001.[7] Sharon was not opposed to the linkage to a final-status negotiation nor to the notion of a Palestinian state. But he had in mind a slower pace and a more modest concept of a future Palestinian state.

A third attempt came in February 2002, when Crown Prince Abdullah, Saudi Arabia's virtual ruler, produced a Saudi initiative that offered a simple formula for a comprehensive Arab-Israeli settlement: full Israeli withdrawal to the lines of June 4, 1967, in return for full peace and normalization of relations. His initiative reflected the growing anxiety of Arab states such as Saudi Arabia, Jordan, and Egypt that the lingering Israeli-Palestinian conflict would undermine their stability. It also demonstrated Saudi Arabia's desire to end the tension that had developed in its relationship with the United States post–September 11. The plan had two main advantages: simplicity, and Saudi Arabia's willingness to endorse the notion of normalization. (During the heyday of the Arab-Israeli peace process in the 1990s, the Saudis had taken exception to the idea of normalizing relations with Israel.) But these advantages were overshadowed by several problems. For one thing, Ariel Sharon and most Israelis were opposed to full withdrawal to the lines of June 4, 1967. And the Saudi initiative would have to be converted into a plan of action that could be endorsed by the Arab world (or at least by the relevant Arab parties). Would Syria sign on to the idea of full normalization with Israel? Would the Palestinians give up the demand for the right of return, which was not included in the Saudi plan?

After investing a strenuous diplomatic effort, the Saudis were successful in persuading the other participants to endorse a modified version of their initiative and turn it into an "All-Arab Initiative" at the Arab summit meeting in Beirut in late March 2002. The new version included an indirect reference to the right of return, referring to resolution of the refugee problem in accordance with UN Resolution 194 (on which the Palestinian insistence on a right of return relies as a source of "international legitimacy"). Furthermore, a second communiqué that specifically mentioned the right of return was issued at the conclusion of the summit. Despite these efforts, however, the Saudi initiative was not pursued and eventually evaporated, in part because its adoption coincided with the Passover suicide bombing in Netanya. The Saudis did not attempt to revive the initiative until 2007.

Finally, in April 2002 the Quartet was launched at a meeting in Madrid as yet another mechanism for bringing about a resolution. As the term implies, four major actors attended the meeting: the United States, the European Union, the United Nations, and Russia. The Quartet was not a product of U.S. diplomacy. It was formed at the initiative of its three other partners and reflected their desire to shape Arab-Israeli diplomacy as well as the failure of the efforts that had been led by Mitchell, Tenet, and Zinni.

Washington's willingness to join this forum stemmed from the need to reduce tensions with partners and even rivals (such as Russia)—whose collaboration Washington needed for the offensive against Iraq's Saddam Hussein—as well as the need to close ranks after the recent exacerbation of Israeli-Palestinian fighting. The Madrid Declaration reflected a shift in Washington's position toward that of the Quartet's other members.

The Quartet's second meeting took place in New York in July 2002, a month after President Bush called for Arafat's removal from power. The decisions adopted at the New York meeting were a compromise, the end result of give-and-take between the United States and its three partners. The Quartet decided to call for the Palestinian Authority to undergo a reform, for elections to take place with Arafat elected to a symbolic position, and for formation of a Palestinian state within three years. In September 2002, the Quartet developed a Road Map for an Israeli-Palestinian settlement, to proceed in three phases: reform within the Palestinian Authority, Israeli withdrawal to the lines of September 2000 (before the intifada), and Palestinian elections; the formation of a Palestinian state within provisional borders and a development of a Palestinian constitution during 2003; and final-status negotiations in 2004 and the first half of 2005.

On October 15, 2002, President Bush published a draft plan for a resolution of the Israeli-Palestinian dispute. These moves were not meant to have an immediate impact; their main importance was in laying guiding principles on the table for the anticipated resumption of the Israeli-Palestinian negotiations once the Iraqi crisis had been resolved. Sharon's government was opposed to the Road Map but chose not to confront the Bush administration over an issue that seemed hypothetical and remote. It finally accepted the Road Map (with fourteen reservations) in May 2003.

THE UNITED STATES AND THE WAR IN IRAQ

In its very early days, the Bush administration established a link between U.S. policy in Iraq and the Israeli-Palestinian crisis. Several spokespersons deprecated the Clinton administration's previous massive investment in Arab-Israeli diplomacy, particularly in view of its meager accomplishments. For the Bush administration, the critical issues of the Middle East lay in the region's eastern part. The administration felt that development of an effective U.S. policy to restrain Iraq and Iran would have a calming effect on the whole region—Israelis and Palestinians included.

The sense that the United States needed "to complete the job" in Iraq and topple Saddam Hussein's regime had deep roots in the Bush administration, beginning with the president's determination to settle the political—and, indeed, a personal, familial—score. This sense rested on the doctrines and arguments of a group of neoconservative intellectuals and Republican activists, some of whom were now appointed to senior positions in the new administration. This group had been sharply critical of Clinton's policies in the Middle East during the latter part of the 1990s, denouncing what they saw as a weak stance taken vis-à-vis Saddam Hussein. From their perspective, beyond eliminating the dangers posed directly by his regime, toppling Saddam would become the cornerstone of a new policy that would weaken and perhaps even eliminate the radical elements in the region. This result would then enable the United States to reorganize and democratize the Middle East, relying on such trusted allies as Israel, Turkey, Jordan, and, according to one version, "the new Iraq" as well.

During its first months in power, the Bush administration did not assign much importance to the matter of reforming the entire Middle East. The energy saved by pulling back diplomatic efforts from the region's western front was not invested in the east. But this state of affairs changed radically on September 11. The Bush administration understood that it had to come up with an impressive response, but it needed to identify a suitable target in the immediate aftermath of the terrorist attack. During the discussions held at the administration's senior level, the Pentagon's team, spearheaded by Deputy Secretary Paul Wolfowitz, advocated attacking Iraq. They argued that it was difficult to target an organization such as al-Qaeda, whereas Iraq was more readily accessible and was replete with targets that should be destroyed in any event. There was no proof of a direct connection between Iraq and al-Qaeda, but a strong case could be made that Iraq was a terrorist-supporting state; moreover, it was crucial to ensure that unconventional weapons were not transmitted to any terrorist group. Beyond these arguments lay the conviction that a change of leadership in Iraq was the key to a larger change within the region.[8] This focus on Iraq exacerbated tensions that had appeared earlier in the administration, separating Secretary Powell on the one hand from Vice President Dick Cheney and Defense Secretary Donald Rumsfeld, with their respective teams in the White House and the Pentagon. Wolfowitz's initiative was rebuffed, for the moment, and the United States chose instead to go to war against al-Qaeda and the Taliban regime in Afghanistan.

But the idea of an attack on Iraq and its link to the new principal theme of the Bush administration was only put on hold. Iraq was mentioned as a potential target of the second phase of the war, and in 2002 President Bush reached the conclusion that he had to act against Iraq before it developed a nuclear weapon. This view put together two separate issues: the war against terror and the effort to deny "dangerous" states, such as the members of what Bush called "the axis of evil" (Iran, Iraq, and North Korea) possession of weapons of mass destruction—nuclear weapons in particular. Central to this argument was the presupposition that rogue states like Iraq were liable to transmit unconventional weapons to terrorist organizations, thereby exposing the United States and its allies to a new level of risk. Once Iraq obtained a nuclear weapon or a delivery system for the biological and chemical weapons already in its possession, the argument went, it would be difficult and perhaps impossible to act against that nation. It was, therefore, crucial for the United States to preempt such a threat.

Later, a third angle was added to this line of argument: in the spirit of President Bush's speech about the Palestinians on June 24, 2002, the idea was offered that war in Iraq could serve as a key to profound change in the region and as an important step on the road to democracy in the Middle East.[9] Three months after that speech, the White House released another important document: a reformulation of the national security strategy of the United States. In this document, the United States explicitly endorsed a doctrine under which it would "act preemptively" in the event "of an emerging threat deriving from the accumulation of unconventional weapons and ballistic missiles or from a terrorist threat to national security." The president stipulated that the United States would act against such emerging threats before they were fully formed.

The road to war in Iraq was rich in mistakes and complications, many of which derived from internecine conflict within the Bush administration or from the need to persuade multiple constituencies that the war was warranted. The main line of conflict within the administration was by now familiar—between Colin Powell and the State Department, on the one hand, and, on the other, Vice President Cheney and Secretary Rumsfeld and their teams.

As chairman of the joint chiefs of staff during the administration of Bush's father, Colin Powell had been reluctant to use American military power overseas. Now, as secretary of state seeking to affect—if not shape—policy toward Iraq, he insisted that the political-diplomatic route be fully explored before a military action was undertaken. Powell and the State Department took exception to the vision of toppling Saddam's regime as a step toward effecting broader change in the region; instead, they advocated continued cooperation with Washington's traditional friends. Within the Israeli-Palestinian context, they supported a return to negotiations rather than insisting on the removal of Arafat.

A clear tension now arose between the need to mobilize American opinion by portraying Saddam in stark terms as an immediate threat, and the need to obtain international support—or at least to mute criticism—by resorting to the Security Council and to the mechanisms established by the UN in the 1990s to neutralize Iraq's capacity to develop weapons of mass destruction and delivery systems. With this end in mind, the Bush administration had to change the definition of its policy goals from changing the regime in Iraq to the enforcement of previous Security Council resolutions, thereby dismantling Iraq's unconventional capabilities and forcing it to collaborate with the international system.

Powell finally succeeded in persuading President Bush to act through the Security Council. True, it was a longer route and full of potential obstacles; the United States was exposed to the risk of a veto that France, Russia, or China could cast at any point. But Powell persuaded the president that international endorsement was important for swaying Congress and American public opinion. These diplomatic moves and the process of military buildup within striking distance of Iraq delayed the war until the early spring of 2003. These preparations also meant that serious decisions regarding the Israeli-Palestinian conflict were postponed again; whatever one's view of this conflict, there was no point in making any serious decisions before the end of the anticipated campaign in Iraq.

Powell's policy had an early success when the Security Council on November 8, 2002, unanimously adopted Resolution 1441, demanding that Iraq surrender all missiles and biological, chemical, and nuclear weapons that it still possessed in violation of previous UN resolutions. This seemed to pave the way for a possible war against Iraq with the Security Council's support. Even Syria voted for the resolution. But the next phase was less auspicious. The new inspection mechanism, installed by the UN under the Swedish diplomat Hans Blix and the International Atomic Energy Agency, reported in February 2003 that it found no evidence that Iraq either possessed or was developing weapons of mass destruction. A dramatic appearance at the Security Council by Colin Powell, in which he used intelligence material in an effort to undermine Blix's case, helped solidify U.S. support for a war against Iraq but failed to build support for a follow-up Security Council resolution endorsing such a war. France and Germany led an international campaign against Washington's quest for war, transforming the issue into the focal point of what was virtually a crusade against unacceptable American hegemony and domination in a unipolar world. A mass protest movement was forming, both around the world and, to a lesser extent, in the United States itself, against Bush's intention to go to war.

Israel occupied an important place in two contexts in this controversy. One was the claim that the United States was being dragged to war not for reasons of state but rather to help Israel. The authors of this thesis seized on the fact that several advocates of the war were Jewish. Such arguments were made by a number of European politicians, by marginal figures in the United States, and by the archconservative politician Pat Buchanan and U.S. Representative Jim Moran (subsequently two American foreign policy scholars elaborated this contention into a full-fledged, influential book).[10] Of greater significance was the fact that President Bush decided to assign much weight, early in 2003, to the argument that a victory in Iraq would pave the way for launching the Middle East Road Map and effecting an Israeli-Palestinian agreement. Bush continued to stress the importance of destroying Saddam's weapons of mass destruction, and of bringing democracy to Iraq and to the region, but he put special emphasis on the link between the war in Iraq and the Road Map. To some extent, Bush, in seeking support for the war from the UN, was motivated by the need to help his closest ally, British prime minister Tony Blair, who was facing sharp criticism at home and in Europe for his support of the war. But Bush's statements also reflected a determination to use the anticipated victory in Iraq as a way of restarting an Israeli-Palestinian negotiation.

A parallel debate was taking place in the Israeli public and political arenas. One school of thought, clearly right-wing in orientation, held a position similar to that of the Pentagon and argued that the war in Iraq and Saddam's fall would weaken Arafat; a path would then be opened for negotiating a settlement with the Palestinians on lines different from those of Clinton's bridging proposal of 2000. The Israeli left, on the other hand, argued that, once the war in Iraq was over, the United States would find the time and the will (and perhaps would be forced) to deal with the Israeli-Palestinian issue, even to the point of imposing a settlement on the parties.

On March 19, the United States finally went to war with Iraq, aided by a broad but not very deep international coalition. Saddam's regime collapsed within three weeks, and Bush on May 1 declared a formal end to combat. The United States and its allies suffered relatively few casualties, and Iraq itself suffered neither heavy civilian casualties nor considerable damage to its economy and infrastructure. Dire predictions to the contrary notwithstanding, the Arab world responded remarkably calmly to the attack on Iraq and to the toppling of Saddam's regime.

But there was a darker side to the picture. Saddam, most of his family, and the hard core of his regime were not captured until much later. Even after an intensive search, the United States failed to find weapons of mass destruction or persuasive evidence that they had ever existed. The Iraqi opposition groups cultivated by the United States before the war failed to provide a base for the rapid construction of a new government. The United States encountered problems in the effort to reestablish normal life in Iraq, was unable to prevent an escalation of sectarian conflict over the following three years, and itself suffered a steady stream of military casualties. The mirage of a liberating army welcomed by a grateful population proved to be just that.

Several ominous trends became apparent. Bogged down in Iraq and, as it turned out, in Afghanistan as well, the U.S position in the Middle East was weakened. Friend and foe alike estimated that Washington was hardly likely to become militarily engaged in a third front in the region.

From the current perspective, the main regional beneficiary of the 2003 war in Iraq and its aftermath has been Iran. Before the war, Bush had included Iran in his axis of evil, and Iran did in fact represent a far more serious threat than Iraq. But Iraq was a much easier target. Saddam had already been demonized and U.S military planners knew full well that despite its formidable image, Iraq's army was no match for the coalition forces. Regarding Iran, the administration adopted a line that Iranian society was antagonistic to the regime and that Saddam's ouster might very well accelerate a domestic change in Iran. That failed to happen. What did happen was that Saddam's fall removed the most immediate challenge to Iran's national security, opened Iraq's Shiite majority to Iranian meddling and influence, and paved the way for an Iranian drive for regional hegemony. After a short hiatus Iran continued its nuclear and ballistic missile program and built the Iran-led "resistance axis" (including Syria, Hizballah, and Hamas) as the most effective opposition to the United States and its allies.

In Syria, Bashar al-Asad was anxious in the war's aftermath that he would also be targeted by the Bush administration—as, indeed, administration officials threatened to do. This fear played a role in Asad's decision to withdraw his troops from Lebanon in 2005 but, on the whole, failed to lead him to a comprehensive change of course. Saddam's fall had a greater impact on Muammar Qaddafi; it accelerated negotiations that had begun during the Clinton years and led him to abandon his chemical and nuclear weapons programs.

The War in Iraq and the Road Map

On January 28, 2003, Ariel Sharon was reelected as Israel's prime minister. Israel's original electoral system having been restored, Sharon was elected on a single ballot and led his party, the Likud, to an impressive achievement: forty members of the Knesset compared with the nineteen elected when Ehud Barak took power in 1999. It took Sharon nearly a month to put together a majority coalition of sixty-six members of the Knesset.

Sharon's major coalition partner was Shinuy, a secularist, middle-class party, which now had fifteen seats. It was joined by two right-wing parties: the National Religious Party and the National Union. The Labor Party was reduced to nineteen seats and chose to remain outside the coalition.

These developments created a dissonance between the platform Sharon presented on the eve of his reelection and the position held by a sizable portion of the coalition and of the Likud's members of the Knesset. During his first term Sharon had maintained a considerable degree of ambiguity regarding a political settlement with the Palestinians. He spoke in favor of settlement, and of his readiness for "painful concessions" to reach it, but refrained from any elaboration on the nature and scope of such concessions. He nurtured the dialogue with the Bush administration but maintained a parallel dialogue with the leadership of the West Bank and Gaza settlers. This latter dialogue, and the determination he showed in fighting the Palestinian Authority, raised questions about the nature of his true position. Did Sharon seek to please all parties? Did he cling to his traditional positions while couching them in softer rhetoric? Or did he come to the conclusion that painful concessions were indeed inevitable—but that he should not play his hand too soon?

As the election date approached, Sharon's position grew more concrete. He announced his acceptance of the idea of a Palestinian state and held on to that position even when it was rejected by the Likud's Party Center. The most complete public articulation of Sharon's position took place on December 4, 2002, in a speech to a national security conference in Herzliya. Regarding the American plan (as distinguished from the Road Map) the prime minister said:

In the second phase of President Bush's outline, Israel will enable the establishment of a Palestinian state within provisional boundaries coinciding with Areas A and B [portions of the West Bank under the Oslo Accords] with the exception of vital security areas. A Palestinian state would be completely demilitarized. It would be permitted to have police and domestic security forces equipped with light weapons. Israel would continue to control all entry and exit points of the Palestinian state and its air space. It would not be permitted to enter into agreements or alliances with Israel's enemies. In the final phase of President Bush's outline, a negotiation would begin for determining the final status of the Palestinian state and its borders. As I have emphasized, we will not move to this phase before a proven state of quieter relations, a change in Palestinian patterns of governance, and an even stronger coexistence are established.

The tensions and contradictions inherent in Sharon's position, the composition of his own party and coalition, and his relationship with George W. Bush could be managed only as long as two essential elements of the status quo remained: the uncertainty concerning the war in Iraq and Arafat's hegemonic position in Palestinian politics. Once the war in Iraq was formally concluded and Arafat acceded to U.S. pressure to appoint Mahmud Abbas as the Palestinian Authority's prime minister, the situation was transformed. From Washington's perspective, the groundwork had been laid for a resumption of the Israeli-Palestinian negotiations. It also became politically important to calm the Israeli-Palestinian arena, and therefore to be able to present the anticipated breakthrough as an American achievement and a by-product of the war in Iraq.

Sharon, in turn, was busy preparing Israel's political system and public opinion for the concessions that would have to be made once the Bush administration launched the effort to resume the Israeli-Palestinian negotiations. The prime minister's efforts were conducted through a maze of political and verbal maneuvers. Politically, he managed to avoid a head-on collision with the settlers and their allies. Rhetorically, he was careful to balance statements concerning anticipated concessions with contradictory pronouncements. And yet, in word and deed (including the adoption of the Road Map), he led Israel—albeit grudgingly—in a

clear direction, toward an interim agreement predicated on the establishment of a provisional Palestinian state and linked to a subsequent
agreement on the permanent borders and status of that state.

On April 13, 2003, *Ha'aretz* published a particularly significant
interview of Sharon by the columnist Ari Shavit. This was Sharon's
first public statement going beyond vague general references to painful
concessions. Sharon's message, moreover, was embedded in a set of
arguments that ran against the grain of both his image and his heritage.
Among other things, he said:

> I think that this [idea of two states for two peoples and the parti-
> tion of the Land of Israel west of the Jordan] is going to happen.
> The situation must be viewed in a realistic fashion: at the end
> of the day there will be a Palestinian state. I look at things pri-
> marily from our perspective. I do not think that we should con-
> trol another people and manage its life. I don't think we have the
> strength for this. It is a very heavy burden on the public and raises
> heavy moral and economic problems.

He went on to say:

> I am determined to make a true effort to reach a true agreement.
> I think that those who saw this awesome entity called the state
> of Israel taking shape perhaps have a better understanding of
> things and a better understanding of the road to a solution. I
> therefore think that this task is for my generation to fulfill. . . .
> I am seventy-five, I have no political ambitions beyond my current
> position. And I regard it as a goal and a purpose to bring peace
> and security to this nation. I will therefore invest great efforts. I
> believe that this is something I should leave [as a legacy]: to try
> to come to an agreement.

On April 16, Sharon once again took a new position in an interview
granted to two other journalists, Nahum Bar-nea and Shimon Shiffer.[11]
But on May 26, having agreed (with reservations) to the Road Map and
having absorbed sharp criticism from the right, Sharon dug in further
with his moral and ideological justification. "It is important to come to
a political settlement," he said to the Likud caucus in the Knesset. "The
idea that one could hold . . . Palestinians under occupation is hard for

Israel. . . . What is happening now is that three million Palestinians are kept under occupation. In my mind this is bad for Israel, for the Palestinians, for Israel's economy. Do you want to stay permanently in Jenin, in Nablus, in Ramallah, and in Bethlehem?"[12]

These developments in Israel were matched by a parallel set of developments in the Palestinian Authority. The United States reached the conclusion that it could not force Arafat's removal and decided to settle on the formation of a cabinet headed by Mahmud Abbas. This cabinet would reduce Arafat's direct control and create an additional power center with an aim of promoting three interrelated tasks: political reform and a campaign against corruption, renewal of the negotiations with Israel, and (as a prerequisite) combating terrorism.

Washington promoted its candidates for key positions in Abbas's cabinet. These were Salam Fayyad, as minister of finance (to advance financial efficiency and accountability), and Muhammad Dahlan, who was seen as the person with the ability to rebuild the Palestinian Authority's security apparatus and use it effectively against terrorism.

Abbas's cabinet was formed in late April. Washington's pressure led the Israeli cabinet to give conditional endorsement of the Road Map on May 25 and to a show of Arab and international support in conferences at Sharm al-Sheikh and Aqaba on June 3 and 4, respectively. Also in June, the World Economic Forum held an economic conference in Jordan in which Arabs and Israelis took part. These moves were designed to help Abbas through a transitional period during which he had to establish his legitimacy and harness the resources that would enable him to act as an effective negotiating partner with Israel.

But the edifice constructed in April and May collapsed in the summer of 2003. In the territories of the Palestinian Authority, a de facto alliance between Yasser Arafat and Hamas was created to obstruct Abbas and the U.S. plan. Arafat had no intention of becoming a "symbolic figure" who was powerless and "irrelevant." He fought for control of the security apparatus and financial resources. Hamas signed a cease-fire (*hudna*) with the Palestinian Authority but was determined to undermine the new diplomatic efforts by using the method that had proven so effective in the 1990s—terrorist acts in Israel proper. Sharon's government, never quite enthusiastic about the Road Map, continued to fight

Hamas through "targeted killings," among other ways. It complained—correctly—that Abbas's government had failed to take on the terrorist infrastructure. In June 2003 a new vicious cycle emerged, as terrorist acts by Hamas were followed by Israeli preemptive action, and vice versa. The Bush administration found itself ever more deeply immersed in Iraq, and its senior echelons significantly reduced their investment of time and attention in the Israeli-Palestinian arena.

In September 2003 Abbas resigned. Arafat nominated Abu Alaa to replace him. If Abbas and Muhammad Dahlan were seen from May to September as the alternative to Arafat's erstwhile domination of Palestinian politics, Abu Alaa and another security chief, Jabril Rajub, were conjured up by Arafat in September as the manifestation of his success in overcoming yet another adversity.

In mid-September, after a new cycle of suicide bombings and targeted killings, the Israeli cabinet decided "in principle" to expel Arafat from the West Bank. It was a declaratory act, allowing Sharon—should he decide at some future point to expel Arafat—to do so without having to convene his cabinet and obtain its approval. The decision was a compromise between those right-wing members of the cabinet and coalition who felt that Arafat's immediate expulsion was indispensable to any progress, and another group, headed by Sharon himself, who realized that expulsion would not be acceptable to the Bush administration. Israeli security forces effectively kept Arafat imprisoned in the Muqata'ah, but his position was enhanced by manifestations of Palestinian and international solidarity.

It is hardly surprising that the war in Iraq failed to break the Israeli-Palestinian deadlock. Whatever the war's long-term effects may be, it failed to create an instant functioning political order in Iraq or to transform political patterns in the larger region. The Bush administration found itself mired in Iraq, its will and ability to sustain the Road Map launched in April 2003 seriously curtailed. In the absence of U.S. chaperoning, the Road Map was doomed: Arafat and the Islamic organizations were determined to block it; and Sharon endorsed it without real conviction or enthusiasm but rather as another compliance with Washington's wishes. He was subsequently criticized by several prominent Israelis, among them the chief of staff of the IDF, for failing to extend real support to Abbas. And so, three years after the outbreak of violence on September 28, 2000, the parties were still engaged in an all-too-familiar vicious cycle without any apparent exit.

SHARON'S ABOUT-FACE AND THE DISENGAGEMENT FROM GAZA 2003–05

The stalemate of the summer and fall of 2003 was broken just months later when Sharon decided to withdraw unilaterally from the Gaza Strip and dismantle all the Israeli settlements in that region as well as four small settlements in the West Bank. This was a historic decision by any standard, one that was made all the more surprising and dramatic by the fact that its author was in many respects the architect and builder of Israel's settlement project, a leader who just recently had stated that "Netzarim [a settlement in the Gaza Strip] was as important as Tel Aviv."

Sharon's decision was soon converted into a series of steps and measures that reshaped Israeli politics and had a profound impact on the Israeli-Palestinian relationship.

Having made the decision late in 2003, Sharon informed the Bush administration and the president of Egypt, which had held the Gaza Strip before the June 1967 war. Only a small circle of Israeli confidants were initially briefed (the chief of staff of the IDF, General Moshe Ya'alon, complained in his memoirs that it was only in January 2004 that the minister of defense, Shaul Mofaz, briefed him on the full extent of Sharon's plan).

The Israeli public had been prepared, in stages, for the revolutionary change. On December 1, 2003, Ehud Olmert, the deputy prime minister, substituted for Sharon at the annual memorial service for David Ben-Gurion. Without prior consultation with Sharon, Olmert (who had a sense of the impending change) delivered a dovish speech and quoted Ben-Gurion's own statements in support of territorial compromise and concessions. Olmert's speech caused a political tempest, but Sharon refrained from criticizing him in private or in public. Encouraged, Olmert gave an interview to the influential columnist Nahum Barnea that was published on December 5 under the headline "Olmert for a unilateral withdrawal." Finally, Sharon himself spoke at the Herzliya Conference on December 18 and stated briefly that in a few months, should the Palestinians continue to fail to implement their part of the Road Map, "Israel will initiate a unilateral measure of disengagement from the Palestinians." He further stated that a disengagement plan would be implemented in close coordination with the United States, and that it essentially was a security measure designed to minimize Israeli-Palestinian friction and maximize Israeli security. It would consist, he said, of redeployment of the IDF and some Israeli settlements (he did not mention Gaza specifically).

The Israeli public was first informed of the full scope of Sharon's plan on February 2, 2004, when another prominent columnist, Yoel Marcus of Ha'aretz, reported on a conversation with Sharon, who told him that thirteen settlements in Gaza and four small settlements at the northern edge of the West Bank—along with their 7,500 settlers—were to be evacuated. During the next eighteen months, events unfolded on several parallel tracks.

In the Israeli political arena, Sharon faced fierce opposition within his own Likud Party and coalition and from the settlers. He was able to get his plan endorsed by the cabinet and the Knesset but could not get the support of the Likud. A group of rebels was organized inside the Likud that was eventually joined by Benjamin Netanyahu, the minister of finance in Sharon's cabinet, who ultimately resigned his post in protest in August 2005.

Sharon's domestic political predicament was exacerbated by a series of criminal investigations and extensive media coverage of charges of corruption and financial wrongdoing by himself and his two sons. His critics, headed by leaders of the settlers' movement, claimed that his sudden shift of orientation was an attempt to please the liberal media and judicial establishment.

In February 2005 Shimon Peres, as chairman of the Labor Party, joined Sharon's coalition and became deputy prime minister, thereby providing Sharon with the requisite parliamentary support for proceeding with his plan.

The second major effort was invested in an effort to obtain from the Bush administration some compensation or reward for a painful step that could be seen as also representing progress toward implementing Washington's own vision of an Israeli-Palestinian settlement. Sharon's decision to withdraw from four small settlements in the West Bank resulted from strong pressure by the Bush Administration that wanted the disengagement to be seen not merely as an attempt by Israel to rid itself of a problem (namely, Gaza), but as a step on the road to resolution of the Israeli-Palestinian process.

This effort resulted in a letter from President Bush to Sharon in April 2004 and a series of tacit understandings between the national security adviser, Condoleezza Rice, and Sharon's chief of staff, Dov Weissglas.

Several elements in Bush's letter were seen as important achievements for Israeli diplomacy: acceptance of Israel's large settlement blocks in the West Bank as "faits accompli," an allusion to continued support of Israel's "nuclear ambiguity," acceptance of the principle of Palestinian refugees' return to a future Palestinian state rather than to Israel itself, and a statement promising that "existing arrangements regarding the patrolling of air space, territorial waters and land passages of the West Bank and the Gaza Strip will continue." The president reiterated his commitment to his own vision, outlined in June 2002 for a Palestinian democracy, and to the Road Map, and he committed that the United States "will do its utmost to prevent any other plans," a reference to an internationally imposed settlement.

A parallel effort was invested in coming to an understanding with Egypt and the Palestinian Authority. Arafat's death in November 2004 and the emergence of a new leadership composed of Abbas as president and Salam Fayyad as prime minister of the Palestinian Authority cast the PA in a new light and as a potential partner. Sharon stayed with his original concept of a unilateral withdrawal from Gaza, but partial cooperation with the Palestinian Authority could be tried (if only half-heartedly).

One key issue to be dealt with by all three partners was access to and from the Gaza Strip in the aftermath of Israel's withdrawal. The Palestinian Authority was expected to establish its control over the area and hopefully pursue the same policies it was pursuing in the West Bank: an accountable and transparent administration and a serious effort to combat terrorism by a U.S.-trained and -supported security service. Still, Hamas had a powerful infrastructure in the Gaza Strip, and the area was inhabited by other radical groups; Sharon and his team were preoccupied with the prospect of men and weapons being smuggled into the strip. The tension between a genuine desire to disengage from the Gaza Strip and Israel's security concerns was inherent in the disengagement plan.

For a while Israel's decisionmakers agonized over the possibility of actually retaining the "Philadelphi Axis," a twelve-kilometer-long, nearly one-kilometer-wide strip along Egypt's border with Gaza. Doing so would be the most effective way of fighting the anticipated smuggling of weapons into Gaza. However, the IDF soldiers stationed there would by definition become sitting ducks, and so the idea was abandoned. Under the government's plan, goods and vehicles would continue to move through the Erez crossing on the Israeli border; the Rafah Crossing on the Egyptian border would continue to be used for crossings by individuals. Rafah would be managed by the Palestinian Authority but monitored by a European team; remote sensing by Israel and Egypt would prevent smuggling from the Sinai. Israel would continue to provide water and electric power to Gaza.

In Israel preparations were made for the evacuation: a legal and administrative infrastructure was put in place and the IDF was prepared with a view to minimizing friction and violence. For the settlers, the evacuation from Gaza was calamitous in its own right as well as a test case for the larger issue of possible future withdrawals from the West Bank, and massive, violent resistance had to be taken into account. The chief of staff of the IDF, General Ya'alon, was seen by Sharon as opposed to the disengagement and was denied the traditional fourth year of his tenure. He was replaced, before the withdrawal, by General Dan Halutz, a former head of the Air Force.

An effort to please the liberal part of the Israeli establishment may well have been part of Sharon's calculus. He was, after all a shrewd politician, and the corruption investigations weighed heavily on his mind (one of his sons would in fact spend time in jail for breaking the law governing political fundraising), but this was probably not his principal motivation. There had been indications during Sharon's first years in power that his outlook on Israel's national security and Israel's future were undergoing a change. This process matured in 2003 when Sharon reached the zenith of his power and popularity. To the Israeli public, Sharon was the leader who defeated the second intifada by retaking military control of main cities in the West Bank and releasing Israel from one of its darkest hours. For General Ya'alon, this was the perfect moment for quashing the Palestinian leadership and perpetuating the status quo. For a transformed Sharon, however, looking at the scene from a position of ultimate responsibility at an age at which leaders think about the sum total of their career and their place in history, this was a moment for consolidating Israel's position vis-à-vis the Palestinians and the Palestinian issue. Sharon had defeated the intifada, but he came to the conclusion that the status quo was untenable. He accepted in fact the Israeli left's demographic argument, namely, that Israel could not hold on to the West Bank and Gaza and also keep its Jewish identity. He also knew that at some point his original policy and that of the Bush administration were bound to diverge. George W. Bush detested Arafat and was willing to support Sharon's campaign against him, but it appeared that Bush would support the quest for independence by a reformed Palestinian Authority led by men like Abbas and Salam Fayyad.[13]

The old Sharon did not vanish completely. He was dubious and skeptical of the Palestinian leaders and did not believe that he could negotiate with them a durable, final-status agreement that would satisfy his definition of Israel's needs and interests. He therefore chose unilateral action. Had he not been defeated ultimately by disease, he would probably have continued in the same vein in the West Bank, although not with a full withdrawal. In his view this arrangement would not have been the definitive final-status agreement that so many people and policymakers had been looking for, but it would have been a solid, stable long-term arrangement that would have consolidated Israel's relationship with the Palestinians. Sharon the warrior would have exited the stage as Sharon the statesman.

The actual disengagement from Gaza (and the four West Bank settlements) was carried out in August and September 2005. It was a traumatic event for the settlers and their many supporters, but it was completed with relative calm.

Sharon's next step was implemented in Israel's domestic political arena. In November 2005 he left his long-time political home, the Likud, and formed a new party, Kadimah. Sharon carried with him a significant group of Likud parliamentarians and also was joined by Shimon Peres and a group of Labor politicians. New elections were called for March 2006, and the formation of Kadimah's candidate list was an opportunity for Sharon to bring several new faces into Israeli politics. The new party was to provide Sharon with the wherewithal for the next phase of withdrawal and to provide the Israeli political system with a stabilizing center. The polls predicted forty seats for Kadimah in the coming elections. But in December 2005 and again in January 2006, Sharon was defeated by his own body when two successive strokes sank him into a coma.

Another important event took place in January 2006, when legislative elections in the Palestinian Authority gave Hamas a victory over the Fatah. Sharon had agreed to facilitate the holding of these elections under heavy pressure from the Bush administration. Ideology remained an important dimension of the latter's policy in the Middle East. From its perspective, having brought a democracy of sorts to Iraq and having supported the 2005 Cedar Revolution in Lebanon, the administration felt it imperative to bring democracy into Palestinian politics. The outcome was more of a Fatah defeat than a Hamas victory, but the immediate result was a split in Palestinian politics. Isma'il Haniyeh of Hamas became prime minister while Abbas remained president. A joint government collapsed in short order, and a year later, in June 2007, Hamas staged a bloody coup that forced the Fatah from power in Gaza. The Palestinian Authority was split between a West Bank governed by Abbas and Salam Fayyad, and a Gaza Strip ruled locally by a Hamas government and from Damascus by the "external" leadership of Hamas.

From a limited perspective of five years, Sharon's unilateral disengagement from Gaza seems at best a partial success. It did put an end to the problematic presence of both Israeli settlers and soldiers in a densely populated Palestinian area. It also demonstrated that a resolute, authoritative (and preferably right-wing or centrist) Israeli leader could stand up to the settler movement and its powerful lobby and implement withdrawal and dismantling of settlements. But as subsequent events amply demonstrated, Israel did not fully disengage from Gaza. The Gaza Strip then came under the local control of Hamas and other radical groups, but also under the influence of Iran and Syria. Rocket attacks from the Gaza Strip created a new front in the Israeli-Palestinian conflict, culminating in an Israeli military intervention (Operation Cast Lead) in December 2008 and January 2009. That operation, the siege of Gaza, and the Turkish flotilla incident (all described in detail in the next two chapters) caused serious damage to Israel's image in the world and exacerbated Israel's deteriorating relationship with Turkey. The relocation of the Jewish settlers from Gaza proved to be a problematic, protracted process, partly because of governmental ineptness and partly because of the settlers' decision to demonstrate with an eye to the future that any such evacuation was an inherently bad idea and bound to fail.

The limited success of a well-intentioned bold step derived from several sources. Unilateral withdrawal was not meant to be a stand-alone measure, and to be successful it had to be fitted into a larger settlement with a Palestinian partner. Sharon's physical collapse, his successor Olmert's limited success in the March 2006 elections, the Fatah's weakness, and Hamas's victory in the January 2006 Palestinian elections—as well as negative input by Iran and Syria—combined to keep Israel's withdrawal from Gaza as an isolated move and to turn the Gaza Strip into an active front in an ongoing conflict. Israel's cooperation with Egypt in dealing with the common challenge of Gaza was constrained both by inherent difficulties and the waning of Mubarak's regime.

These issues are the subject matter of a heated debate among both analysts and political advocates within Israel. Sharon's critics argue, among other things, that had the IDF and the settlements stayed in place, Hamas would not have taken control of the Gaza Strip. His defenders argue that the IDF had essentially been out of Gaza for more than a decade and that it kept a limited presence only to protect the settlements and their inhabitants. Hamas's takeover in June 2007 was an internal Palestinian matter in which the IDF would not have intervened, according to this argument. Be that as it may, the mixed results of the disengagement from Gaza reinforced the school of thought in Israel that has argued since Ehud Barak's departure from South Lebanon in 2000 that unilateralism in the Israeli-Arab context is a bad idea.

6
EHUD OLMERT AND THE
NEW NEW MIDDLE EAST

In the context of Arab-Israeli relations, the term "New Middle East" is associated primarily with the vision presented by Shimon Peres in the early 1990s of Arab-Israeli cooperation—once political peace had been achieved—in building the infrastructure and economic resources for the region to be able to support its swelling population in the coming decades. It was bitterly ironic that a decade later Israel came to confront a very different New Middle East, one defined by Iran's quest for regional hegemony, Turkey's return to the region's politics as an Islamist power, and the construction under Iran's leadership of an axis of resistance composed of Iran, Syria, Hizballah, and Hamas.

In Israel Ehud Olmert, Ariel Sharon's successor, won the March 2006 elections on a dovish platform (called the convergence plan, which envisioned a partial Israeli pullback from the West Bank), but in short order he was challenged by Hamas from Gaza and Hizballah from Lebanon, and he drifted into a problematic war in Lebanon that cast a shadow over the rest of his tenure and led to the shelving of the convergence plan. Olmert conducted another large-scale military operation in Gaza as well as two ultimately unsuccessful negotiations with Syria and the Palestinians before being forced into an early resignation.

Olmert, who had served as acting prime minister after Sharon's stroke and who headed Kadimah's list for the March elections, saw and cast himself as Sharon's successor in the full sense of the term. Like Sharon, he had completed a journey from the hard core of Israel's nationalist right wing to a full-fledged quest for a resolution of the

Israeli-Palestinian conflict. Under Olmert's leadership, Kadimah's platform included as one of its most essential components the convergence plan, which was a modified application to the West Bank of Sharon's disengagement project from Gaza. Olmert preferred a solution agreed upon with the Palestinian Authority, but failing that, envisaged a unilateral withdrawal from most of the West Bank and the dismantling of isolated settlements that did not belong to the three large settlement blocs that were to be left under Israeli control.

On the eve of Sharon's physical collapse, the polls estimated that under his leadership Kadimah would obtain forty (out of one hundred and twenty) seats in the Knesset. As the election campaign proceeded under Olmert's leadership, Kadimah lost ground and ended up with twenty-nine seats. Olmert formed a coalition with the Labor Party (with seventeen seats) as his major partner. Under the circumstances he was forced to offer Amir Peretz, Labor's leader, one of two major portfolios: Defense or Finance. Peretz built his career as head of the trade unions federation, and neither Olmert personally nor Israel's business community wanted him as minister of finance. Olmert's decision to offer Peretz the Defense Ministry and Peretz's decision to accept were soon proven to be grave errors of judgment.

Olmert formed his government on May 4, 2006. The convergence plan figured prominently in the new government's program. On May 23, Olmert traveled to Washington for his first meeting with George W. Bush in his new capacity. The personal relationship between the two leaders was and remained cordial, but Washington was not particularly enthusiastic about another unilateral plan; it preferred a negotiated settlement. Soon thereafter, however, both domestic and international deliberations over a major initiative on the Palestinian track were cut short by challenges from the Gaza Strip and south Lebanon.

As has been described in the previous chapter, Sharon's unilateral withdrawal from the Gaza Strip did not lead to full Israeli disengagement from Gaza, nor did it fully calm this arena of Palestinian-Israeli confrontation. During the twenty-one months that followed the completion of Israel's withdrawal (September 2005 to June 2007), the Gaza Strip under Hamas completed its separation from the West Bank, which remained under the Palestinian Authority's control. The January 2006

Palestinian parliamentary elections (forced by the Bush administration as part of its vision of a democratic Middle East) ended in a Hamas victory. The Palestinian national unity government that was formed, after Saudi mediation, in March 2007 collapsed just three months later, in June. Its collapse was immediately followed by a bloody takeover of the Gaza Strip by Hamas, while the Fatah retained its control of the West Bank.

During the same period violence erupted several times along Israel's new border with the Gaza Strip. These cycles of violence followed a familiar pattern. An effective security fence had been built in stages in earlier decades whose value had been demonstrated during the second intifada. But in the early 2000s, Hamas, the Islamic Jihad, and other radical groups in the Gaza Strip developed primitive short-range rockets (called Qassams, after the military wing of Hamas) that they fired at Israeli targets near the fence, particularly the town of Sderot. A typical cycle of violence would be triggered by the launching of Qassam rockets or mortar fire, Israeli retaliatory attacks, and Israeli sanctions on the movements of goods and people to and from the Gaza Strip. A cease-fire (*tahdi'ah*) was arranged in February 2005, but it was not fully effective and collapsed in 2006.

Developments took a different course further to the north, an arena shaped by the Israeli unilateral withdrawal from south Lebanon in 2000. Hizballah, the Shiite militia, and its Iranian and Syrian patrons saw and presented Israel's departure as vindication of the doctrine of resistance (*muqawamah*), which argued that by persisting in their resistance to Israel, the Arabs were bound to defeat it. Hizballah's leadership justified its refusal to disarm by claiming that the struggle was not over because Israel's withdrawal was not complete (even if it was coordinated with and sanctioned by the United Nations). Hizballah's specific argument was that Israel, by staying in the area known as Shaba Farms (where the borders of Israel, Lebanon, and Syria intersect), remained in occupation of sovereign Lebanese territory and that its military overflights were an infringement of the same sovereignty. During the early 2000s Hizballah was reinforced by the acceleration of Iran's quest for regional hegemony and by the change of leadership in Syria. Hafiz al-Asad had facilitated Iran's support for Hizballah as part of his strategic alliance with Tehran and had cultivated Hizballah as one of Syria's own assets in Lebanon. But while Hafiz al-Asad had treated Hasan Nasrallah, Hizballah's leader, as a client, Asad's son and successor, Bashar, treated Nasrallah as an esteemed, not to say admired, peer.

Hizballah had tested the new rules of the game set by Israel's withdrawal by abducting three Israeli soldiers in October 2000. Ehud Barak, Israel's prime minister at the time, preoccupied by the outbreak of the second intifada and the resulting confrontation with Israel's Arab minority, decided not to respond to the provocation. This policy was continued with some modification by his successor, Sharon, in the face of several additional provocations by Hizballah. Sharon settled on limited punitive raids on Syrian targets in Lebanon and (once) in Syria, signaling that he saw Syria as ultimately responsible for Hizballah's activities. These steps also reflected Sharon's own determination to focus on the Palestinian issue and not to be drawn into a serious entanglement in the north. More significantly, Sharon's decision not to take direct action allowed Hizballah to build an impressive arsenal of long-, medium-, and short-range missiles, as well as an elaborate military infrastructure in south Lebanon that extended to the border fence with Israel.

Hizballah's posture as a resistance movement was essential for its domestic Lebanese agenda. It is a multifaceted entity: a Lebanese Shiite movement and party, a paramilitary (increasingly military) force, a terrorist organization, and an instrument of the Iranian regime. After 2000 it could have transformed itself into a political party and sought to increase its and the Shiite community's share in Lebanon's political system. But this was not its agenda and intent. Furthermore, Hizballah's arsenal of rockets and missiles was, particularly after 2003, part of Iran's deterrence against an Israeli or American attack on its nuclear installations. Keeping active, though discontinuous, "resistance" against Israel was designed to justify Hizballah's refusal to disarm and its ongoing military buildup.

These issues were internationalized by the Bush administration's decision after 2003 to defend Lebanon's sovereignty and democracy against Iran, Syria, and their Lebanese clients. It was both an aspect of the administration's anti-Syrian campaign and part of its quest to democratize the Middle East and to demonstrate how the war in Iraq had contributed to this effort. In September 2004—in league with France and with Saudi Arabia's support—the United States led the Security Council to adopt Resolution 1559, which called for, among other things, the departure of all foreign (namely, Iranian and Syrian) troops from Lebanon and for the disarming of all militias (namely, Hizballah).

The conflict over Lebanon's future was intensified in 2005. On February 14, Rafiq al-Hariri, the former prime minister who was a close ally of Saudi Arabia and a staunch opponent of Syria, was killed by a car bomb in Beirut. Under heavy U.S pressure, Syria announced that it was withdrawing its troops from Lebanon (the withdrawal was completed on April 26). On March 8 Hizballah and Syria's other allies staged a massive demonstration in Beirut. It was eclipsed six days later by a larger demonstration organized by a Christian, Sunni, and Druze coalition. That coalition (called the March 14 coalition, after the date of the demonstration) won the parliamentary elections in May (it obtained seventy-two of one hundred and twenty-eight seats), and Fouad Siniora formed a new government. The victorious coalition chose to include one minister identified with Hizballah in the new cabinet.

This course of events was followed by an exacerbation of Hizballah's attacks on Israel, beginning in May 2005 and continuing intermittently through the first half of 2006. Hizballah attacked both civilian and military targets in northern Israel and invested a particular effort in abducting Israeli soldiers to force Israel into an exchange of prisoners. The IDF prepared two alternative plans for dealing with the prospect of a major confrontation with Hizballah: a massive air raid or a large-scale ground operation.[1]

It was against this background that a two-front crisis erupted in June and July 2006. On June 25 a Hamas squad penetrated Israel's territory through a tunnel dug under the fence from the Gaza Strip, ambushed a tank, killed two Israeli soldiers, and abducted another, Corporal Gilad Shalit.[2] On July 12 Hizballah ambushed an Israeli patrol traveling on the Israeli side of the border fence with Lebanon. Three soldiers were killed and two others were abducted (as it turned out later, they also were killed). An Israeli tank chasing the abductors crossed the border into Lebanon and hit a land mine, which killed five more soldiers. As a diversionary act, Hizballah also launched Katyusha rockets into Israel.

The Israeli government decided on a swift, powerful response. Hizballah's provocation was far-reaching in its own right; coming in the immediate aftermath of the abduction from Gaza, it was perceived as part of a concerted effort to test and undermine the new prime minister. The IDF recommended, and the cabinet endorsed, a massive airstrike against a large number of Hizballah and Hizballah-related targets. Hizballah's attack and Israel's response marked the beginning of a war that ended thirty-two days later, on August 14, when both sides accepted a cease-fire predicated on Security Council Resolution 1701.

In the course of the war, Israel's air force destroyed most of Hizballah's long- and medium-range rockets and missiles, Hizballah's headquarters and the surrounding buildings in the Dahya quarter in south Beirut, and several other bases and command posts in the Beqaa Valley and other parts of Lebanon. The Israeli campaign, however, failed to destroy most of the short-range and some of the medium-range Katyusha rockets that Hizballah had fired into Israel at the rate of at least a hundred a day, hitting several towns (including the major city of Haifa), and wreaking havoc in northern Israel. The IDF refrained initially from large-scale ground activity and encountered fierce, effective resistance when it finally did so. Only on August 9 did the Israeli cabinet approve a large-scale ground operation designed to conquer south Lebanon, cleanse it of Hizballah, and put an end to rocket-launching. The operation was begun but not completed due to the decision to accept Security Council Resolution 1701 (adopted by the Security Council on August 11) and a resulting cease-fire. During the war one hundred and twenty Israeli soldiers and forty-two Israeli civilians were killed. Hizballah lost between six hundred and seven hundred soldiers. A controversy surrounds the number of Lebanese civilians killed, with one estimate putting the number at about one thousand. Significant physical damage was inflicted on both countries.

The 2006 Lebanon war was a significant event in several respects, beyond the immediate deaths and destruction. It was a war between a powerful army and a semi-military guerrilla organization but also was a war by proxy between Israel and Iran and to some extent Israel and Syria. More broadly, it was a contest between Iran's axis of resistance and its regional and international foes. The Bush administration and Iran's Arab rivals were hoping for an Israeli victory and a resounding defeat for Hizballah and its patrons.[3] Israel's failure to achieve a swift, clear victory was thus an achievement for the latter. Also, as time wore on and Arab opinion was agitated by satellite television stations (al-Jazeera in particular), Arab regimes that had tacitly supported the Israeli operation were forced to denounce it.

Israel's public opinion and political system were rattled by the war's management and mixed results, the failure to achieve a clear victory, the military and civilian casualties, and the impact of Hizballah's rocket and missile fire on the civilian population. Under public pressure, Prime Minister Olmert appointed a commission of inquiry to examine the war's conduct. The Winograd Commission published a highly critical interim report in April 2007 and a somewhat milder report at the year's end. The commission decided to refrain from making "personal recommendations" but chided Israel's political and military leadership for going into war without a clear plan, for failing to opt for a ground operation as soon as it realized that the war could not be won from the air, or, alternatively, to end the war much sooner with more or less the same results.

The war's two main achievements were a restoration of Israel's deterrence (as of this writing in late September 2011, Hizballah had refrained from attacking Israel) and the adoption of Security Council Resolution 1701. That resolution reaffirmed Resolution 1559, adopted in 2004, and called for the extension of the Lebanese state's sovereignty and military presence to the southern part of the country, reinforced the UN peacekeeping force in Lebanon (UNIFIL), and called for an end to the smuggling of weapons systems into Lebanon. As time went by this last call turned out to be quite meaningless. Iran and Syria first replenished Hizballah's depleted military stocks and then increased its arsenal dramatically. Hizballah's firepower is now superior not only to that of the Lebanese army but to that of many other states in the region.

For Israel (and indeed for the United States and other states engaged in similar conflicts), the 2006 conflict was yet another demonstration of the difficulties inherent in the conduct of "asymmetrical warfare" against a nonstate militia that is embedded in a civilian population. Such a war is not only difficult to wage without hurting civilians but also to conclude with a clear-cut victory. Israel had done well against its enemies in conventional wars, but it now faced two new challenges: Iran's quest for a nuclear arsenal and the new threat posed by missiles and rockets in the hands of nearby enemies. Israel had been attacked by Iraqi missiles in 1991 and by Katyusha rockets from Lebanon, but these now seemed as minor challenges compared to the ones presented by the arsenals of Iran, Syria, Hizballah, and Hamas.

Nor did the war resolve Israel's underlying problem in Lebanon. Israel's northern neighbor was a failed state where Hizballah, supported by Iran and Syria, kept corroding the state's authority and, as time went on, proved to be increasingly more powerful than the state and its army. At the same time, Hizballah was a legitimate part of the political system and the government. If Hizballah were to attack again, how would Israel plan its response, taking into account the lessons of the 2006 war? To neutralize Hizballah's rockets and missiles, Israel would have to conquer large parts of Lebanon (well beyond the south) and inflict heavy damage on innocent civilians and civilian installations. Or, should the IDF listen to the politicians and experts who argued during the 2006 war (and more vociferously in its wake) that Lebanon was itself becoming an enemy state that was being taken over by Hizballah and therefore that Israel should destroy Lebanon's infrastructure if Hizballah again fired its arsenal at Israel. Alternatively, should Israel target Hizballah's two regional patrons, Iran and Syria, who were cynically blurring the distinction between Hizballah and the Lebanese state? This last option raised the profound question of whether Israel wanted to compound matters by getting into a regional war.

In the short run, Lebanon's Prime Minister Siniora, his government, and the March 14 coalition survived the war's immediate outcome and were temporarily reinforced by Security Council Resolution 1701. Hizballah gained credibility locally and throughout the region by virtue of its ability to stand up to the Israeli military, but it also came under criticism for dragging Lebanon into war and destruction. This criticism was so great that in one of his speeches Hizballah's leader, Hasan Nasrallah, admitted that had he known in advance what the attack of July 12 would lead to, he would not have launched it.[4] In subsequent years, U.S. and French support for the March 14 coalition and Lebanon's sovereignty wore thin, the March 14 coalition itself began to fray, and Hizballah's aggrandizement and creeping takeover of the Lebanese state were renewed in full.

In Israel Prime Minister Olmert's authority was badly damaged by the war, but he survived it. Defense Minister Peretz, the IDF's chief of staff, and three other senior officers resigned their positions, however, because of criticism of their conduct of the war. One important byprod-uct of the 2006 Lebanon war was not immediately visible but acquired significance over time. Olmert and the leaders of Israel's national secu-rity establishment reached the conclusion that the threat posed by the Iran-Syria-Hizballah axis had to be dismantled and that the best way to start dealing with it would be to pull Syria out of it by renewing the Israeli-Syrian negotiation that had collapsed in 2000. Olmert's interest in renewing "the Syrian option" was reinforced by his realization that his convergence plan for the West Bank had to be shelved.

NEGOTIATION WITH SYRIA AND
DESTRUCTION OF ITS REACTOR

A decade of peace negotiations between Israel and Syria had ended in March 2000 after the failure of the Clinton-Asad summit in Geneva (see chapter 4). These negotiations were not renewed during the next seven years for a number of reasons. Hafiz al-Asad died in June 2000, and it took his son Bashar several years to consolidate his rule and build his authority. Ariel Sharon, who became Israel's prime minister in 2001, was simply not interested in renewing the negotiations with Syria. As we saw, he was focused on the Palestinian issue and did not want to spend time, attention, and political capital on a track he did not quite believe in. Sharon grew to accept the notion of territorial concessions to the Palestinians, but he did not want to withdraw from the Golan Heights. His attitude was reinforced by his senior ally, George W Bush, who, as a result of the war in Iraq, became increasingly hostile to Syria and its president. Bush was in no position to use force against Syria, but he did use a UN-sponsored investigation of Hariri's assassination and the prospect of an international tribunal to besiege and isolate the Syrian president. It was this growing isolation that led Bashar al-Asad to send messages and emissaries to Sharon in an effort to renew the negotia-tions. Sharon rebuffed these initiatives.[5]

Upon taking office, Olmert's perspective on Syria was similar to Sha-ron's, but when Olmert was contemplating the idea of reviving negotia-tions with Syria after the war with Lebanon, he had to take into account Bush's attitude. Asad clearly saw the renewal of negotiations with Israel as a way to break out of the diplomatic isolation imposed by the United

States and, to a lesser extent, by France and its European allies. Olmert raised the issue with Bush, who told him that he was opposed to it but that he would not stand in Olmert's way. Olmert then chose to use Turkey as the intermediary. Turkey, under the leadership of Prime Minister Recep Tayyip Erdoğan, was pursuing a policy defined by Foreign Minister Ahmet Davutoğlu as "zero conflict." Rebuffed in its quest to join the European Union, Turkey instead was turning its focus eastward and building a position of influence in its immediate environment. Part of this policy was the termination of long-standing conflicts with such neighbors as Syria. Bashar al-Asad was anxious to collaborate, and a good, eventually close, relationship was built between the two countries and the two leaders. Turkey also was quite eager to become a facilitator and a mediator between Israel and Syria. It was a suitable role for a country seeking regional influence, and it must have been flattering to fill a role performed in the past solely by the United States and denied to such powers as Russia and France.

Turkey's mediation between Israel and Syria began in February 2007 as a secret channel. By agreeing to the format of mediation, Olmert went a long way toward the Syrian position. Syria's traditional view of negotiations regarded procedure as a matter of substance. In several rounds of negotiations during the 1990s, for example, Hafiz al-Asad insisted that Syrian negotiators meet with Israeli counterparts only in an American presence. A direct bilateral negotiation was, to him, a form of diplomatic normalization that he was not willing to authorize at that stage. This rule was broken only once or twice during a decade of give-and-take. Conversely, his willingness to upgrade the level of the negotiations in December 1999 and to dispatch his foreign minister to meet with Israel's prime minister was seen at the time, correctly, as a major breakthrough. In the preparatory talks that preceded the February 2007 negotiations, his son, Bashar, insisted that the Syrian-Israeli track must not begin with a direct negotiation, that third-party mediation precede any negotiation, and that only when he became persuaded that mediation was likely to lead to an agreement acceptable to him, would he agree to direct contact. Since Olmert was providing Asad with a significant dividend by renewing talks in the face of American displeasure, he could have insisted on a different format, but he chose not to.

The rounds of mediation were conducted in Ankara, with Turkish diplomats shuttling and passing messages and texts between the two teams, who did not meet in the same room. This exercise did not remain secret because both parties had an interest in advertising it. Bashar al-Asad wanted to break out of a diplomatic siege imposed by the United States, and Ehud Olmert wanted to send the Israeli public a message of hope during a bleak period. In mid-April 2008, Olmert began to speak of his negotiation with Syria in a series of press interviews on the eve of the Passover holiday. Olmert emphasized that the dialogue was serious and that he was fully aware of the repercussions of a potential agreement: "I only say one thing and am saying it with full seriousness and intent: there is room to conduct a process that will produce an Israeli-Syrian agreement. The Syrians know that I want it. They know my expectations and I think I know theirs." This was in fact a meaningful formulation. It was Olmert's way of conveying to his Syrian interlocutors, in public as well as in private, that he accepted Rabin's "deposit," during the 1990s, of a full Israeli withdrawal from the Golan Heights.

Shortly thereafter, on May 21, 2008, Israel and Syria announced simultaneously but separately that they were holding indirect talks that could develop into a full-fledged negotiation. The timing of the announcement may have been influenced by Olmert's mounting personal legal problems that led to his resignation four months later.

Between the opening of the Israeli-Syrian indirect negotiation in February 2007 and the May 2008 announcement, a startling development took place. On September 6, 2007, the Israeli air force destroyed a nuclear reactor that North Korea was building in Kibar in northeastern Syria. Much has yet to be revealed about this episode, but there is little doubt that the North Koreans were building a reactor modeled on the one they used to develop their own nuclear weapons. When Israeli intelligence obtained clear proof of the enterprise, Olmert turned to George W. Bush and suggested that the United States destroy the reactor. When the Israeli government understood that the United States might not take action and that, in any event, making the decision would take a long time, Israel decided to act on its own. It was a risky operation but it proceeded with relative ease. Compared with Israel's destruction of a reactor in Iraq in 1981 or with the prospect of attacking nuclear sites in

Iran, the Syrian reactor was an easy target, well within range of Israeli bombers. Furthermore, since Asad concealed the reactor operation from his own armed forces, the site was not defended. The real question was what Asad's response would be.[6]

Crisis management in the aftermath of the destruction of the Syrian reactor was facilitated by a convergence of interests. Syria, Israel, and the United States—each for its own reasons—were interested in minimizing news coverage and attention. Asad understood well that extensive news coverage would increase the pressure on him to retaliate. While he was willing to take bold action and collaborate with North Korea in building the reactor, he displayed impressive self-control by deciding that a military response did not serve Syria's interests. His decision was reinforced by the embarrassment of having been caught in illicit cooperation with a member of Bush's axis of evil. For its part, the Israeli leadership was anxious to help Asad save face and evade the pressure to retaliate. Israel therefore imposed and kept total silence, domestically. The Bush administration was preoccupied with the North Korean angle of the affair; it was hoping to reach an agreement with North Korea on that country's own nuclear arsenal and worried that the conservative critics of such an agreement would argue that Pyongyang could not be trusted because while it was negotiating the dismantling of its own arsenal it was busy exporting nuclear technology to other countries. The official U.S. silence was kept well into 2008. Information about the Syrian reactor and its destruction was first released by U.S. officials and was then amplified by reports issued by the International Atomic Energy Agency in Vienna. Israel has kept its official silence to date. Consequently while the fact of Israel's destruction of the Syrian reactor became known in a matter of days, official or semiofficial confirmation came much later.

Once the aftershocks of this episode had abated, the Turkish mediation was renewed. Its course reflected the change that had occurred in the Israeli-Syrian equation since 2000. Syria was still interested in regaining the Golan and in building a new relationship with the United States, but Israel was less interested in diplomatic normalization with Syria. As former U.S. diplomat Martin Indyk formulated it, the notion of territories for peace was replaced by the notion of "territories for strategic realignment."[7] In other words, while Syria still insisted on Israeli withdrawal to the lines of June 4, 1967 (possibly with a loose demarcation of these lines), Israel was less interested in an elaborate definition of what "normal peaceful relations" stood for and more interested in a Syrian undertaking to alter its relationship with Iran and Hamas. During the final phase of their mediation, the Turks passed questions and answers between the parties seeking to clarify their respective positions. Syria gave a list of six sites in the Golan Heights area and wanted to establish that the future border between the two countries would be drawn in reference to those sites. Israel, in turn, wanted specific and concrete answers regarding Syria's future relationship with Iran and Hizballah.

It was against this backdrop that Olmert traveled on December 22, 2008, to Ankara for a decisive meeting hosted by Prime Minister Erdoğan. If all went well, Syria's foreign minister, Walid Muallem, was to join the meeting and a direct negotiation would be launched. But all did not go well, and Muallem failed to arrive. The Syrians were not pleased with the answer they received to their question about lines on the map, but first and foremost they were deterred by the fact that Olmert had resigned in August because of the scandals he faced, and at that point headed a caretaker government. Something like this had happened before (for instance in the negotiations with Peres in 1995–96) and it repeated itself in 2008. Syrians (and Palestinians and others) prefer to conclude agreements with incoming rather than with departing heads of governments. The Ankara meeting had another effect as well. Two days after returning from Ankara, Olmert launched Operation Cast Lead, the large-scale military offensive against Hamas in Gaza. Erdoğan was furious. He felt that he might be portrayed as an accomplice. Turkey's relationship with Israel had been sliding anyway, and Erdoğan, an Islamist sympathizer of Hamas, who had expressed public support for this Palestinian organization, may have responded angrily in any event to Israel's attack, but the personal pique added fuel to the fire.

A FRESH ATTEMPT AT AN ISRAELI-PALESTINIAN SETTLEMENT

Once a cease-fire had been signed in Lebanon in August 2006, Olmert sought to renew his dialogue with Abbas. It was only on December 23 that the two agreed to meet. This was the first in a series of thirty-six meetings that ended in September 2008. While these meetings were under way, the Bush administration decided in 2007 to endorse and lead the quest for a comprehensive Israeli-Palestinian settlement. The initial circumstances were not auspicious. Olmert had been weakened by the 2006 Lebanon War and by persistent allegations and investigations concerning his personal conduct. Abbas was perceived as a weak leader who was unable to reform and rejuvenate his political power base, the Fatah, and who depended on the United States and Israel to maintain his control of the West Bank in the face of the challenge presented by Hamas. Hamas, in turn, consolidated its rule over the Gaza Strip, cultivated the image of a noncorrupt, dynamic entity associated with the aggressive and apparently successful axis of resistance to Israel.

It took President Bush time to warm to the idea of sponsoring and orchestrating a new American effort to resolve the Israeli-Palestinian conflict, but he gradually did. In November 2007, he hosted an international conference in Annapolis, Maryland, and in January 2008 he declared that he intended to settle the Israeli-Palestinian conflict by the time he left office a year later.

The effectiveness of this belated drive was blunted by the weakness of the U.S. position in the region (under the impact of the wars in Iraq and Afghanistan) and by the fact that the president himself, unlike some of his predecessors, did not immerse himself in the effort. The task was left to the secretary of state, Condoleezza Rice. Rice drifted away from the unorthodox approach to the Arab-Israeli conflict that had characterized the policies of Bush's first term (his preoccupation with the war on terror led him to offer unusual support for Israel's policies while staying committed to the basic principles of U.S. policy toward the Arab-Israeli conflict that had been formulated in 1967). Some of the policies associated with Bush's June 2002 speech and the Road Map were retained. Two senior U.S. generals were stationed in the region. General Jim Jones (later to be Barack Obama's first national security adviser) was dispatched as a special emissary to monitor Palestinian and Israeli compliance with the Road Map. General Keith Dayton replaced General William Ward as security coordinator between Israel and the Palestinian Authority and devoted his major effort to building an effective Palestinian security force. Building security, fighting terrorism, reforming governance, and reviving the economy were the foundations of the policy pursued by the prime minister of the Palestinian Authority, Salam Fayyad. Devoid of his own political base, Fayyad adopted a bottom-up approach, laying the foundations for Palestinian statehood. The Bush administration recruited former British prime minister Tony Blair to help these efforts as the representative of the Quartet and tried to persuade the wealthy Gulf States to pour money into the West Bank's economy. The administration argued that success in these efforts should increase Israel's motivation to move forward with negotiations, as well as provide a stark contrast to the state of affairs in Hamas-controlled Gaza.

While these elements represented continuity with the approach underlying the Road Map, both the Bush administration and the Olmert government decided in fact on a radical change of course by agreeing to move quickly to final-status negotiations, skipping over the interim phase, which long had been central to the diplomatic discourse. The change of course was boosted by the Annapolis Conference, held on November 27–28, 2007, at the U.S. Naval Academy. It was an impressive gathering attended by delegations from Israel, the Palestinian Authority, the members of the Quartet, and several Arab and Islamic countries.

Syria's participation was confirmed at a late stage. President Bush was not keen on Syria's participation (while his secretary of state was), and Syria was ambivalent about being a passive participant in a conference designed to upgrade and expedite the Palestinian track. Damascus finally decided on low-level participation.

The pomp and circumstance of the Annapolis Conference was designed to build momentum for the renewed negotiation. The gathering ended with a joint Palestinian-Israeli statement. The parties announced their intention to launch immediately a bilateral negotiation and to conduct it continuously in order to reach an agreement before the end of 2008. Prime Minister Olmert and President Abbas also agreed to meet on a biweekly basis to monitor and facilitate the negotiation. The first negotiating session was held on December 12, 2007.

In practice parallel negotiations were held. On the working level, Abu Alaa (Abbas's de facto second in command) and Israel's foreign minister, Tzipi Livni, and their delegations conducted the bread-and-butter talks. But the more important give-and-take took place between Olmert and Abbas in their numerous meetings. These meetings ended inconclusively on September 16, 2008. Much has been made of their negotiations. Considerable ground was covered and both men made significant concessions that are described in some detail below. In their final meeting on September 16, Olmert went further than any of his predecessors, but Abbas declined—then and later—to respond, either positively or negatively. Given the subsequent stalemate of the years 2009–2011 in Israeli-Palestinian relations and the exacerbation of the Israeli-Palestinian conflict, the failure to consummate that negotiation seems all the more poignant.

The Olmert-Abbas negotiations of 2008 have been unusually well documented. Ehud Olmert wrote extensively and gave numerous interviews about these meetings, and in January 2011 a trove of papers from the archives of (the very professional) Palestinian Negotiations Support Unit was leaked to al-Jazeera. These sources reveal both a considerable narrowing of the gaps between the parties' positions and the persistence of significant disagreements on important core issues.

The parties departed from the underlying concept of most previous negotiations since the 1990s, which had assumed a two-state solution predicated on the lines of June 4, 1967, with land swaps that would minimize the number of Israeli settlers that would have to be evacuated and maximize the contiguity of the future Palestinian state. Abbas began the give-and-take by putting on the table a map showing how Israel could annex 1.9 percent of the West Bank and reciprocate by turning over to Palestinians the same amount of land of its own territory. Olmert's counteroffer asked for 6.3 percent of the West Bank and offered a compensation of 5.8 percent from Israel's land plus a twenty-five-mile-long tunnel that would run from the Hebron hills (in the West Bank) to Gaza. Olmert gave an early indication that he would be willing to accept as little as 5.9 percent of the West Bank. Abbas kept arguing that since the major settlement blocs occupied only 1.1 percent of the West Bank, his offer of 1.9 percent of its territory certainly met Israel's needs (according to his offer, of the 300,000-plus settlers, some 60 percent could stay in place, with their settlements annexed to Israel, but well over 100,000 would have to be evacuated).

A compromise also seemed possible on the specific issue of territory in Greater Jerusalem that would be incorporated into Israel (beyond the original post-1967 war annexation that the Palestinians and the international community do not recognize). Olmert budged over time from his original position, which held that all of Greater Jerusalem was Israeli and therefore not subject to negotiation. Eventually, he agreed that it, too, would in effect be recognized as "occupied territory" and compensation would be offered to the Palestinians.

A fierce argument continued over three large settlements generally considered to be outside the major settlement blocs: Efrat, Ma'aleh Edumim, and Ariel. Olmert argued that no Israeli prime minister would have the political power to evacuate these particular settlements, while Abbas contended that the three, Ariel in particular, would disrupt the contiguity and viability of the future Palestinian state. Over time Ariel remained the unresolved sticking point.

Jerusalem had always been considered, together with the Palestinian claim of a right for refugees to return to Israel, as an intractable issue. In Olmert's negotiation with Abbas, the set of issues composing "the problem of Jerusalem" was addressed with comparative ease although a final agreement was not reached. Both leaders accepted the principle established by the so-called Clinton parameters of late 2000 that the Jewish neighborhoods in Jerusalem would belong to the Israeli part of the city and the Arab ones would constitute Arab Jerusalem. The one unresolved issue in this context was Abbas' adamant refusal to recognize the area known as Har Homa as a legitimate Jewish neighborhood. Olmert was quite flexible with regard to the Jewish, Muslim, and Christian sites in what is often referred to as the "holy basin." He proposed that this area be governed by a kind of custodial committee, made up of five countries: Israel, Palestine, Saudi Arabia, Jordan, and the United States. Abbas agreed in principle, but an important problem remained unresolved: Olmert wanted the nearby neighborhoods of Abu Tor and Silwan and the adjacent City of David to be included in the holy basin, but Abbas insisted that this was unacceptable to the Palestinians.

On the other intractable issue of refugees, Olmert did not explicitly accept the Palestinian demand that Israel agree to the principle of a "right of return" along with the partial implementation of that right through an agreed formula for the number of refugees who could return over a given period of time. Olmert did come quite close, however, to accepting the Palestinian narrative and terminology on the refugee issue; in other words, he agreed to acknowledge that Israel was at least partly responsible for the flight of Palestinians during and after the 1948 war. But he also insisted on including a reference to the suffering of the Jewish refugees who fled Arab countries in the same time period. In practical terms he agreed to accept 5,000 Palestinians into Israel proper and indicated that he would agree to as many as 15,000. In addition to recognizing the pain and suffering of the Palestinian refugees, Olmert agreed to take part in the international endeavor to compensate them. In return, he demanded that the Palestinians agree to the "end of conflict, end of claims" formula that Barak had insisted on in 2000; in other words, he wanted a Palestinian admission that a peace settlement would end the conflict once and for all, with no possibility for further claims against Israel. Olmert's proposals for the number of Palestinian refugees were unacceptable to Abbas, who argued that it was "negligible" compared with the current population of 5 million refugees and their descendants.

Olmert made his final and most comprehensive offer to Abbas on September 16, 2008. It included a map that he put on the table. Abbas wanted to take the map with him, but Olmert declined to give it unless Abbas signed it, which the latter refused to do. Abbas did not reject Olmert's proposal but neither did he respond to it, positively or negatively. Israeli right-wingers see in his refusal proof of their contention that Abbas (or any other Palestinian leader) would not offer Israel finality to the conflict and an end to their claims. A more benign interpretation would center on his reluctance to conclude a final-status deal with a lame-duck Israeli prime minister and the expectation that he could do better once a new president took office in the United States, widely assumed at that point to be Barack Obama. Whatever his calculus and motivation, Abbas's failure to take advantage of Olmert's position and formalize it in some fashion seems to have been a grave error of judgment, from the vantage point of the subsequent deadlock in the Israeli-Palestinian relationship in the years 2009–11.

The Israeli-Palestinian negotiation did not formally end until January 2009, when Bush left office, but for all practical purposes it was finished on September 16. The focus of Israeli-Palestinian relations then shifted to Gaza.

THE GATES OF GAZA

Young Ro'i who left his home in Tel Aviv to build his home at the gates of Gaza to serve as a defensive wall for us. The light in his heart blinded his eyes and he failed to see the shining knife. The yearning for peace sealed his ears and he did not hear the sound of lurking murder. The gates of Gaza were too heavy for his shoulders.

These lines are the concluding passage of Moshe Dayan's eulogy delivered during the funeral of Ro'i Rotberg, who was murdered in the fields of his kibbutz, Nachal Oz, on the border with the Gaza Strip in April 1956. Dayan's eulogy became one of Israel's canonical texts. It reflected the malaise and pessimism of the mid-1950s, and in later years the sense that, in the cluster of issues that make up the Israeli-Palestinian conflict, the problem of Gaza may be the most difficult.

That has certainly been the case since 2006–07, when Hamas won the Palestinian elections and then took control of the Gaza Strip. Hamas's ascension to power in Gaza exposed and exacerbated the deficiencies of Israel's withdrawal from Gaza in 2005. Both Israel and Hamas were hard put to formulate a policy toward each other. Israel faced a non-state entity, ruled by a hostile organization that refused to accept conditions laid down by the Quartet following the Hamas election victory, including renunciation of violence and acceptance of Israel. Hamas remained connected to Iran and Syria but depended on Israel for access to the outside world, supplies, water, and electric power necessary for maintaining life in Gaza. Did Israel wish to topple the Hamas government in Gaza? Could such an attempt succeed? Would Israel have Cairo's and Ramallah's cooperation? And if not, did Israel wish to take advantage of the pragmatic streak woven into the fabric of Hamas's radical rhetoric and seek a modus vivendi that would work until things could be sorted out?[8]

Hamas, whether the local leadership in Gaza or the external leadership in Damascus, also had to make up its own mind. Did it wish to consolidate its rule in the Gaza Strip and use it as a base for extending its control at a future date to the West Bank and to replace Fatah at the helm of the PLO? If so, did it wish to establish a modus vivendi with Israel, or should it choose to practice the doctrine of resistance, position itself as leading the conflict with Israel, and seek to disrupt life in southern Israel and its relations with the Palestinian Authority and with Egypt?

The answer, from both sides, to most of these questions must have been negative since Israel and the Hamas leadership soon found themselves caught in a vicious cycle of escalating violence. One year before its takeover of Gaza, Hamas and its partners launched the operation inside Israel's territory that ended in the killing of two soldiers and the abduction of Gilad Shalit. Israel retaliated both with a military operation inside the Gaza Strip and, eventually, by imposing sanctions on the transit of people and goods into and out of the Strip. Hamas responded by firing rockets into the western Negev. This pattern repeated itself again and again during 2007 and 2008.

When Egypt reached the conclusion that Iran was using Hamas, an offshoot of the Egyptian Muslim Brotherhood, in an effort to destabilize Mubarak's regime, it closed its own border with the Gaza Strip. This made life in Gaza even more miserable than it had been but did not seriously disrupt the flourishing smuggling industry under the border. A significant symptom of the waning of Mubarak's regime was that it was losing control of the Sinai and its Bedouin population, which profited from the smuggling through dozens of tunnels into Gaza. Israel and Egypt cooperated as a rule in dealing with what they saw as a common problem, but the relationship was not free of tension. While Egypt gave public support to Israel's departure from the Gaza Strip in 2005, it was privately critical of the move. Egypt suspected that Israel wanted to lay Gaza back in its lap (Egypt had controlled the Strip before the June 1967 war). Cairo also argued that the demilitarization of the Sinai, an important component of the Israel-Egypt peace treaty of 1979, prevented it from effectively sealing the border with Gaza and stopping the underground smuggling. Israel agreed to some beefing up of Egypt's military presence in the Sinai but resisted any effort to change the terms of the peace treaty.

The uninterrupted supply through the Sinai enabled Hamas and the other radical groups in the Gaza Strip to build more and more sophisticated Qassam rockets as well as to store longer-range Grad rockets. The following table, indicating the numbers of rockets fired from the Gaza Strip into Israel between 2002 and 2008, speaks for itself:

2002	17
2003	123
2004	276
2005	286
2006	1,247
2007	938
2008	1,270

In June 2008 yet another attempt was made to establish a cease-fire between Israel and Hamas. Omar Suleiman, Egypt's intelligence chief, negotiated a cease-fire for six months. It was not kept fully, but the level of violence declined dramatically. Then, in November, Israel discovered a tunnel dug under the border fence between Israel and Gaza, similar to the one used successfully in June 2006 when Shalit was captured. Israel retaliated by closing the border crossings, Hamas fired rockets, and the cease-fire collapsed. It was formally abrogated by Hamas on December 18. Nine days later, on December 27, Israel launched Operation Cast Lead.

The planning and execution of this operation must be seen against the backdrop of the 2006 Lebanon War. Olmert was still the prime minister (though clearly on his way out), Ehud Barak (again the leader of the Labor Party) was the defense minister, and Gabi Ashkenazi (a seasoned army general) was the new chief of staff of the IDF. There were disagreements within Israel's civilian and military leadership as to the scope and purposes of the operation. The maximalist school wanted to reoccupy the Gaza Strip, destroy Hamas' infrastructure and person-nel, occupy and hold the Philadelphi corridor (adjacent to Egypt), and enable the Palestinian Authority to retake control of the Gaza Strip (Abbas indicated discreetly that he did not want to return to Gaza on the strength of the IDF's bayonets). Others argued that Israel might find itself occupying the Gaza Strip for a long time and advocated, instead, a more limited operation that would represent a painful blow to Hamas and reestablishment of effective Israeli deterrence.

As in Lebanon, the operation began with a deadly air raid (killing most of the graduating class in a Hamas police force ceremony) and a land operation designed to destroy Hamas infrastructure and cap-ture and kill Hamas personnel. It was assumed that, in preparing for this much-anticipated operation, Hamas had booby-trapped numerous buildings. In addition, given the costly nature of fighting in urban areas, Israel's military planners put a special emphasis on the use of artillery and other devices that would minimize Israeli casualties—even if this entailed physical destruction and Palestinian civilian losses. Given this approach and given Hamas's own decision to protect its soldiers by min-imizing military resistance, the operation ended with relatively few IDF and Hamas casualties. However, Gaza suffered considerable physical damage and a large number of civilian casualties (the numbers vary and are a matter of controversy, but there were at least several hundred casualties). The operation ended on January 18, 2009. The timing was not accidental. Barack Obama did not wish to start his presidency on January 20 with fighting still going on in Gaza. During the operation, Hamas did use its arsenal of medium-range rockets. The Israeli coastal city of Ashkelon, to the north of the Gaza Strip, had been attacked in an earlier round of fighting. This time Ashkelon, Beer Sheva, and Rehovot were attacked.

From a perspective of three years, it can be said that Operation Cast Lead achieved part of its goals. Rocket fire from the Gaza Strip did not end, but compared with the previous massive attacks that had made life in Sderot and the western Negev unbearable, rocket attacks since the Gaza operation have been marginal. Israel, however, paid a heavy price in terms of its image and international legitimacy. The massive destruction and heavy loss of civilian life as depicted by the international media led to a wave of protest and condemnation. Radical regimes in Bolivia and Venezuela severed relations with Israel. The Islamist government in Turkey issued violent denunciations. The UN's Human Rights Commission appointed a committee headed by a Jewish South African judge, Richard Goldstone, to investigate war crimes that may have been committed. The commission's mandate and composition and Goldstone's own predilections produced a report that condemned Israel in stronger language than used to criticize Hamas. Goldstone eventually recanted some of the findings, but the damage to Israel's image and legitimacy was irreversible.

7

AMERICAN-ISRAELI AUTUMN, ARAB SPRING

The course of Arab-Israeli relations in the years 2009–11 was shaped by three major developments: Barack Obama's election as president of the United States, the victory of the right wing in the Israeli parliamentary elections of February 2009, and the wave of popular uprisings in the Arab world that began in Tunisia in December 2010 and came later to be known as the Arab Spring. Benjamin Netanyahu's return to power in March 2009 was unrelated to Barack Obama's election as president of the United States in November 2008, but the formation of a right-wing government in Israel magnified the impact of several elements of the new American president's view of Israel, the Arab-Israeli conflict, and the Middle East generally. The encounter between a right-wing Israeli prime minister and a U.S. president seeking to break the familiar mold of U.S. policy in the Middle East and to mend America's relationship with the Muslim and Arab worlds (in part by resolving the Israeli-Palestinian conflict) led to a period of tension between Washington and Jerusalem but failed to revive the Israeli-Palestinian peace process. It was hardly surprising that the Obama administration and the Netanyahu government had different perspectives on the chain of events that became the Arab Spring and its relationship to the Arab-Israeli conflict.

BARACK OBAMA, THE MIDDLE EAST, AND THE ARAB-ISRAELI CONFLICT

Barack Obama wasted no time in launching his new policy in the Middle East and in assigning it a high priority within his broader foreign policy agenda. The focus was larger than the Middle East properly defined. The new president believed that he could change both the reality and perception of U.S. conflict with the world of Islam and with large parts of the Arab world that had been associated with the Bush adminis-tration. A significant part of that conflict had to do with the war in Afghanistan, with the complex U.S. relationship with Pakistan, and with the war against al-Qaeda and Jihadi Islam—of which Afghanistan and Pakistan were important arenas.

Then there was the conflict with Iran over a range of issues: its nuclear program, its meddling in Iraq, its support of terrorist organiza-tions, and its quest for hegemony in the Middle East—all of which were seen by several U.S. allies as a direct threat. The new president's promise to withdraw U.S. troops from Iraq was another issue. Could that be accomplished without an embarrassing collapse of the frail edifice built there since 2003? West of Iraq lay a host of other problems and issues for the United States: a hostile relationship with Syria (Iran's close ally), underlying concern with a failure by America's conservative allies in the Arab world to offer their publics more democratic governance, an Islamist Turkish government distancing itself from Washington, and, of course, the festering Israeli-Palestinian conflict.

In the new president's view, resolution of that last conflict was essen-tial for the success of his larger policy in the region. As he saw it, not only the Arab countries but the broader Muslim world as well were offended and radicalized by Israel's continuing occupation of the West Bank and were angered by America's support of Israel and, by exten-sion, of its policies. Obama, in fact, adopted the "linkage theory," which argued that the United States could have a much smoother relationship with Arabs and Muslims but for the impact of the Palestinian issue. He himself made only brief comments in this vein,[1] but other senior mem-bers of his administration spoke about it at greater length. The most explicit articulation of this view was made by General David Petraeus, then commander of the military's Central Command (which covered the Middle East), during a congressional hearing in March 2010:

> The enduring hostilities between Israel and some of its neighbors present distinct challenges to our ability to advance our interests in the AOR [Area of Responsibility]. Israeli Palestinian tensions often

flare up into violence and large scale armed confrontations. The conflict foments anti American sentiments due to a perception of US favoritism to Israel. Arab anger over the Palestinian question limits the strength and depth of US partnerships with governments and peoples in the AOR and weakens the legitimacy of moderate regimes in the Arab world. Meanwhile al Qaeda and other militant groups exploit the anger to mobilize support.[2]

Obama made a clear distinction between America's bilateral relationship with Israel and the U.S. determination to restart the Israeli-Palestinian peace process in hopes of reaching a two-state solution along the lines of the Clinton parameters set out in late 2000. Furthermore, to serve as a credible sponsor of such a peace process, Washington should not be perceived as too closely coordinated with Israel. The intimacy of the Clinton and Bush years had to be abandoned. These convictions were translated into a series of immediate steps. George Mitchell, the former Senate majority leader and peacemaker in Northern Ireland, was appointed on January 22 as special emissary for the Arab-Israeli peace process. Mitchell was quite familiar with the Israeli-Palestinian issue, having headed the international committee that in 2000–01 investigated the outbreak of the second intifada. On January 26 Obama gave an interview (his first as president) to an Arab TV network, *al-Arabiyya,* in which he presented his Middle East policy. When asked at the outset about the Israeli-Palestinian conflict, he indicated clearly that what he had in mind was not necessarily acceptable to all Israelis:

> Now Israel is a strong ally of the United States. They will not stop being a strong ally of the United States and I will continue to believe that Israel's security is paramount. But I also believe that there are Israelis who recognize that it is important to achieve peace. They will be willing to make sacrifices if the time is appropriate and if there is serious partnership on the other side.

During his 2008 campaign, candidate Obama had stated that he would, if elected, seek "to engage" with Iran and Syria. On March 19 he took the first step in his effort to put Washington's relationship with Iran on a different footing and sent a message of congratulations for the Persian New Year. In early April he traveled to Turkey and spoke both to the Turkish parliament and to a group of students. The themes contained in these speeches would be fully developed in a more significant speech in Cairo two months later.

NETANYAHU'S RETURN TO POWER

When Ehud Olmert resigned as prime minister in August 2008, he was succeeded as Kadimah's leader by Foreign Minister Tzipi Livni. Livni failed to keep Olmert's coalition together and form a new government. She had a hard time coming to an agreement with Labor's leader, Ehud Barak, and an even harder time with the leader of Shas, Eli Yishai. Livni and Yishai could not agree on the issue of Jerusalem (in the anticipated peace negotiation) and on the government's financial allocations to the Shas Party's school system. It is quite possible that Yishai had in fact already come to an agreement with Netanyahu to bring about a new election and join his coalition as a first priority. In any event Livni's inability to form a government led to a new election in February 2009; Olmert continued to serve as caretaker prime minister in the meantime.

The February election ended in a right-wing victory. Three years earlier, Olmert had won the elections on a dovish platform, but in the interim the impact of Hizballah's rockets in the north, Hamas's rockets in the south, and the hovering threat of a nuclear-armed Iran had sent a frightened electorate to the right. Kadimah still emerged with the largest caucus in the Knesset (twenty-eight, one more than the Likud's twenty-seven), but Kadimah's success was achieved at the expense of the center (Labor) and left (Meretz). The right wing ended up controlling sixty-five seats. Furthermore, Avigdor Lieberman's Israel Beyteynu ("Israel is our home") Party rose to fifteen seats. Lieberman, who had immigrated to Israel from the Soviet Union in the 1970s, began his political career in the Likud and was the director general of the prime minister's office in Netanyahu's first government in the 1990s. The party he formed was to some extent an ethnic one catering to fellow immigrants from the former Soviet Union. Essentially, however, it was an ultra-nationalist party attractive to voters who believed in strong leadership and simple responses to the difficult challenges facing Israel. Lieberman, who lived in a West Bank settlement, would indicate every so often that demography was more important than geography (thus, recognizing the danger

posed to Israel's status as a Jewish and democratic state by the growing Palestinian population), but as a rule he acted and spoke as a blunt
right-wing nationalist. His campaign for the 2009 elections focused on
the threat, as he saw it, that the disloyalty of the leadership of Israel's
Arab minority presented to the state of Israel.

Once Netanyahu had the support of the right wing and the requisite
sixty-one votes for forming a coalition, he obtained the support of Ehud
Barak and the Labor Party (Kadimah under Livni refused to join the
coalition, while Netanyahu did not really try to have it join). He was
thus able to form a right-wing government tempered to some extent by
Labor's participation and Barak's reappointment to the key ministry of
defense. This tempering was offset by the appointment of Lieberman as
foreign minister. It was this government and coalition that had to cope
with America's new policies in the Middle East.

The centerpiece of Netanyahu's and the Likud's election campaign
was the struggle against the Iranian nuclear threat. Resolution of the
Israeli-Palestinian conflict was relegated to a secondary place. The Likud
and its leaders were critical of Sharon's unilateralism in Gaza and of
the Olmert-Abbas negotiation that emanated from the 2007 Annapolis
conference. Such negotiations, Netanyahu argued, were futile because
the Palestinians were not ready "for a historic compromise that would
end the conflict."[3] Other points in the argument included these: the Palestinians and the Arab world in general were unwilling to accept Israel
as a Jewish state; Israel would not cross red lines including the right to
defensible borders and the responsibility for its own security (responsibility for the Palestinian refugees lay with the Arab states); and a united
Jerusalem under Israeli rule. Since a political settlement was not feasible
under the current conditions, the emphasis should be shifted to an "economic peace." Economic cooperation with the Palestinian Authority
and regional partners such as Jordan would create a climate of hope and
serve as a corridor to an eventual political peace.

On April 1, 2009, during the ceremony marking the transfer of
power to the incoming cabinet, the new foreign minister, Lieberman,
spoke against "the Annapolis process." The way forward, he argued, lay
through a scrupulous implementation of obligations of the parties (the
Palestinians first and foremost) under the early phase of the Quartet's
Road Map.

Against this background it was hardly surprising that Netanyahu's first meeting with Obama and his team on May, 18, 2009, did not proceed well. The president wanted to move rapidly on the Palestinian track while Netanyahu was still unwilling to endorse publicly the notion of a two-state solution. The meeting between the two leaders failed also to produce or even lay the basis for a cordial relationship and a level of trust comparable to the relationships that presidents Bill Clinton and George W. Bush had with several of Netanyahu's predecessors. Such a relationship could have mitigated the genuine differences of opinion between the two leaders. Obama and Netanyahu met several times between May 2009 and May 2011. Some meetings were tense, and some were more cordial, but the fundamental gap and absence of mutual trust did not change. In Obama's view, he was pressing Israel to act for its own good and to adopt a formula that had been acceptable to at least two earlier Israeli prime ministers (Barak and Olmert) and that had been promoted by U.S. presidents who were regarded as very friendly to Israel. If Netanyahu told him that his coalition would not support such a policy, Obama felt that Netanyahu could build a different coalition with Kadimah. Netanyahu suspected that Obama wanted to see him out of office.

Obama and Netanyahu did share one common political interest: both wanted to distance themselves from the legacy of the previous few years. For Obama, it was part of a deliberate effort to disown Bush's legacy; for Netanyahu, it was opposition to the substance of the policies of Sharon and Olmert. When Netanyahu told Obama that he was interested in a "reevaluation" of the peace process, Obama was happy to oblige rather than argue, to take one example, the validity of Bush's April 2004 letter that essentially accepted the reality of Israeli settlements in the West Bank.

The impact of the first meeting between the two leaders was felt in two important speeches delivered in June 2009. On June 4, Obama went to Cairo to deliver a speech directed at the Arab and Muslim worlds. He dwelt on several issues—the tension in U.S.-Muslim relations, Iran's nuclear program, and the quest for democracy—and presented the vision of a two-state solution to the Israeli-Palestinian conflict and his personal commitment to pursue it "with all the patience that the task requires."

There was an edge to this part of the speech. Obama demanded that Israel freeze construction in West Bank settlements and live up to its own commitments in the Road Map by removing travel restrictions and other limitations on Palestinian life in the West Bank, and he went on to criticize Israel's siege of the Gaza Strip.

The insistence on a construction freeze in the settlements was part of a larger strategy designed to jump-start the Israeli-Palestinian talks. The Arab world was asked to reciprocate for this anticipated Israeli concession by offering a measure of normalization. On his way to Cairo, Obama stopped in Saudi Arabia and asked King Abdullah to allow Israeli commercial overflights on the way to Asia, as one such step. The king declined.

In retrospect, the decision to use the idea of a settlement freeze as a starting point for a new negotiation seems to have been a serious mistake. The issue moved to center stage and remained there through the fall of 2010. Netanyahu finally agreed to a ten-month freeze on some construction in existing West Bank settlements, but that window led merely to a brief negotiation. A subsequent U.S. attempt to extend the length of the freeze (in return for an American package of aid and other concessions to Israel) failed. One byproduct of this exercise was the creation of a new bar for the Palestinian leadership. If the U.S. president insisted on a settlement freeze, how could Abbas, then and later, join a negotiation without it?

The second important speech was delivered by Netanyahu at Israel's Bar Ilan University on June 14, 2009. As he did in starting his previous tenure as prime minister in 1996, Netanyahu began a slow, gradual voyage from his original ideological and political position toward the positions demanded by his American ally and Arab partners. In the June 14 speech, Netanyahu accepted for the first time the principle of a two-state solution (had he done that in Washington a month earlier a great deal of acrimony might have been saved). He began the speech by reiterating some of his and the Likud's familiar positions and then stated that:

In the heart of our Jewish homeland now lives a large population of Palestinians. We do not want to rule over them . . . [I]n any vision of peace there are two free peoples living side by side in this small land in good neighborly relations and mutual respect each with its own flag, anthem and government with neither one threatening its neighbor's security and existence.

Netanyahu set several conditions for this vision to materialize, including Palestinian recognition of Israel as a Jewish state. Israel's security would have to be ensured (and for this to happen, the Palestinian state would have to be demilitarized). He added that "Israel needs defensible borders with Jerusalem remaining the united capital of Israel." To Obama's insistence on a construction freeze, Netanyahu responded by saying that the territorial issues would be dealt with in the final-status agreement. Until then, Israel would not build new settlements and would not allocate land for new ones. But he objected to the idea of a construction freeze in existing settlements, arguing that "there is a need to have people live normal lives." The Israeli position was that Obama's demand for a freeze ran counter to Sharon's and Olmert's understandings with the Bush administration. The Obama administration began by claiming that it was not familiar with such understandings and subsequently indicated that even if they existed, it did not feel committed to them.

After further give-and-take, Netanyahu on November 25 announced a ten-month construction freeze. This decision, as well as the Bar Ilan speech, was crafted to mollify the Obama administration without alienating the right wing of Netanyahu's own Likud Party and his coalition partners. The combined effect of these two measures cleared the air between Washington and Jerusalem, if only for the time being, and set the stage for an effort to renew the Israeli-Palestinian negotiation.

STALEMATE 2009–11

Barack Obama's speech on the Middle East delivered in Washington on May 19, 2011, and George Mitchell's concurrent resignation marked the conclusion of a futile two-year effort to restart an Israeli-Palestinian negotiation and see it through.

When America's new president decided to choose the resolution of the Israeli-Palestinian conflict as one of the first, salient, and most urgent issues of his administration's foreign policy, he must not have realized the complexity of his choice. A serious and significant Israeli-Palestinian negotiation had been suspended by Ehud Olmert's resignation the previous year. As we saw, Olmert presented Mamud Abbas with a last-minute, far-reaching proposal, to which the Palestinian leader failed to respond. For Olmert's successor, Netanyahu, that proposal was unacceptable and invalid. In May 2009 he told President Obama that he wanted to reevaluate the whole Annapolis process. This suited the president's own tendency to distance himself from his predecessor's legacy and to shift to a different policy. The Palestinians, in turn, argued that "the negotiations should be renewed at the point at which they had been interrupted." The opening positions presented by the Palestinian chief negotiator, Saeb Ariqat, in February 2009, and Israel's new foreign minister on April 1 seemed irreconcilable. The festering problem of Gaza that Operation Cast Lead failed to resolve compounded matters. So did Barack Obama's call for a settlement construction freeze in his Cairo speech; Mahmud Abbas and other Palestinian and Arab leaders could obviously not settle on less. Abbas, furthermore, felt exposed and weakened by radical criticism in his own Fatah movement and by the presence in Gaza of Hamas. He tried to overcome his weakness by obtaining the Arab League's sanction for entering into indirect and direct negotiations with Netanyahu's government. In earlier decades it had been a high priority for the Palestinian national movement to ensure its "independent decisionmaking"—in other words to release itself from the stranglehold of the Arab states' paternalistic care. A weak Mahmud Abbas reversed that trend when he sought their political backing.

It was against that backdrop that George Mitchell began his effort to renew the Israeli-Palestinian negotiation early in 2009. It proved to be a Sisyphean task. In several trips and rounds of consultation, Mitchell (and occasionally President Obama and Secretary of State Hillary Clinton) could not get past the issue of agreed terms of reference for the negotiation. Abbas refused to enter into a direct negotiation with Netanyahu except on terms of reference acceptable to him and his constituency (a two state-solution based on the 1967 lines plus one-for-one swaps of Israeli land for West Bank land, and a full freeze of construction in the settlements). These conditions were unacceptable to Netanyahu, who insisted on his own demand that the Palestinians recognize Israel as a Jewish state and the national homeland of the Jewish people.

Netanyahu refused to discuss territory (or boundaries) before a discussion of security, arguing that his position on territory would be influenced by the quality of the security regime that should first be agreed on.

George Mitchell's initial approach to his Middle East mission was, quite naturally, influenced by his earlier success in Northern Ireland. This meant a slow, gradual process of working with the parties, leading to incremental change and culminating in a breakthrough. It soon transpired that this approach was not effective in the Israeli-Palestinian context and that his strategy was incongruent with the sense of urgency generated by President Obama, the Palestinians, and other Arab actors.

During the rest of 2009 and throughout 2010 the routine of Mitchell's work was broken by three special events. In September 2009 a trilateral meeting between Obama, Netanyahu, and Abbas was organized in New York where the three attended the UN's General Assembly. It failed to lead to a bilateral negotiation. In March 2010 "proximity talks" were put together as a substitute for direct negotiations, with Mitchell shuttling between Abbas and Netanyahu, once again to no avail. Finally, in September 2010, Abbas agreed to a direct negotiation. It was short-lived. To begin with, Abbas's and Netanyahu's positions remained irreconcilable. A second difficulty was the timing. Netanyahu's settlement freeze had been announced in November 2009 and was now coming to an end, with little prospect of an extension. Abbas would not continue in the negotiations unless the freeze was to be extended. The Obama administration offered Netanyahu a generous package of aid as an inducement, but to no avail; Netanyahu kept walking the fine line that balanced his need to preserve his relations with the United States with his more crucial urge to preserve his governing coalition. Abbas walked out of the brief negotiation.

It took the administration several weeks to accept, as a fait accompli, the failure to put an Israeli-Palestinian in place and to come up with an alternative policy. This policy was presented by Secretary Clinton on December 10, 2010, when she addressed the Saban Forum at the Brookings Institution in Washington:

> It is time to grapple with the core issues of the conflict on borders and security, settlements, water and refugees and on Jerusalem itself. And starting with my meetings this week, this is exactly what

we are doing. We also deepen our strong commitment to supporting the state building work of the Palestinian Authority and continue to urge the states of the region to develop the content of the Arab Peace Initiative and to work toward implementing its vision. . . . We will work toward reaching a framework agreement. The U.S will not be a passive participant. We will push the parties to lay out their positions on the core issues without delay and with real specificity. We will work to narrow the gaps asking the tough questions . . . and in the context of our private conversations with the parties we will offer our own ideas and bridging proposals when appropriate.

From that point on the Arab-Israeli diplomatic arena was shaped by three main issues:

—The expectation that the position articulated by the secretary of state would be translated into concrete steps, perhaps a presentation of Washington's own view of the "core issues" or perhaps even a concrete plan put on the table by the Obama administration.

—The expectation that the Palestinian Authority would take its case to the UN General Assembly in September 2011 and seek a resolution recognizing a Palestinian state based on the 1967 boundaries. As the months went by, this expectation loomed as a more likely course of action as an increasing number of Latin American and other countries promised their support.

—The outbreak and unfolding series of popular uprisings that came to be commonly known as the Arab Spring. These events served both to overshadow the Israeli-Palestinian conflict and to enhance the sense of urgency among some actors, the Obama administration in particular.

These issues came to a head in May 2011. Before turning to that set of events, two other issues need to be analyzed.

WASHINGTON, DAMASCUS, AND TEHRAN

During his election campaign, candidate Obama spoke about his intention "to engage" with Syria (alongside with its senior ally Iran), but as president he was so focused on the Palestinian-Israeli issue that he practically equated the broader Arab-Israeli peace process with the Israeli-Palestinian negotiations. In his two major speeches on the peace process in June 2009 and in May 2011, he spoke at length about the Israeli-Palestinian conflict and the urgent need to solve it, while the Israeli-Syrian conflict was not mentioned. This suited Netanyahu well. He was preoccupied with the Palestinian issue and so a new negotiation with Syria, or creating another controversy over his refusal to accept Syria's insistence on full withdrawal from the Golan as a precondition, was something he could do without. In 1998 he tried to shift from the Palestinian track and was willing to accept the notion of full withdrawal from the Golan (see chapter three), but this was not the case in 2009. A strong lobby inside Israel's national security establishment did advocate a "Syria first" policy, but Netanyahu was not swayed.

George Mitchell's mandate included the Syrian track. One of his deputies was Fred Hoff, a highly respected Syria expert, and between them they traveled several times to Damascus. It soon became evident, however, that with the priority assigned by the administration to the Palestinian track, the problems accumulating on that track, Netanyahu's reservations regarding the Syrian option, and the difficulties inherent in any American give-and-take with Syria, the prospects for launching a parallel track between Jerusalem and Damascus were dim. The Obama administration reverted to a policy that the Bush administration had tried unsuccessfully in its first year—seek to build a bilateral American-Syrian dialogue and mend the two countries' relationship while postponing the quest for a Syrian-Israeli settlement. Efforts to do this were tried through a number of channels: Mitchell and his team, several senior officials headed by Deputy Secretary of State William Burns, and a number of U.S. legislators, most notably John Kerry, the chairman of the Senate's Foreign Relations Committee.

These gambits caused some anxiety in Tehran, so much so that in the aftermath of Burns's visit to Damascus in February 2010, President Mahmoud Ahmadinejad rushed to Syria to shore up the alliance between the two countries. His mission was successful and led to a defiant statement by Bashar al-Asad mocking Secretary of State Hillary Clinton's attempt to lure Syria away from Iran. This episode was, indeed, illustrative of the failure of the larger effort to improve the U.S.-Syrian bilateral relationship. The administration made one additional attempt by appointing a U.S. ambassador to Damascus for the first time since Rafiq Hariri's assassination in Beirut in 2005. Robert Ford, a seasoned diplomat, was nominated in February 2010, but his appointment met with strong resistance in Congress. A significant group of members of Congress argued that on several issues of concern to the United States— from Syria's alliance with Iran to a renewed assault on Lebanon's sovereignty and democracy and ongoing support for anti-American groups in Iraq—Bashar al-Asad's Syria remained a hostile country, deserving sanctions rather than goodwill gestures. Clinton defended the appointment by arguing that the dialogue could be improved by having a senior diplomat stationed in Damascus. Her argument did not satisfy the congressional critics, and the administration was forced to resort to making a temporary recess appointment in December 2010, thus avoiding the need to go through the confirmation process. Ford began his tenure in February 2011—just in time to witness the transformation of Syria's politics by the outbreak of the riots against the government in March.

WASHINGTON, JERUSALEM, AND THE ARAB SPRING

Upheaval in Syria was a comparatively late manifestation of the series of popular uprisings that dramatically altered the Middle Eastern political landscape in 2011. The trend began in Tunisia in December 2010, spread to Egypt in January 2011, and then to Libya, Yemen, Bahrain, and Syria. Other Arab countries, including Jordan and Morocco, were affected by milder forms of agitation and protest. The wave of protest had several common elements: it was directed at authoritarian regimes; it reflected the exasperation of the population, younger groups in particular, with oppression, corruption, lack of participation, and dim prospects for a better future; and it was waged by diffuse groups, using the new social media to mobilize the regime's critics and opponents.

After an early success in toppling the regimes of Ben Ali in Tunisia and Mubarak in Egypt, the revolutionary wave continued to unfold through four tracks:

—In Bahrain a popular revolt by members of the Shiite majority was quashed by the regime with Saudi help.

—In Libya the rebellion against Muammar Qaddafi developed into a civil war, with aerial support by NATO, that finally brought the regime down in August 2011. In Yemen the struggle against the Saleh regime persisted without resolution.

—In Syria, the opposition was able to defy the regime in several towns and cities around the country but not in the two largest cities, Damascus and Aleppo. During the summer of 2011, the regime stepped up its bloody crackdown of the opposition, a move that generated fierce regional and international criticism.

—The royal regimes in Saudi Arabia, Jordan, and Morocco were able, at least temporarily, to calm the opposition by offering moderate political reforms (in Morocco the reforms offered by the king were more significant) along with economic reforms and gestures.

By the summer of 2011 the earlier sense of a political tsunami about to topple several regimes and radically transform the politics of the region was replaced by a more complex reality of ongoing violence in Libya, Syria, and Yemen; an unfolding conflict over the future politics of Egypt; and, more broadly, an sense that Arab publics had been empowered in ways that were still to take shape.

Washington and Jerusalem had quite different responses to these developments. In Washington, an unusual coalition of policymakers and opinion leaders had an early enthusiastic—or at least positive— response to the wave of popular protest and rebellion. Neoconservatives and other conservatives saw a vindication of the Bush administration's policies and their own support for the idea of bringing democracy to the Arab world. Liberals inside and outside the administration were supportive of the movement toward democracy and liberty. The president himself saw a response to several themes raised in his Cairo speech. In June 2009 Obama had refrained from supporting demonstrations against the Iranian regime, but in 2011 his attitude toward the Arab demonstrations was very different.

Yet, as a superpower with vital and diverse interests in the Middle East, the United States was required to formulate complex policies if it was to contend with several immediate challenges. In Tunisia it could offer unequivocal support for the rapid ouster of President Ben Ali. In Egypt, where a more significant ally was attempting to cling to power, a massive U.S. investment and crucial U.S interests were at stake. The administration made an early decision to help ease Mubarak out. This unsettled and angered other allies, notably Saudi Arabia, who felt weakened by Mubarak's fall and exposed by Washington's attitude. What could they expect if threatened by domestic upheaval or external foes?

In Libya, under pressure from such European allies as Britain and France and an in-house liberal interventionist lobby, Obama decided to participate under a NATO umbrella in a campaign designed to protect a diverse rebel group from government attacks but more broadly to topple Qaddafi. The principles invoked in Libya were soon tested in Syria, when a popular rebellion against Bashar al-Asad's regime broke out. This was an important turning point. Until March 2011 most of the regimes that came under assault were pro-Western. In a Middle East divided between Iran's axis of resistance and a group of pro-Western conservative regimes, the fall of Ben Ali and Mubarak and the discomfort felt by Saudi Arabia, Jordan, and Morocco seemed to have been net gains for Iran. But the challenge to Asad's regime in Syria weakened Iran's regional position, gave Hizballah and Hamas pause, and brought to the surface the latent tension between Iran and Turkey.

Washington was hard put to formulate a response to the crisis in Syria, where a dictatorship was killing an increasing number of unarmed civilian protestors. Should the principles invoked in Libya be applied to Syria? Military intervention was not seriously considered, however. The Syrian army and the regime were both controlled by members of the same minority Alawite community, and military intervention would be costly and probably ineffective (Qaddafi's regime proved to be much more resilient than was initially assumed, although it ultimately could not survive a determined onslaught). Even when it came to sanctions and condemnation of Syria, Washington acted cautiously (more so than its European allies). Little was known about the Syrian opposition, and given Syria's location, anarchy in Syria had potential impacts on all of its neighbors: Iraq, Lebanon, Jordan, Turkey, and Israel.

Israel watched these developments with anxiety. Its immediate concern was the future of the peace treaties with Egypt and Jordan. Cold as it was, peace with these two neighboring countries had been a pillar of Israel's national security since 1979 and 1994, respectively. Israelis know that peace with democratic countries is more stable than peace with autocratic or dictatorial regimes. Right-wing Israeli politicians like Netanyahu and Natan Sharansky had argued in the past that Arab and Palestinian transition to democracy should in fact become a precondition for Israeli concessions.[4] But the response to the Arab Spring by Netanyahu (and many others in Israel) was cautious and skeptical. In principle and in the long term, it behooved Israel to be surrounded by democratic neighbors, but in more immediate terms, if the reliable Mubarak was to be replaced by a government dominated by the Muslim Brotherhood (the best-organized civilian force in the country), would the peace treaty survive?

Like Saudi Arabia and other U.S. allies in the region, Israel was jolted by what seemed a swift abandonment of Mubarak, a veteran, trusted ally. As reflected in their May 2011 speeches, Obama and Netanyahu had different views of the Arab Spring's repercussions for Arab-Israeli relations. As Obama saw it, the window for an Israeli-Palestinian agreement was closing. The Arab Spring empowered Arab masses whose attitude to Israel was far more radical than that of the current leadership. Time was not on Israel's side in any event, and it was in Israel's interest to come to an agreement now and remove the Israeli-Palestinian issue from the agenda of Arab revolutionaries. For Netanyahu, by contrast, a time of uncertainty was the wrong time to make irreversible territorial concessions; prudence rather than boldness was the order of the day.

THE MAY 2011 SPEECHES

Several issues discussed above—the policy differences between the United States and Israel over the peace process, the personal tension between Barack Obama and Benjamin Netanyahu, the Obama administration's undertaking to tackle the "core issues" of the Israeli-Palestinian conflict, the impact of the Arab Spring, and the need to deal with the Palestinian threat to seek recognition of a Palestinian state through the UN in September 2011—converged into an extraordinary set of events and speeches in May 2011.

The timing was determined, at least to some extent, by Netanyahu's scheduled visit to Washington to deliver the Israeli prime minister's traditional speech at the annual policy conference of the pro-Israel lobby, the American-Israel Public Affairs Committee (AIPAC). Netanyahu was also invited by House Speaker John Boehner to address a joint meeting of Congress. In the particular context of May 2011, the White House saw this invitation at best as a Republican attempt to gain a political advantage at the expense of a president soon to be seeking reelection or, worse, as a conservative Israeli prime minister meddling in America's domestic politics. Netanyahu was invited to meet the president on May

20, but the president decided to deliver his long-anticipated speech on the Middle East the day before, on May 19, and to include in it his view of the contours of the desired Israeli-Palestinian settlement.

On May 16, on the eve of his departure for Washington, Netanyahu spoke in the Knesset and presented the Israeli public with the essential points of his own vision of an Israeli-Palestinian settlement. The root of the conflict, he said, never was the absence of a Palestinian state, but was always the Palestinian refusal to recognize the Jewish state. It is not a conflict about 1967 but about 1948 "on the very existence of the State of Israel . . . and to our regret they have not had since then a leadership that would be ready to recognize Israel as the national state of the Jewish people. . . ." Netanyahu went on to present his six conditions for an Israeli-Palestinian settlement:

—Palestinian recognition of Israel as the national home of the Jewish people.

—Palestinian acceptance of a settlement as the end of the conflict and the end of claims.

—Resolution of the Palestinian refugee problem outside the boundaries of Israel.

—Establishment of a Palestinian state only through a peace settlement that would not jeopardize Israel's security and that would include a long-term Israeli military presence along the Jordan River.

—Incorporation of the large settlement blocs in the West Bank as part of Israel.

—Continuation of an undivided Jerusalem as Israel's capital.

There were new elements of implicit and explicit flexibility in the speech, but they did not satisfy the White House. As Netanyahu was about to depart for Washington, Secretary Clinton told him (in a telephone conversation) that the president's speech on the 19th would state that the boundary between Israel and the future Palestinian state should be based on the lines of 1967. Netanyahu responded angrily. He resented both the substance of the statement and his being presented with a fait accompli on such a crucial issue before his meeting with the president. His demand or request that this statement be removed from the speech was rebuffed.[5] Barack Obama delivered his speech on May 19 and met Netanyahu the next day. It was hardly surprising that the meeting was extraordinarily tense for all to see.

The encounter in the White House was followed by three additional speeches: Obama's speech to AIPAC (May 22) and Netanyahu's speeches to AIPAC on the same day and then to Congress (May 24). Obama used his AIPAC speech to clarify and somewhat moderate (from an Israeli perspective) his position with regard to the 1967 lines, the issue that irritated Netanyahu and some of Israel's supporters in the United States. He referred to the controversy generated by the position he took on May 19, asserting that "there was nothing particularly original in my proposal" since "this basic framework for negotiations has long been the basis for discussions among the parties, including previous U.S. administrations." He then proceeded to explain "what the 1967 lines with mutually agreed swaps means":

> By definition it means that the parties themselves—Israelis and Palestinians—will negotiate a border that is different from the one that existed on June 4, 1967. It is a well known formula to all who have worked on this issue for a generation. It allows the parties themselves to account for the changes that have taken place over the last forty four years including the new demographic realities on the ground and the needs of both sides. The ultimate goal is two states for two peoples, Israel as a Jewish state and the homeland for the Jewish people and the state of Palestine as the homeland for the Palestinian people.

Netanyahu's speech to Congress was received enthusiastically on both sides of the aisle. Its core was a slightly modified version of his May 16 speech in the Knesset, skillfully wrapped and presented to a supportive American audience.

Obama's two speeches included several elements that could easily be welcomed and endorsed by Netanyahu and his government: an emphasis on the excellent bilateral relationship, particularly in the areas of defense and security; denunciation of the Iranian regime and the affirmation of Washington's "determination to prevent Iran from acquiring nuclear weapons," and endorsement of the formula long used by U.S administrations to endorse Israel's nuclear ambiguity. He also gave indirect support to Netanyahu's demand that its Palestinian and Arab peace partners recognize it as a Jewish state by referring to Israel as such, and, finally, criticized as an "enormous obstacle to peace" an

Egyptian-brokered "reconciliation" agreement between Fatah and Hamas, which had been announced in late April.

While Netanyahu spoke of his willingness for territorial concessions that would affect "some settlements" and laid the basis for accepting the notion of land swaps with the Palestinians, he remained adamantly opposed to Obama's formula regarding the 1967 lines. He objected to the substance of this position and felt that by articulating it Obama was undermining Israel's position in a future negotiation. In the same vein, he said he felt that by stating that boundaries and security should be discussed first, and Jerusalem and refugees at a later phase, the United States was denying him leverage for the difficult haggling over the latter issues. To boot, Netanyahu was unhappy that Obama refrained from stating that the Palestinian refugee problem should be resolved outside Israel's boundaries.

It is important to note the three levels of Obama's references to Iran. Two of them were overt: the denunciation of the regime (so different from the quest for "engagement" announced two years earlier), and the commitment to prevent Iran from obtaining nuclear weapons. Those in the know realized that his emphasis on the close security cooperation between the United States and Israel referred also to their joint campaign—the specifics of which remained secret—to delay the Iranian nuclear project.

During the summer of 2011, American-Israeli diplomacy was governed by the effort to prevent a vote, some time after late September, on Palestinian statehood in the UN's General Assembly and Security Council. Earlier in the year Mahmud Abbas reached the conclusion that his best option for dealing with the diplomatic stalemate and the growing restlessness and disaffection in his own community—where pressure was building to become part of the Arab Spring—was to seek recognition from and possibly membership in the UN. He could reasonably assume that a two-thirds majority could be obtained in the General Assembly to upgrade the PA's status from nonvoting "observer entity" to "observer state" (the same status as the Vatican). But the road to full UN membership leads through the Security Council. The Obama administration objected to this route and stated clearly that it would veto a resolution in the Security Council if need be. The United States was not keen to cast yet another such veto on Israel's behalf, place itself in an isolated position, and antagonize large parts of the Arab and Muslim worlds. It therefore invested in a sustained effort to find a compromise formula that would enable the parties to resume negotiations and enable Abbas to forgo his initiative without loss of face.

When it became clear that the effort had failed and that Abbas was going ahead with his initiative, Barack Obama used his own speech at the General Assembly to criticize the Palestinian's decision and to make an eloquent, powerful presentation of the need to understand Israel's predicament. Obama was clearly motivated by domestic political considerations (the Democrats had just lost a special congressional election in a constituency in New York State that had been theirs for decades, and Obama clearly was concerned about losing Jewish support for his own reelection campaign in 2012), but he was also genuinely critical of Abbas's decision and was concerned by the prospects of violence that could result from either the success or failure of the Palestinian initiative. On September 22 Abbas submitted an application for membership to the UN's secretary general, and on September 23 both he and Netanyahu addressed the General Assembly, each making a forceful argument for his respective position. These dramatic moments were followed by a fresh effort of the United States and its partners in the Quartet to devise a formula for renewing the negotiations as the optimal way forward.

During the rest of 2011 and most of 2012, the Israeli-Palestinian stalemate continued while Israel's national security agenda and its relationship with Washington were dominated by the Iranian nuclear issue. Several trends and developments converged to perpetuate the stalemate. Netanyahu had no personal or political interest in reviving the Israeli-Palestinian track and jeopardizing his right-wing coalition. In fact, through both action and inaction his government facilitated settlement activities and other measures designed to perpetuate Israel's hold over the West Bank, such as the ongoing push to grant a college in the town of Ariel in the West Bank the status of a full-fledged university. The Palestinian leadership, weak, divided, and tired, made no real contribution to reviving the peace process, and the rest of the Arab world was preoccupied with such issues as the Islamist takeover in Egypt and the Syrian civil war. The Obama administration too was preoccupied—with other challenges in the Middle East, with the global economic crisis, and with

President Obama's reelection campaign—and had no desire to sustain another failure in the Middle East.

Israel and the United States had achieved a considerable degree of agreement and cooperation on the Iranian nuclear issue. Obama had reformulated the U.S. position in language that was much more appealing to Israel. He explicitly ruled out the "containment" option and endorsed instead a policy of "prevention," and he articulated Washington's determination to deny Iran a nuclear arsenal—not in the context of a U.S. commitment to Israel's security but as a matter of America's own vital national security interests. The common opposition in Israel and the United States to Iran's nuclear program manifested itself in open and covert cooperation: joint military exercises and planning, sale of new matériel, and joint efforts to slow down Iran's progress.

But there also had been a parting of the ways. During the spring and early summer of 2012, the Israeli leadership, headed by Prime Minister Netanyahu and Defense Minister Barak, reached the conclusion that Obama's policies were not going to stop Iran's race for the bomb. The stiffer sanctions imposed on Iran were painful and had an impact on the country's domestic politics, but they did not seem to affect the leadership's determination to push forward with the nuclear project. The negotiations between the P5 + 1 (the permanent members of the Security Council plus Germany) and Iran were renewed, but they were conducted at a leisurely pace and finally collapsed yet again. Iran made no effort to conceal the fact that it was moving forward in uranium enrichment and in building medium- and long-range missiles capable of carrying a nuclear warhead.

Netanyahu and Barak became persuaded that only a unilateral Israeli military action or the threat of such action could halt the Iranian program or induce the United States and the international community to take effective action. Military action could be taken by either Israel or the United States, but there were significant differences between the two options. An American raid would be far more effective than an Israeli one. The United States had the capacity to destroy Iran's nuclear installations while Israel could at best retard the Iranian effort by eighteen months or so. The United States also had a much larger "window of opportunity." It could wait another year while trying other alternatives and building domestic and international support for the military option. Israel, with its more limited capacity, had to act sooner, if it decided to act.

The November 2012 U.S. presidential elections were another compounding factor. Whatever his ultimate intentions with regard to Iran's nuclear program, Barack Obama had no intention of launching a raid prior to the elections, embroiling his country and the world in a major crisis during such a sensitive period. The Israeli leadership, always suspicious of Obama's real willingness to use a military option, was worried that after the elections he would procrastinate and that in the event of a Republican victory even a more bellicose President Romney would not want to start his term by launching such a raid. Netanyahu and Barack felt that a delay could mean the end of the military option and de facto resignation to the notion of a nuclear Iran. They chose to make a massive investment in Israeli preparations for an attack, which were meant to serve either as a prelude to an actual Israeli raid or as a spur to a U.S. raid (on the assumption that the United States would prefer to act rather than become embroiled in a crisis generated by a less successful or even failed Israeli action). The United States was in fact horrified by the idea of an Israeli attack and mounted a massive effort to prevent it.

Two additional elements then arose in this complex arena. One was the criticism of Netanyahu and Barak's policies voiced by several former members of Israel's national security establishment, who were joined, more discreetly, by senior officers and officials currently in office. The other was the unhealthy link created between this issue and the U.S. presidential elections. Obama and other Democrats felt and complained that Netanyahu was meddling in U.S. domestic politics by trying to help Romney win the election. Romney and other Republicans were only too happy to criticize Obama for his handling of the Iranian issue.

By September 2012 the rift between Obama and Netanyahu became open. Obama refused to meet with Netanyahu in New York when both were in the city for the meeting of the UN General Assembly, and he rejected Netanyahu's demand that the United States draw a "red line" for Iran's nuclear program, which, if crossed, would trigger military action. In fact, Netanyahu employed the notion of a red line in order to abandon the threat of imminent Israeli military action. When rebuffed by Obama, he announced his own red line in his UN speech, indicating that he was willing to wait until the spring of 2013 for the United States and the international community to take effective action. The threat of an Israeli raid and a subsequent regional war was thus delayed but not retracted. In mid-October 2012 it was revealed that in a last-ditch effort, the ground had been prepared through a secret channel for direct U.S.-Iranian negotiations to resolve the nuclear issue. However, negotiations were not to begin before the U.S. presidential elections, in early November. Understandably, the Iranians would want to know the identity of the U.S. president with whom they would be dealing.

8

THE WEB OF RELATIONSHIPS

As we have seen throughout this exploration of the Arab-Israeli conflict, the very term is somewhat misleading—implying as it does the notion that a single conflict pits Israel against the Arab world, and that the ebb and flow of Israel's relations with the Palestinians are linked organically to, say, its rivalry with Iraq or its complex relationship with Morocco. To a considerable extent, this has indeed been true: broad trends have applied across the region. After all, the Arabs collectively rallied against Israel in 1948, participated in the conflict when it festered and swelled, were devastated by the defeat of 1967, condemned Egypt's Sadat in 1977 for moving toward peace, and adopted his formula only a decade later. But under the umbrella of unity, there have always been exceptions, rivalries, and tensions within the Arab world—and those differences have applied to relations with Israel.[1]

EGYPT

For the thirty years between its participation in the Arab invasion of the young Jewish state in 1948 and the Camp David Accords of 1978, Egypt was Israel's most formidable foe. Its decision to enter the war in 1948 had not been a matter of course. It was preceded by a policy debate between two principal schools of thought, one upholding the raison d'état of the Egyptian state, and the other stressing Egypt's Arab and Islamic commitments, as well as the political imperatives of Egyptian leadership and hegemony.[2] The issue was decided at the eleventh hour by King Farouk, who was motivated to join in the war against Israel by dynastic considerations and personal ambition. His decision's momentous consequences included the monarchy's own downfall four years later, and the humiliation of defeat in the war added to Egypt's already complex attitude toward Israel.[3]

The 1948 war launched a quarter-century-long cycle of violence that included four full-fledged wars and a period of low-level conflict known as a war of attrition. On the Egyptian side, the interplay of ideological commitment, state interests, and personal ambition was broadened and intensified with the rise of Gamal Abdel Nasser's revolutionary regime. As the leader of a messianic pan-Arab nationalism, as the head of a military regime, as Moscow's ally, and as the president of the Egyptian state who was angry at the wedge Israel had driven between Egypt and the eastern Arab world, Nasser mobilized hitherto unfamiliar resources against Israel. Israel viewed Egypt as the potential key to a peaceful settlement with the Arab world. Yet during most of the Nasserite period the prospect of a settlement seemed remote. Israel remained deeply concerned that Egypt's military power alone was a threat, and that threat was compounded by Egypt's ability to carry large parts of the Arab world with it. In a crisis during May 1967 that deteriorated into the Six-Day War in June, Egyptian and Israeli misperceptions and misreading of intentions and capabilities were extreme.[4]

Six more years and two more conflicts were required before Israel and Egypt could begin moving to peaceful settlement and reconciliation, but the foundations for these were laid in the 1967 war, during which Israel demonstrated an overwhelming military advantage, acquired territorial assets for a land-for-peace deal, and dealt a devastating blow to Nasser and his regime. When Nasser died in September 1970, his heir apparent, Anwar al-Sadat, was seen by other contenders for power in Egypt as a harmless transitional figure. But Sadat showed himself to be an astute politician, able to outwit his rivals, and emerged as a true international statesman—a dramatic personal evolution that set the stage for Egypt's reconciliation with Israel.

As part of his comprehensive reorientation of his country's politics and policies, Sadat decided that Egypt must disengage from the conflict with Israel. Beginning in 1977, his agenda and that of Israeli Prime Minister Menachem Begin overlapped enough to enable them to conclude the Camp David Accords in 1978 and a peace treaty in 1979. For Sadat, peace with Israel was necessary to regain the Sinai Peninsula and to build a new relationship with the United States. He was willing to dispute with the other Arab states over his and Egypt's right to follow this policy, which gave priority to Egypt's own interests over its commitment to the Arab and Palestinian causes. But at no time did Sadat intend to make a separate deal with Israel or to "divorce" his country from its Arab context—even though these were among the immediate results of the Camp David agreements. Begin, in turn, came to agree to a complete Israeli withdrawal from the Sinai as the price for peace with this most important Arab state. He also presumed that Egypt would willingly acquiesce in a perpetuation of Israel's control of the West Bank and that somehow the Palestinian autonomy plan included in the peace treaty could be finessed.[5] That certainly was not the Egyptian view of things.

Implementation of the bilateral components of the Israeli-Egyptian agreement proceeded smoothly, but the collapse of the autonomy negotiations, the continuation of the Israeli-Palestinian conflict, and Israel's decision to go to war in Lebanon in 1982 combined to produce a very negative effect on the fledgling peace between Egypt and Israel. This negativity was reinforced by Egyptian considerations, including domestic Islamic opposition (both to the government and to peace with Israel), criticism from Nasserite elements, and a desire for conciliation with the rest of the Arab world. Over the years, Egypt, first under Sadat and then under his successor, Hosni Mubarak, adopted a policy of cold peace. Under this policy, which resulted not from a conscious early decision but rather from a murky trial-and-error process, Egypt honored its principal commitments toward Israel, including diplomatic relations, an agreed-on security regime in the Sinai, and allowing Israeli tourism in Egypt. But Egypt also kept economic and trade relations to a minimum, discouraged visits by Egyptians to Israel and cultural relations of all kinds, and signaled that the regime did not really frown upon critics of peace with Israel. Nor did the government curtail virulent verbal attacks against Israel and Jews, but instead invoked its stated commitment to freedom of the press.

This mixed policy, which Israel and occasionally the United States criticized, on the whole functioned reasonably well, and by the late 1980s Egypt's reconciliation with the Arab world was completed. With the Soviet Union's decline, even Sadat's most bitter critic, Hafiz al-Asad in Syria, eventually renewed his country's diplomatic relations with Egypt and indicated his readiness to try to resolve Syria's own conflict with Israel.

The inauguration of the Madrid process in 1991 and, even more so, the formation of the Rabin-Peres government the following year, should have dramatically improved Israeli-Egyptian relations. The separate peace with Israel was now part of a comprehensive peace process; and the new Israeli government used Egyptian help to advance its negotiations with the Palestinians, eventually signing an agreement with them (the Oslo Accords) that was much more attractive, from a Palestinian perspective, than the original autonomy plan had been.

Yet a real improvement in relations between Israel and Egypt failed to happen, either in the 1990s or at any subsequent point. Mubarak's regime could not easily dissociate itself from the cold peace policy, for it was dealing with a radical Islamic opposition, was occasionally pursuing a neo-Nasserist regional and foreign policy, and wanted to signal that it was not Washington's captive. But the additional, larger dimension of Egypt's coolness was a renewed sense of Israel as a competitor. This concern was given a new urgency by the very success of the peace process. Egypt certainly did not wish to see Israel as a regional superpower enjoying a special relationship with the United States and flexing its military and economic muscles throughout the region and beyond.

There was a time, before the Oslo Accords were signed and for a few months afterward, when Egypt appeared reasonably pleased to mediate between Israel and other Arab parties. But when Israel signed a peace with Jordan, began to normalize its relations with the Gulf States and in North Africa, and developed new concepts for regional cooperation, this satisfaction was replaced by alarm.[6] And the principal means Egypt used to articulate its unhappiness was through the issue of nuclear weapons. Egypt, like the rest of the Arab world, had taken it for granted that Israel had a nuclear arsenal, even though Israel adhered to a policy of studied ambiguity in this matter. For years Israeli governments had been using the convenient formula that "Israel will not be the first nation to introduce nuclear weapons to the Middle East," and had consistently refused to sign the Non-Proliferation Treaty, arguing that it was not willing to undertake the treaty's commitments while countries like Iraq and Iran might develop nuclear weapons regardless of having signed the treaty. In the late 1960s, after considerable tension with the United States over this issue, Israel finally arrived at a modus vivendi with Washington; also, Israel's destruction of Iraq's nuclear reactor in 1981 displayed its determination to deny the option of nuclear weapons to other Middle Eastern countries.

As the senior Arab state, Egypt traditionally led the Arab world's campaign at the United Nations and elsewhere against Israel's status as a presumed nuclear power. Also, as a populous country with a large conventional army, Egypt was genuinely opposed to the introduction of nuclear weapons to the Middle East, and it resented Israel's quest for nuclear deterrence and a nuclear monopoly, considering these as symptoms of Israel's hegemonic and exclusivist ambitions. When the security provisions for Israel's withdrawal from the Sinai were negoti-ated at Camp David in 1978, Egypt raised questions about the nuclear issue and was rebuffed. Sadat chose not to insist on the matter so as not to obstruct his main goal—regaining the Sinai. But for the next fifteen years, Egypt continued to raise the issue in the customary diplomatic settings. When a working group on arms control and regional security (ACRES) began to meet in 1992 (part of the multilateral track of the Madrid process), Egyptian-Israeli disagreements over this issue soon emerged, naturally enough. But by late 1994, a qualitative change had occurred: Egypt began to use the issue to slow the diplomacy—first in ACRES, then in the working group on environmental issues (given the issue of nuclear waste), and finally in the Madrid process multilateral steering group.

The change was to some extent due to the UN's approaching April 1995 conference to review the Non-Proliferation Treaty, which was scheduled to expire that year unless it was renewed. The United States wanted the treaty to be renewed indefinitely, and to Egypt this seemed like the last opportunity to bring pressure on Israel to sign the treaty, which it had refused to do. Egypt was able to extract from the United States acceptance of its demand that a Middle East annex be added that did not mention Israel by name but laid a foundation for future Egyp-tian initiatives. Israel recognized Egypt's genuine concern, but it calcu-lated also that Cairo had a much broader agenda: Rabin and Peres could not quite understand why, after years of passive opposition to Israel's nuclear option, Egypt was shifting to active and vociferous opposition precisely when Arab-Israeli peace seemed to be in reach. As they and their advisers saw it, this was part of a deliberate effort to slow down Israel's "normalization" in the Middle East.

Puzzled and angry as they were, Rabin and Peres chose to moderate their reaction to this Egyptian policy. Israel's relationship with Egypt was too precious and fragile to be guided by emotions. They also understood that when conflict between the two countries had ended at Camp David, it had been replaced not by friendship but by peaceful competition. Incidentally, it also was convenient for both Egypt and Israel to pretend that Cairo's anti-Israel moves had been initiated by Foreign Minister Amre Moussa, an ambitious man subscribing to a new version of pan-Arabism. This allowed President Mubarak to stay above the fray as a supreme leader, arbitrating among rival factions in his government while preserving Egypt's relationship with Israel.[7]

After Peres succeeded the assassinated Rabin in 1995, Egypt shared some of Jordan's discomfort with Peres's expansive view of a future Arab-Israeli peace, but Egypt's criticism was milder, concerned principally with Peres's quest for a new regional order. It was also skeptical of his determination to have Israel come quickly to a far-reaching agreement with Syria, a prospect that stirred ambivalent feelings in Egypt. Syria's definition of a "dignified settlement" was expressed in terms that were in contradistinction to the Camp David Accords, and when Israel discussed Syria as the key to a comprehensive Arab-Israeli settlement, Egypt felt put in second place. But, unlike the Jordanians, the Egyptians still hoped to see Peres win in the May 1996 elections, their unhappiness with some aspects of the Labor government's peace policies being minor compared with the prospect of a Netanyahu victory.

When Netanyahu won those elections, Mubarak's unhappiness with the new prime minister and his policies was open and obvious; even so, he maintained a dialogue with Netanyahu's government. The Egyptian government also allowed further degrees of cultural normalization with Israel. Clearly, Mubarak and his aides had come to realize that the policy of cold peace was playing into the hands of the Israeli right wing. At the same time, Egypt took advantage of the political change in Israel to cut the peace process down to size: Egypt did not want this process to transform the regional politics of the Middle East. Having Israel come to a settlement with the Palestinians and eventually with Syria would be one thing; watching Israel use these agreements to develop a network of political and economic relations across the Middle East, to construct new strategic relations with Turkey, and to continue special relations with Washington while retaining a nuclear monopoly—that was another.

The Arab-Israeli armed conflicts of the first decade in the twenty-first century—the Israeli-Palestinian war of attrition (the second intifada) of 2000–03, the Israel-Lebanon War of 2006, and Operation Cast Lead in 2008—all these confronted Egypt with a dual challenge: the decision to maintain its "normal" relationship with Israel, even at a cold peace level, plus the conflict's immediate and potential effect on the Egyptian street. Like other Arab regimes, Mubarak's Egypt had to take into account the repercussions of the media revolution of previous years. In marked contrast to earlier crises, the ubiquitous satellite television stations brought to numerous Egyptian homes graphic, vivid images of these conflicts, thereby agitating Egyptian public opinion.

This challenge was particularly apparent during Israel's 2006 war with Hizballah. Like other Arab regimes, Mubarak's government gave Israel's operation initial tacit support. It viewed Iran and its proxy, Hizballah, as dangerous challengers of their own legitimacy and stability and were hoping that Israel would deliver a swift, deadly blow to Hizballah. When that failed to happen and the new war lingered for a month, public outrage built up, and Egypt and other conservative regimes became vociferously critical of Israel's policies.

During the same decade, conditions also changed in the Gaza Strip and the Sinai. Egypt was rattled by the Hamas takeover of Gaza. Egypt now had on its border an entity ruled by the Palestinian offshoot of the Muslim Brotherhood and allied with Iran. Cairo was concerned by the large-scale influx of Palestinians from the impoverished, overpopulated Gaza Strip and by penetration of agitators and weapons into its own territory. At the same time it was pressured by Israel to prevent smuggling into Gaza of weapons, missiles, and rockets in particular—whether above ground or in underground tunnels. Egypt did close the border with Gaza, with very limited exceptions, thus becoming in fact a party to the siege of Gaza, but its efforts to prevent smuggling into Gaza were half-hearted and not entirely effective.

Egypt's difficulties in this regard derived in large part from the Mubarak regime's declining ability to control the Sinai's Bedouin population. Hamas, and to a lesser extent al-Qaeda, spent large amounts of money buying Bedouin cooperation in the flourishing Gaza smuggling industry and in facilitating occasional terrorist activities in and from the Sinai. Another lucrative trade was the smuggling of thousands of African migrants and refugees through the Sinai and across the long, unprotected Israeli-Egyptian border.

The nuclear issue remained another bone of contention between Egypt and Israel. Egypt could not do much in this regard during the Bush years. But Barack Obama made reduction of the world's nuclear arsenal one of his priorities, and he was less sensitive to Israel's concerns than his predecessors had been. When a nuclear security summit was convened in Washington in 2010, Egypt's diplomats were able to draw on the 1995 agreement to get Israel mentioned specifically by name and obtain a resolution that stipulated further discussion of the issue in 2012.

The Mubarak regime's loss of control over the Bedouin in the Sinai was an early harbinger of its decline and ultimate fall in the revolution of January-February 2011. Israel followed these events with manifest concern. Intellectually, Israelis realized that in the long range a democratic Egypt and a democratic Arab world would be partners for a stable peace. But in more immediate terms they were concerned by the fall of a familiar regime that was, if not friendly, at least reliable—and by the prospect that the Muslim Brotherhood and other radical elements might end up as partners in any new regime and possibly even its masters. For more than thirty years, peace with Egypt, cold as it was, had been a cornerstone of Israel's national security. Israel's view of the revolutionary changes in Egypt was shaped primarily by Jerusalem's concern with the durability of this peace. In the late winter and early spring of 2011, several statements by Egypt's new foreign minister, Nabil al-Arabi, and other officials, and the increased influence of Islamist groups in the country, exacerbated Israel's concern that Egypt, while not abrogating the peace treaty with Israel, had mounted a path leading to a different regional orientation and to a still colder, more limited, relationship with Israel. These concerns were heightened by a terrorist attack on August 18, 2011. It was launched by a small Palestinian organization from

Gaza through the Sinai against Israeli vehicles traveling to Eilat along the Israeli-Egyptian border. The terrorists wore Egyptian uniforms and may have had support from some local Egyptian forces. Israeli troops who fought and killed most of the terrorist also killed a number of Egyptian soldiers. This led to a large anti-Israeli demonstration in Cairo and to fresh demands by opposition groups to break the relationship with Israel. Matters came to a head on September 11 when an Egyptian mob stormed the Israeli embassy in Cairo. General Mohamed Tantawi and his colleagues on the Supreme Council of the Armed Forces were reluctant to engage in yet another confrontation with the "street" and refrained from acting against the rioters. It took the personal intervention of President Obama to get them to send commando troops to help salvage from the building six Israeli security guards, protecting the premises after the evacuation of diplomatic personnel, and to prevent a bloodbath. Israel now has a minimal presence in Cairo and Israeli-Egyptian peace is hanging by a thread.

SYRIA

Israel's current relationship with Syria has been shaped by a legacy of hostility and rivalry, by twenty years of intermittent and unfinished negotiations, and by new realities: the transition from Hafiz to Bashar al-Asad, Israel's departure from south Lebanon, the war in Iraq and the ensuing deterioration in Syria's relationship with the United States, and Syria's alliance with Iran.

For four decades in the aftermath of the 1948 war, Syria was Israel's most bitter enemy among the Arab states. Syria's self-perception as "the Arab Nation's pulsating heart," its particular closeness to Palestine and the Palestinians, and the radicalization and militarization of its politics positioned it as Israel's fiercest enemy. But the collapse of its Soviet patron and the circumstances created by the first Gulf War led Syria to come to the Madrid Conference in 1991 and endorse the notion of a negotiated peace settlement with Israel.

When Yitzhak Rabin jump-started the Madrid process in 1992, he (and most of his successors) acted on the assumption that they had to sequence their progression in the peace process—that the Israeli political system would not be able to sustain simultaneous major concessions in both the West Bank and the Golan Heights. As a result all Israeli prime ministers since 1992 (except for Ehud Barak during part of his tenure) have felt that they had to choose between a "Syria first" and a "Palestine first" policy. In the 1990s the Israeli leadership and the Clinton administration tended to assign priority to the Syrian track primarily for three reasons. First, the Syrian-Israeli conflict is "simpler" than the Israeli-Palestinian one because it is essentially a territorial conflict as distinct from the clash of Israeli and Palestinian nationalisms. Second, unlike the fragmented Palestinian political system, Syria was an orderly state with a powerful, authoritative government. Third, Hafiz al-Asad (in contradistinction to Yasser Arafat) was seen as a reliable, if difficult, partner.

And yet, and despite the major investment made by President Clinton and his administration, Israel and Syria could not reach agreement and negotiations collapsed in 2000. Even so, the shape of a settlement was adumbrated during these years. Israel accepted (hypothetically and conditionally) the notion of full withdrawal from the Golan, and Syria agreed to adopt the main components of the peace treaty signed by Egypt in 1979: contractual peace, diplomatic relations, normalization, and security arrangements. What was most glaringly lacking was simultaneous political will to make the concessions and sign the deal.

The watershed year in the history of this negotiation turned out to be 2000. Hafiz al-Asad died and was succeeded by his son Bashar; and Israel withdrew fully from Lebanon and severed the Gordian knot between its Lebanese problem (discussed below) and the Syrian negotiation. In early 2001 Ehud Barak was replaced by Ariel Sharon, who focused on the Palestinian issue and had no interest in a Syrian deal, and Bill Clinton was succeeded by George W. Bush, who at the outset of his term sought to disengage from the Israeli-Arab peace process and shortly thereafter found himself on a collision course with Syria's new president.

Hafiz al-Asad had been a master of straddling the line. At the height of the cold war, he maneuvered between the United States and the Soviet Union, taking advantage of Washington's desire to lure him away from Moscow. During the 1990s he negotiated a peace agreement with Israel but supported a propaganda campaign by Hamas and other Palestinian "rejectionists" against Arafat's "capitulation" to Israel. He also supported Hizballah's military campaign against Israel in Lebanon, both because he wanted Israel out of Lebanon and because he believed that diplomacy had to rest on force and power, and therefore pressure had to be exerted until an agreement was reached.

His son and successor tried to emulate this strategy. The double game Bashar Asad played in Iraq before and after the American invasion earned him George W. Bush's hostility. With regard to peace talks with Israel, he also pursued a two-track line. From an early point in his presidency, he argued that he wanted to renew the peace negotiations with Jerusalem. He changed the terms of the peace agreement he had in mind several times, but on the whole he indicated that he was willing to adhere to the terms that had tentatively been agreed to in the previous decade. But he also stated that he was preparing a military option should the diplomatic one fail. In addition to buying advanced weapon systems from the Soviet Union and to deploying Scud missiles, he struck a secret agreement with North Korea to build a nuclear reactor in northeastern Syria. Whereas his father had been Iran's ally since 1979, Bashar gradually lost the status of Tehran's peer and became the subordinate partner. Under Bashar, Syria became the most important component in the "resistance axis" constructed by Tehran. Hizballah, Hamas, and (the Palestinian) Islamic Jihad were the other partners in this camp, which pitted itself against the United States, Israel, and such moderate or conservative Arab states as Mubarak's Egypt, Saudi Arabia, and Jordan. The doctrine of resistance argued that by persevering, Muslims and Arabs could stand up to both the United States (as in Iraq and Afghanistan) and Israel. Peace with Israel meant capitulation and was to be avoided. Israel's unilateral withdrawals from Lebanon and Gaza were touted as prime examples of the ability to defeat Israel and as harbingers of its ouster from the whole of Palestine.

Syria's main contribution to Iran's efforts during these years was by affording it access to Lebanon and Gaza (by hosting the external headquarters of Hamas in Damascus). Asad and his team knew full well that Hizballah was ultimately an arm of the Iranian regime, but they saw it also as an ally in preserving Syria's own position in Lebanon. They were instrumental in building Hizballah's huge arsenal of missiles and rockets. This arsenal was deployed there primarily to deter Israel and the United States from attacking Iran's nuclear installations, but it also was seen as part of Syria's own deterrence against Israel.

During his tenure as prime minister, Ariel Sharon had no interest in negotiating with Syria, and he rebuffed a number of Syrian attempts to renew the dialogue with Israel. After 2003 Bashar al-Asad's efforts were motivated at least in part by his desire to break the diplomatic siege laid by the Bush administration. For Sharon, who was focused on the Palestinian issue, this was yet another reason to reject the Syrian gambits. Sharon had built an excellent working relationship with the Bush White House and he did not wish to jeopardize it by talking to the president's bête noire. This was also Ehud Olmert's policy during his first year in office, but in February 2007 he changed his mind and, as has been described in an earlier chapter, authorized Turkey's prime minister, Recep Tayyip Erdoğan, to start a mediation process with Damascus. This effort lasted for almost two years until it collapsed in December 2008. Olmert copied a page from Asad's own book, and when he found out that Syria and North Korea were building a nuclear reactor, he sent his air force to destroy it in September 2007. Israel refrained from taking credit for this action, in part to help Asad overcome the humiliation and to keep him from retaliating.

During these years the focus of the Israeli-Syrian give-and-take shifted significantly. In the 1990s the concept of a prospective Israeli-Syrian peace deal was modeled on Israel's peace with Egypt. Predicated on the principle of territories for peace, the core of the deal would be full withdrawal from the Golan in return for a (cold) peace agreement and a security regime. By the early 2000s the crucial issue for Israel was Syria's intimate alliance with Iran and the manifestations of that alliance in Lebanon and Gaza. Israel, without abandoning the expectation of peace and normalization, began to insist that Syria had to disengage from Iran and end its support for Hizballah and the radical Palestinian organizations if it wanted an Israeli withdrawal from the Golan. It is precisely this state of affairs that turned Israel's national security establishment into the chief advocate of an Israeli-Syrian deal. Looking at Israel's national security challenges, the leaders of this establishment argued in recent years that an agreement with Syria would be a crucial step in the effort to dismantle the challenge presented by Iran and in loosening Hizballah's stranglehold on Lebanon.

This view is not shared by Prime Minister Netanyahu. As a previous chapter noted, during his first term in the 1990s, he tried to shift from the Palestinian track to the Syrian one by employing his friend Ronald Lauder as an emissary to Syria. But in his 2009 election campaign, and once in office, he was consistent in rejecting the idea of withdrawal from the Golan. In January 2009 George W. Bush, Asad's foe, was replaced in the White House by Barack Obama, who in his own election campaign had promised "to engage" with Syria (as well as with Iran). As president, however, Obama invested his major effort on the Palestinian track. He failed in his attempt to persuade Damascus to remain patient and settle for the time being on an improvement in Syria's bilateral relationship with Washington.

Israel's ambivalence toward Bashar al-Asad and his regime cut deep. The Israeli leadership was fully aware of the damage Syria inflicted on Israel in Lebanon and Gaza and by the destructive potential of a regime that had tried once to acquire nuclear weapons. But when confronted with the prospect of a regime change, Israelis pondered whether the current regime may not be preferable to the alternative, whether that is a regime dominated by Islamists or a long period of instability. After all, it was an unstable Syria that triggered the May 1967 crisis. In 2005, when President Bush seemed to be targeting Bashar al-Asad and his regime, his Israeli partners were not enthusiastic. In 2011, when the Arab Spring reached Syria and serious protests erupted, Israelis were once again uncertain what to think. They saw the weakening of the Iranian camp as a net gain but were not at all convinced that Asad's putative fall would be in Israel's immediate interest. This did not prevent Asad, when he finally addressed his people on March 30, from arguing that the unrest in Syria was not a domestic phenomenon but a conspiracy hatched from the outside by the United States and Israel. Israelis could only wish that they had such influence on the course of events in Syria.

On May 10, 2011, as the pressure on Asad's regime mounted, his cousin, Rami Makhluf, gave an unusual interview to the *New York Times* in which he threatened, among other things, that there would be no stability in Israel if there was no stability in Syria. Four days later, on what they call Nakba Day, hundreds of Palestinian demonstrators in Syria, clearly encouraged by the Asad regime, broke through the fence to Majdal Shams, a Druze village in the Golan Heights. It was the first serious infringement of Syria's 1974 Disengagement Agreement with Israel and also a message from the Asad regime that it did not intend to go down quietly.

In the late spring and early summer as the demonstrations and bloody suppression continued and as the United States, the major European countries, several Arab states, and Turkey denounced Bashar al-Asad as an illegitimate ruler, Israel maintained a passive stand. It had no influence over the course of events in Syria and did not seek any. The issue of a new peace negotiation with Syria was off the agenda for the foreseeable future, and the country had to prepare quietly for the possibility that Asad, on his way down or out, would try to inflict one final blow on Israel.

In 2000, after the failure of the Clinton-Asad meeting in Geneva and before Hafiz al-Asad's death, the Syrian intellectual Sadiq al-'Azm published an essay in the *New York Review of Books* in which he asserted that the Syrian public (by which he meant primarily Damascene society) had accepted the notion of peace with Israel.[8] The only remaining question, he said, was when the peace would be negotiated. (Al-'Azm's concept of peace was a different matter; it was quite far from Israel's most modest concept of peace with Syria.) Al-'Azm is well known as an independent, courageous intellectual and definitely does not speak for the Ba'ath regime, but his essay should be read with an awareness of the limits of free expression in Syria, particularly regarding such a sensitive issue as peacemaking with Israel.

Eleven years after its publication, al-'Azm's essay can be read with more than a touch of irony. It seems far removed from the present realities. But it remains significant. Present realities can change swiftly and dramatically—as the 2011 events in the Arab world demonstrated—and the deep currents of Syrian public opinion could once again become relevant.

LEBANON

In the 1950s and 1960s a political cliché was current in Israel to the effect that "Lebanon will be the second Arab state to sign a peace with Israel," simply because Lebanon did not have the regional clout to be the first. The cliché, clearly not borne out by the course of events, was inspired by earlier contacts between Zionist diplomats and some Maronite Christian leaders in Lebanon and on a mistaken perception of the nature of Lebanese politics. Many Lebanese Christians thought of Israel as another non-Muslim state that was or could be a bulwark against pan-Arab nationalism—and thus Israelis thought of them as potential allies. But most of these Christians also viewed Lebanon as a part of the Arab world and wanted to preserve the delicate domestic and external balances so indispensable to Lebanon's precarious survival.[9]

Those balances were upset in the early 1970s, and the Lebanese state and political system essentially collapsed during the 1975–76 civil war. From Israel's perspective, the civil war and lingering crisis in Lebanon had several negative results: the Lebanese state was incapable of exercising authority over Lebanese territory, Syria had become the paramount power and military presence in Lebanon, and the Palestinians built a territorial base in Beirut and southern Lebanon under the PLO's direction. Israel eventually responded in various ways: a tactical indirect understanding with Syria to preclude a Syrian military presence in southern Lebanon, an Israeli "security strip" inside Lebanon, and a strategic alliance with several Maronite groups in Lebanon. But the Lebanese front was the main arena of the PLO's armed conflict with Israel during the 1970s. The growing Palestinian and Syrian challenge and a misguided belief that Israel could place a friendly government in Beirut and change the strategic configuration in the region led Menachem Begin's government to invade Lebanon in 1982.

For both Lebanon and Israel, the 1982 war had momentous, mostly unintended consequences. The PLO's leaders and troops were forced to move to Tunisia; Syria's hold over Lebanon, after an initial setback, was reinforced; and the Christian communities preserved some of their political privileges but lost much of their power. But the war's single most important outcome was the acceleration of a process that had been apparent earlier: the mobilization of the hitherto underprivileged Shiite community and its quest for a political position commensurate with its demographic strength in Lebanon. This trend was reinforced when Iran's Islamic revolution of 1979 was projected into Lebanon and its Shiite community, so far its only successful foreign destination.[10] The Shiite militias of Amal and Hizballah were propelled not by nationalism but by religion, and they introduced into the conflict such then-novel elements as suicide bombings.

By 1985 Israel had given up any claim to figure in Lebanon's national politics and focused on the defense of its northern frontier. It withdrew to an expanded security zone in south Lebanon maintained by the Israel Defense Forces with the help of a local militia. After that point, the security zone and occasionally Israel itself were attacked primarily by Hizballah, under direction from Tehran and with the tacit cooperation of Syria.

In October 1989 an Arab conference held in Taif, Saudi Arabia, tried to consolidate and formalize the situation. The compromise embodied in the Taif Accord envisaged Syria's military withdrawal from Lebanon, albeit as a remote prospect. But the accord remained a dead letter. In fact, Syria took advantage of its participation in the American-led coalition during the 1990–91 Persian Gulf crisis and Gulf War to consolidate its hold over Lebanon, fourteen years after its original invasion in response to the civil war. Syria finally controlled Lebanon through a functioning local government—maintaining a significant military presence there not as an army of occupation but as a guarantor of its hegemony, as a defender of the western approaches to Damascus, and as a potential threat to Israel. Syria made a point of acting as the guardian of the trappings of Lebanese statehood, but in subtle and less-than-subtle ways it ensured Lebanon's acquiescence to its will and interests. Thus, no progress was to be made in Lebanese-Israeli negotiations so long as a breakthrough had not occurred in Syrian-Israeli relations. Syria undertook, once such a breakthrough occurred, to obtain a comparable agreement for Lebanon, and Lebanon's territory was to be used to pressure Israel to come to terms with Syria.

In 1994 the broad lines of an understanding about Lebanon were, in fact, worked out between Israel and Syria through their ambassadors in Washington. Provided that a Syrian-Israeli agreement was reached, Syria was willing to endorse an Israeli-Lebanese peace agreement to be implemented within nine months—a time frame that coincided with the nine months that Rabin envisaged in his discussions with Secretary of State Christopher for the first phase of a prospective agreement with Syria. But no such agreement was reached.

Unfortunately, there was also a violent side to this story. Hizballah's offensive against Israel's security zone in southern Lebanon and occasional Katyusha rocket attacks on northern Israel kept up a permanent cycle of violence along the Lebanese-Israeli border. Twice—in July 1993 and April 1996—Israel launched large-scale land operations in Lebanon in an effort to break the cycle. Both operations led to "understandings" between Israel and Hizballah that limited the violence but failed to end it.

Soon after the formation of his government in June 1996, Netanyahu sought to promote a "Lebanon first" initiative, which he hoped would win Syrian endorsement. But Syria suspected this effort was an attempt to drive a wedge between Damascus and Beirut and wasted no time in rebuffing the gambit. That September, a redeployment of Syrian troops in Lebanon led to a brief war scare, when some in Israel wrongly interpreted it as a preparation for launching an attack, and Syrians then wrongly interpreted Israel's statements and responsive movements as preparations for an attack. Eventually, reassuring messages were exchanged and a confrontation was averted, but the episode showed how explosive the Israeli-Syrian-Lebanese triangle was.

As the months went by and the number of Israeli casualties grew dramatically, so did public and political pressure to extricate Israeli soldiers from southern Lebanon. A mixed coalition of concerned parents, left-wing politicians, and Golan settlers who were eager to sever the diplomatic link between southern Lebanon and the Golan Heights led a movement calling for Israel's unilateral withdrawal from Lebanon. Netanyahu's government responded with a novel tactic—a conditional acceptance of Security Council Resolution 425, which in 1978 had required Israel to leave Lebanon after an earlier intervention. This put Lebanon's President Elias Harawi and Prime Minister Rafiq Hariri in a difficult position: it was hard for them to explain why they were refusing to take Israel up on its offer to withdraw. Their predicament enhanced Syria's suspicions that they might seek accommodation with Israel on their own, and Syria made highly visible efforts to keep Lebanon's government in tow.

As has been described above, this state of affairs was transformed by Ehud Barak's decision to withdraw the IDF from south Lebanon, a decision that was implemented in May–June 2000. Barak took care to execute the withdrawal in close coordination with the United Nations (not a common practice in Israel's diplomatic tradition) and obtained the UN's stamp of approval for the completion of Israel's withdrawal to the international boundary. But Hizballah, and subsequently the government of Lebanon, complained that Israel's failure to withdraw from the Shaba Farms and the village of Ghajar (Syrian territory according to Israel and the UN) and Israeli overflights constituted ongoing acts of aggression. Hizballah used these complaints to justify the maintenance of regular low-level pressure on Israel's northern borders with occasional outbursts of more spectacular attacks.

Hizballah continued its campaign against Israel on two levels. It used its complaints about Israel's "aggression" and other open-ended issues to legitimize its claim that the resistance had to continue, and to argue that Hizballah was a more effective defender of Lebanon than the country's army and therefore could not be asked to disarm. On a deeper level, it acted as a spearhead of the larger resistance axis in the Middle East on Iran's behalf to demonstrate that there was no point in coming to terms with America and Israel and that perseverance was bound to end in victory. With help from Iran and Syria, Hizballah built a massive arsenal of rockets and missiles, a small but well-trained military force, and an extensive military infrastructure in south Lebanon, stretching all the way to the Israeli border. Following Israel's withdrawal from south Lebanon in 2000, Hizballah staged occasional attacks against Israel, seeking first and foremost to abduct Israeli soldiers. One such attack in July 2006 triggered the 2006 war.

Lebanon went through several twists and turns during the 2000s, but by the decade's end, several trends and facts seem to have been established. Iran and Syria were the paramount external powers in Lebanon, and with their help Hizballah established itself as the paramount political force in the country. The March 14 Coalition, with American and French backing, did well in the elections of 2005 and won a less impressive victory in the election of 2009. In 2010, however, Hizballah, after demonstrating in a brief confrontation that it could, if it wanted, take over the government by force, was able to use political pressure to topple the government of Sa'd al-Hariri (the son of the assassinated former prime minister) and to form a cabinet headed by Najib Miqati, a Syrian political client.

For its part, Syria had been forced to end its long occupation of Lebanon in 2005 after Rafiq Hariri's assassination. But Syria's ouster was never complete, and it regained its position, though not its military presence, by the end of the decade. Likewise, Iran, by building and rebuilding Hizballah's massive arsenal of rockets and missiles, obtained the ability to retaliate against Israel's cities and infrastructure in the event of an American or Israeli attack on its nuclear installations—as well as to provoke a major crisis at will.

Israel faced these developments with mounting concern. The moderate Lebanese parliamentary republic had flourished and been a harmless neighbor during the decades when a balance of domestic and external forces sustained its unique pluralistic system. But if the current trends continue and Lebanon remains dominated and shaped by Hizballah with the support of Iran and Syria, Israel and Lebanon face the danger of additional, far more destructive wars and the added danger of becoming outright enemies. The Israeli policy of distinguishing between a benevolent Lebanon and the hostile elements that operate from its territory may no longer remain valid.

JORDAN

Israel shares its longest border with Jordan, and the two countries have immense actual and potential impact on each other's national security and economy. Their relationship, however, is, and for a long time has been, primarily affected by their respective and common relations with a third party—the Palestinians.

Jordan's very birth as a modern state was intimately linked to this issue. When Great Britain decided in 1921 to create ex nihilo a principality for the Hashemite potentate Amir Abdullah, it needed to placate him personally and the Hashemite family in general for what the family considered a betrayal—their receipt of only a meager share in the postwar settlement in the Middle East. Britain's solution was to detach the East Bank of the Jordan River from the territory of Mandate Palestine and turn it into the Emirate of Transjordan. In doing so, Britain was also trying to reduce the impact that the formation of the promised Jewish "national home" in Palestine would have on the region.

During the next twenty-five years, Abdullah, with British help, developed a genuine polity in Jordan, and in 1946 his principality became a kingdom. At the same time, a significant political relationship grew between Abdullah and the leaders of the Jewish community in prestate Israel, the Yishuv. This understanding was predicated on their common enmity to radical Palestinian-Arab nationalism, as personified by

Haj Amin al-Husayni, the mufti of Jerusalem. Abdullah was hostile not merely to the mufti personally but to his political style and to the brand of Arab nationalism that he represented. Never satisfied with the desert principality assigned to him, Abdullah also was eager to extend his rule to more significant territories and cities—Syria and Damascus, or Palestine west of the Jordan, and Jerusalem.

When the idea of partitioning Palestine into Jewish and Arab states came to the fore in 1937, a new dimension was added to Abdullah's relationship with the Yishuv. If this partition came to pass, he might assume the Arab leading role on Palestine and provide the stability and pragmatism that had been so glaringly absent from the scene. The term "Jordanian option" was coined later, but the concept originated then: the solution of Israel's Palestinian dilemma by means of Jordan. This option became viable after the UN's partition resolution of November 1947.

The Jewish leaders had accepted the notion of Palestine's partition and were quite content to go along with part of Abdullah's annexation plan. But they disliked what became another aspect of Abdullah's policy: his part in the Arab states' invasion of Palestine on May 15, 1948, the day after the founding of the state of Israel. By participating in that war, Abdullah sought to facilitate his own takeover of the area assigned to be a Palestinian-Arab state in the UN's partition plan.

During the war, Abdullah's army, the Arab Legion, was a resolute and effective enemy that inflicted on the young Israel Defense Forces some of its most painful defeats, and at the war's end Abdullah was indeed in control of what became known as the West Bank and East Jerusalem. His annexation of these territories was formally recognized by only two foreign governments, but, whatever the legal aspects, it transformed the Jordanian polity. (The kingdom was called Transjordan until 1946 and Jordan thereafter.) Palestinians now made up a majority of its population; many of them regarded Abdullah, his kingdom, and his act of annexation as illegitimate.[11] And in the years before Abdullah was assassinated by a Palestinian in 1951, the transformation of his kingdom's traditional politics as a consequence of the annexation of this large, better-educated, politically mobilized, and embittered Palestinian population had become apparent. In 1949–50, a treaty between Israel and Jordan was negotiated and initialed but was not finalized, because

Abdullah realized that he had neither the power nor the de facto authority to carry his country with him to a peace settlement with Israel.[12]

During the next fifteen years, the issue for Jordan was not territorial annexation but survival. Following a brief regency period, the eighteen-year-old Hussein ascended the throne that he was to occupy for forty-five years. The young monarch proved to be extremely determined, astute in maintaining external support and facing down domestic opposition, and unusually skillful and lucky at aborting plots and evading assassination attempts. By this point, revolutionary Arab nationalism (as exemplified by Egypt) held sway over much of the Middle East, and the king's Palestinian subjects were among its staunchest supporters. Yet at the same time, Jordan, reflecting the new demographic realities and in keeping with its claim to embody the Palestinian issue, was the only Arab state that offered citizenship to Palestinians. In 1967 King Hussein joined Egypt and Syria in their war against Israel, and he paid dearly by losing the West Bank and East Jerusalem. Jordan now had no West Bank but a Palestinian majority in the East Bank; yet by then many Palestinians had been "Jordanianized" and had come to accept Jordan as their country and state. Yearning for Palestinian self-determination was one thing, and the realization that life under the Hashemites is quite attractive was another.[13]

So, the Six-Day War reopened "the question of Palestine." For the first time since 1949, all of the territory that had been Mandate Palestine was placed under a single authority. Israel was in control of the sizable Palestinian population living in the West Bank and in the Gaza Strip, in addition to its own Palestinian Arab minority. The debate over the future of the West Bank and the Gaza Strip became the governing issue of Israeli politics. For Israel, three principal alternatives presented themselves: reviving the Jordanian option; seeking or accepting the creation of an independent or autonomous Palestinian entity; or perpetuating Israeli control, either as a deliberate policy or, more likely, by failing to make painful choices.

The Hashemite regime's initial preference was to come to an agreement with Israel, but the king insisted that he could do so only on the basis of Israel's full withdrawal from the occupied territories. With the passage of time, Israel's attachment to the West Bank grew stronger, as did the PLO's stature and power, and so the prospects for this Jordanian option waned. Nor did various notions of a Jordanian-Palestinian federation turn into a magic formula.

Its protestations of formal support notwithstanding, Jordan had consistently opposed or at least been uneasy about the idea of a Palestinian state in the West Bank and the Gaza Strip. For Hashemite Jordan, a small Palestinian state in part of the West Bank and the Gaza Strip could not be a durable, satisfactory solution to the Palestinian problem, and Palestinians were likely to direct their irredentist claims eastward and to seek the allegiance of Jordan's Palestinian majority. True, many of the kingdom's Palestinian subjects viewed themselves as Jordanians, but why expose their loyalty to such a challenge?[14] So, for many long years, staying with the status quo proved to be the easiest choice for Jordan, too. A channel of communication with the Israeli leadership was kept discreetly open (but not publicized) for nearly three decades. Several attempts were made to reach a settlement, various practical issues were sorted out, and a dialogue was maintained between King Hussein and most of Israel's prime ministers. A community of interests was established with both Labor and Likud leaders, based on shared opposition to the PLO and to the notion of Palestinian statehood.

One tenet of this relationship—the Israeli belief that the survival of the Hashemite regime and its control of the East Bank were important Israeli national interests—was shaken when, in 1970, the Likud adopted the slogan "Jordan is Palestine" and took the position that there was no need to establish a second Palestinian state. The argument also presumed that, once the Palestinians took over the reins of government in Amman, their claim over the West Bank would weaken.[15] The issue came into stark relief that September, when Israel was key in facilitating King Hussein's victory over Syria and the PLO (discussed in chapter 1). Golda Meir and Yitzhak Rabin believed that the king's survival and American-Israeli strategic cooperation should be Israel's paramount considerations; their decision was subsequently criticized by Ariel Sharon, leader of Israel's radical right, who argued that the government had missed an opportunity "to let nature take its course."

In the rich chronology of Israeli-Jordanian history during these years, several defining events stand out: King Hussein's decision not to join the Arab war coalition in October 1973; Henry Kissinger's inability to effect an Israeli-Jordanian interim agreement in the spring of 1974; the

Arab summit's decision in October 1974 to designate the PLO (rather than Jordan) as the legitimate claimant to the West Bank; the London Agreement of April 1987, which was Israel's last attempt to exercise the Jordanian option, albeit in a modified version; Jordan's formal disengagement from the West Bank in 1988;[16] and the 1990–91 Persian Gulf crisis and Gulf War, which represented the culmination of Iraq's threat to Jordan's independence.

The signing in 1993 of the Oslo Accords affected this history paradoxically. The Hashemites resented Israel's latest choice of a Palestinian option but decided that they had to draw closer to Israel, the better to affect the course of events. The emergence of a Palestinian state had grown more likely but was not a foregone conclusion, and Jordan and Israel still shared a significant agenda. But there was another side to the same developments. By signing the Oslo Accords with Israel, the PLO enabled Jordan and other Arab states to pursue their bilateral agendas with Israel. This was not such a simple matter, however, because any dealings with Israel ended up involving an ever-present third party, the United States. There were also complex regional issues to be dealt with, such as strategic cooperation with Turkey and the future of Iraq.

Meanwhile, Israel's commitment to the survival of King Hussein's regime was buttressed by a close personal relationship between the king and Yitzhak Rabin. This relationship played a crucial role in enabling the two states to sign a peace agreement in October 1994 and to formalize their relationship. This relationship changed during Peres's brief tenure as Rabin's successor. The king was worried that his policies would lead all too quickly to an independent Palestinian state and to Israeli-Syrian and Syrian-Lebanese agreements; these would jeopardize and dwarf Jordan's position. On the eve of the May 1996 elections, Jordan indicated its preference for Benjamin Netanyahu and a peace policy managed at a more deliberate pace.

Yet these hopes were not fulfilled. For, although Jordan was opposed to an accelerated peace process, it found a viable one essential, particularly vis-à-vis the Palestinians. The collapse of Israeli-Palestinian negotiations, let alone outbreaks of Israeli-Palestinian violence, would make Jordan's peace with Israel hardly tenable. This might have been a tall order, but the Hashemites expected from Israel finesse and subtlety in the conduct of a delicate, fragile relationship. They soon came to believe that Netanyahu in the late 1990s was a prime minister who could not manage that relationship, who could not keep the king's personal trust, and whose real intentions with regard to the peace process could not be divined. The king vented his frustration in a scathing letter to Netanyahu, the text of which became available to the international media. Yet the king kept the lid on: most of the interests that kept Jordan wanting a peace with Israel were still valid, and the cost of an open break with Israel still outweighed the benefits it might produce. And so, for the time being, Israeli-Jordanian peace survived, but the expectations of a special relationship, a warm peace, and a mutually beneficial web of economic and development projects failed to materialize.

In February 1999, King Hussein died of the cancer he had fought during the previous few years. On his deathbed he removed his brother Hasan, who had served as crown prince for more than thirty years, and appointed his oldest son, Abdullah, as his heir. After ascending the throne, the young king reassured Israel on several occasions that he was committed to the peace his father had signed. Yet Israeli apprehensions about Jordan's ability to contend with potential and external threats were exacerbated by the simultaneous loss of two brothers who had been experienced and familiar partners.

King Abdullah's early decisions and the change of government in Israel in the late spring of 1999 improved the atmosphere in the two countries' relationship, but the intimacy and special relations of the Rabin-Hussein years were not restored. Jordan anxiously watched the new Israeli prime minister Barak's apparently swift progress toward far-reaching agreements with Syria and the Palestinians (as it had under Peres). It was particularly alarmed by Barak's willingness to give up a permanent presence in the Jordan Valley, thereby laying the groundwork for Jordan's uncomfortable contiguity with a future Palestinian state. But in keeping with a long-established tradition, Jordan did not express such concerns in public and chose to pay lip service to Palestinian nationalism.

Jordan must not have lamented the collapse of the Israeli-Palestinian negotiation in July 2000. But the outbreak in short order of the al-Aqsa intifada created new pressures on a state with a Palestinian majority that had made and maintained peace with Israel. Amman lowered the profile of its relations with Israel and took security precautions. It was a tacit source of inspiration for what was initially known as the Saudi Initiative (adopted at the Beirut Arab Summit of 2002) and eventually as the Arab Peace Initiative. Together with Egypt, Jordan became the chief promoter of this initiative.

Jordan's role reflected its growing concern with the impact on its own politics of the unresolved Israeli-Palestinian conflict. Such events as the al-Aqsa intifada, the 2006 Lebanon War, and Operation Cast Lead in Gaza agitated the Palestinian majority in Jordan. And as the first decade of the twenty-first century wore on, Jordan's traditional anxiety about the repercussions of the potential formation of an irredentist Palestinian state gave way to growing criticism of Israel for the failure to move toward a resolution of the Palestinian issue. The king kept the essential elements of the peace with Israel, but he and other prominent members of the Jordanian establishment made no secret of their unhappiness with its policies.[17]

Early in 2011 the agitation that toppled Tunisia's Ben Ali, Egypt's Mubarak, and Libya's Qaddafi and that affected large parts of the Arab world also rattled the Hashemite regime, if only temporarily. Significantly, many of the chief protestors were not Palestinian but East Bankers, the monarchy's traditional power base.

THE PALESTINIANS

In November 1975, a senior State Department official and long-time specialist in Arab affairs, Harold Saunders, testified at a hearing held by a subcommittee of the House of Representatives' Committee on Foreign Affairs. In his prepared written text, Saunders referred to the Palestinian issue as the core of the conflict between Arabs and Israelis in the Middle East.[18] At the time, little attention was paid to Saunders's testimony, but it subsequently drew considerable attention and animated objections from Israel's government. Israel was then in the midst of a complex diplomatic process orchestrated by the United States and predicated on the assumption that the key to the Arab-Israeli conflict lay in Israel's relations with the major Arab states. Saunders's argument ran against the grain of U.S.-Israeli policies and was, indeed, a harbinger of the change that came with the subsequent Carter presidency. If the Palestinian issue was the core question of the Arab-Israeli conflict, did it not make sense to predicate the quest for Arab-Israeli peace on a resolution of the problem that lay at its heart? Indeed, the Carter administration, and Saunders as its top Middle East diplomat, acted in the Middle East on the dual assumption that it could resolve the Palestinian problem and that its success would offer the key to a comprehensive Arab-Israeli peace.

But was such a resolution feasible? Since 1948 Israeli attitudes toward the Palestinians were to a large extent shaped by a sense that the Israeli-Palestinian dispute is a zero-sum game, that Palestinian demands and expectations could be met only on intolerable terms. It was much easier for Israel and Israelis to think of Israeli-Arab reconciliation by means of negotiations and agreements with states like Egypt, Jordan, and Syria, which could focus on such issues as boundaries and water.[19]

This frame of mind was for many years reinforced by the course of Palestinian history and the drift of Palestinian politics. Between 1949 and 1964, the Palestinians were absent from the Middle Eastern arena as an independent force. They were crushed, fragmented, and dispersed. Their traditional leaders were discredited, and most young Palestinian activists invested their zeal in ideological parties that promised a remedy to the Palestinian predicament within a larger, pan-Arabic scheme. The Arab states, in turn, were eager to assume control of the Palestinian issue and to suppress the efforts made by Palestinian groups to take charge themselves. For more than a decade, the vast majority of them were under the spell of Gamal Abdel Nasser and his brand of messianic pan-Arab nationalism. They believed that when Nasser defeated the enemy—the unholy trinity of Western imperialism, Zionism, and domestic reactionary forces—and united the Arab homeland, Arab Palestine also would be liberated and redeemed. It was only with Nasser's and Nasserism's decline in the late 1960s that an authentic Palestinian national movement could assert itself.

The PLO was founded by the Arab states in 1964 as their instrument, but was taken over in 1968 by the authentic Palestinian groups that had emerged a few years earlier. Yet, for another twenty-five years, most Israelis did not consider the PLO an acceptable interlocutor. It had drafted a charter that called for Israel's destruction, and it used terror as a principal instrument to achieve that end. All efforts to persuade the PLO's leader, Yasser Arafat, to take positions that would enable the PLO to join the peace process in the 1970s were to no avail. The

PLO only slowly adopted the formula of a two-state solution. Nor was Israel, the more powerful party to the conflict, ready or willing to take the initiative.[20]

Thus, while Israel and Egypt went ahead toward their peace treaty of 1979, armed conflict between Israel and Palestinian nationalists and their struggle over the land of the West Bank continued. The ambivalence and equivocation about building Jewish settlements in the West Bank that marked Israel's Labor governments was replaced after the Likud victory in 1977 with open encouragement to do so. These efforts created (mostly by design) a new reality under which a workable compromise with the Palestinians became ever more difficult to achieve. Yet at the same time, the sight of expanding Israeli settlements persuaded many Palestinians, particularly in the West Bank and the Gaza Strip, that time was not necessarily on their side and that reaching a settlement was imperative.

In 1988 Arafat finally endorsed the principle of a two-state solution, and on that basis diplomacy began between the PLO and the United States. The changes of position in Washington and the PLO amplified the considerable impact of the intifada, which began later that year, and increased the pressure on Israel's second national unity government to renew, after a seven-year hiatus, negotiations about Palestinian self-rule. The profound disagreement between the government's Labor and Likud components over this issue expedited the collapse of the talks in March 1990. When Israeli-Palestinian negotiations began again in 1991, they were part of the Madrid process, and they played out against the backdrop of other great changes: the breakup of the Soviet Union, the end of the Cold War, the Persian Gulf crisis and Gulf War, and a fresh wave of emigrants from the former Soviet Union to Israel.

In the course of putting the Madrid process together, Secretary of State James Baker discovered that Prime Minister Shamir's resistance to the very notion of negotiating with the Palestinians could be mitigated by shifting emphasis from the Palestinian issue to a parallel channel of diplomacy with Israel's Arab neighbors. This blunted the Palestinian edge of the Madrid process, which was further reduced by the formal incorporation of the Palestinian delegation into a Jordanian-Palestinian delegation. The junior status thus assigned to the Palestinians, and the

PLO's formal absence from the Madrid process, reflected the PLO's decline in the Arab world after the Gulf War, though the effect of this humiliating turn of events was limited at first, since no progress occurred during the first nine months of the post-Madrid negotiations. But when the Rabin government was formed, the PLO's hold over Palestinian politics acquired fresh significance. An Israeli-Palestinian agreement became a key to any progress; whether Israel would come to such an agreement without the PLO or deal with the PLO and find an acceptable formula became a crucial issue on its diplomatic agenda.

We have seen how Rabin pondered the comparative advantages of the Syrian and Palestinian options. In early August 1993, the hypothetical vacillation turned into an actual policy choice. Then, by signing the Oslo Accords, Israel predicated the new phase of the peace process on its agreement with the PLO, and not with a major Arab state such as Syria. This action resulted in a radical change of perspective. Having signed a framework agreement with representatives of Palestinian nationalism, Israel now argued that the core issue of the Arab-Israeli conflict had been addressed and the chief obstacle to Arab-Israeli reconciliation and normalization had been removed. A hitherto unfamiliar mutual dependence was created between the government of Israel and the PLO leaders.

The Oslo process was a very complex and fragile mechanism; genuine cooperation and a genuine sense of partnership were indispensable to its success. As we have seen, these were achieved to only a limited degree.

Moreover, the signing of the Oslo agreement did not mean that the Israeli-Palestinian conflict was over. In both societies, powerful forces were opposed to reconciliation and continued to try to abort it. Competition for control of the West Bank and Jerusalem continued, and the leaders, cooperating as they did in implementing the agreements they had signed, still had very different visions of the final-status agreement. Both societies had yet to think through, separately or together, some fundamental issues. Were Israel and the Palestinians interested in separation, or in some form of cooperation or integration within the Israeli-Jordanian-Palestinian triangle? And if separation was what they wanted, was it feasible? What sort of relationship could be envisaged between societies separated by such social and economic gaps? How would as many as fifteen million Israelis and Arabs share the limited resources of land and water in the space between the Mediterranean and the Jordan early in the next century?

The Oslo process ran its course during the 1990s without the Israeli-Palestinian dispute being resolved. We have seen how Benjamin Netanyahu failed to maneuver among the forces that buffeted his Palestinian policy, and how Ehud Barak shifted from the preference he had assigned to the Syrian track to the boldest effort yet by any Israeli leader to reach a final, comprehensive agreement with the Palestinian national movement. The collapse of Barak's negotiations with Arafat and the outbreak of violence in September 2000 set the stage for a resumption of a full-blown conflict between the two protagonists.

The Palestinian-Israeli war of attrition in 2000–03 (commonly known as the second intifada) exacted a high toll from both parties. Coupled with an economic crisis of the same years, this period was one of the darkest in Israel's history. The war also inflicted heavy damage on the Palestinians and eliminated many of the gains made during the 1990s. Israel won the war, but the military victory did not resolve the broader conflict. Arafat's death in November 2004 was preceded by political decline for two of the entities he headed: the Palestinian Authority and the Fatah movement. He was criticized by many Palestinians for resorting to violence and subjecting them to its consequences, and he was gradually emasculated by Sharon's siege of his compound in Ramallah and his own physical decline.

The Bush administration's original effort to diminish Arafat's role and provide the Palestinian Authority with a different type of government could now be implemented. With Mahmud Abbas as president and Salam Fayyad as prime minister, the Palestinian Authority mounted a new track. Fayyad became the real leader of the effort to build a clean, accountable government and, with U.S. help, an effective security force to combat terrorism. In Fayyad's vision, this was to be a bottom-up effort to create the foundations of a Palestinian state. Israel saw in Fayyad an excellent partner, but at a certain point the interests of the two parties diverged. Fayyad was determined to achieve statehood, and if Israel did not accommodate him, he was ready to take unilateral action.

But "Fayyadism" was only part of the picture. Fatah did not undergo a process of reform and was seen by many Palestinians as tired and corrupt. When the Bush administration insisted on free elections in the West Bank and Gaza, Hamas won, in January 2006. After a prolonged period of political uncertainty, Hamas in June 2007 staged a violent coup and took control of Gaza. The Palestinian polity was now divided physically and ideologically. Hamas, an Islamist movement, rejects the notion of a final-status agreement with Israel. Hamas's impact is matched to some extent by the decline of secular Palestinian support for the idea of a two-state solution, since that solution proved to be so elusive. Quite a few Palestinian intellectuals and political activists have come to the conclusion that, ultimately, time is on their side and that in a decade or so a "one-state solution" could become a reality.

Hamas presents Israel with a manifold challenge. It is firmly in control of the Gaza Strip and, as we saw, Israel has failed to come up with a solution to the "problem of Gaza." Hamas was weakened, at least temporarily by the Syrian crisis of 2011, but it remains closely allied to Iran and is a beneficiary of Egypt's current weakness. It continues to challenge Fatah's hold over the West Bank and to present an alternative strategy that many Palestinians find attractive. As long as Hamas is in control of Gaza, any agreement that Israel might make with Abbas can be implemented only in the West Bank, with Hamas possessing the ability to obstruct it by restarting a cycle of violence from the Gaza Strip.

In 2008, during the final phase of his tenure, Ehud Olmert negotiated with Abbas and went even further than Barak did in 2000 (see above). Abbas did not respond to Olmert's final offer. Abbas and other Palestinians have since explained that there was less to the offer than met the eye and that there was no point in signing a deal with a departing Israeli prime minister. This may be true, but Abbas has yet to demonstrate that he is willing to offer Israel finality, an end of claims and acceptance of Israel as the Jewish people's national state in return for Israeli willingness to accept a Palestinian state with a territory comparable to the 1967 lines and a capital in Jerusalem.

The quest for a renewal of the Israeli-Palestinian negotiation was reinforced by Barack Obama's election as America's new president. The new president made the resolution of this conflict a priority, an important component of his effort to ameliorate the tension between the United States and the Muslim and Arab worlds. But Obama also encountered a right-wing Israeli government that was once again headed by Benjamin

Netanyahu. The Israeli electorate that had elected Ehud Olmert in 2006 on a dovish platform was pushed to the right by the Iranian threat and by the impact of the 2006 Lebanon War, Hamas's control of Gaza and Operation Cast Lead in 2008–09. Prime Minister Netanyahu grudgingly accepted the notion of Palestinian statehood, but that did not suffice to get the process restarted. Nor was it certain that Obama could find a willing and effective Palestinian partner for his effort. For much of 2011, the Palestinian preference seemed to be adoption by the UN General Assembly of a resolution that would recognize a Palestinian state in the lines of 1967. The impact of the Arab Spring of 2011 on Palestinian politics and on the Palestinian-Israeli equation was also unclear. President Obama and others suggested that it actually made an Israeli-Palestinian deal more urgent and more feasible. Netanyahu's government and quite a few Palestinians argued that major decisions could not be made in times of flux and uncertainty. In Gaza the Hamas leadership was biding its time, hoping that the kindred Muslim Brotherhood would become more influential in Egypt. Both the Fatah and Hamas leaderships were concerned that their constituencies might be affected by the prevailing mood in the Arab world and take to the streets, while Israel was concerned that the same mood could lead to a third intifada.

FROM "ISRAELI ARABS" TO "ISRAEL'S PALESTINIAN CITIZENS"

In the original terminology of the Arab-Israeli dispute, the conflict in and over British Mandate Palestine was conducted between an Arab side and a Jewish side. It was only after the establishment of the state of Israel and the conclusion of the 1948 war that a stark distinction was drawn between Israelis and Palestinians as the successors of the Jewish and Arab communities in Palestine. In Israeli usage, the term "Arab" came to refer to the people who lived in the larger Arab world beyond Israel's borders, while the term "Palestinian" referred to Palestinians residing outside Israel. Israel's own Arab or Palestinian citizens were strictly referred to as "Israeli Arabs," as members of Israel's "Arab minority" or "sector." This curious choice of terms well expressed Israelis' uneasiness about the Palestinian issue. It was, in a way, easier to cope with a national minority pertaining to an amorphous Arab world than with a people who laid specific claim to Israel's own land.[21] For twenty years or so, Israel's Arab citizens accepted this terminology and used it themselves, but by the 1970s, they began to refer to themselves as Palestinians or as Palestinians who happened to be Israeli citizens. This was but one of many profound changes in the complex relationship between the Israeli state and its Arab citizens.

When the 1948 war ended, some 160,000 Palestinian Arabs remained in the territory of the independent Jewish state and became its citizens. As a result, the fledgling state of Israel had a population of just over one million, and its Arab citizens constituted a minority of about 15 percent. In the aftermath of a brutal war, the victorious Jews considered this Arab minority as a potential fifth column, liable to be used by a hostile Arab world in an inevitable, imminent "second round." This underlying attitude was translated into a policy of control embodied first and foremost by the imposition of a system of military government on the Arab population, which was abolished only in 1966 by Israel's third prime minister, Levi Eshkol.

This policy of control was carried out in an ambivalent context. Israel was hard put to decide whether as a Jewish state it wanted to separate the Arab minority from the mainstream of Israeli public life or, as a democratic state dominated by a social-democratic political establishment, to integrate it. Ironically, integration was first accomplished, after a fashion, in the political realm. As full-fledged citizens of the state of Israel (though not as truly equal members of Israel's body politic and society), most Israeli Arabs voted for Zionist parties through satellite political party lists and, in fact, helped to perpetuate Labor's hegemony.

During these early years, the Arab minority, predominantly rural and Muslim, can best be described as powerless, traumatized, and confused. Its members had to adjust to defeat, to minority status, and to isolation from the other parts of the fragmented Palestinian community and from the larger Arab world. There also was an acute problem of leadership: the pre-1948 Palestinian Arab elites were now beyond Israel's borders (for example, in East Jerusalem), and those who had stayed tended to be poorer and less educated. Arab political opinion and activity in Israel spanned a spectrum that went from pragmatic acceptance of the reality of the Jewish state to nationalist opposition to and rejection of it. Pragmatism was manifested by most Arabs' voting for the major Zionist parties, and opposition was manifested primarily through the Communist Party. Attempts to form a local Arab nationalist party (notably a grouping called al-Ard, or The Land) collapsed when faced with an insurmountable obstacle: to qualify as such, the party would adopt a platform negating Israel's very existence and legitimacy as a Jewish state, and then the government and courts would label it seditious. A subtler, politically easier way for members of the intellectual Arab elite in Israel to express their rejection of the Israeli state was in literary prose and verse.

As in so many other respects, 1967 was a watershed year in the evolution of Israel's Arab minority. The reemergence of an authentic and effective Palestinian nationalist movement and the removal of the physical barrier that had once separated them from the Palestinian and Arab worlds beyond Israel's borders induced a process of Palestinianization. But the balance that had been achieved in practice between Israeli and Arab nationalist components in the community was upset. It was a measure of this change that the term "Israeli Arab" was discarded, and Israel's Arab citizens came to refer to themselves as Palestinians. This nationalist awakening, coupled with socioeconomic improvements—a higher standard of living, a higher level of education, the partial breakdown of the extended-family system, the transformation of several villages into towns—led to a new phase of political activism. On March 30, 1976, a massive protest was organized, under the title The Day of the Land, against the expropriation of Arab-owned land in the Galilee (in northern Israel). In clashes with security forces, six people were killed. March 30 became an annual day of protest for Palestinians in Israel and in the West Bank and Gaza.

Yasser Arafat and the PLO turned the day into an all-Palestinian event, but as a rule the PLO did not view Israel's Arab minority as part of its constituency. Long before the PLO formally accepted the notion of a two-state solution, its leaders had presumed that would be the eventual outcome, while most Arabs in Israel, though galvanized by the idea of Palestinian nationalism, continued to see their future within the state of Israel. Some Israeli Arabs crossed a physical and mental line and joined the PLO and its orbit, but the vast majority continued to live within the Israeli state and system. Israel's Arab minority did not join either the violent conflicts between the PLO and Israel or either of the intifadas.

Still, the patterns of organization and activity in Israeli-Arab political life underwent profound changes after 1967. The Zionist parties'
satellite lists disappeared, and nationalist Arab parties were formed that
found a way of operating within the boundaries of Israeli law (most
notably Abdel Wahab Darawshe's Arab Democratic Party, founded in
1988). Semipolitical civic groups like the Committee of Heads of Local
Arab Councils emerged. In the late 1970s a powerful Islamic fundamentalist movement appeared, partly as a reflection of regional trends and
partly in response to particular local conditions. Muslim fundamentalists in Israel are primarily a religious and social phenomenon, but their
potential political power is enormous.[22]

In the post-1976 political chronology of the Israeli state's relationship
with its Arab citizens, three events stand out as particularly significant
turning points. One was the signing of the Oslo Accords between Israel
and the PLO in 1993. The mutual recognition between Israel and the Palestinian national movement, the establishment of the Palestinian Authority, and the prospect of Palestinian statehood complicated the self-view
and political perspective of Israel's Arab minority. Most significantly, its
members tended to "localize" their outlook and focus it on their position in and relationship with the Israeli state. This tendency was largely
a by-product of the PLO leadership's decision to avoid dealing with the
issues of the group known in Arab and Palestinian parlance as "the Palestinians of 1948." Because the issues of 1948 were to be dealt with in
the final-status negotiations, Israel's Arabs saw no point in antagonizing
the Israeli leadership and public by raising these sensitive issues earlier.

This being the case, Israel's Arab citizens felt that it was up to them
to deal with their position and status in Israel. Several developments
and forces combined to radicalize their quest. What had been a minority of 160,000 after the 1948 war had, in subsequent years, crossed the
1 million mark. Villagers became urban dwellers, and an increasingly
large number of university graduates were frustrated by a lack of jobs
or unsatisfactory employment. Successive Israeli governments failed to
draw appropriate lessons from the March 1976 outburst and formulate
a comprehensive policy for the Arab minority; they settled, at best, on a
piecemeal approach to this cardinal problem (the one exception to this
rule was the Rabin government of 1992–95). The rise and expansion
of the Islamic movement introduced into the equation a powerful actor

that claimed to be apolitical but had in fact a considerable, radicalizing political impact.

Many, if not most, Arab citizens of Israel were primarily preoccupied with mundane issues of integration and equality: educational opportunities, a larger slice of the national economic pie, and progress toward economic and civic equality. But the political and intellectual elites intensified their critique of the very foundations of the state, rejecting the prevalent description of Israel as of a Jewish and democratic state and advancing such themes and ideas as a "bi-national state," the status of a national minority, "reopening the files of 1948" and the *Nakba* (catastrophe) narrative. *Nakba* is the common Arabic term for the events of 1948 and stands in sharp contrast to the Israeli-Hebrew narrative of independence and liberation.

The second event was the wave of violence that burst out in Israel on October 1, 2000, a response to the outbreak three days earlier of Palestinian violence that came to be known as the al-Aqsa intifada. In the clashes between the Israeli police and Arab demonstrators and rioters, thirteen Arab citizens of Israel were killed. It is difficult to overstate the importance of an event that had a traumatizing effect on both sides of the Arab-Jewish divide. On the Jewish side, the violent clashes of early October joined the outbreak of the intifada in creating the sense of the end of an era. If the peace process of the 1990s generated expectations for the normalization of life in Israel, the events of the autumn of 2000 underscored the fact that such normalization remained a remote prospect. In certain respects, the Arab-Jewish clashes inside Israel were more ominous than the outbreak of violence with the Palestinian Authority, in that they exposed the pernicious potential of the tension between the Israeli state and a national minority of nearly 20 percent. Critical or even hostile rhetoric by an Arab intellectual or member of the Knesset can be seen as releasing tension and frustration in a legitimate fashion; but blocking roads or clashes of thousands of angry demonstrators with the police are a different matter. From the Arab perspective the use of firearms by the Israeli police was seen as unjustified and as yet another manifestation at the Israeli state's hostility.

On the eve of the February 2001 elections, Ehud Barak formed a commission of inquiry headed by a Supreme Court Justice (the Or Commission) to investigate the government's (particularly the police's) conduct during the October crisis. The formation of the Or Commission served to calm the atmosphere and to suspend full discussion of Arab-Jewish relations in Israel for nearly three years—the time taken by the commission to complete its work.

The Or Commission published its report in September 2003. The bulky report chided political leaders (former prime minister Barak, former interior security minister Shlomo Ben-Ami, a number of Arab members of the Knesset, or MKs), and the leadership of the police, and recommended sanctions against several police officers. But the importance of the report (coauthored by Professor Shimon Shamir and Justice Hashem Khatib) was in the thorough analysis of the relationship between the state of Israel and its Arab citizens. The commission was critical both of the conduct of the leadership of the Arab minority and of the Israeli government's failure over the years to deal thoroughly with the political and socioeconomic problems of the Arab minority.

Unfortunately, the Or Commission's policy recommendations were essentially filed away and the rift between majority and minority in Israel grew ever wider. One outcome of this state of affairs was the publication between December 2006 and May 2007 of four papers authored by groups of Arab academics and civic leaders that came to be known as the vision documents. The documents, collectively and separately, present the boldest challenge to date to the current fabric of Arab-Jewish relations in Israel.

The vision documents constitute a total rejection of the current identity and makeup of the Israeli state. They are predicated on a refutation of the dominant Israeli-Zionist narrative. Israel is presented as an essentially imperialist, expansionist entity. The Arabs in Israel are an integral part of the Palestinian Arab people and are the abused, indigenous, or native people. Two broad alternatives are offered to restore their lawful rights: a bi-national state as a comprehensive solution to the Israeli-Palestinian conflict; or a two-state solution with far-reaching changes in the character of the Israeli state, transforming it from a Jewish state to "a state for all its citizens."[23]

The civic activism and radicalism of the Arab nongovernmental organizations in Israel has long been matched in the political arena by the Arab members of the Knesset. The Arab minority in Israel now constitutes some 17 percent of the population (the Arab residents of East

Jerusalem not included) and (given the young age of the Arab population) 14 percent of the electorate. In Israel's fragmented-political system, when a few votes in the Knesset determine the fate of coalitions
and governments, 14 percent of the electorate could in theory elect fifteen MKs and constitute a swing vote in Israeli politics. But that would
require full acceptance of the rules of the game in Israeli politics and a
high degree of coherence and unity. Neither of these have been the case.
Over the years, the percentage of Arabs voting for what can be called
Arab Zionist parties (those willing to participate fully in Israel's political
process) declined dramatically, from 52 percent of the total Arab vote in
the 1992 elections to 18 percent in the 2009 elections. Of the 15 Arab
MKs in 2009, just four were from Arab Zionist parties. Turnout among
Arab voters has also steadily dropped, from nearly 70 percent in 1992
to 53 percent in 2009.

The trajectory on the Jewish side of the equation appears as a mirror
image of the dominant trends on the Arab side. The bulk of the Jewish
population has for many years been oblivious of and indifferent to this
difficult, fundamental problem and has been rattled only occasionally,
including by the violent outbreaks of 1976 and 2000 and by occasional
egregious statements or acts by Arab members of the Knesset. But over
time a significant part of the Jewish right wing came to assign growing
importance to what it views as a domestic Arab challenge to Israel's
national identity and security.[24]

In this respect, the signing of the Oslo Accords in 1993 was a turning point for the Jewish right wing as it was for the members of the
Arab minority. If the fate of the Land of Israel was to be decided,
should Arab voters be able to tilt the decision? The elections of 1996
were to a large extent a referendum on the Oslo process, and one of
Netanyahu's campaign slogans used his nickname to claim that "Bibi
is good for the Jews." Netanyahu won by a small majority; had Peres
won by an equally small majority, his authority to continue the Oslo
process would in all likelihood have been challenged by right-wing
opponents claiming, among other things, that he was elected by Arab
votes and had no moral right to partition the "Land of Israel." (In the
1996 elections, thirteen Arab MKs were elected, compared with ten in
the previous Knesset, and nine of them were affiliated with Arab and
Jewish-Arab (non-Zionist) parties.)

As the Israeli-Palestinian negotiations wore on, and the idea of a land swap became part of the agenda, a new idea took hold about exactly what land should be swapped. In return for the 5 percent or so of the West Bank that would be annexed to Israel (along with some 80 percent of the settlers), the Israeli territory transferred to the future Palestinian state should not be a piece of southern Israel contiguous to the Gaza Strip, but rather a part of Israel with a sizable population of Israeli Arabs. The argument (made by Israeli right-wingers) was that such a transfer would consolidate the Jewish majority and character of Israel and would ensure that a "two-state solution" would indeed rest on the country's partition between a purely Arab and a predominantly Jewish state.

Such a swap would in fact be "a transfer in place," whereby a quarter of a million Israeli-Arab citizens would remain in their homes but lose their Israeli citizenship and become citizens of a new Palestinian-Arab state. The idea's proponents argued that this was hardly a calamity, since the population viewed itself as Palestinian. But the idea met with fierce opposition, some of it from Israeli Jewish liberals, and most of it from Israeli Arabs who argued that they wanted to remain citizens of a transformed Israeli state rather than become the citizens of an ill-defined Palestinian one. In short order, though, the centrist advocates of this idea were overshadowed by right-wing activists. Most prominent among the latter was Avigdor Lieberman, head of the Israel Beyteynu Party, who turned the issue of the Arab minority's loyalty (or lack thereof) into the centerpiece of the 2009 election campaign that brought his party into Netanyahu's coalition and landed him in the respectable position of foreign minister.

Lieberman and his party persisted in their campaign against what they call Arab "disloyalty" to the Israeli state. This campaign culminated in March 2011 in the passage of the third reading of a Knesset bill that came to be known as the *Nakba* bill. It stipulated that the minister of finance was entitled to reduce the budgets of state-funded organizations and local municipalities should they reject the existence of the state of Israel as a Jewish and democratic state. Upholding the *Nakba* narrative (that the establishment of Israel was a catastrophe for Arabs) was cited as the prime example of such conduct. The law's authors had a harsher version of their legislation in mind as well as other measures but had to reach a compromise with other coalition members who were reticent on grounds of principle or prudence to escalate the tension with the Arab minority. But even this milder version marked a further escalation in the vicious spiral that has come to characterize Israel's relationship with its Arab minority.

ISRAEL AND IRAQ: CONFLICT WITHOUT RELATIONS

Iraq occupies a special place among all of Israel's relationships with Arab nations. Iraq is sufficiently remote from Israel to have chosen to act as a "nonconfrontation" state, but for a variety of reasons its rulers have preferred over the years to participate in military conflict with Israel even though it does not share a border with Israel. Indeed, the absence of a common border has radicalized the Iraqi-Israeli relationship. Arab-Israeli peace has mostly been predicated on two foundations—that the cost of war is prohibitive, and that "land" can be exchanged for "peace." Neither is an element in the Israeli-Iraqi equation, and the conflict between the two countries has been nourished by other sources.

The pattern was established early. Iraq played an important part in the 1948 war, by pushing for Arab participation and by sending an expeditionary force to join the Arab campaign. But, unlike Israel's immediate neighbors, Iraq chose not to end the war with an armistice agreement, and in similar fashion it dispatched expeditionary forces in 1967 and 1973 but took no part in the diplomatic activities that brought these wars to an end.[25]

Israel's conflict with the conservative Iraqi regime in power during the decade after the 1948 war was muted. But the overthrow in 1958 of the Iraqi monarchy and its replacement by a succession of revolutionary and postrevolutionary regimes changed the situation. Moved by their own ambitions for Arab leadership and their competition with Egypt and Syria, Iraq's leaders from Abd al-Karim Qassem to Saddam Hussein tended to take the most radical positions concerning Israel and to pursue them from the comparative safety afforded by distance. Israel, in turn, was worried by the prospect of having to confront Iraq's full potential as a participant in future wars, either as the linchpin of an eastern front comprising Iraq, Syria, and Jordan, or as an immediate neighbor if Iraq took over Jordan. To keep such possibilities at bay,

Israel pursued two principal policies: it helped the Kurdish secession-
ists in northern Iraq (hoping to keep Baghdad's leaders preoccupied on
that front), and it cultivated a strategic alliance with the shah's Iran.
(This latter had a broader agenda, but common enmity with Iraq was
an important component.) These Israeli actions, needless to say, were
well-known to the Iraqis and helped to develop their view of Israel as a
dangerous national enemy.[26]

This configuration was altered in the late 1970s when Egypt signed
its peace treaty with Israel, when Israel lost its alliance with Iran in the
wake of the Islamist revolution there, and when the Kurdish rebellion
collapsed. Saddam Hussein's rise to power in 1979 thus ushered in a
period of domestic stability in Iraq. Over time, Saddam built an outsized
army of sixty divisions and also sought to obtain nuclear weapons and
other weapons of mass destruction. Along with Hafiz al-Asad, Saddam
led the opposition to Sadat and the Egyptian-Israeli peace, but he and
his country were soon absorbed in Iraq's eight-year war with Iran.[27]

Israel was worried not so much about Iraq's conventional military
buildup as about its actual or potential acquisition and development of
weapons of mass destruction—chemical weapons, Scud missiles, and,
most ominously, nuclear weapons. Israel was not necessarily the only
likely target: Saddam's army used chemical weapons against Kurdish
civilians, and Scud missiles were launched against Iran. But the notion
that a regime like Saddam Hussein's might be in possession of nuclear
weapons was unacceptable to Israel. When, in June 1981, an Israeli air
raid destroyed Iraq's nuclear reactor at Ossirak, Iraq did not respond or
retaliate, but Israel's action further exacerbated Iraq's hostility.[28]

The end of the Iran-Iraq war in 1988 had the effect of releasing the
huge military machine that Saddam Hussein had constructed. He was
determined to use it to aggrandize his regime, and he saw Israel as a principal foe and an obstacle to his schemes. In April 1990 he publicly warned
that Iraq possessed "binary chemical weapons" and threatened to "make
fire eat up half of Israel if it tries to do anything against Iraq." He may
have been thinking of his plans for the conquest of Kuwait, or of Israel's
anticipated opposition to any Iraqi act of aggrandizement, but he was
also trying to deter Israel from interfering with his plans and to couch his
expansionist schemes in anti-Israeli terms.[29] In the event, Saddam chose
to carry out his aggrandizement in the Persian Gulf; he occupied Kuwait

and threatened Saudi Arabia, thus triggering the crisis of 1990 and the war of 1991. He positioned himself as a latter-day Nasser fighting for the Arab cause against the West and against Israel, depicting his occupation of Kuwait as part of a broader challenge to the colonial order that had been imposed on the Arab world at the end of World War I. This was hollow posturing, and most of the Arab world saw it as such. But some mistakenly either accepted Saddam's claims or believed that he would somehow emerge victorious. The PLO's leaders and many Palestinians in the Gulf were among those who made these errors.[30]

During the Persian Gulf War, Saddam fired about forty Scud missiles at Israel, primarily in hopes of drawing Israel into the war and thus splitting the Arab coalition the United States had organized against him. Prime Minister Yitzhak Shamir's government, partly of its own volition and partly under American pressure, did not respond—restraint that paid off handsomely. The U.S.-led coalition decimated Iraq's military machine, and the constraints imposed on Iraq by the United States through the United Nations at the war's end led to the destruction of almost all, if not all, of Iraq's missiles and unconventional arsenal. In addition, a sanctions regime severely limited Iraq's oil exports and oil revenues. Washington's "containment" of Iraq has thus denied it any effective role in the Middle East since 1991.

In the 1980s, at the height of its war with Iran, and then in the 1990s, Iraq sent some indirect messages to Israel that it was interested in entering into a tacit dialogue. Some Israeli politicians and strategic planners supported this idea, arguing that it could balance the threat posed by Iran or provide leverage vis-à-vis Syria. Others argued that Saddam was not credible, that Israel should support U.S. policy to contain Iraq and not subvert it, and that in any event Iraq was not seriously interested in dialogue but, at best, in buying some goodwill in the United States. The latter arguments prevailed, and a tacit dialogue, whether or not Saddam intended it, never developed.

Israel, alongside the United States, closely monitored Iraq's compliance with the UN regulations imposed on Baghdad at the end of the Gulf War. With almost all of Iraq's arsenal of weapons of mass destruction and ballistic missiles destroyed, as well as its capacity to reproduce them, and with Iraq's oil exports limited to the bare minimum, this edge of Iraq's offensive capabilities was blunted. Saddam's limited resources were invested instead in his regime's very survival. But he was also remarkably consistent in his drive to escape this situation, to erode Middle Eastern and international support for Washington's policies, and to maintain or restore at least a measure of Iraq's offensive capability. On several occasions, the United States responded to these challenges with limited military action and in February 1998 prepared the ground for, but did not carry out, a large-scale operation.

As already discussed in chapter 5, George W. Bush's election to the presidency, the terrorist attack of September 11, 2001, and ultimately Washington's decision to invade Iraq and topple Saddam's regime transformed this dynamic. It is still not clear what Iraqi state and what Iraqi political system ultimately will emerge from this unfinished saga. At this point, Iraq does not play an active role in regional politics, and it has yet to formulate its own distinct policy vis-à-vis Israel.

Israel has no reason to regret Saddam's removal, but it has been adversely affected by the resulting weakening of America's position in the Middle East and by the boost given to Iran's regional ambitions through the removal of its archrival.

9

PEACE AND NORMALIZATION

In the mid-1970s an unusual book was published in Egypt under the title *After the Guns Fall Silent,* written by the Egyptian left-wing intellectual and journalist Muhammad Sid-Ahmed.[1] It was the first presentation of an Arab vision of accommodation with Israel, the first Arab effort to spell out what the Middle East might look like after the establishment of Arab-Israeli peace. The author of this bold, pioneering work was roundly criticized in Egypt and elsewhere in the Arab world for breaking a taboo and endorsing and propagating the idea of peaceful accommodation with Israel. The criticism came even though the book was written after the signing in 1974 of the Israeli-Egyptian and Israeli-Syrian disengagement agreements and after two Arab summit conferences had redefined the Arab consensus to embrace the principle of a political settlement with Israel. But a full-fledged vision of Arab-Israeli peace written by a major Egyptian intellectual with left-wing credentials was still difficult for those who remained ideologically and emotionally committed to the struggle against Israel.

In fact, a great deal of ambivalence and vacillation is evident at the very core of Sid-Ahmed's book. The author began by posing this question: "What shape will the Middle East take after a just and permanent peace?" He then explained that "among Arabs the topic is taboo, condemned as a notion by the bulk of public opinion as well as by most of the intelligentsia. It is condemned because there is a deep-rooted conviction in the Arab psyche that the only conceivable settlement would entail complete surrender." But, he argued, after the October War of

1973, which brought more balance to the Israeli-Arab equation, a change occurred in the Arab view of a political settlement. The Arab world decided to settle, "but as long as the settlement with Israel and the future of peace in the region is not embodied in a clearly defined vision, Israel will never admit that the Arab goal is genuine: it will continue to cast doubts on the sincerity of their overtures and maintain that the Arab position is basically unchanged."[2]

It is precisely that "clearly defined vision" that Sid-Ahmed set forth. As he saw it, an enduring peace would require Israel to play a "functional role" in the Middle East, comparable to but different from that of Lebanon. "There is . . . more or less tacit acknowledgement that the existence of Israel within secure and recognized borders is unavoidable after the Arabs recover their occupied territories and after the establishment of some Palestinian entity." Then, once settlement is achieved along these lines, the chief psychological barrier to Israel's integration into the region could be addressed: "The stumbling block has always been the Arabs' fear of Israel's technological superiority and her ability, if peace came to the region, to dominate the Arabs economically and to prevent them from becoming masters of their own fate."[3]

But Arabs after the October War, buttressed by the use of the "oil weapon" and having accumulated huge revenues, "acquired a new confidence that Israeli superiority could no longer deprive them of their freedom of decision—even in the case of peace. . . . Israeli quality could no longer neutralize Arab quantity. . . . For the first time some kind of match between Israeli technological know-how and Arab capital can be envisaged in certain quarters." Moreover, in the spirit of "complementarity," there need be no contradiction between security arrangements and economic interests. Security arrangements do not necessarily have to rely on "negative sanctions" (like demilitarized zones or areas policed by UN forces) but can actually go hand in hand with "positive incentives" to "promote the interest of the protagonists to abstain from war."

Industrial projects could conceivably be set up in Sinai, the Negev, the Gaza Strip, the West Bank, in various parts of a Palestinian state, and even on the borders separating Israel from Syria and South Lebanon. Petrochemical plants might possibly be erected in some of those regions, and more and more of the crude oil that now goes to the West could be retained to feed these petrochemical complexes. This Arab asset could be exported not in the form of crude alone but also in the form of finished and semi-finished products.[4]

Sid-Ahmed saw several advantages in matching security arrangements with economic development schemes. Capital could be mobilized for projects that might not be feasible otherwise. Countries like Egypt would benefit by shifting part of their population from densely populated regions to desert areas. Advanced industries in an area like the Sinai could also include "nuclear plants to desalinize sea water for irrigating wide areas of the desert to meet growing food requirements." Industrial projects "erected inside the Palestinian state will invalidate the argument that this state is not viable."

After a first phase of this kind, during which Israel would be reluctantly but inevitably absorbed into the life of the Middle East, a second phase could develop in which Arabs "could use Israeli human and technological assets to achieve a Middle East conglomerate able to stand up to the big geopolitical conglomerates expected to coalesce at the turn of the century." Curiously, some of Sid-Ahmed's paragraphs read like the vision of Arab-Jewish coexistence that T. E. Lawrence had sketched out more than half a century earlier. Most of the time Sid-Ahmed wrote and thought as a Marxist, dialectically—the course of events being determined by the interplay between "contradictions." It is thus fully in character that, after completing the presentation of his impressive ideas about Arab-Israeli peace, he argued the opposite case: that the obstacles inherent in the situation are so great that implementation is quite unlikely; indeed, that another Arab-Israeli war may yet be launched.

Most of the "stumbling blocks" the author identified had to do with Israel itself. Sid-Ahmed had come to accept, in fact advocate, the idea of accommodation with Israel, but he retained a critical, not to say negative, attitude toward the Jewish state, anticipating Israeli attempts to break up the settlement into a number of separate agreements in the hope that partial agreements would allow it to neutralize the weaker links instead of dealing with all Arab parties as equals. But even if a total settlement is achieved, there will be a problem concerning Israel itself. The only justification for its existence is as the embodiment of the Zionist design, and it would lose its raison d'être if its role is reduced to that of an economic instrument that the Arab environment would have digested and used for its own development.[5]

Furthermore, Sid-Ahmed predicted, "If a settlement is reached, many Arab Jews will eventually return to their original homelands as Israeli emissaries or end up by resettling. Israel has always derived its strength by claiming that its very existence was at stake. Can it continue to obtain foreign aid once this argument loses credibility?" He concluded on a pessimistic note: "For all these reasons Israel will resist being absorbed into the region with all the means at its disposal. That is why a fifth war is likely."[6] (Sid-Ahmed held a view common in Egypt that Jews of Middle Eastern extraction are "Arab Jews" whose ultimate identity has yet to crystallize.)

More than forty years after its publication, *After the Guns Fall Silent* stands out as a unique and exceptionally prescient work in a number of ways. Not merely was it the first work in Arabic to offer and endorse a vision of Arab-Israeli peace, but for many years it remained the only work of its kind. (Not until 1997 was it supplemented by Hazim Saghiyya's *In Defense of Peace*.) Sid-Ahmed understood correctly that beyond an agreement enabling Israelis and Arabs to sort out their differences and settle their conflicts lay complex and difficult questions regarding Israel's own essence, its view of itself, and its role in the region. For a peace settlement to be durable, Israel would have to become part of the Middle East and to have a "function," as he calls it, in its development. For that to happen, he assumed that Israel would have to undergo a transformation, and then he posed a legitimate question: could Israel become an integral part of the Middle East and retain its own character and cohesion?

Sid-Ahmed's ideas regarding the actual cooperation possible between Israel and the Arab states—industrial zones in border areas, nuclear-powered desalinization plants in desert areas—are remarkably far-sighted. But his ambivalence is as telling: the traces of lingering hostility to Israel, his doubts, his questions.

Yet the term "peace" has occupied a prominent place in the vocabulary of Arab-Israeli relations for more than fifty years. This had not been the case during the early decades of the Arab-Jewish conflict in and over Palestine, when the contenders sought victory, accommodation, or political settlement. The UN partition resolution, the establishment of the state of Israel, the 1948 war, and Israel's victory in it created an entirely different situation. The war consolidated Israel's existence, but it also expanded and exacerbated the conflict between the new state and its Arab environment. Yet, to normalize its position and to proceed with its agenda, the new state needed peace. And peace was for the Arabs to give or deny; this capacity, and the adamant and persistent refusal to extend it, soon became their principal weapon against Israel.

Recent scholarship has shown that Israeli and Arab attitudes toward the notion of a peaceful settlement during the very early stages of the conflict were more complex than assumptions in subsequent decades, which were characterized as Israeli craving for and Arab rejection of the very idea. During the final phases of the 1948 war and immediately thereafter, several Arab protagonists were willing to discuss peace, but Israeli policy as shaped by David Ben-Gurion preferred armistice agreements to peace treaties. Israel thought the terms demanded by the prospective Arab partners were dangerous, unwarranted, and unacceptable. It preferred to consolidate its existence and preserve its achievements through a more modest series of armistice agreements, and to seek full peace later, on a more secure base. Then, during late 1949, when Israel's calculus and policy changed, full-fledged peace agreements proved elusive. King Abdullah of Jordan was the only Arab leader then to conduct—and in fact complete—a peace negotiation with Israel, but when it came to implementation in early 1950, he discovered that he no longer had the authority or the political base for such a bold move.[7]

This brief quest for Arab-Israeli peace was followed by nearly two decades during which peace was an abstract, remote notion. On the Arab side, peace with Israel became equated with capitulation and betrayal. When Habib Bourguiba, the president of Tunisia, proposed in 1965 that the Arab world adopt a "phased strategy"—recognize Israel and continue the struggle through peaceful means—he was denounced as a traitor. Two years later, right after the Six-Day War, the Arab summit conference in Khartoum reiterated and reformulated Arab nationalism's categorical rejection of the very notion of peace with Israel.

On the Israeli side, peace was increasingly considered in mystical terms and as inaccessible, while actual policies focused on meeting Arab political and military challenges. The outcome of the 1967 war altered the situation. The United States shared Israel's view that its victory must be converted into nothing less than a full-fledged peace settlement, and initiated the "land-for-peace" policy, which, through several variations, has guided its conduct to this day. Yet the very idea was initially unacceptable to the defeated Arab states and their supporters and was never accepted by Israel. And, though the notion of land-for-peace informs Security Council Resolution 242, given the UN's need to satisfy diverse and contradictory interests, references to territorial concessions and contractual peace were indirect or coded. Thus the search for peace in the full sense of the term was postponed for another decade, and Middle Eastern diplomacy focused instead on more modest forms of accommodation. When, in February 1971, Egypt's new president, Anwar al-Sadat, communicated through the UN envoy, Gunnar Jarring, his willingness "to enter into a peace agreement with Israel," he probably did not have in mind the full-blown peace treaty he ended up signing in 1979, and Israel did not take his regime and his offer seriously.[8]

DEFINING THE MEANING OF "PEACE"

Only after the 1973 October War was serious thought given to, and work done toward reaching, a peaceful resolution of the Arab-Israeli conflict. On the Israeli side, the principal figure was Yitzhak Rabin during his first tenure as prime minister, in 1974–77. (Golda Meir and Moshe Dayan, whose policies collapsed during the war in 1973, negotiated and carried out the disengagement agreements with Egypt and Syria, but Rabin was left to deal with the long-term consequences.)

Rabin's policy was based on two premises: that, with Arab economic power and international political influence at a peak during the energy crisis, it was not to Israel's advantage to seek a comprehensive settlement; and that Israel could not and should not accept one based on withdrawal to the June 4, 1967, lines. He therefore collaborated with Henry Kissinger in the "step-by-step" diplomacy that led to the September 1975 Israeli-Egyptian interim agreement, pledging to resolve their differences "by peaceful means." On the Arab side, the principle of settling the conflict politically was formally endorsed at a summit conference in Algiers in November 1973. But political settlement meant, as the final communiqué expressed it, acceptance of the Arabs' two premises: that Israel had to withdraw from all Arab territories occupied in June 1967 (including Jerusalem); and that the Palestinians must recover their "established national rights." This was rather vague and could be and indeed was interpreted in more than one way. But Egypt kept edging toward a bolder concept of a peaceful settlement.[9]

Egypt's political and intellectual elite more or less agreed that Egypt must disengage from the policy it had followed vis-à-vis Israel for a quarter-century. Egypt had paid a terrible price for the Six-Day War and the subsequent war of attrition; the oil-producing states of the Gulf had accumulated wealth and influence while Egypt declined. So Cairo's priorities had to be altered. Thus a will to disengage from the conflict with Israel was clear, but it was not matched by a clear sense of how this could or should be achieved. Debates raged. Muhammad Sid-Ahmed drew his bold scenario of peace and "complementarity," while others advocated a theory of Israel's "withering" with a more hostile edge: the Arabs would make peace with Israel if the latter withdrew from all territories occupied in June 1967. An Israel "reduced to its natural dimensions," a "second Lebanon," was an entity Egypt and the Arab world could accept. In any event, a shriveled Israel was not viable and would lose coherence and sense of purpose, internal contradictions would come to the fore, and the Israeli state would wither over time.[10] A slightly milder approach was offered by Boutros Boutros-Ghali, then a senior scholar and member of Egypt's foreign policy establishment and later UN secretary-general:

In any case, the front-line states may in the near future accept a de jure recognition of Israel, but not the possibility of instituting diplomatic, commercial or cultural relations with it. This is not to say that such relations are inconceivable in the more distant future. It will remain for the State of Israel to prove to the interstate community of the Arab world that it wishes to and is able to integrate itself into the region. This willingness on Israel's part would have to include a vast program of Arabization in which Arabic would become a language of Israel on equal footing with Hebrew[, and] an active process of cultural and social decolonization, in which the policies of both immigration and emigration would be calculated to encourage the integration into the Israeli population only of elements that could adapt to this profound change in the nature of Israeli society. The author does not underestimate the difficulties that would be created in Israeli society by this sort of change[, but] only a change of this nature can incur the passage of the front-line states from a stage of confrontation to one of coexistence and, from there, to a level of active cooperation without which there can be no real or durable peace in the area.[11]

The debate ended in 1978 with the direct Egyptian-Israeli negotiation predicated on the principle of land for peace. The bilateral part of the Camp David Accords and the subsequent peace treaty rested on a clear formula: Israel's full withdrawal from the Sinai Peninsula in return for contractual peace, "normalized" relations, and a satisfactory security regime. But the same clarity did not apply to the framework for peace concerning the Palestinians. Disagreements over the implementation of Camp David's proposed autonomy plan for Palestinians marred the new relationship, and the initial hopes that Israel's relations with the Arab world would be transformed were dashed.

Before this turn of events, Israelis had time to think seriously about the meaning of peace. It was no longer an abstract notion wrapped in mist but had become a concrete, accessible goal. Egypt was opened to Israeli tourists in 1979 and thousands traveled to Cairo, Alexandria, and Upper Egypt. Israelis were engaged in drawing up bold plans as well as in soul-searching. When borders were open and people could move in both directions, would Israel lose its coherence and identity? Would Israeli Jews of Middle Eastern extraction perhaps feel more comfortable in Egypt than in Israel's Westernized culture?[12]

But by 1981 it had become clear that the framework for peace was doomed. The cold peace meant that diplomatic relations and some elements of normal relations were implemented and maintained, that Egypt would adhere to the security regime in the Sinai, but a critical, negative tone came to characterize Cairo's attitude and policy toward Israel.

This selective policy enabled Egypt to maintain the basic, most important elements of its new relationship with Israel and to cultivate its new relationship with the United States while at the same time placating Islamist and leftist opposition and mending fences in the Arab world. Some Israelis criticized and complained: this was not the peace they had yearned for and envisioned. Among other Israelis, who had felt uncomfortable with the prospects of opening up to the Arab world, of losing the comfort of a familiar way of life, there was a lack of genuine interest in Arab social and cultural life. (It is significant that no correspondent for an Israeli newspaper or television station has been stationed over time in Cairo.) In January 1999 Ariel Sharon, addressing a closed session of Israeli diplomats in New York, expressed the atavistic discomfort most Israelis seem to have with the prospect of open borders between Israel and her Arab neighbors: "If we keep open borders—which may be a vision of this peace process—Israel would be swamped by many vehicles, would become a country of transit; hundreds of thousands of Arab visitors would come carrying not swords in their hands but olive leaves in their mouths. . . . This is a very complex issue that will have to be thought through."[13]

This Israeli frame of mind might conceivably have been altered with the gradual development of new ties, but that was not allowed to happen. Instead, both sides settled into the new reality of a limited and selective relationship. Thousands of Israelis went to Egypt as tourists; very few Egyptians came to Israel. Curiously, an Israeli Academic Center was allowed to open in Cairo, but it was rendered controversial by the unruly media, and its effect was in any event limited because it was boycotted by Egypt's hostile intelligentsia and academic establishment.

The Israeli assumption that peace with the largest, most important, and most powerful Arab state would go a long way toward ending the Arab-Israeli conflict proved wrong. That Egypt had made a full peace with Israel had no profound immediate effect elsewhere in the Arab world. The termination of the military conflict between Egypt and Israel tended to telescope rather than limit the Arab-Israeli conflict. Indeed, resolution of the Israeli-Egyptian conflict only exacerbated the Palestinian, Syrian, and Lebanese dimensions of Israel's situation. Hardly less damaging was the realization that peace could be made and maintained without a genuine reconciliation. Menachem Begin had wanted a separate peace with Egypt, and at this he proved to be quite successful, but it fell short of being the peace Israelis yearned for.

The lengthy suspension of the peace process during much of the 1980s finally ended with the Madrid Conference in October 1991 and its new concept of four tracks of bilateral negotiations (with Israel's immediate neighbors: Syria, Lebanon, Jordan, and the Palestinians) and a parallel track of multilateral negotiations. As we have seen, the multilateral efforts were made by five working groups concerned with refugees, water, arms control and regional security, environmental problems, and economic development. Arab states from the Gulf and North Africa and interested states from other parts of the world were invited to join these working groups. By dealing with issues that were meant to be solved after the resolution of Israeli-Arab political disputes, the parties could glimpse the prospect of regional cooperation, and this in turn could facilitate the difficult bilateral negotiations. This proved to be a particularly productive idea. The multilateral talks were successful both in their own right and as a launch for the regional economic conferences that were the high-water mark of the peace process in the mid-1990s.

It was through these multilateral talks that a nation like Saudi Arabia came to participate in the peace process. The Saudis had been sharply critical of Sadat's original peacemaking with Israel, but time had changed their perspective and priorities. The Iranian revolution of 1979, the rise of a powerful Iraqi state, and the tidal wave of radical Islam all over the Middle East presented new and ominous threats to the kingdom's survival and prosperity. In the perspective afforded by these developments, the Israeli challenge lost much of its edge. In fact, Egyptian-Israeli peace and stabilization at the core of the Middle East came to be seen in Riyadh as a positive development, for it would help contain Iran, Iraq, and the radical Islamist tide in the Gulf. The signing of the Oslo Accords legitimized a significant measure of Saudi-Israeli normalization. It was a first step, still a far cry from the Arab definition of a "just peace," but if "the sole legitimate representative" of Palestinian nationalism had crossed the threshold and agreed to mutual recognition with Israel, why should Saudis, Omanis, and Tunisians refuse to discuss future regional projects with Israelis in a multilateral working group?

Rabin approached all these new developments in his customary pragmatic way. Israel faced both an opportunity and a duty. The availability of the Madrid framework, the evident changes in Arab attitudes, the hospitable regional and international arenas all offered unusual chances to move the peace process forward, and it was Israel's duty to take advantage of them. But it was not at all clear how far and along which course the peace process could be moved. As Rabin saw it, Israel should indicate its willingness, explore the options, make progress where progress could be made, and make fresh decisions along the way.

Rabin's approach was incrementalist. As he had in the mid-1970s, he shied away from a sweeping approach to a comprehensive or swift settlement. A final resolution was not feasible, and whatever version of it was available came with a prohibitively high cost. Israel's first step should be made with either the Palestinians or the Syrians, and the next step should depend on that first breakthrough and be tailored to the circumstances. And so it was that the first agreement was with the PLO and that it was followed by peace with Jordan. Rabin was surprised by the willingness of other Arab states to normalize relations with Israel and to participate in the regional economic conferences in Casablanca and Amman. But without an agreement with Syria, the road to a formal resolution of the Arab-Israeli conflict was closed. Still, Rabin was not in a hurry. Much had been accomplished in only a few years, and the difficult job of completing the final-status negotiations with the Palestinians and the arduous negotiation with Syria would have to be carried out during a second term, one that never came.

In his role as Rabin's foreign minister, Peres, as we have seen, approached the peace process in an entirely different way. He was mindful of all the difficult political and territorial disputes between Israel and its Arab neighbors, but to him these were not the crucial matter. They would be addressed in the first, transitional phase, during which trust and confidence should build, but "in the second, decisive phase of the peace process the specific nature of peace is the dominant issue."[14] And its nature would be determined by the interplay between Arab-Israeli relations and the larger regional developments of which they were a part. In short, a durable solution to the Arab-Israeli problem could be achieved only when the Middle East had established a regional system, and the formation of such a system depended on the resolution of the Arab-Israeli conflict. Put differently, Israel could not enjoy a stable peace so long as the Middle East was beset by severe social and economic problems, and Israel's neighbors could not overcome their problems so long as they failed to settle their conflict with Israel. The foreign minister's vision was stated boldly:

> Peace between Israel and its Arab neighbors will create the environment for a basic reorganization of Middle Eastern institutions. Reconciliation and Arab acceptance of Israel as a nation with equal

rights and responsibilities will sire a new sort of cooperation—not only between Israel and its neighbors but also among Arab nations. It will change the face of the region and its ideological climate. . . . The problems of this region of the world cannot be solved by individual nations. . . . Regional organization is the key to peace and security. . . . Our ultimate goal is the creation of a regional community of nations . . . modeled on the European community.[15]

As Rabin's partner, Peres was given considerable scope to try to implement some of his ideas. He helped initiate the "donors' conference" in Washington, two weeks after the Oslo Accords signing ceremony on the White House lawn; this initiative was intended to orchestrate a large-scale international boost to the Palestinian economy and to raise living standards in the Gaza Strip and the West Bank. Indeed, the point was to recast the economic relationship between Israel and the West Bank and the Gaza Strip (the legal framework was defined in the Paris Protocol in July 1994). This campaign was motivated by more than the obvious and familiar idea that Arab peacemakers should be rewarded economically. As American and Israeli policymakers saw it, Hamas and the other fundamentalist groups who opposed Arafat fed on poverty; by creating new sources of employment, by providing housing projects and better schools, the Palestinian Authority could better build a constituency that supported peace with Israel. A different way of saying much the same thing was to argue that over time it would be hard, if not impossible, to maintain peace between a society enjoying a per capita income of $18,000 a year and a society with a per capita income of less than $1,000 a year. That is difficult enough between neighboring states separated by clearly defined boundaries, and even more so in the case of two societies whose lives are closely intertwined.

Israel's effort to obtain financial and economic aid for the Palestinian Authority was a controversial aspect of the Rabin-Peres policy—controversial in Israel and among Jewish communities abroad. After years of mobilizing *against* Arafat and the PLO, it was difficult to accept the reconciliation, the recognition, the symbolism of a handshake, and even harder to imagine Israeli leaders and diplomats lobbying to obtain financial resources for yesterday's enemies. Yet acceptance of the Palestinians as partners went to the core of the new reality that Israeli policymakers were seeking to shape. Israelis have yet to decide whether they want a clear-cut separation from the Palestinians or some form of association or integration. But whatever shape the final settlement takes, the very existence of the Oslo Accords means that it has ceased to be a zero-sum game. Mental adjustment to this revolutionary truth has lagged far behind, for understandable reasons. The Rabin government and Foreign Minister Peres in particular were way ahead of the public in adjusting to this new reality and molding it to fit into a new policy about Israel and its Arab environment.

Under Peres's direction, then, experts affiliated with the Foreign Ministry prepared an impressive dossier of joint economic projects. Of particular significance were the industrial parks proposed for several sites along the lines separating Israel from the West Bank and the Gaza Strip, to be financed by international agencies and private investors, and intended to provide employment for Palestinian workers while facilitating Israeli-Palestinian economic cooperation and minimizing friction or the appearance of Israeli economic domination. (The similarity to some of the ideas raised nearly twenty years earlier by Muhammad Sid-Ahmed is quite striking.) In short order, a similar approach was likely for Israel's relationship with Jordan. King Hussein made clear that he expected "peace dividends"—debt relief and military aid from the United States and massive investments in Jordan's economy that would make up for the loss, following the Persian Gulf War, of remittances from Jordanian workers in the Gulf. He also indicated that he was willing to develop a "warm" peace with Israel, in stark contrast to Egypt's proverbial "cold" policy. The Foreign Ministry responded with a thick volume of projects focused on the Jordan Rift Valley. This portfolio included spectacular infrastructure projects (for example, a canal leading from the Dead Sea to a single Red Sea port just above the Gulf of Eilat, and a joint international airport for Eilat and Aqaba) as well as more conventional industrial parks in border areas.

It was during Peres's secret visit with King Hussein in November 1993 that an international business conference was first proposed. (Peres wanted to hold it in Amman.) The Israeli effort to take advantage of the Oslo Accords to finally make peace with Jordan had just begun, and Peres was seeking to expand the agenda. In the winter of 1993–94, the king was not quite ready for such a bold move, but the

Clinton administration was persuaded to endorse the idea and helped to recruit support from Morocco's King Hassan: the first conference took place in Casablanca a year later, the second one in Amman in October 1995. Both conferences were impressive and successful gatherings of many Israeli, Arab, and international businessmen, though it is difficult to point out many joint Arab-Israeli business ventures that grew out of them. Still, as a demonstration of the potential inherent in the peace process, they were most effective. So Peres pushed on and tried to put together a regional bank for the Middle East, modeled after regional banks in other parts of the world. He came quite close to seeing this project through, but neither the Clinton administration nor most Arab states had been fully supportive of this concept, and with the waning of the peace process it was shelved sine die.

The differences between Rabin's and Peres's approaches to peace-making were underlined by the changes Peres introduced when he assumed power in November 1995, after Rabin's assassination, in the conduct of Israel's negotiation with Syria. Rabin had assumed that Israel could not expect to obtain more than a cold peace with Syria, tailored by Hafiz al-Asad to offer less than Sadat had given. A warmer, closer relationship could develop only over time. But a contractual peace and satisfactory security regime would remove the danger of conventional war, push Iran back to the margins of the Middle East, resolve Israel's problem in Lebanon, and consolidate the agreements with Jordan and the Palestinians. These achievements would justify the concessions Israel would have to offer Damascus.

Peres was not interested in yet another version of Egypt's cold peace and thought it would be difficult to persuade the Israeli public to withdraw from the Golan Heights in return. But if Syria's economy could be tied more closely to the global economy, if investments were brought to it, if joint Israeli-Syrian ventures could be launched (even, if necessary, with American sponsorship or partnership), a web of interests would develop that would reduce the danger of renewed conflict. And if some of these joint ventures were established in the Golan Heights, this cordon would be hardly less valuable as security protection than yet another line of fortifications. Syria would have to think twice before embarking on a course that would jeopardize its investments and interests in the Golan. Joint ventures in the Golan would also make Israeli concessions easier, blunting the sense of loss and departure. In the terminology of conflict-resolution theory: whereas Rabin was seeking a "settlement" with Syria, Peres was aiming at a "resolution."

Further, Peres wanted to make a prospective agreement with Syria a stepping-stone to a comprehensive Arab-Israeli settlement. In his discussions with the Clinton administration, he explored the idea of a regional security system in the Middle East, although the Americans regarded it as premature. Meanwhile, discussions between Israel and Turkey matured to produce a formal agreement on strategic cooperation. In theory, this Turkish-Israeli relationship could fit into a regional system inclusive of the major Arab states, but in practice Israel's Arab interlocutors, first and foremost Syria, viewed it as an anti-Arab measure, a revival of David Ben-Gurion's "alliance of the periphery" in the late 1950s.

Nor was Hafiz al-Asad enamored of the economic aspects of Peres's peace policy, which he had already denounced as an Israeli scheme directed against Arab nationalism. He found the notion of joint businesses an offensive intrusion: any Israeli involvement in projects in the Golan Heights would be interpreted as perpetuating its presence there and denying him the chance for a full liberation of Syrian territories lost in 1967. As Asad's biographer, Patrick Seale, put it: "Most Syrians would have seen such a settlement as exposing their society, nascent industries, cultural traditions and national security to hostile Israeli penetration. For Asad it would have made a mockery of his entire career."[16]

It is telling that negotiations between Israel and Syria collapsed in March 1996 for reasons that had little to do with this dim view of economic relations with Israel in the event of peace and more to do with Asad's response to the initiative of an Israeli prime minister who was eager to come to an agreement with him. Asad had negotiated with Israel resentfully and grudgingly because it was something he had been forced to do, and now his policy options had diminished. As a reluctant peacemaker, he would agree only to what he could not avoid, and he would demonstrate his dissatisfaction with the way things were going. Asad criticized everyone who deviated from the course he had tried to prescribe—who, in his view, gave Israel too much and undermined him—and at the same time was criticized by Syrians and others adamantly opposed to peace with Israel, who expected or wanted him to uphold the ideas and principles with which he had once been identified. For those who said that terms like "revolution," "Arab unity," and "Arab socialism" had long ago lost their meaning and that the Ba'ath too had become hollow, but who also were hoping against hope that Asad would hold the line, his willingness to sign a contractual peace with Israel was a bitter disappointment.

The lines separating Asad's position from that of his critics and from that of the objects of his own criticism are landmarks, and when we try to map out—and understand—Arab attitudes to peacemaking with Israel, we must understand where those lines are. Each end of the spectrum is clear and distinct: the wholehearted opposition of Islamic and other ideological opponents to any peace or reconciliation, and at the other end, open and unambiguous advocacy of full peace with Israel. In the middle of the spectrum, subtle differences separate halfhearted endorsement of reconciliation from a grudging reluctance to agree to peace and normalization with Israel.

As we saw above, in the twilight of Asad's reign it was his foreign minister, Faruq al-Shara, who presented in an apologetic fashion the regime's version regarding its willingness to sign a peace treaty with Israel. In essence, this version stated that signing the peace treaty with Israel meant transition from "a struggle with an existential enemy" to competition with an adversary.

"Orphaned peace" is the term Fouad Ajami, the prominent American scholar of the Middle East, uses to describe a diplomacy that Arab opinion has accepted with many reservations.[17] Popular opinion in any country is difficult to measure, and certainly so in Arab countries, but there seems to be no discrepancy in this case between popular opinion and the positions articulated by public intellectuals and the intelligentsia. They are all informed with a sense of defeat. The 1990s were not good years in the Arab world. Old ideologies died or became stale and were not replaced; the great hopes of the "oil decade" were dashed long before. Saddam Hussein was defeated in the Persian Gulf War, and though his immediate neighbors were relieved, those who had hoped for a revival of revolutionary zeal, spirit, and ideals were badly disappointed. The end of the Cold War and the disintegration of the Soviet Union left the United States with undue influence in the Middle East. Political Islam, a source of both threat and regeneration, seemed to have peaked. And even if the Arab regimes seemed remarkably resilient, durability does not go hand in hand with openness and innovation. Against that backdrop, peace with Israel achieved on terms closer to the Israeli than to the Arab position was received as yet another humiliation.

The expatriate Syrian poet Nizar Qabbani, one of the most eloquent and bitter critics of the "Arab order," wrote a particularly powerful and poignant poem, published in October 1995, expressing his disgust with the Oslo Accords and with the "Arab condition" exposed by them. "The last walls of embarrassment have fallen," he wrote. "We were delighted and we danced and we blessed ourselves for signing the peace of the cowards."[18] This was a humiliating surrender, with Arabs scrambling to kiss the shoes of "the killer. . . . In our hands they left a sardine can called Gaza and a dry bone called Jericho. . . . After the secret romance in Oslo, we came out barren. They gave us a homeland smaller than a single grain of wheat." And it was a deal made in the United States— "the dowry was in dollars . . . the cake was a gift from America." But Qabbani's real rage was directed at the Arabs' own political establishment, whom he held responsible for the misery and humiliation in the terms of the peace with Israel and for the larger decline of which the Oslo Accords were both a consequence and a symptom:

Who would ask the rulers
about the peace of cowards
about the peace of selling in installments
and renting in installments
about the peace of the merchants
and the exploiters?
Who could ask them
about the peace of the dead?
They have silenced the street
and murdered all the questions
and those who question.

What Qabbani said in verse, others said in prose. The most prominent Palestinian intellectual, Edward Said, who had been one of Arafat's supporters several years earlier, denounced the Oslo Accords as a sellout. In *The Politics of Dispossession*, he wrote:

With some of the euphoria dissipated after the great celebration surrounding the breakthrough, it now becomes possible to reexamine the Israeli-PLO agreements with the required common sense. What emerges from such scrutiny is a deal that is more flawed and weighted unfavorably for the Palestinian people than many had first supposed. The show biz front of the White House ceremony on September 13, the degrading spectacle of Yasir Arafat thanking everyone for the suspension of most of his people's rights and the solemnity of Bill Clinton's performance . . . all these only temporarily obscure the truly astonishing proportions of the quite sudden Palestinian capitulation, which smacks of the PLO leadership's exhaustion and of Israel's shrewdness. . . . In sum, we need to move up from a state of supine abjectness with which, in reality, the Oslo [agreement] was negotiated . . . into the prosecution of parallel agreements with Israel and the Arabs that concern Palestinian national, as opposed to municipal aspirations. But this does not exclude resistance against the Israeli occupation, which continues indefinitely.[19]

Qabbani's poem was entitled *Al-Muharwilun* (The hurried ones)—a castigating term for the Arabs who rushed to normalize relations with Israel. This term, used by an angry poet to denounce the Arab governments for endorsing hated agreements, diplomacy, and policies—the Egyptian and Syrian governments, notably—was the very term Arab governments themselves used to criticize those whom they accused of eagerness to "normalize" relations with Israel too rapidly. This fact underlines two important aspects of the Arab attitude to peacemaking with Israel in the 1990s: the centrality of the notion of "normalization," and the complex relationship between the ruling political classes and their societies on this particular issue. As Ajami correctly pointed out, reservations with regard to peacemaking with Israel were one issue on which autocratic governments and their "civil societies" could agree, and in which they could have agreed on a division of labor, as it were. If it suited Sadat and Mubarak to keep the peace with Israel cold, they might as well also let Egyptian professional associations boycott their Israeli counterparts, or let the Egyptian press vent their anger and frustration in anti-Israeli diatribes. By the same token, for a Syrian regime that was negotiating a peace with Israel and trying to achieve its extremely narrow concept of peace, statements made by Syrian writers or journalists condemning "normalization with Israel" would be useful. Nor could Arafat complain of Edward Said, Hisham Sharabi, or other prominent Palestinian intellectuals for criticizing the Oslo process when he himself publicly indicated that "the struggle continues."

FROM COLD PEACE TO NORMALIZATION

During the mid-1990s, "normalization" came to replace "cold peace" as the key term in discussing the nature of Arab-Israeli peace. Curiously and significantly, this shift in terminology focused the debate on a notion that had been so cardinal to the original purpose of Zionism, which sought to normalize the condition of the Jews by establishing a state in which the Jewish people could develop a normal society and a normal economy. As we saw, that failed to happen. A Jewish state was founded and survived the 1948 war, but it could not obtain the Arab states' acceptance of its very existence. The most effective weapons in the Arabs' conflict with the Jewish state were refusal, rejection, and boycott. So the new state was rejected by its immediate neighbors, by the Muslim world, and later by the Soviet bloc and much of the Third World. Israel did very well nonetheless, but its regional and international positions were not normal. Peace with the Arabs was the key to normalizing both of these positions. The end of the Cold War and the inauguration of the Madrid process improved Israel's international position, but normalizing "the Israeli condition" could not be achieved without resolution of the Arab-Israeli conflict.

As new agreements were being negotiated, signed, and implemented in the years 1992–95, normalization acquired two different meanings: the establishment of bilateral normal peaceful relations between Israel and each of its principal Arab counterparts; and the further normalization of Israel's position in the Middle East through its participation in regional and international forums along with Arab and other partners. The Arabs' response to Israel's quest for normalization varied greatly. Syria's original position in the bilateral negotiations of 1992–93 was that normalization fell outside the scope of the peace legitimized by the Arab consensus for regaining the territories Syria had lost in 1967.

The Syrians grudgingly accepted the notion of a contractual peace, but continued to argue that the Israeli definition of normality—in cultural, commercial, and economic relations, for instance—concerned issues that "the society" and not the government should agree to, and that conditions allowing for such relations could develop only over time. In August 1993, when Rabin made his "hypothetical gambit" and included normalization in Israel's peace proposal, Asad responded by telling Warren Christopher that he "disliked" and "had difficulties" with that term. It took Syria another year of trilateral negotiations with Israel and the United States to agree to a limited, well-defined normalization as part of its prospective peaceful relationship with Israel. This Syrian attitude clearly reflected the Asad regime's negotiating style. All issues and details were a matter of hard bargaining: the more eager Israel was for normalization, the higher the price it would have to pay for it.

Understandably, Syria also was trying to follow the Egyptian precedent of cold peace. Egypt had signed a full-fledged peace treaty, with numerous annexes concerning normalization across the board, and it had subsequently found a way to turn these agreements into a dead letter while keeping the essence and formality of a nonbelligerent relationship. Perhaps Syria could accomplish the same result by avoiding the normalization issue altogether. Moreover, Asad felt he must do better than merely replicate Egypt's agreement with Israel (if his agreement with Israel looked like a copy of the Camp David Accords, he would be hard put to explain why he had not made it fifteen years earlier) and tried to achieve something that at least in one major aspect would seem an improvement over the peace made by Sadat. In time, Asad discovered that he could not cite the precedent Egypt had set in obtaining full withdrawal of Israeli troops from its territory without offering an equivalent full contractual "peace with normalization," at least on paper.

Beyond these considerations lay genuine fears of Israel's ambitions and schemes in the event of peace. Asad was not about to open Syria up to Israeli business and technology, or to contemplate the creation of a "new Middle East" on the ruins of what was, after all, a predominantly Arab world. The thesis has been advanced that Asad was so deeply concerned with the destabilizing effects of peace with Israel that he did not actually want to consummate the deal and conducted negotiations in an "idle" mode.[20] But this is an overstatement. Asad believed that his regime could cope with the effects of peace and limited normalization with Israel, but his aim was to contain Israel, not to integrate it into the Middle East. In October 1995 he lashed out against the very idea:

> I wonder about this notion in the far Arab future and what its values and role at present and in the future will be. . . . This is the objective they are seeking. . . . Why is the Middle East being established? The Middle East already exists. The strange thing is that the Middle East is being presented as an alternative to Arabism.[21]

As I have tried to make clear, Asad in 1995 was locked in an awkward position vis-à-vis Peres, the Israeli architect of an envisioned "new Middle East" who was willing to move much farther than Rabin had been, but who insisted on "quality" and "depth" in the new peaceful relationship and who saw normalization and economic cooperation as key to it. Assad's difficulties with this very approach were an important element in the subsequent failure to achieve a breakthrough.

As for Egypt, although its negativism about normalization with Israel had a domestic dimension,[22] the accent was clearly on the regional dimension. Egypt shared Syria's anxieties about a new Middle East, but whereas Damascus voiced opposition and criticism from the sidelines, Cairo was forced, by virtue of being both a pillar of the peace process and a critic of its excesses, to adopt a much more complex policy. Its dilemmas were simplified by Netanyahu's 1996 victory and by the subsequent decline of peace diplomacy. With Israel's regional role diminished, Cairo could shift from subtle, indirect criticism of overly eager, hurried, and premature Arab willingness to normalize relations with Israel to outright criticism of normalization as such. "Normalization is an Israeli invention," stated Osama al-Baz, a particularly thoughtful Egyptian policymaker, "which means the establishment of a special relationship. Such a relationship must be predicated on a common concept of and common interests in the future, and these are absent of true progress and of a national, normal Israeli conduct, which meets legal criteria; normal relations cannot be maintained lest the balance be upset."[23]

Jordan formulated its peace policy in yet a third way. It was willing to offer Israel a distinctly "warm" peace in return for rewards it expected to gain from other dimensions of its relationship with its neighbor. After the Oslo Accords, the Hashemite regime had no qualms about the effect of normalized relations with Israel in its own domestic sphere or about Israel's playing a regional role at the expense of some of Jordan's rivals. But the course of events in subsequent years made this policy untenable. Rabin's assassination, public resistance at home, the failure of the anticipated "peace dividends" to materialize, and the general decline of peace diplomacy forced King Hussein to turn down the volume on peace and normalization. And now Israel's relationship with Jordan does not appear very different from its relationship with Egypt.

At the same time, the Palestinian approach is remarkably uninhibited with regard to the idea of normalization. This may sound surprising, given the ferocity of the Israeli-Palestinian conflict, but it is quite understandable when the realities of two societies intertwined with one another are taken into account. In any event, the Palestinians' leverage in the peace process derives primarily from their centrality in determining the legitimacy and finality of a settlement. This crucial issue goes to the core of Israel's relationship with the Arab world. Israel appears to Arabs as a powerful, aggressive, and threatening entity, but in fact it is a country haunted by a sense of vulnerability and persecution. Arabs believe as a rule that time is on their side, and many Israelis agree. But the two sides have different views of a final settlement as a result. As Israelis see it, they are offering, irreversibly, to give up tangible assets, and they would like to be reassured that the consequent settlement is definitive and final, not open-ended. This is matched by a tendency on the Arabs' side to deny Israel that very asset—a reassuring sense of finality.

THE ARAB PEACE INITIATIVE

Since the Arab summit conference in Cairo in June 1996, there has been a formal Arab definition of the terms under which a comprehensive Arab-Israeli peace might be established (and, implicitly, the Arab-Israeli conflict might end):

> Adhering to their national responsibility, the Arab leaders assert that the establishment of a comprehensive and just peace in the Middle East requires Israel's complete withdrawal from all

occupied Palestinian territories, including Arab Jerusalem, and enabling the Palestinian people to exercise their right to self-determination and to establish an independent state with Arab Jerusalem as its capital. This is because the Palestinian issue is the crux of the Arab-Israeli conflict. The Arab leaders also call for Israel's complete withdrawal from the Syrian Golan Heights to the June 4, 1967, line and for Israel's full and unconditional withdrawal from southern Lebanon and the western al-Biqa to the internationally recognized borders, in implementation of Security Council Resolutions 242, 338, and 425 and the principle of land for peace. On these bases, they call for the resumption of talks on all tracks.

The Arab countries' commitment to continue the peace process to achieve a just and comprehensive peace under the aegis of international legitimacy is a goal and a strategic option. This commitment requires similar serious and unequivocal commitment on the part of Israel, which must work to complete the peace process in a way that will restore the rights and occupied territories and ensure balanced and equal security for all the states of the region, in accordance with the principles agreed upon at the Madrid Conference, especially the land-for-peace principles, and the assurances given to the parties.

The Arab leaders stress their adherence to the UN resolutions, which do not accept or recognize any situation resulting from Israeli settlement activity in the occupied Arab territories. They consider this settlement activity illegal, unlawful, and nonbinding. They consider the building of settlements and bringing settlers to them a violation of the Geneva Convention and the Madrid framework and an obstruction of the peace process. They call for a halt to all settlement activity in the occupied Syrian Golan Heights and the occupied Palestinian territories, particularly Jerusalem, and for the dismantling of these settlements. They also reject any change to the character and legal status of Arab Jerusalem. They emphasize that a comprehensive and just peace in the Middle East cannot be achieved unless a solution is found for the issue of Jerusalem and for the problem of *Palestinian refugees,* who *have the right to return* [italics mine] in accordance with international legitimacy and the UN resolutions.[24]

By citing the Palestinian "right of return" as yet another condition, the Arabs introduced an element likely to perpetuate indefinitely the debate on a settlement. It is hard enough to formulate a definition of terms for a final settlement that will be acceptable to a large and diverse group, and within that group particularly important parts are played by the Palestinians and by Egypt. The right of return is an important issue of principle particularly for Palestinians living in the diaspora, but it is significant first and foremost as an issue likely to keep the peace process open-ended.

The 1996 Arab consensus position regarding peace with Israel was replaced in March 2002 by the "Saudi Peace Initiative" that was adopted by the Beirut Arab summit and thus became the "Arab Peace Initiative." Jordan, worried by the impact of the Israeli-Palestinian impasse on its own position, and Saudi Arabia, which in addition to the same concern was also worried about its own image in the aftermath of the September 11 attacks against the United States, were the prime movers in amending the Arab consensus on the shape of a final-status solution. The text approved by the Beirut summit reaffirmed the resolution taken in 1996 and then went beyond it. The core of this revised initiative was the following:

—Full Israeli withdrawal from all the territories occupied since 1967 including the Syrian Golan Heights to the June 4, 1967, lines as well as the remaining occupied Lebanese territories in the south of Lebanon.

—Achievement of a "just and agreed" solution to the Palestinian refugee problem in accordance with UN General Assembly Resolution 194.

—The acceptance of the establishment of a sovereign, independent Palestinian state on the Palestinian territories occupied since June 4, 1967, in the West Bank and the Gaza Strip, with East Jerusalem as its capital.

After Israel has withdrawn from the territories and a Palestinian state has been established, the Arab countries said they would: Consider the Arab-Israeli conflict ended and enter into a peace agreement with Israel and achieve security for all states of the region; and "Establish normal relations with Israel in the context of this comprehensive peace, which assures the rejection of all forms of Palestinian resettlement (*tawtin*) which conflict with the special circumstances of the Arab host countries."

It should be noted that a separate final communiqué of the Beirut summit included a very different reference to the right of return issue. The ambiguity of the initiative's text was replaced in this document by an explicit demand for "guaranteeing the Palestinian refugees' right of return, based on the international legitimacy's resolutions and international law including UN Resolution 194" and rejected any solution which included "their patriation (or naturalization) away from their homes." Curiously, the Arab League summit in Riyadh in 2007 endorsed the Arab initiative without repeating the text of the 2002 final communiqué.[25]

The Arab Peace Initiative can be approached from two very different perspectives. One is textual. It put the emphasis on the precise meaning and implication of key terms and phrases. In this context the initiative generated a lively debate among Israeli experts (as well as nonexperts) on two main aspects of the persistent issue of the right of return. There is no explicit mention of the claim of return in the text, but the text does insist on the traditional Arab demand for "a just" solution of the refugee problem and reference to UN resolution 194 on which the claim for a right of return has been drawn. This demand is somewhat balanced by addition of the term "agreed" in reference to a solution, which in theory would enable Israel to disagree with any Palestinian claim it refuses to accept. Another debate concerns the term *tawtin,* which some read as "resettlement" or "patriation" and others as "naturalization." This is somewhat of a moot point. Whether the opposition is to "patriation" or "naturalization" of Palestinian refugees in the Arab countries where they have been living, the question remains as to the future of the Palestinian refugees and their descendants and the formula that would be adopted in any final-status agreement.

A second school of thought pays less attention to textual hairsplitting and attaches more significance to the prospect of embedding an Israeli-Arab settlement within a larger regional settlement. But this very approach of shifting the accent from legalistic fine points to political and diplomatic realities encounters difficulties of a different sort. The Arab Peace Initiative is simple but terse; to have any real effect, it needs to be developed into a full-fledged plan of action. It also depends on an Israeli leader who wants to endorse it as a point of departure and who will agree at the outset to a full withdrawal on both the Palestinian and Syrian fronts. This difficulty explains why dovish Israeli leaders like Prime Minister Ehud Olmert and Foreign Minister Tzipi Livni, who wanted to move toward a settlement and toyed with the idea of responding to an improved version of the peace initiative, ended up pursuing the more limited traditional avenues of negotiation.

During the first decade of the current century, the Arab Peace Initiative became one of the issues separating the two contending non-Israeli camps in Middle Eastern politics. The moderate or conservative camp led by Egypt, Saudi Arabia, and Jordan was the promoter of this plan. Its leaders saw Iran, not Israel, as the major threat to their interests and they genuinely sought a resolution of the conflict with Israel in order to be able to proceed with their main agenda (namely the Iranian threat).

That camp was indeed opposed by Iran, which had built the so-called resistance (*muqawama*) axis. Resistance was both a frame of mind and a concrete policy of opposition to the United States and to Israel. Iran and its allies (notably Syria, Hizballah, and Hamas) negated the very idea of peace with Israel. The peace process of the 1990s and its sequels were seen as an attempt to subjugate the Arab world and fit it into "an American order." For Iran and its allies and clients, resistance to the United States, Israel, and the peace process was both an ideological edict and a mindset. The notion of peace with Israel had to be rejected and defeated and the alternative—resistance and victory—upheld.[26]

This attitude was common but not uniform. In Iran since 1979 nuances could be detected, occasioned by personal and political changes. On the whole, however, rejection of Israel and its right to exist—supplemented by Shiite Muslim negative attitudes toward Jews and Judaism—remained a fundamental policy as well as an instrument in the conduct of Iran's regional policy. For the ayatollahs' regime, making (a U.S.-sponsored) peace with Israel was an act of capitulation and had to be fought and defeated. Successful resistance to Israel would demonstrate the futility of capitulation. Over time this view acquired a new motif: Israel was diabolical but not all-powerful. It was declining and its defeat was feasible and imminent.

Among Tehran's allies and clients, Hizballah's position has been the closest to Iran's. In May 2000, after Israel's unilateral withdrawal from south Lebanon, Hizballah's leader, Hassan Nasrallah, delivered in the town of Bint Jubail his "spiderweb" speech, which was a graphic way of referring to Israel as an odious but weak and defeatable entity. A more recent comprehensive and eloquent presentation of Hizballah's position is "the political document" that was put together by the organization's eighth general conference and was presented by Nasrallah on November 30, 2009:

We are facing two contradictory paths. The first combines active resistance (*muqawaqmah*) with [a] passive one (*mumana'ah*). This path is based on military victories and political successes . . . it reflects persistence, despite the huge challenges it is facing, to the point of having succeeded in altering the regional balances in favor of the resistance and its supporters. The second path—American Israeli domination and domineering . . . this path sustained military defeats and failures and political defeats. . . . Today we are in the midst of historic changes that are the harbingers of the US retreat as a hegemonic power. . . . we are also witnessing an accelerated process of the Zionist entity's decline.

Nasrallah proceeded to describe Hizballah's successful history of resistance from 1982 to 2006 and to denounce Israel's very nature and existence:

The Zionist movement is a racist movement and the product of Western domineering and arrogance. Essentially its project is one of settlement, Jewification and expansion. The struggle we are waging against the Zionist and colonialist project is an existential duty and self defense against the occupation, aggression and usurpation by Israel which threatens our very existence.

The natural outcome is that this usurpatory and artificial entity finds itself in a state of existential predicament. . . . It is the duty of the whole nation not to recognize this entity, whatever the pressures and challenges. Instead we must act to bring about the liberation of the land that had been robbed and the rights that had been squandered even if this takes a long time and requires numerous victims. Our position with regard to the option of a diplomatic settlement and the agreements that had already been made . . . was and is a position of absolute opposition to the very idea of the political option. The same applies to the very principle of any settlement with the Zionist entity that is predicated on recognition of its existence and on conceding the land in Arab and Islamic Palestine that this entity had squandered. This position of ours is consistent, permanent and final.[27]

Ironically, Iran's chief Palestinian client, Hamas, has been forced by its role in Palestinian politics to depart occasionally from its fundamental position. As manifested in its 1988 charter, it is not just an anti-Zionist organization but an anti-Semitic one as well. Hamas views the whole of Palestine as an Islamic religious endowment (*waqf*), no part of which can be "renounced." It rules out peace initiatives, "the so-called peaceful solutions and the international conferences" to resolve the Palestinian problem.[28]

This position has been endorsed and articulated by any number of Hamas leaders and spokesmen during the past two decades. At the same time, when the Hamas leadership felt the need to articulate more moderate or pragmatic positions, various leaders and spokesmen found ways of moderating their stance. Examples of this seeming flexibility came when Hamas agreed to participate in the 2006 elections, when a reconciliation agreement with Fatah was signed in Mecca in 2007 but never implemented, and when the Saudis exerted pressure on Hamas to refrain from criticizing the Arab Peace Initiative.

The most notable manifestation of such pragmatism was the idea of *hudna* (armistice with an enemy, as sanctioned by Islam) that would be declared for five years and would be based on the establishment of a Palestinian state within the 1967 boundaries with its capital in Jerusalem, the dismantling of all Israeli settlements, and Israel's acceptance of the right of return without formal recognition of Israel by the Palestinians and without ending the conflict. On other occasions. Hamas spokesmen revived the notion of "a strategy of phases" that had been current in the 1970s. Under this strategy Hamas would establish Palestinian sovereignty over any piece of land it was able to liberate and continue that expansion in phases until "the final goal" was achieved. But the Hamas leadership was quite skillful in blunting the effect of such statements by having other spokesmen issue denials or simply make contradictory statements.[29]

Even more than Hamas, Syria—while it acted and served as Tehran's most important ally and client—pursued a complex policy with regard to peacemaking with Israel. Syria accepted the Arab Peace Initiative (which had been modified to accommodate its interests and sensibilities), engaged in peace negotiations with Jerusalem as late as 2008, and did not rule out the possibility of signing a peace treaty with Israel even when that negotiation failed. The issue of an Israeli-Syrian peace negotiation became moot—at least for the time being—after the eruption of domestic turmoil in Syria in March 2011. Even so, it is still instructive to read the distinction made by Bashar al-Asad in late January 2011 (in an interview with the *Wall Street Journal*) between a peace treaty and peace itself:

> But actually when you sign the treaty, it is the very beginning of the peace. . . . Because it is only the treaty and not the real peace. Peace is when you give normal relations. . . . Many people do not understand the difference between peace and a peace treaty. And we always talk about comprehensive peace, because if you want to have real peace with normal relations between people . . . because in Syria we have 500,000 [Palestinians] and in Lebanon you have another half a million Palestinians. They have all their rights in Syria except voting because they are not citizens . . . so people are sympathetic to them and if you do not find a solution with them, you can not have real peace . . . so having [a] peace treaty only with Syria could be one step that can not be peace.[30]

Rejectionism, ambivalence, and ambiguity on the Arab side of the equation have their counterparts within the Israeli political spectrum. But while the settler movement and other radical right-wing groups remain opposed to any settlement that requires meaningful territorial concessions, the moderate right wing headed by Prime Minister Netanyahu has by now accepted the notions of Palestinian statehood and Israeli withdrawal from large parts of the West Bank. The mainstream in the Israeli political discourse ponders and debates the gamut of issues and conditions that Netanyahu raised in his May 2011 speeches to the Israeli Knesset and the U.S. Congress, but it is primarily preoccupied with the finality of a prospective solution to the Palestinian-Israeli conflict. During the previous decade the term *finality* came to replace *normalization* as Israelis contemplate, debate, or negotiate peace. Finality is addressed directly as an Israeli demand (end of conflict, end of claims) or indirectly when Israelis insist on Palestinian and Arab acceptance of Israel as a Jewish state or when they object to the Palestinian insistence on the right of return. The interplay between the current Arab concepts of peace and resolution and their Israeli counterparts are analyzed in some detail in the conclusion.

Conclusion

In the fall of 2012 Israel's relationship with the Arab world and its strategic position in the Middle East reached an especially low point. To a considerable extent, this state of affairs was the result of trends and developments over which Israel had no, or at most limited, influence. One was the chain of events known as the Arab Spring. As discussed, by the middle of the previous decade Israel found itself in a bleak regional environment. In confronting this new reality, Israel relied on a number of assets that were among the pillars of the old regional order—foremost, its peaceful relations and limited security cooperation with Egypt and Jordan. The events of the Arab Spring destroyed, or threatened to destroy, those assets.

As the Arab Spring began to unfold, Israel was anxious that the fall of Hosni Mubarak's regime in Egypt and the growing opposition to Jordan's king, Abdullah II, would undermine its crucial relations with these two neighboring countries. Israel watched with concern as during 2011–12 its traditional Egyptian partners, the leaders of the national security establishment, lost their grip and positions and the Muslim Brotherhood won the parliamentary and presidential elections, establishing a new regime headed by Mohamed Morsi.

Morsi himself and other Islamist spokesmen have made a variety of statements, some of them contradictory and most of them ambiguous, about the future of the peace treaty with Israel. As he has done with other issues on which the Muslim Brotherhood's ideology and Egypt's interests and needs collide, Morsi has been maneuvering. It seems that whatever his own and the Brotherhood's real feelings are with regard to Egypt's relations with Israel, Morsi intends, for now at least, to keep the essence of the peace treaty, avoid direct contact with Israel, and assign the conduct of the limited relationship between Egypt and Israel to the military and the intelligence community. But the relationship is tenuous and fragile. It is difficult to maintain such a complex relationship when the regime's clear if not explicit message is that Israel is essentially illegitimate. A major crisis—in the Sinai, in Gaza, or in the region—is liable to jeopardize the current relationship.

Under these circumstances, developments in the Sinai Peninsula have acquired particular significance. During Mubarak's years of waning, three interrelated developments occurred: Mubarak's regime lost control of the Bedouin population, that population played a major role in smuggling weapons and goods into the Gaza Strip and African immigrants into Israel, and jihadi elements established themselves in this barely governed part of the country. After Mubarak's fall, those elements took on the weak Egyptian civilian and military administration, paralyzed the export of natural gas from Egypt to Israel and Jordan, and began to launch terrorist attacks across the long, poorly defended border with Israel. One such raid in August 2011 was especially effective: in addition to killing seven Israeli civilians, the perpetrators managed to pit Egyptian border policemen against Israeli soldiers. The loss of Egyptian life reverberated in Cairo and led to an attack on the Israeli embassy there. It took President Obama's personal intervention to get the Egyptian authorities to intervene and to prevent a blood bath and a major crisis.

Ironically, it took the new government, led by the Muslim Brotherhood, to launch a serious campaign against the jihadis entrenched in the Sinai. That required allowing forces larger than the ones allowed by the Egyptian-Israeli Peace Treaty of 1979 to enter the Sinai. The two countries' defense establishments were able to navigate that diplomatic minefield as well as overcome the effects of another major terrorist raid in 2012, but the explosive potential in the Sinai, both on its own and in relation to the adjacent Gaza Strip, remains high.

Israel's relationship with Jordan is jeopardized by a dual challenge. King Abdullah is confronting his own version of the Arab Spring. In a curious and significant shift, the current criticism of the Royal House comes less from the traditional Palestinian opposition and more from Islamist groups and the monarchy's East Bank supporters. The king, in turn, has escalated his criticism of Israel and of Netanyahu's government, whose failure to move forward with the Palestinians is, he claims, the real source of his domestic problems.

As seen, a two-year effort led by the Obama administration to move Israeli-Palestinian negotiations forward failed due to mistakes and policy decisions by all three partners in the effort: the United States, Israel, and the Palestinian Authority. Not much has happened in this regard since the evaporation of the Palestinian Authority's effort to obtain UN recognition of Palestinian statehood in September 2011. The Obama administration has been preoccupied with other issues. The Middle Eastern arena is dominated by other problems, such as the Syrian civil war, the conflict over Iran's nuclear program, and Egypt's domestic convulsions. Israel's right-wing government is consumed by the Iranian nuclear issue and is drifting into de facto annexation of the West Bank. The Palestinian Authority is busy dealing with domestic unrest and managing the competition with Hamas. Hamas, in turn, is overseeing its mini-state in Gaza and managing its transition from the Iranian-Syrian orbit to that of its neighbor and parent movement, the Egyptian Muslim Brotherhood. And yet the Palestinian issue remains cardinal and explosive.

The ebb and flow of Turkey's quest for a leading role in the Middle East has been another important dimension of the region's politics and of Israel's strategic predicament. The formation in Turkey of a durable Islamist government, the European Union's refusal to admit Turkey to the EU, and the vacuum left by the decline of U.S. power and influence prompted Turkey during the last ten years or so to build a position of influence in its surrounding environment. The prospect of taking the lead in the region had a dramatic effect on politics in Turkey, a former imperial power possessed of a population of more than 80 million, a strong economy, a powerful military, a unique geopolitical location, and a functioning mode of Islamic democracy. At the outset, Turkey drew close to the radical Iranian-Syrian axis without joining it and boosted its position vis-à-vis the conservative-moderate axis, led at the time by Egypt and Saudi Arabia. But its position changed in 2011, when Prime Minister Erdogan and Foreign Minister Davutoğlu discovered the complexities of Arab politics.

Turkey's rapprochement with Syria, a hallmark of its early Arab policy, was transformed into open hostility by the Syrian rebellion. Erdogan was snubbed when Bashar al-Asad rejected his advice to solve the crisis by offering political reform. Ankara is worried by the rebellion's potential impact on Turkey's national security—chaos on its southern border, the flight of refugees into Turkey, and, most important, the creation of a second autonomous Kurdish region on its border. The Syrian crisis also has contributed to the transformation of the tension that had been implicit in Turkey's relations with Iran into overt competition over the political future of both Syria and Iraq. The Kurdish issue, it should be noted, creates both common interests and tension between Ankara and Tehran.

Turkey seeks to build a new relationship with post-Mubarak Egypt. There is an evident affinity between the two Islamist regimes, and Turkey relishes its leader's popularity in the "Arab street" and the perception that it is a successful model of a working Islamic democracy. Erdogan is consciously cultivating his image as a supporter of the Palestinian cause, a critic of Israel and of Netanyahu's government, and an Islamist leader who knows how to stand up to the United States and Israel while preserving the essence of Turkey's relationship with Washington.

The transition from the close Turkish-Israeli alliance of the 1990s to the current problematic relationship unfolded gradually during the previous decade. Erdogan became prime minister in 2003, but the change in Turkey's attitude toward Israel emerged fully only after the consolidation of his position in 2007. Erdogan began to voice strident criticism of Israel's Palestinian policy and to express his support of the Palestinian cause, specifically of Hamas, an Islamist movement kindred to his own party, the AKP. Turkey's role as mediator in trying to restart Israeli-Syrian peace negotiations in 2007–08 moderated Turkey's disengagement from Israel, but the collapse of the mediation, Operation Cast Lead in Gaza, and the embarrassment for Erdogan caused by Olmert's visit to Ankara on the eve of the Gaza campaign produced a barrage of anti-Israeli statements, the most notable being Erdogan's verbal assault on President Peres in Davos in January 2009.

The deterioration of relations was further expedited in July 2010, when the IHH, a Turkish nongovernmental organization with close ties to Erdogan's party, dispatched a six-ship flotilla to Gaza in an effort to break the Israeli siege there. The incident culminated in a violent takeover of the *Mavi Marmara,* the largest of the six ships, by Israeli commandos. They met with fierce resistance, and in the ensuing clashes nine of the passengers, most of them Turkish citizens, were killed and several Israeli soldiers were wounded. Erdogan and other Turkish spokesmen demanded that Israel apologize, pay damages, and put an end to the siege of Gaza, and they threatened to take severe punitive measures should Israel fail to respond to their demands.

The two countries negotiated discreetly for about a year in an effort to find a formula that would enable Israel to apologize without admitting guilt or responsibility and to end the incident without loss of face and exposure to legal suits. At the same time, the incident was investigated by the UN-appointed Palmer Commission. Turkey had a clear interest in bringing the issue to closure prior to the publication of the Palmer report, but Netanyahu's government decided not to sign the fairly mild text agreed on by Turkish and Israeli negotiators. As a consequence of Netanyahu's refusal and the publication in September 2011 of the Palmer report (which criticized both countries), Erdogan decided to lower the level of Turkey's diplomatic relations with Israel and expelled Israel's ambassador from Ankara. He also issued new, far-reaching threats against Israel.

Erdogan was clearly carried away by a sense of power and success. He threatened to use the Turkish navy to break the siege of Gaza and made dark allusions to Israel's future. Soon after that he warned Cyprus against prospecting for gas in its own "economic waters" without the agreement of Northern Cyprus, the occupied Turkish part of the island. At that point he may have felt—or was told—that he was getting carried away by his own rhetoric, and he began to tone it down.

In the intra-Israel debate that followed those events, Netanyahu and other spokesmen of his government argued that an apology to Turkey was not warranted and that, in any event, Israel's relationship with Turkey could not be restored. His critics argued in response that indeed the relationship could not be restored to its formal level but that it still was in Israel's interest to moderate Turkey's hostility even if doing so entailed a certain loss of face. Furthermore, so the argument went, given the difficulties encountered by Turkey's Middle Eastern policy in 2011, there was a good prospect of at least some improvement in the bilateral relationship.

The final section of chapter 7 reviews Israel's preoccupation with the Iranian issue during most of 2012 and the tension that it produced between the Netanyahu government and the Obama administration. It was not a new issue. During the second half of the previous decade, Iran's quest for a nuclear weapon and for regional hegemony and the presence that it had established in Lebanon and Gaza were cardinal issues on the Middle Eastern security and diplomatic agendas. The United States and its European allies invested considerable effort in checking Iran's nuclear and other plans and, in parallel, in dissuading Israel from launching any unilateral military action against Iran's nuclear program. They share Israel's concern with the regional and international ramifications of a nuclear Iran, but Israel's concern is much more profound. Many Israelis suspect that rhetoric aside, the United States and certainly its European allies are liable to recoil from action when the moment of truth arrives and resign themselves to living with a nuclear Iran. In Israel, even those who refuse to define the threat of a nuclear Iran as "existential" still feel that if Iran should obtain a nuclear weapon, Israel would be confronted with hitherto unfamiliar national security challenges.

Iran's regional rivals, headed by Saudi Arabia, are equally perturbed by the prospect of a nuclear Iran. They suspect, correctly, that under a nuclear umbrella the Iranian regime would step up its campaign against them. They would be relieved if the United States were to destroy Iran's nuclear installations or, short of that, if Israel were to do so. But the Israeli leadership knows full well that that would not prevent them from denouncing an Israeli raid, should it be carried out.

The Iranian regime is coping with political unrest and infighting as well as severe economic difficulties caused for the most part by international sanctions, but it continues to push forward with its nuclear program and its regional agenda: extending its influence in Iraq, trying to salvage the Asad regime in Syria, and dealing with the fallout from the Syrian crisis in Lebanon and Gaza.

Israel is clearly coping with difficult regional and international environments. In the Middle East and in the Arab world, hostile forces and trends have gained momentum; in the international arena, it is coping with delegitimization and isolation. The Obama administration has reduced its role in the Middle East, and its relationship with Netanyahu's government is difficult. Nonetheless, the complex new reality in the Middle East also creates new opportunities for Israeli initiatives and actions. Israel's ticket into the new diplomatic arena is twofold: normalization of relations with Turkey and renewal of the peace process with the Palestinians. With respect to Turkey, the road is open for signing a mildly apologetic text comparable to the one that it refused to sign in 2011. Renewing the peace process is a more complicated matter. The Syrian option is off the table, at least for now, and renewing negotiations with the Palestinian Authority would be a difficult task. So far the Palestinian leadership has insisted on discussing nothing short of a final status agreement and on renewing the negotiations at the point that they were interrupted toward the end of Olmert's tenure. The proposal presented by Olmert on September 16, 2008, is not acceptable to Benjamin Netanyahu and his coalition. As mentioned, the Obama administration failed in a two-year effort to overcome those difficulties. At present, the prospect of starting and concluding negotiations on final status is dim. Progress is feasible on two tracks: reaching a long interim agreement or deciding on a partial unilateral Israeli withdrawal that, unlike the departure from Gaza, would be coordinated with the Palestinian Authority. A change in the positions of both the Palestinian Authority and the current Israeli government would be required for either alternative to be seriously explored.

The current Israeli government's response to the geopolitical and diplomatic challenges faced by Israel has been shaped to a large extent by the nationalist, right-wing, and aggressive ideology through which most prominent members of the cabinet view the region and the world. This government does confront a tougher and bleaker environment and a critical, impatient international community. Those are difficult barriers, but they can be overcome. As seen earlier, nationalist leaders from the right wing of the political spectrum like Menachem Begin and Ariel Sharon knew how to cope with similar challenges, to cut themselves free from their past, and to adopt new, bold positions. It can only be hoped that at the end of the day Benjamin Netanyahu will be able to do the same.

Chronology

November 29, 1947
United Nations votes to partition Palestine between Jewish and Arab states. Jewish side accepts; Palestinian Arab side rejects. Civil war erupts.

May 14, 1948
Declaration of Israel's independence, followed by invasion by Arab states' armies.

1949
War ends with a series of armistice agreements.

1949–51
Several futile efforts to resolve the conflict.

October 29–November 6, 1956
Suez Sinai campaign.

1964
The road to the Six-Day War: Israel completes overland water carrier. First Arab Summit Conference convened. PLO is formed. Unified Arab Command established to support diversion of tributaries of the Jordan River.

1965
First terrorist act by Fatah (Yasser Arafat's movement).

May–June 1967
Egypt remilitarizes the Sinai, reimposes blockade of Strait of Tiran (separating the Red Sea from the Gulf of Aqaba). Israel launches Six-Day War and captures the Sinai, the Gaza Strip, the West Bank, East Jerusalem, and the Golan Heights.

November 1967
Security Council Resolution 242 lays out principles for Arab-Israeli settlement.

1968–70
Arab states launch war of attrition. PLO, now under Arafat, launches attacks through Jordan valley and terrorist acts abroad.

September 1970
Jordan expels the PLO ("Black September").

October 6, 1973
Egypt and Syria launch the October War, won by Israel.

1974
Israel signs disengagement agreements with Egypt and Israel; U.S. Secretary of State Henry Kissinger engages in "shuttle diplomacy" between Israel and the Arab states.

September 1975
Egyptian-Israeli interim agreement about the Sinai.

November 1977
Egyptian President Anwar al-Sadat travels to Jerusalem and addresses the Knesset; the beginning of Egyptian-Israeli peace negotiations.

March 1978
Israel launches Operation Litani against the PLO in south Lebanon following massive terrorist attacks inside Israel.

September 1978
Signing of Camp David Accords between Israel and Egypt.

March 1979
Signing of the Egyptian-Israeli peace treaty.

June 7, 1981
Israel destroys Iraq's nuclear reactor.

June 6, 1982
Israel launches war in Lebanon.

December 1987
Outbreak of the first intifada.

1988
First declaration of Palestinian statehood; short-lived U.S.-PLO dialogue.

October 1991
Madrid Conference, which begins the Arab-Israeli peace process.

September 1993
Israel and the PLO sign the Oslo Accords on the White House lawn.

October 1994
Israel and Jordan sign peace treaty in a ceremony at the Arava/Araba border crossing.

November 4, 1995
Israeli Prime Minister Yitzhak Rabin assassinated. He is succeeded by Shimon Peres.

May 2000
Israeli unilateral withdrawal from Lebanon.

March–September 2000
Collapse of the peace process; failed Clinton-Asad summit in Geneva; failed Israeli-PLO summit at Camp David; outbreak of the second intifada.

November 2004
Arafat dies; Mahmud Abbas becomes head of the PLO and the Palestinian Authority.

August 2005
Israeli disengagement from the Gaza Strip.

January 2006
Israeli prime minister Ariel Sharon falls ill and is succeeded by Ehud Olmert. Hamas wins Palestinian legislative elections.

July 2006
War between Israel and Hizballah in Lebanon.

June 2007
Hamas takes control of the Gaza Strip during a violent confrontation with Fatah.

2008
Collapse of Israeli Prime Minister Olmert's negotiations with Syria and the Palestinian Authority.

December 2008–January 2009
Israel's Operation Cast Lead in Gaza.

2009–11
Israeli-Palestinian stalemate.

NOTES

1. The Background

1. For two overviews of the Arab-Israeli conflict, see Elie Kedourie, "The Arab-Israeli Conflict," in *Arabic Political Memoirs* (London, 1974), pp. 218–31; Shimon Shamir, "The Arab-Israeli Conflict," in *The Middle East: Oil, Conflict and Hope,* ed. A. L. Udovitch (Lexington, Mass., 1976), pp. 195–231. For more detailed accounts, see Nadav Safran, *Israel—The Embattled Ally* (Cambridge, Mass, 1981); Don Peretz, *Palestinian Refugees and the Middle East* (Washington, D.C., 1993); Fred Khourie, *The Arab-Israeli Dilemma* (New York, 1968).

2. On the Madrid process, see James A. Baker, *The Politics of Diplomacy* (New York, 1995), pp. 417–20, 425–28, 447–49, 454–57, 459–63, 468–69, 487–89, 500–07; Eithan Ben Tzur, *Haderekh Lashalom Overet be Madrid* (The road to peace goes through Madrid) (Tel Aviv, 1997).

3. For an original, classic account of the Cold War in the Middle East, see John Campbell, *Defense of the Middle East* (New York, 1960). For a subsequent complete study of U.S. policy in the Middle East and relations with Israel, see Steven Spiegel, *The Other Arab-Israeli Conflict* (Chicago, 1985).

4. William Quandt, *A Decade of Decisions* (Berkeley, Calif., 1997).

5. Benny Morris, *1948 and After* (Oxford, 1994) and *Righteous Victims: A History of the Zionist-Arab Conflict* (New York, 1999); Avi Shlaim, *The Politics of Partition: King Abdullah, The Zionists and Palestine 1951–1911* (Oxford, 1990) and *The Iron Wall: Israel and the Arab World since 1948* (New York, 1999); Ilan Pappe, *The Making of the Arab-Israeli Conflict 1941–1951* (New York, 1988); Efraim Karsh, *Fabricating History: The New Historians* (London, 1997); Shabtai Teveth, "Charging Israel with Original Sin," *Commentary* 88 (September 3, 1989): 24–33; Zeev Sternhell, *The Founding Myths of Israel: Nationalism, Socialism and the Making of the Jewish State* (Princeton, N.J., 1998); Rami Tal, "No Subject Is Taboo for the Historian" (an interview with Anita Shapira),

in *Zionism—The Sequel,* ed. Carol Diament (New York, 1998). See also Itamar Rabinovich, "Palestine Portrayed," *Jewish Review of Books,* October 2010.

6. Itamar Rabinovich, *The Road Not Taken* (New York, 1991); Neil Caplan, *Futile Diplomacy,* vol. 3 (London, 1997); Neil Caplan and Laura Zittrain Eisenberg, *Negotiating Arab-Israeli Peace* (Bloomington, Ind., 1998).

7. For a cogent presentation of an Arab point of view, see Boutros Boutros-Ghali, "The Arab Response to the Challenge of Israel," in Udovitch, *The Middle East: Oil, Conflict and Hope,* pp. 231–50. See also Laura Zittrain Eisenberg and Neil Caplan, *Negotiating Arab-Israeli Peace: Patterns, Problems, Possibilities* (Bloomington, Ind., 2010).

8. Yehoshafat Harkabi, *Arab Attitudes to Israel* (Jerusalem, 1974) and *Arab Strategies and Israel's Response* (New York, 1977).

9. Shimon Shamir, "The Middle East Crisis: On the Brink of War (14 May–4 June)," in *Middle East Record 1961,* ed. D. Dishon (Tel Aviv, 1971), pp. 183–204; Michael Oren, "Six Days of War: June 1967 and the Making of the Modern Middle-East" (New York, 2002). For the domestic Israeli dimension, see Ami Gluska, "Eshkol, Give the Order!" (Tel Aviv, 2004) (in Hebrew).

10. For a penetrating assessment of the major currents of opinion and the national mood in Israel, see Amos Oz, *In the Land of Israel* (London and New York, 1983).

11. Fouad Ajami, *The Arab Predicament* (Cambridge, 1982).

12. Helena Cobban, *The Palestine Liberation Organization* (Cambridge, 1984); Avraham Sela and Moshe Maoz, eds., *The PLO and Israel* (New York, 1997).

13. Shlomo Avineri, *Israel and the Palestinians* (New York, 1971).

14. For the Israeli and American perspectives on the September 1970 crisis in Jordan, see Yitzhak Rabin, *The Rabin Memoirs* (Boston, 1979), pp. 186–89; Henry Kissinger, *The White House Years* (Boston, 1979), pp. 597–617. For a contemporary exposition of Likud's view that "Jordan is Palestine," see Benjamin Netanyahu, *A Place among the Nations* (New York, 1993), pp. 343–45.

15. For a critical view of Israeli policy at the time, see Ezer Weizman, *On Eagles' Wings* (London, 1976), pp. 279–95.

16. Zeev Laqueur, *Confrontation* (London, 1974).

17. William B. Quandt, *The Peace Process* (Washington, D.C., and Berkeley, Calif., 1993); Malcolm Kerr, ed., *Rich and Poor States in the Middle East* (Boulder, Colo., 1982); Moshe Dayan, *Breakthrough* (New York, 1981).

18. Henry Kissinger, *Years of Upheaval* (New York, 1982), pp. 747–98.

19. Rabin, *Memoirs,* pp. 253–300; Itamar Rabinovich, "The Challenge of Diversity: American Policy and the System of Inter-Arab Relations 1973–1977," in *The Middle East and the United States,* ed. I. Rabinovich and H. Shaked (New Brunswick, N.J., 1980), pp. 181–96.

20. Kissinger, *Years of Upheaval;* Rabin, *Memoirs,* pp. 799–853.

21. Jimmy Carter, *Keeping the Faith* (Toronto, 1982), pp. 269–329, and *The Blood of Abraham* (Boston, 1985, passim); Cyrus Vance, *Hard Choices* (New York, 1983), pp. 16–256.

22. Quandt, *Peace Process*.

23. Ze'ev Schiff and Ehud Ya'ari, *Israel's Lebanon War* (New York, 1984); Itamar Rabinovich, *The War for Lebanon, 1970–1983* (Ithaca, N.Y, and London, 1984).

24. Fouad Ajami, *The Dream Palace of the Arabs* (New York, 1998).

25. Shimon Peres, *Battling for Peace* (London, 1995), pp. 258–70.

26. Baker, *Politics of Diplomacy;* Uri Savir, *The Process* (New York, 1998); Itamar Rabinovich, *The Brink of Peace* (Princeton, N.J., 1998).

2. MADRID AND OSLO: YEARS OF HOPE

1. Studies and memoirs regarding this period include Itamar Rabinovich, *The Brink of Peace* (Princeton, N.J, 1998); Uri Savir, *The Process* (New York, 1998); David Makovsky, *Making Peace with the PLO* (Boulder, Colo, 1996); Warren Christopher, *In the Stream of History* (Stanford, Calif, 1998); Hanan Ashrawi, *This Side of Peace* (New York, 1995); Mahmud Abbas, *Through Secret Channels* (Reading, UK, 1995), Bill Clinton, *My Life* (New York, 2004), and Madeleine Albright, *Madam Secretary: A Memoir* (New York, 2003). Practically all members of the U.S. peace team published books and memoirs. For a review of these works, see Itamar Rabinovich, "Making Peace and Writing About It," *Bustan*, vol. 1, 2010, pp. 21–28.

2. Joseph Alpher, "What Went Wrong?" (New York, 1998).

3. Robert Slater, *Rabin of Israel* (London, 1996). See also the memoir by Rabin's widow, Leah Rabin, *Our Life—His Legacy* (New York, 1997).

4. For Baker's surprisingly brief version of this, see James A. Baker, *The Politics of Diplomacy* (New York, 1995), pp. 555–57.

5. Foreign Broadcast Information Service (FBIS), "Final Statement Issued," July 27, 1992, pp. 5–6.

6. On Hamas and Islamic Jihad, see Ziad Abu-Amr, *Islamic Fundamentalism in the West Bank and Gaza* (Bloomington, Ind, 1994); Hisham H. Ahmad, *From Religious Salvation to Political Transformation: The Rise of Hamas in Palestinian Society* (Jerusalem, 1994).

7. Martin Indyk, "Dual Containment," lecture at the Washington Institute, May 18, 1993.

8. Yossi Beilin, *Laga'at BaShalom* (To touch peace) (Tel Aviv, 1997).

9. Shimon Peres, *Battling for Peace* (London, 1995).

10. For a detailed version of this episode, see Rabinovich, *Brink of Peace*, pp. 108–15. My version of the event is contested by the Syrian view that Rabin actually "committed Israel to a withdrawal from the Golan." For the Syrian version,

see Ambassador Walid Muallem's interview in *Journal of Palestine Studies* 26, no. 2 (Winter 1997): 401–12.

11. The only detailed account of the Israeli-Jordanian negotiations is in Moshe Zak, *Hossein Oseh Shalom* (Hussein makes peace) (Ramat Gan, 1996).

12. Savir, *The Process*, pp. 346–50.

13. Shimon Peres, *The New Middle East* (New York, 1993).

14. Foreign Broadcast Information Service, "Radio on Al-Assad's *Al-Ahram* Interview," October 12, 1995, pp. 50–61,

15. Shai Feldman, *Nuclear Weapons and Arms Control in the Middle East* (Cambridge, Mass., 1997), pp. 7–15, 153–58.

3. YEARS OF STAGNATION

1. See the official text: "The Wye River Memorandum Signed at the White House, Washington, D.C," United States Information Center.

2. Two biographies of Benjamin Netanyahu have been published in Hebrew. I give their titles in English here: Ben Kaspit, *Netanyahu: The Road to Power* (Tel Aviv, 1997); and Ronit Vardi, *Bibi—Who Are You, Mr. Prime Minister?* (Jerusalem, 1997).

3. See the interview with Ben Zion Netanyahu in *Ha'aretz*, September 18, 1998.

4. Benjamin Netanyahu, *A Place among the Nations: Israel and the World* (New York, 1993), pp. 256–328.

5. Ibid., pp. 350 ff.

6. Ibid., pp. 351–53.

7. For an illuminating study of the 1996 elections and their social context, see Daniel Ben Simon, *Another Country* [in Hebrew] (Tel Aviv, 1997); also Daniel J. Elazar and Shmuel Sandler, *Israel at the Polls: 1996* (London, 1998).

8. See Netanyahu's interviews with David Makovsky, *Jerusalem Post*, May 10, 1996, and with Shimon Schiffer, *Yediot Ahronoth*, May 23, 1996.

9. Ibid.

10. Foreign Broadcast Information Service (FBIS), "Likud Issues Platform," May 23, 1996, p. 4.

11. Interview with Makovsky, *Jerusalem Post*.

12. FBIS, June 18,1996, "Netanyahu Government Presents Basic Guidelines," pp. 32–36.

13. FBIS, June 24, 1996, "Final Communiqué Issued by Arab Summit," pp. 13–16.

14. Itamar Rabinovich, *The Brink of Peace* (Princeton, N.J, 1998), pp. 256–64.

15. See the chapters on Israel in Bruce Maddy Weizman, ed., *Middle East Contemporary Survey, 1996* and *1991* (Boulder, Colo.).

16. For an excellent synoptic survey of the events that led to the signing of the Wye Agreement, see David Makovsky's article in *Ha'aretz*, December 4, 1998.

17. For a critical biography of Ariel Sharon, see Uzi Benziman, *He Does Not Stop at the Red Light* [in Hebrew] (Tel Aviv, 1985).

18. The document was first published in *Ha'aretz,* November 16, 1998.

19. For the fullest account of the Lauder mission, see the memoirs of Gen. Danni Yatom, *The Confidant* [in Hebrew] (Tel-Aviv, 2009), pp. 194–214. Yatom served as an aide to Rabin, Peres, and Barak and was head of the Mossad under Peres and Netanyahu.

4. EHUD BARAK AND THE COLLAPSE OF THE PEACE PROCESS

1. The first book written on the Barak period was by the journalist Raviv Druker, *Hara-kiri* [in Hebrew] (Tel Aviv, 2002). It is a critical book, relying mainly on interviews with disappointed assistants and partners and internal material from the Prime Ministry Office that was handed to the author. Later on another book was published, Ran Edelist, *Ehud Barak: His War against the Demons* [in Hebrew] (Tel Aviv, 2002). This book attempts to form a reaction to Druker's book, and it is based, although this is not explicitly stated, on long hours of conversations with Barak himself as well as with other participants in the events of the period. Danny Yatom's book, *The Confidant* [in Hebrew] (Tel-Aviv, 2009), offers a detailed, less critical account of Barak's tenure.

2. Aluf Benn in *Ha'aretz,* July 19, 1999.

3. Yatom, *The Confidant.*

4. For an overview of the Israeli-Syrian negotiations during Barak's period, see Eyal Zisser, "The Israel-Syria Negotiations, What Went Wrong?" *Orient 42* (June 2, 2001): 225–51. Barak's negotiation with Syria is described, often from a critical perspective, by several members of the U.S. peace team. See my review essay, "Making Peace and Writing about It," *Bustan,* no. 1 (2010): 21–28.

5. Uri Savir, *The Process* (New York, 1998), pp. 298–326, and Itamar Rabinovich, *The Brink of Peace* (Princeton, N.J., 1998), pp. 248–93, 305–19.

6. For the public diplomacy in the Israeli-Syrian negotiations, see Itamar Rabinovich, "Public Diplomacy and Apologetics—the Israeli-Syrian Negotiations during the End of Asad's Reign," in Itamar Rabinovich, *The View from Damascus* (London 2008).

7. Ibid.

8. Druker, *Hara-kiri,* pp. 70–110, and U.S. ambassador in Israel Martin Indyk in *Yediot Ahronoth,* March 16, 2001. Ehud Barak's version was published in an interview for *Ha'aretz,* May 19, 2000; Uri Sagie (during a conversation with the author, May 2003). Another American version is that of Robert Malley, a member of the National Security Council during the Clinton administration; see Robert Malley, "Middle East Endgame III: Israel, Syria and Lebanon—How Comprehensive Peace Settlements Would Look," *International Crisis Group Middle East Report* 4 (July 16, 2002): 4.

9. Robert Malley and Hussein Agha, "Camp David: The Tragedy of Errors," *New York Review of Books*, August 9, 2001. For two different, often contradictory accounts, see Martin Indyk, *Innocent Abroad: An Intimate Account of American Peace Diplomacy in the Middle East* (New York, 2009), and Yatom, *The Confidant*.

10. Zisser, "The Israel-Syria Negotiations," p. 237.

11. Aluf Benn in *Ha'aretz*, January 4, 2000.

12. Rabinovich, "Public Diplomacy and Apologetics."

13. Ibid.

14. Zisser, "The Israel-Syria Negotiations"; Malley, "Middle East Endgame III." Additional details of the negotiations can be found in Madeleine Albright, *Madam Secretary* (New York, 2003), pp. 476–82.

15. For an analysis of the new power equation created in south Lebanon, see Robert Malley, "Old Games in Search of New Rules," *International Crisis Group Middle East Report* 7 (October 29, 2002).

16. Druker, *Hara-kiri*, pp. 189–208.

17. Ibid., pp. 167–78.

18. Shlomo Ben-Ami, interviewed by Ari Shavit, *Ha'aretz*, September 14, 2001. See as well Shlomo Ben-Ami, *Scars of War, Wounds of Peace: The Israeli-Arab Tragedy* (New York, 2006); Gilead Sher, *Within Reach, the Peace Negotiation 1999–2001: A Testimony* (Tel Aviv, 2001), pp. 80–96.

19. Ben-Ami interview of September 14.

20. Ibid., and Sher, *Within Reach*, pp. 153–235. A Palestinian version of the course of affairs can be traced in the notes of Akram Hanieh, which were published originally *in Al-Ayyam* (between July 29 and August 10, 2000). A shorter version was published in English: Akram Hanieh, "The Camp David Papers," *Journal of Palestine Studies* 30, no. 2 (Winter 2001): 75–97.

21. Sher, *Within Reach*, pp. 360–74.

22. Ibid., pp. 397–415; Yossi Beilin, *A Guide for a Wounded Dove* [in Hebrew] (Tel Aviv, 2001), pp. 198–222.

23. *Ha'aretz*, January 28, 2001.

24. For the dispute regarding Taba, see Ari Shavit, "Taba's Principle of Return," *Ha'aretz*, July 11, 2002, and Yossi Beilin, "What Really Happened in Taba," *Ha'aretz*, July 15, 2002.

25. Michael Hirsh, "Clinton to Arafat: It's All Your Fault," *Newsweek*, June 27, 2001.

26. Edelist, *Ehud Barak: His War against the Demons*.

27. *Ha'aretz*, January 28, 2011.

28. Clyde Haberman, "Dennis Ross's Exit Interview," *New York Times Magazine*, March 25, 2001.

29. Daniel Mandel, "Dennis Ross: The Man in the Middle," *The Review* 26, no. 6 (June 2001).

30. Dennis Ross, "Camp David: An Exchange," *New York Review of Books,* September 20, 2001. These points are elaborated by Ross in *The Missing Peace: The Inside Story of the Fight for Middle East Peace* (New York, 2004).

31. Elsa Walsh, "The Prince: How the Saudi Ambassadot Became Washington's Indispensable Operator," *New Yorker,* March 24, 2003.

32. See my review essay "Making Peace and Writing About It," (2010): 21–28.

33. Malley and Agha, "Camp David: The Tragedy of Errors."

34. Beilin, *Wounded Dove.*

35. Uri Savir interviewed by Ben Kaspit, *Ma'ariv,* March 9, 2001.

36. Ron Pundak, "From Oslo to Taba: What Went Wrong?" *Survival* 43, no. 3 (2001): 31–46.

37. Norman Podhoretz, "Oslo: The Peacemongers Return," *Commentary,* October 2001.

38. Amos Gilead during a lecture at the Jaffa Center for Strategic Studies, Tel Aviv University, May 23, 2002.

39. Moshe (Bogi) Ya'alon, *The Longer Shorter Way* [in Hebrew] (Tel Aviv, 2008).

40. Henry Kissinger, *Does America Need a Foreign Policy?* (New York, 2001), pp. 164–88.

41. Menachem Klein, *Shattering a Taboo: The Contacts towards a Permanent Status Agreement in Jerusalem, 1994–2001* (Jerusalem, 2001).

5. Sharon, Bush, and Arafat

1. See chapter 3. Also see Sharon's autobiography, Ariel Sharon and David Chanoff, *Warrior* (New York, 1989).

2. Uzi Benziman, *He Does Not Stop at the Red Light* [in Hebrew] (Tel Aviv, 1985).

3. Bob Woodward, *Bush at War* (New York, 2002).

4. Ibid., pp. 60–61.

5. Mahmud Abbas, "Call for a Halt to the Militarization for the Intifada," *Journal of Palestine Studies* 32, no. 126 (2003): 74–78.

6. Khalil Shikaki, "How to Reform Palestinian Politics," *New York Times,* July 9, 2002. See also Dr. Mahdi Abdul Hadi, "Reforms in Palestine," *Passia* (Palestinian Academic Society for the Study of International Affairs, Jerusalem), July 2002. 1 am indebted to Brigadier General (reserve) Shlomo Brom, a senior researcher at the Jaffe Center for Strategic Studies, Tel Aviv University, for most useful conversations about these issues.

7. *Ha'aretz,* December 24, 2001.

8. Woodward, *Bush at War,* pp. 17–18. See also George W. Bush, *Decision Points* (New York, 2010). For a description of the infighting within the Bush administration see Peter W. Rodman, *Presidential Command* (New York, 2009).

9. For an in-depth analysis of this issue, see Fouad Ajami, "Iraq and the Arab's Future," *Foreign Affairs,* January–February 2003.

10. John Mearsheimer and Stephen Walt, "The Israel Lobby and U.S. Foreign Policy" (New York, 2007).

11. *Yediot Ahronoth,* April 16, 2003.

12. *Ha'aretz,* May 27, 2003.

13. Nahum Barnea and Ariel Kastner, "Backchannel: Bush, Sharon and the Uses of Unilateralism," Saban Center monograph 2, December 2006.

6. EHUD OLMERT AND THE NEW NEW MIDDLE EAST

1. Dani Haloutz, *Straightforward* [in Hebrew] (Tel-Aviv, 2010).

2. Gilad Shalit's capture and captivity became a major issue in Israel's public life and the conflict with Hamas for the next five years. In October 2011 a deal was negotiated with Hamas in return for the release of more than 1,000 Palestinian prisoners.

3. George W. Bush, *Decision Points* (New York, 2010).

4. As broadcast on al-Manar, September 22, 2006,

5. Itamar Rabinovich, "The Bush Administration, Israel and Syria, 2001–2008," in Rabinovich, *The View from Damascus* (London, 2008), pp. 341–54.

6. Ibid.

7. Martin Indyk, *Innocent Abroad: An Intimate Account of American Peace Diplomacy in the Middle East* (New York, 2009), pp. 413–15.

8. Daniel Byman and Gad Goldstein. "The Challenge of Gaza: Policy Options and Broader Implications," Saban Center Analysis Paper 23 (Washington, July 2011).

7. AMERICAN-ISRAELI AUTUMN, ARAB SPRING

1. Quoted in Abraham Ben-Zvi, *From Truman to Obama* [in Hebrew] (Tel-Aviv: 2011), pp. 231–81.

2. Quoted in Zaki Shalom, "Israel–US Relations: Approaching a Turning Point?" *Strategic Assessement* (Institute of National Security Studies, Tel-Aviv University), vol. 13, no. 1, July 2010. For a refutation of the linkage theory, see Dennis Ross and David Makovsky, *Myths, Illusions, and Peace* (New York, 2009).

3. See Netanyahu's speech at the Herzliya Conference in January 2008.

4. See chapter 3 and Natan Sharansky, *The Case for Democracy* (New York, 2006). For an analysis of Israel's attitude toward the prospects of democratization of Egypt in a conservative Israeli periodical, see Asaf Sagiv, "Egyptian Democracy and Israeli Democratophobia" [in Hebrew], *Tchelet,* 43, spring 2011, pp.15–28.

5. See www.dailykos.com/story/2011/05/20/977636/-Sparks-Fly-in-Angry-Phone-Calls-between-Clinton-and-Netanyahu,-US-Will-Use-Veto-for-Israel.

8. THE WEB OF RELATIONSHIPS

1. Elie Kedourie, "The Arab-Israeli Conflict," in *Arabic Political Memoirs* (London, 1974), pp. 218–31; Shimon Shamir, "The Arab-Israeli Conflict," in *The Middle East: Oil, Conflict and Hope,* ed. A. L. Udovitch (Lexington, Mass., 1976), pp. 195–231.

2. Shimon Shamir, ed., *Egypt from Monarchy to Republic* (Oxford, 1995); Israel Gershoni, *The Emergence of Pan-Arabism in Egypt* (Tel Aviv, 1981); and *Rethinking the Egyptian Nation: 1930–1945* (Cambridge, 1995).

3. Abraham Sela, "The Question of Palestine in the Inter-Arab System, from the Foundation of the Arab League until the Invasion of Palestine by the Arab Armies, 1945–1948" [in Hebrew], Jerusalem, 1986.

4. P.J. Vatikiotis, *Nasser and His Generation* (London, 1978), *Conflict in the Middle East* (London, 1971), and *The History of Modern Egypt* (London, 1991).

5. William B. Quandt, *The Peace Process* (Washington, D.C., and Berkeley, Calif., 1993).

6. Fouad Ajami, *The Dream Palace of the Arabs* (New York, 1998).

7. On the nuclear dimension of Israeli-Egyptian relations, see Shai Feldman, *Nuclear Weapons and Arms Control in the Middle East* (Cambridge, 1997), pp. 206–24.

8. Sadiq al-'Azm, "The View from Damascus," *New York Review of Books,* June 15, 2000.

9. For the history of Israel and the Zionist movement's contacts with various groups in Lebanon, see Laura Zittrain Eisenberg, *My Enemy's Enemy* (Detroit, 1994); Benny Morris, "Israel and the Lebanese Phalange: The Birth of a Relationship 1948–1951," *Studies in Zionism* 5, no. 1 (1984): 125–44.

10. Ehud Ya'ari and Ze'ev Schiff, *Israel's Lebanon War* (New York, 1994); Itamar Rabinovich, *The War for Lebanon, 1910–1983* (Ithaca, N.Y, and London, 1984).

11. Avi Shlaim, *Collusion across the Jordan* (Oxford, 1988); Dan Shiftan, *Optzia Yardenit* [Jordanian option] (Efal, 1986); Moshe Zak, *Hossein Oseh Shalom* [Hussein makes peace] (Ramat Gan, 1996), and "Israel and Jordan: Strategically Bound," *Israel Affairs* 3, no. 1 (Autumn 1996): 39–60. See also Uriel Dann, *Studies in the History of Transjordan, 1920–1949* (Boulder, Colo., 1984).

12. See my *The Road Not Taken* (New York, 1991), pp. 111–67.

13. For a Jordanian version of the 1967 crisis and war, see Samir Mutawi, *Jordan in the 1961 War* (Cambridge, 1987).

14. Asher Susser, *On Both Banks of the Jordan* (London, 1994).

15. See chapter 1, note 14.

16. It is significant that, though King Hussein publicly announced his country's disengagement, the formal annexation act was never abrogated, nor has Jordan's constitution been amended. It still stipulates that the "territory [of the kingdom] is indivisible and no portion of it may be ceded." The Constitution of the Hashemite

Kingdom of Jordan, chap. 1, art. 1, as found in Muhammad Khalil, ed. *The Arab States and the Arab League* (Beirut, 1962).

17. For a Jordanian perspective on these developments see Marwan Muasher, *The Arab Center* (New Haven, Conn., 2008). For a recent analysis of the growing tension between Jordan and Israel, see Asher Susser, "Falling Out," in *Tablet Magazine*, January 2011.

18. Harold Saunders, *The Other Walls* (Princeton, N.J., 1991).

19. For several classic statements of Israel's outlook on the Palestinians, see Shlomo Avineri, *Israel and the Palestinians* (New York, 1971).

20. For a sympathetic history of the Palestinian national movement, see Helena Cobban, *The Palestinian Liberation Organization* (Cambridge, 1984).

21. For two basic and very different views on the subject, see Jacob Landau, *The Arabs in Israel: A Political Study* (London, 1969), and Ian Lustick, *Arabs in the Jewish State: Israel's Control of a National Minority* (Austin, Tex, 1980).

22. Majid Al Haj and Henry Resenfeld, *Arab Local Government in Israel* (Tel Aviv, 1988); Jacob Landau, *The Arab Minority in Israel, 1961–1991: Political Aspects* (London, 1994); C. Klein, *Israel as a Nation State and the Problem of the Arab Minority in Search of a Status* (Tel Aviv, 1987); David Kretzmer, *The Legal Status of the Arabs in Israel* (Tel Aviv, 1987); Sammy Smooha, *Arabs and Jews in Israel*, 2 vols. (Boulder, Colo., 1989–92); Elie Rekhess, "Resurgent Islam in Israel," *Asian and African Studies* 27, nos. 1–2 (March–July 1993), and Rekhess, ed., "Arab Politics in Israel at a Crossroad," *Occasional Papers 119* (Tel Aviv, 1991); Nadim Ruhana, "The Political Transformation of the Palestinians in Israel from Acquiescence to Challenge," *Journal of Palestine Studies* 18 (1989).

23. For a sharp response to the documents and the broader challenge to the "Israeli order" by members of the Arab minority, see Dan Schueftan, *Palestinians in Israel: The Arab Minority's Struggle against the Jewish State* [in Hebrew]. Tel-Aviv: 2011.)

24. Elie Rekhess, "The Arab Minority in Israel: An Analysis of the 'Future Vision' Documents," www.ajc.org/site/apps/nlnet/content3.aspx?c=ijITI2PHKo G&b=843137&ct=5161971.

25. After the 1948 war, the Iraqi government conducted a study of the Arab debacle in Palestine that offers important early insights into the Arab, and specifically Iraqi, view of the conflict. See Shmuel Segev, *In the Eyes of an Enemy* [in Hebrew] (Tel Aviv, 1954).

26. Shmuel Segev, *The Iranian Triangle* (New York, 1988).

27. On the Iran-Iraq war, see Anthony H. Cordesman and Abraham R. Wagner, *The Iran-Iraq War* (Boulder, Colo., 1990). On Saddam's Iraq, see Efraim Karsh, *Saddam Hussein: A Political Biography* (London, 1991); Ofra Bengio, *Saddam Speaks on the Gulf Crisis* (Tel Aviv, 1992); Amatzia Baram, *Culture, History and Ideology in the Formation of Ba'thist Iraq, 1968–1989* (Hampshire, U.K., 1991); and Samir Al Khahil, *Republic of Fear: The Politics of Modern Iraq* (New York, 1990).

28. See Avner Yaniv, "Israel Faces Iraq: The Politics of Confrontation," in *Iraq's Road to War,* ed. Amatzia Baram and Barry Rubin (New York, 1996).

29. *Al Thawra,* April 3, 1990. See also "President Warns Israel, Criticizes U.S., April 1, 1990," in Bengio, *Saddam Speaks on the Gulf Crisis.*

30. Judith Miller and Laurie Mylroie, *Saddam Hussein and the Crisis in the Gulf* (New York, 1990).

9. PEACE AND NORMALIZATION

1. Muhammad Sid-Ahmed, *After the Guns Fall Silent* (London, 1976).

2. Ibid., p. 67.

3. Ibid., p. 111.

4. Ibid., pp. 111–13, passim.

5. Ibid, p. 114.

6. Ibid., p. 115.

7. Itamar Rabinovich, *The Road Not Taken* (New York, 1991), pp. 135–67.

8. The debate still continues as to whether an agreement could have been made and an opportunity was missed by Golda Meir's government in 1971. For a detailed account by a member of Meir's cabinet, see Gad Ya'akobi, *On the Razor's Edge* [in Hebrew] (Tel Aviv, 1989).

9. S. A. Sela, *The Decline of the Arab-Israeli Conflict* (Albany, N.Y., 1998), pp. 156–57.

10. Some of those ideas were put forth in the debate that followed the publication of Sid-Ahmed's book. See *Al-Hawadith* (Beirut), May 30, June 13, June 20, 1975.

11. See Boutros Boutros-Ghali, "The Arab Response to the Challenge of Israel," in *The Middle East: Oil, Conflict and Hope,* ed. A. L. Udovitch (Lexington, Mass, 1976).

12. For impressions and reflections of an Israeli intellectual after a first visit to Egypt, see Amos Elon, *Flight into Egypt* (New York, 1980).

13. *Ha'aretz,* January 7, 1999.

14. Shimon Peres, *The New Middle East* (New York, 1993), p. 86.

15. Ibid., pp. 62–64.

16. Patrick Seale, "Asad's Regional Strategy and the Challenge from Netanyahu," *Journal of Palestine Studies* 26, no. 1 (Fall 1997): 36.

17. Fouad Ajami, *The Dream Palace of the Arabs* (New York, 1998).

18. Cited in ibid., pp. 256–58.

19. Edward Said, *The Politics of Dispossession* (New York, 1995), pp. 34, 45.

20. Daniel Pipes, "Just Kidding," *New Republic,* January 8 and 15, 1996, pp. 18–19.

21. "Interview with President Assad," *Al-Ahram,* October 11, 1995, p. 1.

22. Thus the argument has been raised that "this reality was translated among Egyptian national security circles into a growing fear of the future. According to

these circles the Egyptian market will be dominated by foreign powers, moreover by Israel. It has even been claimed that Israel will achieve economically what it has failed to achieve militarily." See Abdel Monem Said Aly and others, *National Threat Perceptions in the Middle East* (Geneva, 1995.)

23. Interview with Syrian television, November 16, 1997, quoted in *Al-Ra'y al-'Amm* (Kuwait), November 17, 1997.

24. Statement issued by attendees of the Cairo conference as broadcast on Radio Cairo, June 23, 1996.

25. Quoted in Joshu Teitelbaum, *The Arab Peace Initiative: A Primer and Future Prospects* (Jerusalem: 2009)

26. David Menashri. "Iran, Israel and the Middle East Conflict," *Israel Affairs* 12, no. 1 (January 2006): 107–22.

27. Al-Manar Television, November 30, 2009.

28. Among other places, the Hamas charter is available at http://avalon.law. yale.edu/20th_century/hamas.asp.

29. For description and analysis of Hamas's position see Meir Litvak, "The Hamas: Unique Muslim Brotherhood Palestinian Movement," in *The Muslim Brotherhood: Eighty Years* [in Hebrew], ed. Uri Kupferschmidt and Meir Khatina (Tel-Aviv, forthcoming).

30. Interview with Bashar al-Asad in the *Wall Street Journal*, January 31, 2011.

INDEX

Surnames starting with al- are alphabetized under the subsequent part of the name.

Iraq: Bush policies on, 131; Iran-Iraq war (1980–88), 20–21, 247; Kuwait invasion (1990), 21; nuclear reactor destroyed by Israel, 212; and Persian Gulf War (1991), 24; and Syria, 218; U.S. war in, 145–56; and war on terror, 134; web of relationships, 246–49
Islamic Jihad: and Hebron Agreement, 77; and Madrid Conference, 34–35; in resistance axis, 218; terrorist attacks by, 52, 137
Israel Beyteynu Party, 188, 245
Israeli-Egyptian track: and cold peace, 269; overview, 2; and peace process, 16, 143, 255–56; peace treaty (1979), 2, 17, 26, 210. *See also* Egypt
Israeli-Palestinian track: and *al-Aqsa intifada*, 108–09; and Barak, 101–13; and Camp David conference (2000), 107–08; and Clinton's bridging proposals, 110–12; and Stockholm talks, 105–07; and Taba Conference, 112–13; views on collapse of, 113–27. *See also* Palestine Liberation Organization (PLO); Palestinian Authority (PA)
Israeli-Syrian track: Annapolis conference (2007), 177; and Arab Peace Initiative, 275, 277–78; and Olmert, 171–75; and Oslo Accords, 36; and peace process, 42–43, 269–70. *See also* Syria

Jabotinsky, Ze'ev, 57
Jarring, Gunnar, 255
Jerusalem: in Clinton's bridging proposals, 110; and collapse of peace process, 124; Olmert's policies on, 178–79; and Stockholm talks, 106
Jones, Jim, 176
Jordan: and Arab Peace Initiative, 275; and Arab Spring, 197, 198, 279, 280–81; and Camp David conference (2000), 107; and Madrid Conference, 258; and Netanyahu, 66, 69,

230–31; and normalization, 270–71; and Oslo Accords, 230; and Palestinian nationalism, 9–10; peace treaty with Israel, 2, 27, 29, 42, 199; and quest for Arab-Israeli settlement, 143; and Sharon, 81; and Six-Day War, 8, 228; Syria conflict with, 10; web of relationships, 226–32
Jordan Valley, 106, 107, 110
Judea. *See* West Bank

Kadimah party, 160–61, 163–64, 188–89
Karin A (ship), 135
Karmi, Raid, 138
Kerry, John, 196
Khatib, Hashem, 243
Khomeini, Ayatollah, 20
Kidnappings. *See* Abduction of soldiers
Kissinger, Henry, 10, 13–15, 123–24. *See also* Step-by-step diplomacy
Klein, Menachem, 124–25
Kuwait invasion by Iraq (1990), 21, 247–48

Labor Party (Israel): and elections of 1992, 29–30; and elections of 1999, 88; and elections of 2003, 151; and elections of 2006, 164; and elections of 2009, 189; loss of power, 13; and Netanyahu, 80
Land for peace, 4, 245, 254
Lauder, Ronald, 84, 90, 220
Lauder Mission, 84, 90, 220
Lebanon: Barak's policies on, 92; Bush policies on, 166; Cedar Revolution (2005), 161; civil war (1975–76), 20, 222; and Hizballah, 99, 109, 165, 223, 225, 226; Iran's influence in, 53; Israeli war (1982), 20, 22, 222; Israeli war (2006), 167–69, 183, 238; and Madrid Conference, 258; Netanyahu's policies on, 68; PLO in, 12; and Syria, 222, 223; web of relationships, 221–26; withdrawal from, 99, 165, 224
Levy, David, 75, 92, 104

BROOKINGS The Brookings Institution is a private nonprofit organization devoted to research, education, and publication on important issues of domestic and foreign policy. Its principal purpose is to bring the highest quality independent research and analysis to bear on current and emerging policy problems. The Institution was founded on December 8, 1927, to merge the activities of the Institute for Government Research, founded in 1916, the Institute of Economics, founded in 1922, and the Robert Brookings Graduate School of Economics and Government, founded in 1924. Interpretations or conclusions in Brookings publications should be understood to be solely those of the authors.

Board of Trustees

John L. Thornton
 Chair
Glenn Hutchins
 Vice Chair
Suzanne Nora Johnson
 Vice Chair
David M. Rubenstein
 Vice Chair
Strobe Talbott
 President
Liaquat Ahamed
Dominic Barton
Robert M. Bass
Alan R. Batkin
Crandall Bowles
Hanzade Doğan Boyner
Paul L. Cejas
John S. Chen
Abby Joseph Cohen

Howard E. Cox
Arthur B. Culvahouse Jr.
Paul Desmarais Jr.
Kenneth M. Duberstein
Cheryl Cohen Effron
Alfred B. Engelberg
Bart Friedman
Ann M. Fudge
Ellen Futter
Jeffrey W. Greenberg
Brian L. Greenspun
Shirley Ann Jackson
Benjamin R. Jacobs
Kenneth M. Jacobs
Richard A. Kimball Jr.
Nemir Kirdar
Klaus Kleinfeld
Philip H. Knight
Rajan Bharti Mittal

Nigel Morris
James Murren
Thomas C. Ramey
Edgar Rios
James Rogers
Victoria P. Sant
Leonard D. Schaeffer
Lynn Thoman
Larry D. Thompson
Michael L. Tipsord
Andrew H. Tisch
Antoine W. van Agtmael
John H. White Jr.
John W. Wilhelm
Tracy R. Wolstencroft
Daniel Yergin
Daniel B. Zwirn

Honorary Trustees

Robert J. Abernethy
Elizabeth E. Bailey
Zoë Baird Budinger
Rex J. Bates
Richard C. Blum
Geoffrey T. Boisi
Louis W. Cabot
James W. Cicconi
William T. Coleman Jr.
Alan M. Dachs
Kenneth W. Dam
Steven A. Denning
Vishakha N. Desai

Mario Draghi
Lawrence K. Fish
Cyrus F. Freidheim Jr.
David Friend
Lee H. Hamilton
William A. Haseltine
Teresa Heinz
Joel Z. Hyatt
James A. Johnson
Ann Dibble Jordan
Vernon E. Jordan Jr.
Herbert M. Kaplan
Donald F. McHenry

Arjay Miller
Mario M. Morino
Samuel Pisar
Charles W. Robinson
James D. Robinson III
Warren B. Rudman
Haim Saban
B. Francis Saul II
Ralph S. Saul
Michael P. Schulhof
John C. Whitehead
Stephen M. Wolf
Ezra K. Zilkha

CPSIA information can be obtained at www.ICGtesting.com
Printed in the USA
LVOW082318031212

309781LV00006B/11/P